Sheffield Hallam University
Learning and IT Services
Collegiate Learning Centre
Collegiate Crescent Campus
Sheffield   S10 2BP

101 930 224 0

D1356001

KEY TEXT
REFERENCE

Sheffield Hallam University
Learning and Information Services
Withdrawn From Stock

Anarchism and utopianism

Manchester University Press

Anarchism and utopianism

edited by Laurence Davis
and Ruth Kinna

Manchester University Press
Manchester and New York

distributed in the United States exclusively by Palgrave Macmillan

Copyright © Manchester University Press 2009

While copyright in the volume as a whole is vested in Manchester University Press, copyright in individual chapters belongs to their respective authors, and no chapter may be reproduced wholly or in part without the express permission in writing of both author and publisher.

Published by Manchester University Press
Oxford Road, Manchester M13 9NR, UK
and Room 400, 175 Fifth Avenue, New York, NY 10010, USA
www.manchesteruniversitypress.co.uk

Distributed in the United States exclusively by
Palgrave Macmillan, 175 Fifth Avenue, New York,
NY 10010, USA

Distributed in Canada exclusively by
UBC Press, University of British Columbia, 2029 West Mall,
Vancouver, BC, Canada V6T 1Z2

British Library Cataloguing-in-Publication Data
A catalogue record for this book is available from the British Library

Library of Congress Cataloging-in-Publication Data applied for

ISBN 978 07190 7934 4   *hardback*

First published 2009

18 17 16 15 14 13 12 11 10 09   10 9 8 7 6 5 4 3 2 1

The publisher has no responsibility for the persistence or accuracy of URLs for any external or third-party internet websites referred to in this book, and does not guarantee that any content on such websites is, or will remain, accurate or appropriate.

Typeset
by SNP Best-set Typesetter Ltd., Hong Kong
Printed in Great Britain
by the MPG Books Group

SHEFFIELD HALLAM UNIVERSITY
RS
335·83
AN
COLLEGIATE LEARNING CENTRE

This collection is respectfully and with great sadness dedicated to the memory of Nicholas Spencer.

Contents

Notes on contributors

John P. Clark is the Gregory F. Curtin Distinguished Professor in Humane Letters and the Professions at Loyola University, New Orleans. His books include *Max Stirner's Egoism* (Freedom, 1976); *The Philosophical Anarchism of William Godwin* (Princeton University Press, 1977); *The Anarchist Moment: Reflections on Culture, Nature and Power* (Black Rose, 1984); *Anarchy, Geography, Modernity: The Radical Social Thought of Elisée Reclus* (Lexington Books, 2004, co-editor); and *A Voyage to New Orleans: Anarchist Impressions of the Old South* (Glad Day Books, 2004, co-editor and co-translator). He is currently working on a reformulation of social ecology, a political ecology collection, and a historical and philosophical work on social crisis in New Orleans in the mid-nineteenth century. He is a long-time activist in the green movement and advisor to the Environmental Action Committee of the Loyola University Community Action Programme.

Laurence Davis teaches politics at the National University of Ireland Maynooth. He was awarded a doctoral degree in politics by Oxford University, and has taught at a range of universities in the UK and Ireland, including Oxford University, Ruskin College, and University Colleges Dublin and Galway. His current research interests include anarchist and utopian political thought, social radicalism and the arts, and the politics of work and love. He is the editor, with Peter Stillman, of *The New Utopian Politics of Ursula K. Le Guin's The Dispossessed* (Lexington Books, 2005).

Uri Gordon is an Israeli activist, writer and lecturer. He holds a doctorate in politics from the University of Oxford and is the author of *Anarchy Alive! Anti-authoritarian Politics from Practice to Theory* (Pluto Press, 2008). While completing his doctoral research in the UK and Europe he organised with community initiatives and with anti-capitalist networks including Dissent!, Indymedia and Anarchists Against the Wall. Currently he lives on an ecological kibbutz in Israel's southern desert and teaches Israeli, Palestinian and Jordanian students at the Arava Institute for Environmental

Studies. His research continues to focus on anarchist political theory and grassroots sustainability.

Brian Greenspan is Director of the Hypertext and Hypermedia Lab and Associate Professor in the Department of English and the Institute for Comparative Studies in Literature, Art and Culture at Carleton University in Ottawa. His published research focuses on satire, utopian literature and new narrative media. He is currently writing a historical study of Australian dystopias.

Judy Greenway is a Visiting Research Fellow in Cultural Studies at the University of East London. Most of her writing has been on gender, sexuality, anarchism and utopianism, and her chapter in this book derives from a longer work in progress on anarchism, feminism and sexual utopianism in Britain between the 1880s and the 1930s. She is a member of the editorial board of *Anarchist Studies*.

Gisela Heffes is an Assistant Professor in the Department of Hispanic Studies at Rice University, Houston, Texas. She is the author of the annotated edition *Judíos/Argentinos/Escritores* (Atril, 1999) and has published numerous articles, reviews and interviews in both Spanish and English. Her recent book, *Las ciudades imaginarias en la literatura latinoamericana* (*Imaginary Cities in Latin American Literature*), is a study of the literary representations of non-existent urban spaces and their significance in the wider political and cultural framework of Latin America. Besides her academic work, she is also an active fiction writer, having published the novels *Ischia* (Paradiso, 2000) *Praga* (Paradiso, 2001) and *Ischia, Praga & Bruselas* (Beatriz Viterbo, 2005) and several short stories and fictional chronicles.

Ruth Kinna teaches political thought at Loughborough University. She completed her doctorate on Kropotkin's theory of mutual aid and has since published on late nineteenth-century anarchism and socialism. She is the author of *William Morris: The Art of Socialism* (University of Wales Press, 2000) and *Anarchism: A Beginner's Guide* (One World, 2005) and editor of the three-volume collection, *Early Writings on Terrorism* (Routledge, 2005).

Brigitte Koenig, PhD, is Associate Professor of History and Co-director of the Elizabeth Ann Seton Center for Women's Studies at Seton Hall University, South Orange, New Jersey. This essay has evolved from her larger study of anarchist cultural politics in the United States, *American Anarchism: A History* (forthcoming from Oxford University Press).

Peter Marshall has a doctoral degree in the history of ideas from Sussex University. He has taught philosophy and literature at several British universities and is now a full-time author. He has written fifteen books translated into as many languages. They include *William Godwin* (Yale University Press, 1984); *William Blake: Visionary Anarchist* (Freedom Press, 1988; new edition, 2009); *Nature's Web: Rethinking our Place on Earth* (Simon & Schuster, 1992; new edition, M.E. Sharpe, 1996); *Demanding the Impossible: A History of Anarchism* (HarperCollins, 1992; new edition Harper Perennial, 2008), and *Riding the Wind: Liberation Ecology for a New Era* (Cassell, 1998; new edition Continuum, 2009). His website is www.petermarshall.net.

Saul Newman (PhD UNSW 1998) is a Reader in Politics at Goldsmiths, University of London. His research is in the area of continental and poststructuralist political theory, and contemporary radical politics. He is the author of *From Bakunin to Lacan* (Rowman & Littlefield, 2001); *Power and Politics in Poststructuralist Thought* (Routledge, 2005); *Unstable Universalities* (Manchester University Press, 2007), and *Politics Most Unusual* (Palgrave, 2008), as well as numerous journal articles.

Dominic Ording is Assistant Professor of English at Northern Michigan University in Marquette, on the shores of Lake Superior in Michigan's Upper Peninsula. His research interests this season include masculinity and LGBTQ (Lesbian Gay Bisexual Transgender and Queer) studies and the presence of philosophy, religion and spirituality in diverse literatures and communities.

John A. Rapp, Professor of Political Science at Beloit College, in Beloit, Wisconsin, teaches classes in comparative politics and Asian studies, including courses on anarchism, Daoism and Chinese politics. His research focuses on modern Chinese Marxist dissidents as well as Daoist anarchists of ancient and medieval China. His publications include the co-authored book (with Anita M. Andrew) *Autocracy and China's Rebel Founding Emperors: Comparing Chairman Mao and Ming Taizu* (Lanham, Maryland: Rowman & Littlefield Publishers, 2000), and two articles for the journal *Anarchist Studies*, 'Daoism and Anarchism Reconsidered' (1998) and 'Maoism and Anarchism: Mao Zedong's Response to the Anarchist Critique of Marxism' (2001).

Nicholas Spencer was an Associate Professor in the Department of English at the University of Nebraska-Lincoln. His publications include *After Utopia: The Rise of Critical Space in Twentieth-Century American Fiction* (University of Nebraska Press, 2006), articles in journals such as *Contemporary Literature*, *Arizona Quarterly* and *Angelaki*, and essays in various edited book collections. He died in 2008.

Peter G. Stillman is Professor of Political Science at Vassar College, Poughkeepsie, New York, where he has taught since 1970. His primary teaching interests lie in modern political thought from the Renaissance through to the present. His research interests are in Hegel's political philosophy, Marx's political theory, ecological political thought and utopian thought. He has published more than thirty articles and book chapters on these topics, as well as editing two collections of essays, one with Laurence Davis entitled *The New Utopian Politics of Ursula K. Le Guin's The Dispossessed*. He is currently working on utopian thought and on the politics of New Orleans since Hurricane Katrina.

Judith Suissa is Lecturer in Philosophy of Education at the Institute of Education, University of London. Her research interests include radical and libertarian theories of education, political education and philosophical aspects of the parent–child relationship. Her book, *Anarchism and Education: A Philosophical Perspective*, was published by Routledge in 2006.

Preface

Paradise is where the sun shines on both sides of the hedge (Old Devon saying)

A map of the world that does not include Utopia is not worth even glancing at . . . (Oscar Wilde)

Utopia is an ideal society in an imaginary country. 'Utopia' in Greek means 'No place', and utopias are frustratingly to be found on faraway islands, continents or planets which are difficult to reach. In their literary form, they are intended to fire the imagination by presenting what the poet Philip Sydney called 'a speaking picture'. Not surprisingly, utopians are often dismissed by the sensible and the practical as idle dreamers at best or dangerous maniacs at worst. They are deemed irredeemably fanciful, naive and escapist. In short, to be utopian means to be 'unscientific', that most heinous of sins and Engels' greatest crime. God save us from such people. In the meantime, the best one can hope for, our rulers tell us, is the closed space of state-regulated global capitalism. History and ideology have come to an end. The age of dreams is over. Or is it?

Utopian thinking and reverie have been with us a very long time, ever since our ancestors on the African savannah first lifted up their heads and wondered what kind of society might be over the horizon or on the other side of the mountain range. This ability to imagine what is not, to think otherwise, to envision an alternative future seems peculiar to humans. It can be paradoxical and has undoubtedly on occasion got us into trouble but it has also conjured up some wondrous visions of freedom and love.

Associated with the idea of utopia is the golden age, a period of peace and plenty at the beginning of time. Any fundamental change from this pristine dawn was considered a tragic decline. Only within the Judaeo-Christian tradition, with its teleological myth of a beginning and an end, has the idea of progress emerged in the west. Since the Enlightenment, it has been exported with capitalism throughout the world.

For many, the golden age is now seen not in the distant past but in a mythical future, usually brought about by science, technology, reason and the free market. Work hard now, defer joy, consume as much as you can, obey your rulers and all shall be well. This is the dead-end that liberal democracy serving capitalism has to offer, the only form of government and society said to be universally valid. Trouble is, not everyone enjoys living in such a world, nor, given the limited resources of the planet, can they. And, as recent events have shown, the anti-utopia of global capitalism and industrial civilisation is beginning to collapse due to its own internal contradictions and excesses.

Not to be outdone, the monotheistic religions have offered their own versions of utopia, not on earth but in heaven. Their crude descriptions of paradise include compliant virgins, trumpeting angels, never-ending fountains and pearly gates. This prospect of endless pie in the sky has been used to justify the ways of God to man and to keep the oppressed, especially women, in their place. To be sure of admittance into this utopia of the afterlife, one must obey the priests, curb unruly desires and never leave the straight and narrow path of righteousness.

Naturally, philosophers and writers have followed the prophets and been quick to offer their own versions of utopia. While anarchism has always had a utopian dimension in the sense of imagining a free society without the state, not all literary utopias have been anarchistic. The mainstream of utopian writing, from Plato onwards, has been authoritarian and totalitarian, offering an ideal form of centralised government which controls a rigid and hierarchical society. Like Thomas More's *Utopia*, they describe a centralised state promoting virtue through the rule of a rational elite. They sacrifice freedom for security, individuality for comfort (contemporary echoes there). The setting – the *topos* – for their city states is neat and ordered. Nature is conquered. Time is banished. There is no room for change. Woe betide the poet, the artist and the individualist who would like to stick out her tongue or pull a funny face. That ubiquitous troublemaker Freedom, who would turn the world upside down, is locked out of the city gates and must roam in the tangled wilderness beyond.

There are of course real dangers in being swept away by such utopias, especially when they are offered by charismatic leaders. The utopias of the authoritarian communists are as bad as those of the fascists. Indeed, most so-called utopias which deny personal autonomy and individuality would be best described as dystopias. Nevertheless, without the utopian imagination it would be impossible to imagine a different world from the one in which we live. We would be stuck in the cloying mud of abject deference, endless toil and grinding poverty of body and spirit. Without the generous vision of a better society, there would be little hope and less change.

While the utopian mainstream has been authoritarian and based on hierarchy and domination like the cultures which have produced them, there has fortunately in the history of ideal societies been a powerful undertow of imaginative libertarian utopias. In the oral tradition, from the Land of Cockaigne to the Big Rock Candy Mountain, the poor and oppressed have enjoyed songs and ballads which celebrate a country of freedom and abundance, a country where there are no kings and priests, no bosses and police, where sex is easily available, food falls from the sky and alcohol runs in streams. It is a place where the sun shines on both sides of a hedge which no longer serves as a boundary to private property but as a haven for wildlife and a resting place for travellers.

Ever since Lao Zi (or those associated with his name) launched a rural idyll of peace and contentment over two thousand years ago there has also been a rich tradition of libertarian literary utopias which depict a world without coercive government, laws and authority. They offer sexual freedom without shame, fulfilment without force. Rabelais, Diderot, Morris and Le Guin have among others offered such inspiring and life-affirming 'talking pictures'. Paradoxically, their utopias often have a strong sense of *topos*, of place, and are rooted in a flourishing landscape.

Critics of anarchism have dismissed it as utopian in the negative sense of being 'nowhere' and incapable of being realised. Yet many successful libertarian and utopian experiments have taken place in the past, ranging from the medieval communes of the sisters and brothers of the Free Spirit, the Ranters and Diggers of the English Commonwealth, the breech-less sections of the French Revolution, the assemblies of the Paris Commune and the council democracy in the early days of the Russian Revolution, to the agricultural and industrial collectives during the Spanish Civil War. Since then, intentional communities, free schools, cooperatives and the affinity groups and temporary autonomous zones of the green, peace and global justice movements have all taken on a libertarian and utopian dimension. 'Another world is possible,' they declare.

They have created flowing alternative spaces in the cracked shells of existing states and the burgeoning wastelands of post-industrial civilisation. Even their horizontal and decentralised ways of organising are libertarian utopias in-the-making. They engage in pre-figurative politics and constructive direct action, living out what they hope to create, walking the talk, being the change. If such diverse experiments have succeeded in the past, however short-lived, they are undoubtedly part of the collective experience of humanity, and can take place on a larger scale in the continuously developing present.

The elements of an anarchist society have always been with us, like seeds in a desert, ready to blossom whenever the life-giving rain begins to fall and the earth gives up its bounty. While state jugglers lead us to 'no place' worthwhile, anarchist principles, enlivened by the utopian imagination, can take us to a genuinely free society in harmony with the natural world. Unlike the square, static, blueprint utopias of statists, libertarian utopias like anarchism itself tend to be dynamic, fluid, organic and open-ended, delighting in change and endless experimentation. There is no revolutionary closure: they offer a process, not an end; a journey rather than arrival.

Anarchist utopias value mutual aid and solidarity as well as personal freedom and autonomy. Rather than imposing a repressive morality, they provide ample room for personal creativity and the free satisfaction of desire. Work, now depressing the spirit and avoided like the plague, is transformed into meaningful play fulfilling the all-rounded personality. The individual is able to blossom in the bosom of the community. Unity in diversity is encouraged in society as well as in nature. The anarchist utopia is not the closed space of a perfect society but engages in constant struggle against protean forms of domination, hierarchy and exploitation. It is the active creation of a more generous, loving and free society. It operates in the present tense.

In one sense, Oscar Wilde is right: 'Progress is the realization of Utopias'. But in a deeper sense, utopia need not be looked for in some imaginary country or in a mythical future but can be discovered and created here and now. The utopia of a free society is an ever-present possibility. As William Blake observed, if we cleanse 'the doors of perception', 'every thing that lives is Holy'. If we can only see it, the everyday world is infinitely meaningful and beautiful and full of promise.

Unless troubled and duped by rulers, oligarchs and soldiers, for most of human history people have tended to be cooperative, peaceful and kind. They prefer to love rather than to kill and maim. Such libertarian tendencies are always around us and within us. The golden age is not therefore to be found in the remote past or in the faraway future, but is a flaming fire within us all waiting to shine forth. It is not therefore unrealistic to live freely in our everyday lives, to demand what the rulers and cynics call impossible.

This wide-ranging and lively collection of essays not only reveals the visions underlying libertarian utopian thinking but shows how anarchism and utopianism have both enriched each other. Utopianism is valuable for stimulating critical thought and for conjuring up different alternatives to existing political and social realities. Anarchism is utopian in holding up the vision of a free society but it is also realistic in drawing on existing libertarian trends and recognising that means are ends-in-the-making.

These colourful and stimulating essays mirror their own subject, breaking out of neat classifications and occasionally disagreeing with each other. They show the great variety of anarchist thinking, feeling and imagining. The reader can admire the splendid views from the open road of freedom as well as wander off on less travelled paths to hidden clearings of joy, hope and beauty. Above all, these essays vividly demonstrate that libertarian utopias are not only eminently desirable but also immediately realisable. So I say: 'All power to the utopian and anarchist imagination!'

Peter Marshall

Acknowledgements

We would like to express our deep thanks to all those who have been involved in this project, work on which began in the summer of 2005. First, to our contributors, who have demonstrated an enormous commitment to it by their patience and by their inexplicably cheerful responses to seemingly endless requests to read and re-read their work. We would like to thank our editors at Manchester University Press, not only because they have also been very patient with us but also because we know how extraordinarily reluctant publishers are to consider edited collections. We have benefited greatly from Jon Purkis's diligent, perceptive and encouraging reviews of the proposal and draft manuscript, and we are extremely grateful to Peter Marshall for lending his support to the project. Finally, we thank the organisers of the autumn 2006 meeting of the Society for Utopian Studies in Colorado Springs, USA, and the summer 2006 meeting of the European Utopian Studies Society in Tarragona, Spain, for facilitating discussion of the book's contents in such congenial surroundings.

Laurence Davis and Ruth Kinna

Laurence Davis

Introduction

Anarchism is one of the most vital impulses of contemporary radical politics. A practice-grounded way of seeing the world that provides a framework for understanding and acting upon some of the most pressing problems of our times, it is currently thriving in the decentralised networks of the alter-globalisation movement, as well as in countless experiments in co-operative production and distribution, alternative media and art, and collective living. Fired by the conviction that it is possible to create another world far better than the upside down one we currently inhabit, those now inspired by anarchist ideas have refused to acquiesce to the prevailing consensus that there is no alternative to a way of life based on domination and hierarchy.

Yet most such activists are also notably reticent about articulating detailed conceptions of what might take its place. Wary of the many potential pitfalls of utopian speculation and, in particular, of the ways in which it may constrain free thinking rather than enrich it, many anarchists are now united far more by what they are against than what they are for. The primary aim of this book is to encourage further reflection on the wisdom of such blanket anarchist anti-utopianism. It does so by assembling the first collection of original essays to explore the *relationship* between anarchism and utopianism and, in particular, the ways in which their long historical interaction from the Warring States epoch of ancient China to the present day has proven fruitful for emancipatory politics.

A collection of essays about the relationship between anarchism and utopianism would, on the face of it, appear to be an unlikely endeavour. After all, what could Kropotkin's *Fields, Factories and Workshops* and the *Daodejing* of Lao Zi, or the anarchist collectives in republican Spain and the utopian eco-communes of the late 1960s, possibly have in common?

One plausible answer to this question is that they are all thoroughly impractical. From such a 'pragmatic' point of view, neither anarchist nor utopian ideas are worth taking seriously because they cannot possibly be realised in practice.

The difficulty with this line of reasoning is that it fails to distinguish between different senses of 'impossibility'. While some things are indeed impossible, others are 'impossible' only because humanly created institutions make them so. For example, many people would dearly like to engage in a wide variety of creative work without needing to worry about whether it would yield them a sufficient 'income'. However, this is not a realistic option in societies where income is tied to waged work and capital. On the other hand, it would be a realistic option in a society that guaranteed a decent livelihood for all. Hence the need for anarchist and utopian thought experiments and experiments in living that expose the partiality of currently dominant perceptions of reality, and thus facilitate free choice from among a fuller range of practical social alternatives.

Another, more sophisticated, answer to the question of the relationship between anarchism and utopianism is that they in fact have very little in common, because while both may expand the horizons of the possible they do so in very different ways. Whereas utopians from Plato to More to Bellamy have dreamt of a rational social order administered by a centralised state, anarchists have instead insisted on the value of individual freedom and resolutely maintained that society can and should be organised without the coercive authority of the state.

While true in some respects, this reply is also too simplistic, insofar as it fails to account for the numerous instances in which the two traditions have overlapped or intersected. As several of our contributors point out, the state-centric tendency of much utopian writing is not a defining feature of the genre. Hence the rationale for this book, and for its original treatment of the subject fields under study.

The fourteen international and interdisciplinary chapters that we ultimately accepted for publication following a rigorous review process fall into two distinct, though not impermeable, generic categories. The first set of papers addresses the topic in broad philosophical fashion, by analysing the historically variable conceptual nature of the relationship between anarchist and utopian ideas, movements and communal experiments. The second illuminates it by focusing more narrowly on specific case studies of instances in which the traditions converged, be it in literary works, dissident spiritual philosophies, anthropological studies, unorthodox lifestyles, self-consciously political expressions of gender and sexuality, experiments in alternative education, ecological communities or revolutionary social movements.

Our organisation of this material reflects two primary considerations: first, the assessments we made about the continuities between the individual essays; and second, our wish to incorporate into the structure of the book topics that would exemplify the creative relationship between anarchism and utopianism. The volume opens with John Clark's impressively wide-ranging analytical survey of the history of that relationship. As Clark points out, Plato's *Republic* and Lao Zi's *Daodejing* are the original, paradigmatic utopias of world literature. The former is a work of civilisation, and in expressing the *telos* of civilisation seeks to banish the remnants of the pre-civilised and to exclude that which remains outside of, and resistant to, civilisation. The latter, by contrast, constitutes the first great rebellion of poetic thought against the civilised order. It looks to those natural and cultural forces that are the devalued and rejected 'other' of civilised domination, and affirms their reality and worth. Implicit in the opposition between these two primordial visions of the ideal – one statist and the other anarchic – is the entire history of the dialectic of utopia that has unfolded over the past two and a half millennia. In the modern world, Clark suggests, the anarchic utopia is perhaps most compellingly represented in three types of utopian imagination: the utopia of aesthetic creativity, the utopia of desire, and socio-historical manifestations of utopia evident in certain communal experiments and revolutionary movements.

We reflect these concerns in the editorial structure of the book by commencing with fresh assessments of two classic literary utopias that challenged the dominant norms of civilised rationality. We then proceed to consider in turn exemplary anarchist utopian expressions of aesthetic creativity and sexual desire during the past two centuries, and conclude with four theoretically rigorous chapters analysing contemporary forms of revolutionary practice.

The first section of the book following Clark's introductory survey is entitled 'Antecedents of the anarchist literary utopia', and includes complementary chapters by John Rapp and Peter Stillman re-examining two of the most influential of such antecedents, Lao Zi's *Daodejing* and Diderot's *Supplément au voyage de Bougainville*. Both Rapp and Stillman are particularly concerned to assess the radicalism of their respective subject texts in the historical contexts in which they were written, and in this respect at least reach some very similar – though not entirely consonant – conclusions. Just as the *Daodejing* draws on the norms and practices of a peaceful, pre-existing tradition of stateless agrarian community in order to oppose the increasing centralisation of state power in the late Warring State epoch of ancient China (ca. 400 to 221 BCE), so the *Supplément* draws on the norms and practices of eighteenth-century Tahiti in order to criticise the imperial French state. However, whereas according to Rapp the *Daodejing* harkens back to a temporarily lost natural order, Stillman interprets the *Supplément* as an enigmatic utopian text in which the 'natural' turns out to be a complex, ambiguous and uncertain standard.

The next section of the book, entitled 'Anti-capitalism and the anarchist utopian literary imagination', features four essays exploring the challenges posed by anarchist utopian literary works of the nineteenth and twentieth centuries to the currently dominant, capitalist global order associated with the ruthless exploitation of nature, ever-expanding production for profit and the increasing rationalisation of society. Laurence Davis does so by evaluating the profoundly romantic revolutionary aesthetic legacies of William Morris, Oscar Wilde and Ursula K. Le Guin, all of whom imagined post-capitalist, non-coercive societies in which artistic creation would replace profit-driven economy as the fundamental aim of social life; Nicholas Spencer by analysing sophisticated models of egalitarian social power in selected works of B. Traven and Pierre Clastres inspired by the indigenous populations of Latin America; Gisela Heffes by focusing on the treatment of emotion in undeservedly neglected anti-capitalist utopias of early twentieth-century Argentina and Mexico; and Brian Greenspan by elucidating the anti-colonial impulses of an exceptionally rich but largely forgotten Australian manuscript that identified in the slums of Melbourne a dialectical link between the communal societies of the pre-capitalist past and a utopian, post-capitalist future. While the geographical scope of these chapters is quite wide, all of them call into question modern conceptions of progress and recall the organic communities of the pre-modern past in order to inspire and inform contemporary libertarian struggles for a more humane future.

The fourth part of the volume, entitled 'Free love: anarchist politics and utopian desire', provides a focused case study of a particular set of issues raised by the interplay of anarchism and utopianism, insofar as all three of the featured essays examine the theory and practice of free love as an expression of anarchist politics and utopian desire. Inspired in part by feminism, gay liberation and contemporary queer theory, these chapters illuminate the relationship not only between anarchism and utopianism, but also between the personal and the political – in particular the links and tensions between sexual and social radicalism. Judy Greenway does so by tracking anarchist advocacy of free love in fin de siècle Britain, during a critical period when it grew from a private conviction to a public expression of utopian desire; Brigitte Koenig by exploring the themes of maternalism, sexuality and reproduction in contemporaneous works of American anarchist utopian fiction unjustly forgotten by historians and literary critics; and Dominic Ording by considering the utopian and anarchist impulses in a set of autobiographical texts written by politically active gay men in the years immediately following the 1969 Stonewall rebellion. If there is a dominant theme in these chapters, it is the idea of speaking/living/being utopia as a manifestation of the anarchist emphasis on the inextricable interrelationship of means and ends.

Very importantly, nearly all of the utopias examined in Parts II–IV are open and dynamic and organically linked to anarchic social practices. And our authors consistently highlight the differences between these utopias and the rationally fixed and transcendent utopias associated with escapism and/or domination. There is a consensus that such anti-perfectionist and anti-authoritarian utopias do not represent a form of abstraction from the world. On the contrary, they help to shape social practices by converting the given confines of the here and now into an open horizon of possibilities.

These themes are also taken up in the final section of the book, 'Rethinking revolutionary practice'. In this section all four authors make use of the tools of normative political philosophy in order to analyse the shifting role of utopian thinking in contemporary anarchist revolutionary practice. At one level, their conclusions are quite similar. From different perspectives, all of them highlight the perils of perfectionist conceptions of utopia understood as a rational and rigidly fixed projection of a perfected society of the future to be realised once and for all 'after the revolution'. Beyond this common floor of agreement, however, their conclusions differ dramatically. At the level of historically oriented textual analysis, Saul Newman and Ruth Kinna disagree directly about the epistemological and political functions of science in Kropotkin's anarchist utopian revolutionary theory. At a much broader political and philosophical level, both Newman and Uri Gordon associate 'classical' nineteenth-century anarchist utopian thinking with a Marxian-influenced conception of utopia as the harmonious closure of the revolutionary project. They also comment approvingly about what they regard as the relatively recent rise of a strongly open-ended (Gordon) and present-tense oriented (Newman and Gordon) tendency in utopian thinking. In stark contrast, Kinna (implicitly, given her primary focus on the fraught relationship between anarchism and Marxism in the nineteenth century) and Judith Suissa (explicitly) argue that the anarchist utopia has never been an end-state model like Plato's *Republic*, but has the commitment to constant experimentation and flux built into it. Indeed, according to Suissa, these qualities constitute the essence of the anarchist utopia, which has always been focused first and foremost on transforming the present as part of an organic process in which already existing historical tendencies are actively engaged with, nurtured and built upon.

Like the open-ended utopian works it examines, this book does not purport to offer final and definitive answers to the very large questions it raises. Nor does it aspire to achieve a comprehensive treatment of the subject matter. Rather, its aim is to stimulate further reflection and informed dialogue about an intrinsically interesting but relatively neglected topic that has taken on renewed political significance with the rise of the contemporary alter-globalisation movement and the emergence of new anarchist forms of feminism, gay and black and indigenous liberation, post-colonialism, pacifism and ecologism. Hence the rich diversity of opinions and the wide variety of perspectives in the pages that follow. As editors of the volume, we hope that you the reader will take pleasure reflecting on it in the anarchist utopian spirit in which it is intended: namely, as an open, dynamic and socially engaged contribution to a continuing conversation with significant implications for emancipatory politics.

PART I

Historical and philosophical overview

| John P. Clark

Anarchy and the dialectic of utopia

The highest aspirations of the imagination are called utopia. But utopia is just as much the *enemy* of the imagination, and is our nemesis today. We live in the shadow of a terrifying utopia and must search the shadows for those other utopias that have been eclipsed. The dominant utopia is the utopia of endless material progress, based on a fundamental utopian fantasy of infinite powers of production and infinite possibilities for consumption. This utopia inspires the system of superpower that is expanding its global domination and threatening the very future of life on earth.

The ultimate telos of this dominant utopia is the reduction of the world to the most literally utopian state; to the condition of a nowhere. Yet its everyday reality is presented as an inevitable march of progress that promises everything to everybody everywhere. As Ronald Reagan, the great utopian salesman, once said, '[p]rogress is our most important product!'[1] Through this march, it drives relentlessly toward the destruction of all diversity and complexity – of ecosystems, cultures, personalities and imaginations. It progressively undermines any 'sense of place' but, more fundamentally, it demolishes or dissolves the actual rich specificity of natural place, the biological diversity upon which that cultural sense rests materially. Beyond its everyday reality is its ultimate triumph and ultimate utopian nightmare. That is its ontological breakthrough: its actual attainment, through its nuclear technologies, of the power to transform our world into its most radically utopian state, into the ultimate nowhere of non-being.

Fortunately, there are other utopian possibilities, other utopian spaces and other utopian times, for us to choose. For every empty space there is a richness of place; for all empty duration there is a fullness of time.

The origins of utopia

The divergent paths of utopian thinking had already been travelled by the time of the original, paradigmatic utopias of world literature: the *Republic* of Plato and the *Daodejing* of Lao Zi. Of course, even these 'original' utopias have origins deep in history and prehistory. Plato's utopian project is a work of civilisation. It is situated in the evolution of civilisation, it is a product of civilised self-consciousness, and it is an effort to legitimate the institutional structure of civilised domination. In that sense, it is not only written *in* history but written *on behalf of* history. In expressing the telos of civilisation, it seeks to banish the remnants of the pre-civilised and to exclude that which remains outside of, and resistant to, civilisation.

On the other hand, Lao Zi's utopia constitutes the first great rebellion of poetic thought against the civilised order. It looks back to pre-civilised personhood and the pre-civilised community (*the Uncarved Block*) and finds there a realm that escapes the order of domination. It looks to those natural and cultural forces that are the devalued and rejected other of civilisation and affirms their reality and worth. In this sense, it is a work written *against* history.[2]

Plato's *Republic* (except to the degree that the project unconsciously subverts itself) represents the effort of civilised rationality, the logos of domination, to banish the forces of resistance, and to establish itself, once and for all. The forces of resistance are exactly those encountered by the archetypal Hero of Greek civilisation, Odysseus: the powers of nature, desire, the unconscious, the primitive, and the feminine. Odysseus, through the exercise of rational self-repression and rational assertion of will, conquers these forces in their mythical guise – as Circe, Calypso, the Lotus-Eaters, Scylla, Charybdis, and so forth. Plato's task was to translate this story into philosophy.

Thus, Plato presents the same process of conquest in non-mythical form (though he reserves for myth an important place as an arm of theory). He theorises it as the quest for the ideal state, ruled by the wise. It is a state in which reason itself is said to dominate through their edicts, in which desire and the body are subjected to the control of reason and its rational representatives, and in which knowledge and power are unified in this system of rule.

A truly utopian – and totalitarian – conception of justice is finally attained. For justice (the theme of the work) is discovered to be that harmony in which all contradictions are resolved, all conflict pacified, all resistance broken. Plato's subject matter is how to subject matter (the world of untamed nature) to the rule of reason, so that even the most irrational and unruly forces are brought under control.

It is pertinent that the title of Plato's work is not *Polis* but rather *Politeia*. While he presents us with a depiction of an 'ideal state', to do so is not its primary function. As Allan Bloom points out, the title can more accurately be translated as 'The Regime'.[3] He divulges the usually well-kept secret (a philosophical 'purloined letter') that the unifying theme of the book is less the abstract idea of justice than the concrete reality of power, its attainment, its exercise, and its systematisation.[4] We might call it the original utopia of state power.

The *Daodejing*, on the other hand, is the original utopia of stateless freedom. Ironically, this work has sometimes been interpreted as a manual for the cunning ruler. Literal-minded readers east and west have seen it as a book of advice on how to rule successfully, a do-it-yourself book for the crafty prince who wants to learn how to control his subjects without appearing to dominate them.[5] And, granted, the title itself has been aptly translated as the 'Book of the Way and Its *Power*'.

But this is a subtle work, and is among the most dialectical and poetic of the classics of world literature. What less would one expect from an author whose name has been interpreted not only as 'the Old Sage' but also as 'the Old Child'? He is one who unites wisdom and spontaneity, experience and innocence, seriousness and play. What the Old Boy tells us is that the Daoist prince is the ruler who rules without ruling, the Empire is the realm beyond force and coercion, and the power is the very negation of domination. This is why the *Daodejing* can appropriately be called 'The Anarchist *Prince*', and Lao Zi the 'anti-Machiavelli'.

The *Daodejing* depicts an Empire in which all beings are allowed to follow their 'natural' course of development, their *Dao*. The result is a world in which humanity and nature are in harmony, in which human beings live together peacefully and cooperatively, and in which universal self-realisation is fostered. However, the Daoist harmony is not that of a pacified or homogenised world in which all conflict, opposition, and otherness are dissolved. Rather it is a discordant harmony, in which unity is expressed through multiplicity and difference, and in which beings are mutually determined by and even contain within themselves the other.

The Daoist utopia is not achieved through domination in any of its forms, whether political, economic, patriarchal, technological, or even epistemological. Rather, through an ontology of unity-in-difference, the other is given authentic recognition. Knowledge becomes sympathetic understanding and participatory consciousness, as opposed to conquest and subjugation. The hierarchies of the utopia of domination (reason over desire, form over matter, soul over body, male over female, adult over child, humanity over nature, civilised man over the primitive, consciousness over the unconscious, and so on.) are thus rejected. Apparent opposites are shown to interpenetrate, to complement one another, and to be necessary elements of a larger whole (that is, of course, also a non-whole). The Daoist utopia, expressed as a mythical golden age to be re-attained, is such a unity-in-diversity, in which self-realisation is maximised for all beings.

The entire history of utopia that has unfolded over two and a half millennia is implicit in the opposition between these two primordial visions.

Utopia as domination

Throughout history, there have been utopian expressions of the quest for domination. Such utopias project the existing system of domination into a perfected future order in which the contradictions that cannot be reconciled in the real world are resolved through an act of sovereign imagination. The resulting images of static perfection can then be used as weapons against the evil and the unenlightened, in short, against all the forces of resistance. Vaclav Havel, while writing as a dissident under actually existing dystopia, called such a utopia 'a more or less rationalist attempt to think up an abstract better world, to conceive "on paper" how it should be organised. It is an attempt to produce a blueprint of the best possible system and then to try to put it into practice.' The Czechs, he says, have 'lived through the failure of one great utopia, and this has given us a very skeptical and critical view of utopianism in general'.[6]

The dystopia that they endured is only one specific form of the generic utopia of domination that lies at the imaginary core of civilisation's project of universal conquest. It is closely allied to the conception of knowledge as power, a conception with roots at the beginnings of civilisation, but which has only achieved fulfilment with the rise of the nation-state, transnational capital, and the global megamachine. Havel's critique touches on this relationship of utopia to the quest for unlimited domination, for a world of 'total administration', in which all other realities, whether cultural, spiritual, psychological, or personal, are subordinated. Utopianism, he says, is 'an arrogant attempt by human reason to plan life', that 'inevitably ends up homogenizing, regimenting, standardizing and destroying life, as well as curtailing everything that projects beyond, overflows or falls outside the abstract project'.[7] He concludes that there is 'a direct and logical progression from beautiful utopias to concentration camps', which are 'but an attempt by utopians to dispose of those elements which don't fit into their utopias'.[8]

Havel is perceptive enough to have noted at times that the complementary utopianism of the corporate capitalist west leads in a direction similar to the one he detected in the state capitalist east. The utopia of consumption does not of course rely heavily on concentration camps (though it seems to be moving a bit more in that direction lately) but its tactics are in many ways similar to those Havel points out. The elements that are most threatening to its utopian illusion are also concentrated – in ghettos, in reservations, in human and ecological sacrifice zones – as the unthinkable horrors on the margins of utopia. However, such dystopian dimensions of the everyday can be ideologically banished in a world in which everyone who can shop at Walmart and dine at McDonald's can self-identify as middle class, and is convinced, in any case, that 'There Is No Alternative'. Thus, it becomes increasingly evident that totalitarianism reaches its greatest perfection in the utopia of consumption. Its only remaining rival of any consequence is the competing totalitarianism of religious fundamentalism. And though the battle between these totalising systems continues to intensify, there is no doubt that the overwhelmingly more powerful one at this moment in history on a global scale remains the 'empire of consumption'.

Totalitarianism today is not on the deepest level a matter of sovereignty. Nor does it depend on the state's formal abolition of all competing forms of social organisation (though the evils embodied in this political totalisation process and its system of oppression and terror cannot be overemphasised). The ultimate totalitarian achievement is the capture of the imagination, and the reinforcement of that conquest as the dominant order is legitimated through processes of sublimation and banalisation. The consuming subject is over-awed by the sublime consumptionist spectacle and automatised by the realities and rituals of everyday productionist and consumptionist life.

The economistic system's values are not yet universal but are, however, hegemonic. This means they are enshrined in the reigning 'common sense' or dominant 'reality principle'. Furthermore, they are constantly extending their dominion, especially in their consumptionist dimension. The growing success of the totalitarian project depends on the efficacy of the consumptionist utopia and its image of the good life. It is a life of happiness, health, love, sex, beauty, power, fun, and immortality. And it is available to all who buy the right commodities and know how to perpetually *refashion* their very selves into the right kind of commodities. It is available, that is, in the form of the fundamental fantasy of the world of consumption. It is with good reason that a popular version of this fantasy is called 'the American Dream'.

Utopia as elitism

The history of utopianism contains abundant evidence of its ideological use for purposes of power and manipulation. Plato, again, outlined the essentials of the programme quite well. First, the utopian order is defined as a harmony in which all contradictions are resolved. Next, an ideology is devised in which the system of power is identified with the order of nature and social domination is redefined as universal self-realisation. And, finally, the rule of the elite is mystified further as an expression of the divine will. This 'noble lie' has been more than a mere philosophical fiction. Its basic structure has remained intact over history, requiring only an updating of the content (as when, for example, historical inevitability is substituted for divine will).

But utopian elitism has infected not only the more obviously authoritarian utopian ideals. It has been exemplified as well in seemingly libertarian tendencies, such as the heresy of the free spirit. In a sense, the free spirit was one of the most anti-authoritarian movements in history. Flourishing in the thirteenth and fourteenth centuries, it followed Joachim of Fiore's teaching of the coming of the third stage of history, the age of the holy spirit, which would see 'the illumination of all, in mystical democracy, without masters and Church'.[9] It proclaimed that the law of Church, state and traditional morality were all abolished for those who enter into the Joachimite utopian realm. In its extreme antinomianism, the movement adhered in a sense to the most radically anarchistic position.

However, this anarchic rejection of law disguised certain profoundly authoritarian dimensions of the movement. In particular, there remained a hierarchy between the more advanced adepts of the movement and the masses drawn to it. According to Norman Cohn, 'after "becoming God", a new adept began to seek contact with pious souls who wished to "attain perfection". From these he exacted an oath of blind obedience, which was made on bended knees . . . they gave a promise of absolute obedience to a human being and received in return an assurance that they could do no sin.'[10] Moreover, there are serious problems even with the sexual iconoclasm and eroticism that have often been seen as evidence of the movement's libertarian rejection of traditional morality. One must judge as, to say the least, less than emancipatory the view that 'just as cattle were created for the use of human beings, so women were created to be used by the Brethren of the Free Spirit'.[11]

The tradition of utilising utopian mythology to justify authoritarianism and domination has continued through the modern period. The vagaries of the Leninist manipulation of the vision of the utopia of communism are too familiar to repeat. A more instructive example is Bakunin, who, while launching an authentic and indeed powerful critique of various forms of domination, in turn used the myth of the anarchist utopia to justify elitism and personal power. He correctly described the goals of anarchism as the destruction of all the forces that restrain human freedom and the achievement of a free, cooperative society of equals acting in solidarity. Yet, in the name of this utopian ideal he was capable of advocating the control of the revolutionary movement by an enlightened elite of revolutionaries. He proposed for various secret societies an oath of 'absolute obedience' to the group, fanatical and ascetic commitment from all members, and a hierarchical relationship between levels of organisation. The justification for these authoritarian measures was their supposed temporary nature and their necessity as a means toward the imminent achievement of the utopian future.

Bakunin was finally capable of calling for an 'invisible dictatorship' that is 'all the stronger for having none of the paraphernalia of power'.[12] It is true that he counterposes to his vanguardism a multitude of anti-authoritarian declarations. The danger, however, is that to the extent that the vanguardist project is realised, the anti-authoritarian utopia will remain in a state of complete invisibility, while the putatively invisible dictators will retain a certain degree of materiality.

Utopia as escapism

It is clear that utopia may function to support an oppressive system of power and it may also become a means to establish new forms of domination. But the dangers do not end there. For even when it is not used to dominate, it may still fail to liberate. Indeed, it may function merely as an inert and impotent illusion, a utopia of escape. The lure of escapist utopianism is great for those who profess a certain idealism, but who have been frustrated in their efforts to realise their dreams, or whose situation in society renders the idea of praxis entirely unnatural.

The former situation is typical of various leftist sectarians, ranging from 'democratic centralists' to 'libertarian municipalists', whose blueprint for the future demands only earnest and dedicated propagation of the correct set of ideas which will revolutionise the world if only the masses finally learn how to pay attention and fall in line with the intended course of history. According to such an abstract idealist worldview, the tenacity with which these masses continue to hold on to their unenlightened views only reinforces the need for more vigorous propagandising and validates the virtuousness of those who fight the good fight.

The latter case pertains especially to many academic utopians. Such utopologists are the counterparts of the better-known Marxologists, who have found an even more firmly established intellectual niche. The logos of these 'ologists' is not the 'way of things' with which engaged dialectic concerns itself but rather their own 'words about things' that are always one step removed from the dynamism of the real. Utopologists are often the most well intentioned and progressive of thinkers; however, they fail to bridge the gap between good intention and effective action or grasp the connection between the movement of ideas and the movement of reality.

Escapist utopianism of all varieties remains in the vacuous realm of what Hegel called the beautiful soul, the sphere of those dreamers of moral perfection who are unable to cope with the ambiguities and uncertainties of the world and history, and therefore cling to a more manageable and immediately gratifying ideal world.

The utopia of escape has powerful attractions. So often we are inclined to believe because belief fulfils certain needs and satisfies, or even creates and then satisfies, certain desires. Accordingly, utopia can serve as a means of escape from the imperfections of the world and their inevitable reflection within our own being. It can be an escape from the exigencies of the real, from history and its unavoidable tragedies. It can be an escape from the minutiae of the everyday. It can offer an imaginary compensation for being denied real power or having real efficacy. In this sense, utopia is neurosis, a defence mechanism, a convulsive reaction against self and world. It offers an imaginary revenge against a recalcitrant reality.

Utopia as critique

In opposition to the utopianism of domination and the utopianism of escape is a utopianism that is a critique of domination and a vision of a reality beyond it. Ricoeur contends that the 'deinstitutionalization of the main human relationships' is 'the kernel of all utopias', and that though it 'may be an escape', it is also 'the arm of critique'.[13] Mannheim's classic definition of utopia also stresses its character as a challenge to the status quo. He contends that a utopian orientation is one that is, first, 'incongruous with the state of reality within which it occurs', and that secondly, 'transcends reality'. When utopian perspectives 'pass over into conduct', he says, they 'tend to shatter, either partially or wholly, the order of things prevailing at the time'.[14]

Ricoeur's analysis of the critical dimension of utopia is among the most profound, in that he situates it in relation to the social imagination. Utopia, in his view, is the corrective to that other powerful construct of the imagination, ideology. He refers to 'the eccentric function of imagination as the possibility of the nowhere', and asks, 'is not this eccentricity of the utopian imagination at the same time the cure of the pathology of ideological thinking, which has its blindness and narrowness precisely in its inability to conceive of a nowhere?'[15] Ideology is an expression of the conservative, systematising processes of the social imagination. Utopianism, in contrast, expresses the creative, self-transcending, liberating tendencies.

In reality, no ideology is 'pure' ideology, and elements of utopia are embedded even in ideology itself. It is for this reason that the process of 'immanent critique' can move from ideological premises to utopian conclusions. Nevertheless, Ricoeur's point concerning the critical, oppositional nature of utopia is well taken. He notes that there are two distinct aims for the utopian imagination in its rejection of the established order: 'to be ruled by good rulers – either ascetic or ethical – or to be ruled by no rulers. All utopias oscillate between these two poles.'[16] The first utopian option has already been described. It is the dominant authoritarian and hierarchical utopian ideal from the *Republic* of Plato to the modern fantasyland of technological progress and endless consumption.

The second option is exemplified by what Marie Louise Berneri calls, in *Journey Through Utopia*, 'the libertarian utopias'. Libertarian utopians 'oppose to the conception of the centralized state that of a federation of free communities, where the individual can express his [or her] personality without being submitted to the censure of an artificial code, where freedom is not an abstract word, but manifests itself concretely in work'.[17] Indeed, as illustrated in the utopias of Fourier and Morris (to be discussed shortly), one of the distinctive attributes of the most radically libertarian utopias is the emergence of a realm of freedom in which the very division between work and play dissolves, and does so not in some distant and endlessly mediated future, but here and now.

Utopia of desire

The civilised order has always been faced with the problem of taming or repressing passion to serve the needs of exploitative and hierarchical institutions. A primary function of civilised morality has been to subordinate individual fulfilment to the requirements of domination, which is expressed in mystified form as the universal good or the moral law. Kant stated this first principle of civilisation in section one of the *Foundations of the Metaphysics of Morals*, when he explained that if human happiness were the 'real end of nature', then our destiny would most certainly be attained best through following our instincts (that is, through the passions). However, he continues, reason tells us that this is not our true end, which is to follow the moral law merely because we recognise it to be the law.[18]

Kant grudgingly admits that it would be possible for all the members of society to renounce repression and what he sees as their higher duties for the sake of 'indulgence in pleasure'. But he hastily adds that one 'could not possibly will' that such a social order should exist, for it would mean that we would live a life 'like the inhabitants of the South Sea Islands', that is, we would 'allow our talents to rust' while we foolishly pursued a life of 'idleness, indulgence, and propagation'.[19] Significantly, Kant takes as his example of what a 'rational' human being would never choose the society that perhaps more than any other inspired the imaginations of those (Diderot, Gauguin) who sought a world in which pleasure, beauty, freedom and harmony could be reconciled. In rejecting in absolute horror the thought of any civilised person going Tahitian, Kant was exorcising the spectre of an existing society that offered evidence that unrepressed passion and human self-realisation could coexist, that utopia could have a material basis, that real world history could prefigure a new passionate order that would in turn inspire a new utopian social order.

In fact, such possibilities are precisely the premises on which Fourier bases his vision of a utopia of passionate attraction. Much as Proudhon contends that 'freedom is the mother, not the daughter of order', Fourier asserts that the passions, far from destroying social order, are the source of the most perfect harmony in society. The problem is not to bring the passions under rigid control but rather to determine how their fullest expression can contribute to a sublime harmonisation of the whole of society.

In his view, all the natural inclinations and passions of individuals can be directed freely toward activity that is beneficial for the community. He contends that under civilisation long hours of unfulfilling work activity have been dictated in the name of productivity and economic need, but that in reality all the labour required to satisfy the needs of society and indeed to produce abundance can be furnished without the infliction of such undeserved punishment. He notes that even highly pleasurable activities become boring after several hours, and asks quite sensibly how human beings can possibly be expected to engage even this long in labour that is only mildly agreeable, much less the kind that is truly unpleasant or even repugnant. Such absurdities will end, he assures us, as humanity abandons obsolete Civilisation and enters into Harmony. Through the creation of more fulfilling forms of labour, limitation of periods of work, and rotation of jobs, work will then become a form of expression of the passions, rather than a restraint on them. The same principle of harmonisation of passions that is applied to work will be expressed in all areas of social life, and indeed will be even easier to realise in other realms of social interaction, such as personal relationships, recreation, and cultural activities.

William Morris is perhaps the one other figure who ranks with Fourier among nineteenth-century utopian imaginative geniuses. Morris's contribution to utopianism includes his political essays, his work in the creative arts, and his authorship of *News from Nowhere*, one of the most notable works of utopian fiction. Morris made an enduring contribution to the liberatory utopian tradition by emphasising the importance of art, the aesthetic, and the imagination to the achievement of the good society and by exhibiting these dimensions so capably in his own work. It is common for admirers of nineteenth- and early twentieth-century radical social theory to apologise for its economism and uncritical acceptance of high technology by noting that those who formulated the theories were a product of their time, which was an epoch of the unleashing of astoundingly vast powers of production and of rapid and impressive material progress. Nevertheless, Morris was also a product of those times, and reacted to them not by internalising the values embodied in the prevailing system but rather by creating a vision of a qualitatively different society with radically different values.

He envisioned a social order in which the creative capacities of all would be allowed free expression. Human productive activity would be valued as a good in itself, rather than as a means toward accumulation of property and power. The goal of labour would be the collective creation of a community in which beauty, joy, and freedom would be realised. Morris's utopia is the quintessence of what Mumford described as 'the community as a work of art'. In imagining such ideals, utopian thinkers such as Morris and Fourier are important for creating a life-affirming, positive vision of the future as an alternative to the increasingly destructive and repressive society of their day.

This was a notable achievement; however, radical thought has become ineffectual in more recent times in part because it has continued to conceive of the social dialectic in similar terms of this stark opposition between oppressive, restrictive forces and emancipatory, liberating ones. Meanwhile the dominant system has revolutionised itself as it has moved from the productionist to the consumptionist era. It has passed beyond the highly repressive stage reflected in Kant's obsessive moralism into what Marcuse called the stage of 'repressive desublimation'. In this period desire, instinct, and passion are 'liberated', but only to the degree that they can serve the needs of an ideologically mystified system of domination. Many anarchist and utopian thinkers have continued to depict the dominant order as if it were still the same repressive system that it was in the productionist age of capital accumulation. This approach fails miserably, since those who live within the system find that the critique describes a world that does not correspond to their everyday life experience. An adequate critique must focus not only on the system's negative moment of domination but also its positive utopian one that allows it to harness the social imagination.

Perhaps the most notable recent case of such a failure is Bookchin's account of the system of domination, which suffers in large part from an inability to get beyond what Foucault called the 'repressive hypothesis'. Foucault contributes to a more subtle understanding of the mechanisms of domination by pointing out the ways in which various strategies and tactics made possible by the constraints of the system itself are sources of pleasure and gratification. The Situationists and Castoriadis make further contributions in bringing 'the spectacle' and the social imaginary, with their highly positive and constitutive dimensions, to the centre of analysis. A consideration of the role of what Bourdieu calls 'habitus', the repertoire of dispositions that internalise social structure, brings another essential dimension to light. And finally, Zizek's Hegelian–Lacanian theory goes perhaps furthest in uncovering the deepest mysteries of social subjectivity in his diagnosis of the role of the 'fundamental fantasy' and of 'enjoyment' within the social order. As Zizek often points out, the categorical imperative dictated by the superego (or Big Other) in late capitalism is 'You must enjoy!' Consequently, well-socialised postmodern subjects feel guilty not because of their fear of 'transgression' against repressive law, but rather because their level of enjoyment is never quite up to par (and usually miserably below). The most humiliating moral flaw is a failure to inhabit the imaginary consumptionist utopia.

If we take into consideration all these positive dimensions of the dominant utopian project, we can see how a utopianism of the passions and aesthetic sensibility in the tradition of Fourier and Morris, if decoupled from naive anti-authoritarian ideology, offers certain elements of what is needed in an effective alternative. Such a utopianism, by confronting the dominant system on its own utopian ground, is capable of revealing the contradictions, limitations, and falsehoods of the utopia of consumption, and of then re-channelling in a liberatory direction the desires and passions that have been captured.

The presence of utopia

It would be a disastrous error to look to utopian thinking only, or even primarily, for visions of the *future*, no matter how libertarian, just, peaceful, ecological, or desirable in any other way that future may be. For utopianism is above all about the *present*. The most utopian of utopianisms is also the most practical one. It demands Heaven on Earth and explores the extra-ordinary realities latent in the seemingly ordinary present.[20] Its ideal was expressed best by that most utopian of poets, Blake, when he asserted that when the doors of perception are opened we perceive all things as infinite. The most utopian community would be one in which the members could find the kind of numinous reality that Blake was capable of discovering in a literally quotidian event, the rising of the sun: 'What it will be Questiond When the Sun rises do you not see a round Disk of fire somewhat like a Guinea O no no I see an Innumerable company of the Heavenly host crying Holy Holy Holy is the Lord God Almighty I question not my corporeal or Vegetative Eye any more than I would Question a Window concerning a Sight I look thro it & not with it.'[21] This does not mean that every one of their experiences must be a Blakean mystical epiphany; however, it may very well mean that each member of the community would become the kind of 'truly experienced person' who, according to Gary Snyder, 'delights in the ordinary'.[22]

The most liberatory utopianism affirms this existence of the eternal, the sublime, the marvellous, as a present reality and an object of present experi-ence. It does not propose any 'metaphysics of presence' that posits an unmediated essential reality that somehow reveals to us its full being. Rather it is a *radical empiricism of presence* that allows what is present to present itself, to give itself as a miraculous gift. What appears may be medi-ated, but the mediations, the layers of appearance, are also present, they are part of the gift. There is however no need for what is present to be mediated by various ideas of essence or ultimate reality, all of which take us one step away from what is presented.

Such a perspective breaks radically with the ideology of progress, which demands a continual alienation from *present* realities and repression of *present* experience for the sake of some future attainment of reality or value. This perspective negates the idea of the present as a realm of accumulation with a view to some ultimate cosmic payoff. It asserts the identity of means and ends. It thus uncovers the hoax of all utopias of power. It holds before us the lotus flower and invites us to look upon it, perhaps in serenity, perhaps in bliss, perhaps in laughter and amusement.

Erazim Kohak has suggested that 'real success is not that time is transformed in its flux but that, in each moment, value ingresses in it, that each moment humans glimpse the glory of the true, the good, the beautiful, the holy'.[23] Utopianism finds such value, not in some higher realm or some indefinite future, but in the depths of our being and the heights of our experience. Indeed, it finds it even in the false, the evil, the ugly, and the profane. Utopia is present in all the creative play of energies, in spiritual and material voyages of discovery, and, of course, in everything touched by the transformative imagination.

Even if it can never be attained, utopia is already present or it is a fraud.

Hyper(topian) text

If this is true, it might seem that literary utopias would not be of great significance, for they are about what is merely imagined rather than what actually is. However, they cannot in fact be dismissed in this way. The greatest of the fictional utopias are as much about evoking the deepest of our past and present experiential realities as they are about envisioning future possibilities. Thus, the most powerful utopian works are also profoundly *topian* – they create a vivid sense of place, of topos, that is grounded in deeply experienced realities. Utopianism finds its fulfilment in topianism, indeed, we might even say in *hypertopianism*, the most intense sense of being somewhere, in a specific place at which reality shines forth.

One of the great achievements in this venture is Robert Nichols' series, *Daily Lives in Nghsi-Altai*.[24] In this remarkable tetralogy, Nichols envisions the nature of a communal, yet highly individualised society in which decentralised democracy, ecological sensibility, bioregional principles, and liberatory technologies are integrated into a traditional culture. It is a vision of utopia emerging out of the thickness of history and lived experience. While *Daily Lives* is not widely known, it is one of the most important contributions to both literary and theoretical utopianism.

Nichols creatively incorporates concepts of utopian anarchist and decentralist writers and imagines what they would mean in a rich cultural embodiment. In Nghsi-Altai they are realised not in a utopia of static perfection, but rather in a generally peaceful but still mildly chaotic world in which people live a good but still slightly messy life, and achieve an expansive yet communally bounded freedom. What is so compelling about this work is its extraordinary synthesis of utopianism with an acute sense of both the universals of the human condition and the ineluctable specificity of culture. Nichols brilliantly creates a sense of the utopian ethos. It is not surprising that Ursula Le Guin has recognised the importance of Nichols' influence in her development of a utopian project that culminates in a social anthropology of utopia.

Le Guin has created a series of major landmarks in the history of utopianism. In *The Left Hand of Darkness*[25] her protagonist confronts the challenge of relating personally and humanly to a literally androgynous species. The work is of major significance for its confrontation of the question of otherness and difference with a subtlety rare not only in utopian writing but in literature in general. *The Dispossessed*[26] quickly became a utopian classic for exploration of the contrasts between the anarchist 'ambiguous utopia', Annares, and the corrupt, earthlike planet, Urras. Le Guin's grasp of anarchist social theory in the work, which is expressed as the teachings of Odo, the founding mother of Annares's political system, far surpasses that of most academic and partisan writers on the subject. But what is most notable about the work is the protagonist's ruthlessly anarchistic critique of Annares itself. It is, in effect, an anarchist critique of anarchism and a utopian critique of the dangers of utopia.

But finally, in *Always Coming Home*[27] Le Guin produced her masterpiece and, indeed, what is perhaps the masterpiece of utopian literature to date. The work includes the familiar Le Guinian themes of the good society versus the corrupt society and the departure from, and return to, one's spiritual centre. It is also implicitly an anarchist utopia, though without the overt discussion of anarchist theory that is found in *The Dispossessed*. But the great achievement of the book is the richness of detail, the development of particularity and 'suchness', at the level of the person, the group, and the culture. Le Guin's evocation of the good society is compelling because she has, more than any other utopian writer, succeeded in creating a topos and an ethos. Indeed, *Always Coming Home*, with its songs, stories, myths, legends, music, rituals, and accounts of lives, is less a utopian novel than an anthropological sourcebook of another world that tells us important things about the deepest truths of our own world.[28] Le Guin's great achievement is that she has given to utopia – nowhere – the strongest possible sense of place.[29] Utopian literature has finally become truly *topian*.

There is perhaps only one work of fiction that has made a major contribution to anarchistic utopianism since the appearance of Le Guin's classic work. This is Starhawk's *The Fifth Sacred Thing*[30] in which she depicts a non-violent, cooperative, communal anarchist society based on eco-feminist values. Four of the 'five things' alluded to in the title are the four elements that make up the natural world and which must be treated with care and respect. A person or community that does so gains access to the 'fifth sacred thing', which is spirit.

The book is remarkable in that it creates a powerful sense of a qualitatively different society through its convincing depiction of values, practices, and institutions in many spheres that reinforce one another. But though the society is qualitatively different from our world, it does not seem as experientially distant from present reality as do most utopias. The characters and situations that express truths about cooperation, non-violence, equality, freedom, love and care, creativity, sensuality, and joy do not seem so far from what many readers may have experienced if they have had some contact with the feminist, ecology, peace, and global justice movements, and particularly their more anarchistic dimensions. *The Fifth Sacred Thing* suggests that a great many people and small groups are right now creating in their own lives the elements of a utopian world, and it offers a compelling vision of what that utopian world might be like if many such people were to join these elements together in a community that transformed them into an all-embracing way of life.

Utopia in history

The importance of literary utopias such as those just discussed should not be underestimated. However, it would be a mistake to look at utopia primarily as a literary genre, as is often done today. The abundant legacy of utopian practice in the real world and in actual history was first, and most extensively, delineated by Elisée Reclus in his six-volume magnum opus of social theory, *L'Homme et la Terre*.[31] Reclus showed that a fertile history of radical freedom has existed and developed alongside the long story of domination that has been so central to world history. This 'other history' has included cooperative and egalitarian tribal traditions, anarchistic millenarian movements, dissident spiritualities, anti-authoritarian experiments in radical grassroots democracy and communalism, movements for the liberation of women, and the radically libertarian moments of many of the world's revolutions and revolutionary movements.

Millenarian movements, despite the elitist and authoritarian aspects that have been noted, illustrate the extent to which the utopian social imagination can inspire the absolute negation of apparently immovable social institutions, such as the state, the church, patriarchy, and repressive morality. Bloch observes that in the Joachimite tradition, 'the Kingdom' becomes radically immanentised. It is 'more decidedly of this world than anything since the days of early Christianity. Jesus is once again the Messiah of a new earth, and Christianity operates in reality, not just in ritual and empty promises; it operates without masters and property, in mystical democracy.'[32] Such millenarian movements, for all their flaws, have shown the extent to which the utopian social imagination could radically subvert the dominant order, even during what have been thought of as the more conservative periods of history.

Particularly in their most radical early stages, modern revolutions have often contained a deeply utopian dimension. In these periods, a decisive

break with existing systems of power is undertaken, and hierarchy, domination, and authoritarianism have been vigorously combated. It is true that
the system of domination, or some pseudo-revolutionary mutation of it,
has always triumphed. This proves that the technique of social domination
is far more advanced than the art of social liberation. But as a result of
these 'revolutions within the revolutions', we are left with a heritage
of utopian practice that continues to inspire the radical imagination. The
multitude of impressive historical examples in this tradition includes
the direct democracy of the section assemblies of the French Revolution,
the civic democracy and egalitarianism of the Paris Commune, the council
democracy of the early Russian Revolution and the Hungarian Revolution,
and the democratic self-management in the anarchist industrial and agricultural collectives of the Spanish Revolution. What has been less evident
but perhaps most important in these emancipatory moments has been the
flowering of creativity on the microsocial level, which has been expressed
in personal change and the transformation of intimate relationships, the
proliferation of small action and affinity groups, and the emergence of
liberatory social and cultural spaces at the grassroots level. Such phenomena
have been accorded little attention by historians, whether of the mainstream
or radical varieties.

These neglected historical phenomena relate to a final important sphere
of utopianism in history, the creation of liberatory intentional communities.
Ronald Creagh, in his important study *Laboratoires de l'Utopie*, presents
abundant evidence of the rich history of experiments in libertarian communalism carried out across the North American continent, from the
Owenite and Fourierist colonies of the early nineteenth century to libertarian counter-cultural communes of the 1960s and beyond. Many problems
concerning the project of social emancipation can only be confronted
through investigation and experimentation on the microsocial level. The
social history of utopianism helps one to appreciate the centrality of personal life, in all its particularity, to the project of social emancipation.

Creagh shows that the North American intentional communities confronted in practice numerous issues related to interpersonal relations
and everyday life that are often overlooked in theoretical analyses and
sometimes only superficially touched upon in imaginative utopias.[33] They
posed questions concerning sexual and affectionate relationships, the nurturing of children, the balancing of solitude and community, the tensions
between individuality and solidarity, the threats of charismatic authority,
the complexity of achieving just and democratic decision-making in
all spheres, and the problem of consciously confronting the heritage of
domination carried in each psyche. The story of successes, and just as
importantly, of failures in the long tradition of liberatory striving is an
invaluable legacy for inspiring the utopian imagination and guiding future
utopian creation.

The end of utopia

Utopia has had a long history, both as a form of visionary art and literature and as a political practice aiming at radical social transformation. However, for most of the past century social commentators have been announcing the death of utopia, and the end of radically utopian thinking, at least in so far as it significantly affects history and social movements.

Mannheim argues that the modern period is an epoch of rationalisation in which utopian thought must in the long run decline. He recognises that this poses a threat to society, since 'the complete elimination of reality-transcending elements from our world would lead us to a "matter-of-factness" which would ultimately mean the decay of the human will'.[34] Indeed, he goes so far as to judge that, 'with the relinquishment of utopias, man would lose his will to shape history and therewith his ability to understand it'.[35] Yet he seems reconciled to the fact that utopia will play at most a minor role in the modern world. In fact, he seems to think that in the European intellectual world the death of utopia was in his time already a *fait accompli*. He refers to 'the complete disappearance of all reality-transcending doctrines – utopian as well as ideological',[36] a situation that he believes to have resulted from the success of historicism, critique of ideology, psychoanalysis, and other intellectual trends in demonstrating the relativity of all values. He asks whether in an increasingly rationalised and disenchanted world, such developments as 'the gradual reduction of politics to economics', 'the conscious rejection of the past and of the notion of historical time', and 'the conscious brushing aside of every cultural ideal', will not result in 'a disappearance of every form of utopianism from the political arena'.[37]

However, the world has demonstrated a tendency to resist instrumental rationality and remain more 'enchanted' than Mannheim imagined. He believes that 'radical anarchism', which he calls the 'relatively purest form of modern Chiliastic mentality', by his own time has 'disappear[ed] almost entirely from the political scene'.[38] He concludes that the 'disintegration of the anarchist ecstatic utopia was abrupt and brutal, but it was dictated with a fatal necessity by the historical process itself'.[39] Ironically, Mannheim's obituary for anarchism was written in 1929, seven years before the Spanish Revolution, the period of the most extensive and socially creative experimentation in anarchist organisation in the history of Europe. Despite the 'fatal necessity' that dictated anarchism's demise, its supposed corpse not only quickly showed signs of life but soon reached a state of unprecedented vigour.

Utopia was to be re-interred several times in the half-century after Mannheim, most notably by the 'End of Ideology' theorists (Bell, Lipset, and so on) of the 1950s. According to this school, ideology in general and utopian ideology in particular had been superseded in the west, and was to be elsewhere, by a pragmatic, non-ideological outlook typically embodied in the modern state and corporation. As Daniel Bell stated in 1960, there had come 'an end to chiliastic hopes, to millenarianism, to apocalyptic thinking – and to ideology'.[40] So anarchism and utopianism were again buried by the theorists – only to re-emerge shortly thereafter in the 1960s in a form that was even more challenging to conventional reality than the rather traditionalist versions of the 1930s.

But the ferment of the 1960s did not put an end to grandiose speculation concerning the imminent end of both ideology and utopia. Not so long ago Francis Fukuyama, at the time the Deputy Director of the Policy Planning Department of the State Department, announced the latest end of ideology, and with it the end of any utopian aspirations. 'What we may be witnessing is not just the end of the cold war, or the passing of a particular period of postwar history, but the end of history as such: that is, the end point of mankind's ideological evolution and the universalization of western liberal democracy as the final form of human government.'[41]

As he says, *we may be witnessing* this. But as it turned out, we were not. For a brief triumphalist moment, history, viewed through the thick mist of neo-con ideology, could seem to Mr Fukuyama and the Department of (Steady?) State to have reached its end. One could imagine a gathering of neo-conservative intellectuals in 1992 to celebrate the end of history, perhaps under a huge banner declaring 'Mission Accomplished!' But then history, with all its deep and complex contradictions, its dialectical reversals, its tragedies and its absurdities, decided, as it always does, to move on.

The return to nowhere

So history goes on, as does the quest for utopia. If the history of utopianism shows anything, it is that the sources of inspiration for utopian visions are myriad. The idea that an end has already come to the quest for a reality that radically transcends the existing one was a naive idea indeed. Not the least of its absurdities was that it ignored the dependence of the existing system upon its own vision of utopia, which drives it toward self-transcendence and self-destruction. But it is not only the utopia of domination that will live on. As long as the radical imagination exists, the anarchistic utopia, with its values of freedom, mutuality, joyfulness, and creativity, will continue to exist, and human beings will seek to realise it with diverse degrees of passion, imagination, and rationality. Whether it will in any given future epoch be successfully marginalised or instead realised to varying degrees through powerful upsurges of social creativity cannot now be determined.

What we do know from past history is that hunger, thirst, sexual desire, religious passion, the quest for truth, the desire for self-actualisation, envy, resentment, maliciousness, hatred, will to power, neurosis and psychosis of every variety, can, by cultural alchemy, be transformed into, or expressed through, utopian striving. We do not know whether the future will be more a dream or more a nightmare, but we do know that it is quite likely that it will have a utopian dimension.

Notes

1 Ronald Reagan was for years the main spokesperson for the General Electric corporation's PR campaign. See www.smecc.org/frontiers_of_progress_1961_sales_meeting.htm.

2 For a more extensive discussion of the *Daodejing* as an anarchist and utopian classic, see my 'Master Lao and the Anarchist Prince', in *The Anarchist Moment: Reflections on Culture, Nature and Power*, pp. 165–90.

3 Plato, *The Republic of Plato*, trans. A. Bloom (ed.), pp. 439–40.

4 Of course, the work is also about justice, but in the end the two values are identified, for Plato adopts the maxim 'justice is the interest of the stronger'. Of course, along the way he rejects this principle in its vulgar Sophistic form, only to embrace it in its sublated, perfected form. One of the most exquisite expressions of Socratic irony is Socrates' brutal demolition of Thrasymachus's flimsy parody of this principle in order to throw the naive reader off the track and disguise Plato's own argument for this principle of power in its most sublime form.

5 In recent anarchist history, the best example was erstwhile anarchist Murray Bookchin, who reiterated repeatedly his theory that Lao Zi was not only not an anarchist but indeed an authoritarian manipulator of peasants who sought to instil in them a quietistic, 'passive–receptive' outlook to the benefit of their feudal overlords. Bookchin failed to offer much evidence of Lao Zi's fronting for feudalism but was quite convincing in his ultimate conclusion that he himself was not an anarchist.

6 V. Havel, 'Conversation with Vaclav Havel', *East European Reporter*, 2:3 (1986), 15.

7 *Ibid.* 17.

8 *Ibid.* It should be noted that despite this scathing attack on 'utopia', Havel praised the early green movement (which had at the time a distinctively utopian dimension that has largely been lost since) for raising issues that 'concern the meaning of life, such as whether there is any reason in the constant drive for increased production when it is to the detriment of future generations' (p. 17).

9 E. Bloch, *The Principle of Hope*, II:509.

10 N. Cohn, *The Pursuit of the Millennium*, p. 181.

11 *Ibid.* p. 179.

12 A. Lehning (ed.), *Michael Bakunin: Selected Works*, p. 180.

13 P. Ricoeur, *Lectures on Ideology and Utopia*, p. 300.

14 K. Mannheim, *Ideology and Utopia*, p. 192.

15 Ricoeur, *Lectures on Ideology and Utopia*, p. 17.

16 *Ibid.* p. 299.

17 M. L. Berneri, *Journey Through Utopia*, p. 8.

18 I. Kant, *Foundations of the Metaphysics of Morals*, p. 11.

19 *Ibid.* p. 41.

20 We might still say that the present will always be in some ways haunted by the absence of the fully realised ideal that we imagine, yet the greatest reality of that absent ideal is that aspect of it that is already present here and now.

21 W. Blake, notes to 'A Vision of the Last Judgment', in David Erdman (ed.), *The Complete Poetry and Prose of William Blake*, pp. 565–6.

22 G. Snyder, *Practice of the Wild*, p. 153.

23 E. Kohak, *The Embers and the Stars*, p. 217.

24 R. Nichols, *Daily Lives in Nghsi-Altai*. The series consists of *Arrival, Garh City, The Harditts in Sawna*, and *Exile*, and was preceded by an introductory work, *Red Shift*. A new (unfortunately abridged) edition has appeared. See R. Nichols, *Travels in Altai*.

25 U. Le Guin, *The Left Hand of Darkness*. Le Guin is profoundly influenced by Daoism, as she recognises in various essays and in her own version of the *Daodejing*. Her work is perhaps the most notable contemporary expression of the anarchistic utopian tradition founded (and not founded) by the great (and possibly non-existent) sage Lao Zi.

26 U. Le Guin, *The Dispossessed*.

27 U. Le Guin, *Always Coming Home*.

28 The book is consciously influenced by Nichols' work, which more explicitly draws on anarchist and decentralist ideas. In *Always Coming Home*, when 'The Five People' ask where they came from and 'The Wise Old Man' and 'The Talking Woman' give rather unsatisfying metaphysical replies, Coyote finally answers, 'From the west you came, from the west, from Ingasi Altai, over the ocean, dancing you came, walking you came' (p. 170). So when The Five People migrated across the ocean long ago they brought along many of the libertarian and decentralist values Nichols describes in *Nghsi-Altai*.

29 It is for this reason that the novel, with its emphasis on person, community, culture, nature, and place, has been an inspiration to those interested in bio-regionalism, the project of reinhabiting the land, and the re-establishment of the connections between self, culture, and nature.

30 Starhawk, *The Fifth Sacred Thing*.

31 Elisée Reclus, *L'Homme et la Terre*, 6 vols. This 3500-page work was the culmination of half a century of research in radical social geography. Discussion of this history and extensive translation from this work can be found in J. Clark and C. Martin, *Anarchy, Geography, Modernity: The Radical Social Thought of Elisée Reclus*.

32 Bloch, *The Principle of Hope*, II:511.

33 R. Creagh, *Laboratoires de l'Utopie: Les Communautes Libertaires aux Etats-Unis*.

34 Mannheim, *Ideology and Utopia*, p. 262.

35 *Ibid.*, p. 263.

36 *Ibid.*, p. 255.

37 *Ibid.*, p. 256.

38 *Ibid.*, p. 248.

39 *Ibid.*, p. 244.

40 D. Bell, *The End of Ideology*, p. 370.

41 F. Fukuyama, 'The End of History', *The National Interest*, 16 (1989), 3.

References

Bakunin, M., *Michael Bakunin: Selected Works*, ed. Arthur Lehning (New York: Grove Press, 1973).

Bell, D., *The End of Ideology* (Glencoe, IL: The Free Press, 1960).

Berneri, M. L., *Journey Through Utopia* (New York: Schocken Books, 1971).

Blake, W., *The Complete Poetry and Prose of William Blake*, ed. David Erdman (Garden City, NY: Doubleday, 1982).

Bloch, E., *The Principle of Hope* (Cambridge, MA: The MIT Press, 1986).

Clark, J., 'Master Lao and the Anarchist Prince', in *The Anarchist Moment: Reflections on Culture, Nature and Power* (Montreal: Black Rose Books, 1984), pp. 165–90.

Clark, J. and C. Martin, *Anarchy, Geography, Modernity: The Radical Social Thought of Elisée Reclus* (Lanham, MD: Lexington Books, 2004).

Cohn, N., *The Pursuit of the Millennium* (New York: Oxford, 1970).

Creagh, R., *Laboratoires de l'Utopie: Les Communautes Libertaires aux Etats-Unis* (Paris: Payot, 1983).

Fukuyama, F., 'The End of History', *The National Interest*, 16 (1989), 3–16.

Havel, V., 'Conversation with Vaclav Havel', *East European Reporter*, 2:3 (1986), 12–17.

Kant, I., *Foundations of the Metaphysics of Morals* (Indianapolis: Library of Liberal Arts, 1959).

Kohak, E., *The Embers and the Stars* (Chicago: University of Chicago Press, 1984).

Le Guin, U., *The Left Hand of Darkness* (New York: Berkeley Publishing Group, 1969).

——*The Dispossessed* (New York: Harper and Row, 1974).

——*Always Coming Home* (New York: Harper and Row, 1985).

Mannheim, K., *Ideology and Utopia* (New York: Harcourt, Brace and World, 1936).

Nichols, R., *Daily Lives in Nghsi-Altai* (New York: New Directions Books, 1977–9).

——*Red Shift* (Thetford, VT: Penny Each Press, 1977).

——*Travels in Altai* (Enfield, NH: Glad Day Books, 1999).

Plato, *The Republic of Plato*, trans. with notes and an Interpretive Essay by Allan Bloom (New York and London: Basic Books Inc., 1968).

Reclus, E., *L'Homme et la Terre*. 6 vols (Paris: Librairie Universelle, 1905–08).

Ricoeur, P., *Lectures on Ideology and Utopia* (New York: Columbia University Press, 1986).

Snyder, G., *Practice of the Wild* (San Francisco: North Point Press, 1990).

Starhawk, *The Fifth Sacred Thing* (New York: Bantam Books, 1993).

PART II

Antecedents of the anarchist literary utopia

2 John A. Rapp

Daoism as utopian or accommodationist: radical Daoism re-examined in light of the Guodian manuscripts

Introduction

Though philosophical Daoism[1] undoubtedly contains utopian anarchist strains, whether these tendencies can be traced back to the text known as the *Daodejing* (Tao Te Ching in Wade–Giles romanisation, hereafter abbreviated DDJ) is more open to debate.[2] Those who find a radical utopian[3] argument in Daoism stress especially the DDJ's critique of the Confucian ideal of humane rule. Below this critique is traced to previously received versions of the DDJ that date to approximately 200–250 BCE. Nevertheless, bamboo strips unearthed in 1993 from a tomb in China's Hubei province present a major challenge to the idea that radical utopianism goes back to the earliest roots of Daoist philosophy.

Perhaps the most important find in this tomb were portions of what later became the DDJ, thus marking the text as much as a century older than any previously known version.[4] As the news about the strips spread, some scholars began to claim that the Guodian manuscripts proved that Daoism was more accommodationist toward government than was previously thought.[5]

This essay will first present the provisional case for that 'accommodationist' view of Daoism. Next we will review the utopian anarchist strands of Daoism that can be traced back to at least a century after the Guodian manuscripts were transcribed, which will then lead us to question whether the Guodian texts really present such a major challenge to radical Daoism. The essay will conclude with a discussion of what the identity of the owner of the Guodian strips may tell us about the ultimate meaning of the Guodian texts.

The Guodian challenge examined

The Guodian manuscripts present three main challenges for the view of Daoism as a radical utopian doctrine. The first is the absence from the

Guodian bamboo strips of many DDJ chapters that explicitly oppose direct attempts to rule, including, most dramatically, the absence of the entire last third of the received DDJ. The second challenge is the lack in the Guodian texts of clear anti-Confucian language in what became chapter nineteen of the received DDJ. The third challenge is the relative absence of a 'law of return' in the Guodian texts that would explain how humans could ever have fallen away from the stateless utopia. All three potential challenges are based on the fact that the Guodian text is the oldest known edition of what became the DDJ and thus that the clearly anti-statist and utopian statements in the received text may be later additions by other authors.

The absence of the most anti-statist and utopian sections of the DDJ

Absent from the Guodian strips are some of the most direct criticisms of other political philosophies and the most anti-statist statements of the received DDJ. Most importantly, the Guodian text does not contain the explicit, influential utopian chapter eighty of the DDJ. As Ursula Le Guin retranslates that chapter (based mostly on Arthur Waley's 1935 translation),

> Let there be a little country without many people.
> Let them have tools that do the work of ten or a hundred
> and never use them.
> Let them be mindful of death
> and disinclined to long journeys.
> They'd have ships and carriages,
> but no place to go.
> They'd have armor and weapons,
> but no parades.
> Instead of writing,
> they might go back to using knotted cords . . .
> The next little country might be so close
>   the people could hear cocks crowing
>   and dogs barking there
>   but they'd get old and die
>   without ever having been there.[6]

Others have argued that this chapter contains the heart of the Daoist critique opposed to technological innovation that would aid the oppressive centralisation and militarisation of state power, a critique that can be found clearly in Daoist texts of the Warring States period (403–221 BCE), an era that culminated in the foundation of a centralised imperial state.[7]

Absent as well from the Guodian text are some of the most dramatic examples of Daoist advice to rule by non-interference in the affairs of the world (*wushi*), including the end of chapter forty-eight of the received DDJ:

In wanting to rule the world
Be always non-interfering in going about its business;
For in being interfering
You make yourself unworthy of ruling the world.[8]

The Guodian strips also leave out the severe critique of Legalism, a political philosophy that would later be highly influential on the imperial state. This anti-Legalist stance can be seen in chapters in the received DDJ missing from the Guodian strips which contain criticism of rule by harsh punishments (chapter seventy-four) and the idea of suffering and rebellion as caused by over-taxation and the oppression of the rich over the poor (chapter seventy-five).[9] Finally, the Guodian text leaves out much of the attack on the Confucian ideal of rule by the morally virtuous, as in chapter three of the received text which is missing from the Guodian strips:

If we stop looking for 'persons of superior morality' [xian] to
put in power, there will be no more jealousies among the people.
If we cease to set store by products that are hard to get, there will be
no more thieves.[10]

Also absent from the Guodian strips is the explicit critique of the negative political evolution that occurs if Daoist principles are lost, as in chapter thirty-eight of the received DDJ:

After the 'power' [de] was lost, then came human kindness [ren].
After morality was lost, then came ritual [li].
Now ritual is the mere husk of loyalty and promise-keeping
And is indeed the first step towards brawling.[11]

Chapter nineteen and the Guodian accommodation to Confucianism

By far the most highly publicised example of the seeming accommodation towards government in the Guodian strips lies in what became chapter nineteen of the received DDJ. The received versions contain language that directly mocks the Confucian values of sageliness (sheng), benevolence or humanity (ren), and righteousness (yi), values at the heart of the ideal of paternalistic rule. As the received DDJ puts it,

Eliminate sageliness, get rid of knowledge,
And the people will benefit a hundredfold.
Eliminate humanity, get rid of righteousness,
And the people will return to filial piety and compassion.
Eliminate craftiness, get rid of profit,
And there will be no robbers and thieves . . .[12]

As opposed to this direct critique, the Guodian text uses the following language:

Eliminate knowledge, get rid of distinctions,
And the people will benefit one hundredfold.

Eliminate artistry, get rid of profit,
And there will be no robbers and thieves
Eliminate transformation, get rid of deliberation,
And the people will return to filial piety and compassion . . .[13]

To critics, this chapter shows clearly that Confucian and Daoist thought
were not so opposed at the time when the Guodian texts were transcribed
and that both philosophies argued for a humane rule based on paternalistic
values of filial piety and benevolence,[14] not a stateless utopia as some later
Daoists from the Warring States to the Wei-Jin period (ca. 220–316 CE)
explicitly favoured. Thus the Guodian text prefigures scholar-officials who
later used Daoist principles to defend the supposedly limited and light rule
of the former Han dynasty (ca. 206 BCE–8 CE). Perhaps the best evidence
for such an accommodationist position can be found in chapter fifty-four
of the received DDJ, which is also in the Guodian strips with only minor
differences and gaps due to broken or missing slips (for which Henricks
puts extrapolations in italics):

If you cultivate it in your self, your virtue will be pure;
If you cultivate it in your family, your virtue will be overflowing;
If you cultivate it in your village, your virtue will be longlasting;
If you cultivate it in your state, your virtue will be rich and full;
If you cultivate it throughout the world, *your virtue will be widespread.*
Look at the family *from the point of view of the family*;
Look at the state from the point of view of the state;
Look at the world from the point of view of the world . . .[15]

As many commentators have long pointed out, this chapter is remarkably
similar to the later Confucian text, the *Da Xue*, or 'Great Learning', which
says that great sages of antiquity who wished to order their own states,

first regulated their own families, for which they first corrected their own
hearts, for which they first regulated their own intentions, for which they first
perfected their own knowledge.[16]

The *Da Xue* later became one of the four classic texts that all would-be
officials had to master in order to pass the imperial examinations, thus
showing how Confucianism became a legitimating formula under which the
role of the ruler was similar to that of head of a family. Thus critics of
Daoism as a radical doctrine point to this chapter of the DDJ to say that
early Daoism was not opposed in principle to the idea of rule as long as it
was limited and humane.

The lack of a 'law of return' in the Guodian texts

Finally, the Guodian strips lack what could be termed the Daoist 'law of
return' that exists in the received DDJ.[17] This law is important in that it
helps Daoists both to explain how a 'fall' from a stateless utopia could ever
have occurred and to predict the oppressive forms of rule other political

philosophies of the time would bring if ever put into practice. This law is most explicit in chapter fifty-five of the received text, which is absent from the Guodian strips:

> Whatever has a time of vigor also has a time of decay.
> Such things are against Tao
> And whatever is against Tao will soon be destroyed.[18]

In other words, those who try to impose political order either by indoctrinating people with ideas of goodness (Confucianism) or through harsh laws and punishments (Legalism) will only bring about a reaction of nature that will destroy their ideal states.[19] Also, under this principle Daoists can explain the 'fall' from the natural, stateless society not as something unnatural, which would be self-contradictory to a naturalistic philosophy, but instead only as a temporary change that is doomed to fail. Without this law of return, the Daoist critique of other political philosophies is arguably much weaker.

In the Guodian version of what became chapter thirty of the received DDJ, which opposes war and militarised rule, the lines containing the most famous example of the law of return are absent:

> One who uses the Way to assist the ruler of men,
> Does not desire to use weapons to force his way through the land.
> *Such deeds easily rebound.*
> *In places where armies are stationed, thorns and brambles will grow.*
> *Great wars are always followed by great famines.*
> One who is good at such things achieves his result and that's all.
> He does not use the occasion to make himself stronger still.[20]

Thus the Guodian version seems to call for modest, humane rule that avoids war if possible but refrains from opposing *any* attempt to use force of arms, which would undermine the idea of Daoism as anarchistic.

Other minor linguistic differences between the Guodian and the received DDJ for many scholars demonstrate that the Guodian text is the oldest version of what became the DDJ and that much of the received DDJ was not present at the time of Confucius (b. 579 BCE), but instead was added during or after the third century BCE.[21] Thus, according to the 'accommodationist' view, the elements of the DDJ that contain the anti-Confucian critique must have also been added during the late Warring States era, while the utopian anarchist aspects must have been non-intrinsic additions of later writers.

The case for radical Daoism

To make the case for radical Daoism as genuine and intrinsic, one should start with unambiguous anarchist Daoism of the Warring States and Wei-Jin periods and work backwards to the time of the Guodian texts.

First, later radical thinkers definitely used Daoist language to describe a stateless utopia.[22] These utopian depictions included explicit opposition to Confucian moral virtue and Legalist rewards and punishments, ideas that legitimated succeeding Chinese imperial dynasties. Radical Daoism developed to its fullest extent in the early Wei-Jin period (ca. 220–316 CE).[23] The poet Ruan Ji took Daoist anarchism to its height in his poem, 'The Biography of Master Great Man', which describes the stateless utopia in terms based on the received DDJ:

> There was no fleeing from harm, no fighting for profit . . . The bright did not win because of their knowledge; the ignorant were not cowed by oppression, nor did the strong prevail by force. *For then there was no ruler, and all beings were peaceful; no officials, and all affairs were well ordered.*[24]

Ruan Ji has the Great Man denounce serving in government, based on the famous Daoist text, the *Zhuang Zi* (see below). Based also on received versions of the DDJ, Ruan Ji in this poem criticises Confucian and Legalist ideas of rule as 'nothing more than the methods of harmful robbers, or trouble-makers, of death and destruction . . .'.[25]

Ruan's harsh, anti-Confucian tone is continued in the tract of the obscure Daoist philosopher Bao Jingyan, ca. 300 CE:

> The Confucian literati say: 'Heaven gave birth to the people and then set rulers over them.' But how can High Heaven have said this in so many words? Is it not rather that interested parties made this their pretext? The fact is that the cunning tricked the innocent and the innocent served them. It was because there was submission that the people, being powerless, could be kept under control. Thus servitude and mastery result from the struggle between the cunning and innocent, and Blue Heaven has nothing whatsoever to do with it.[26]

Bao also presents the Daoist stateless utopia found in other Wei-Jin writers, but in very direct and forceful language:

> In remote antiquity, princes and ministers did not exist . . . There were no roads and paths in the mountains, nor were swamps crossed by bridges or boats. Because rivers and valleys could not be crossed, wars of conquest between states did not occur . . . Greed for power and profit had not yet budded in the hearts of men, and therefore unhappiness and confusion did not arise . . . In mystical equality [*xuantong*], the ten thousand creatures forgot each other in the 'Way', epidemics and pestilence did not spread, and the people became very old as a result. Pure and innocent as they were, men had no cunning in their hearts. They felt at ease when they could simply eat their fill, and walked about stroking their stomach. It would have been impossible to multiply taxes to bleed the people, or to introduce strict punishments to [en]trap [them].[27]

These Wei-Jin Daoist anarchists took their language directly from the 'outer' chapters of the *Zhuang Zi*, which were written either shortly after

the death of Zhuang Zhou (late fourth or early third century BCE, as argued
by Liu Xiaogan) or at the latest during the later years of the Qin dynasty
(209–202 BCE, as argued by A. C. Graham).[28] As the utopia is depicted in
the (outer) chapter ten of the *Zhuang Zi*:

> Long ago, the people knotted cords and used them [instead of writing systems].
> They relished their food, admired their clothing, enjoyed their customs, and
> were content with their houses. Though neighboring states were within sight
> of each other, and could hear the cries of other's dogs and chickens, the people
> grew old and died without ever traveling beyond their own borders. At a time
> such as this, there was nothing but the most perfect order.[29]

This account is highly resonant of chapter eighty of the received DDJ, which
scholars date to at least 250–200 BCE. As in chapters eighteen and nineteen
of the received DDJ, chapter ten of the *Zhuang Zi* also blames Confucian
and Legalist 'sages' for bringing oppression into the world, if in much
harsher language:

> Cudgel and cane the sages and let the thieves and bandits go their way; then
> the world will at last be well ordered! . . . if the sage is dead and gone, then
> no more great thieves will arise. The world will then be peaceful and free of
> fuss. . . . Cut off sageliness, cast away wisdom, and then the great thieves will
> cease . . . Destroy and wipe out the laws that the sage has made for the world,
> and at last you will find you can reason with the people.[30]

The writer of the (outer) chapter nine of the *Zhuang Zi* presents the Daoist
utopia where the world is free of sages trying to order the world:

> In this age of perfect Virtue men live the same as birds and beasts, group
> themselves side by side with the ten thousand things. Who then knows any-
> thing about 'gentleman' or 'petty man'? Dull and unwitting, men have no
> wisdom; thus their Virtue does not depart from them. Dull and unwitting,
> they have no desire; this is called uncarved simplicity [*si* and *pu*, two key
> terms from the DDJ]. In uncarved simplicity people attain their true nature.[31]

This utopian picture relates to language of the inner chapters of the
Zhuang Zi and the DDJ itself concerning the need to 'return to the root'
and reject technological refinements that came with the increasing centralisation of power in the Warring States era.[32] Even if these accounts from the
outer *Zhuang Zi* chapters and the received DDJ were later extrapolations,
there is no doubt that their utopian ideal harkens back to a pre-existing
tradition of a stateless agrarian community. This community was supposedly begun by the mythical founder of agriculture, Shen Nung, a legend
repeated by one Xiu Xing, who argued with the thinker Mencius around
315 BCE.

   According to A. C. Graham, the Shen Nung ideal 'appears to be
an anarchistic order based on mutual trust in small communities' that is
'ancestral to all Chinese utopianism'.[33] Graham's argument would backdate
the utopian Daoist ideal to a time at least roughly contemporaneous with

the historical Zhuang Zhou himself, if not earlier, even if this ideal was later sharpened during the harsh Qin dynasty (221–207 BCE).

Graham's argument supports the view that even the inner *Zhuang Zi* chapters suggest the spontaneous order that exists in the universe without human intervention and thus the lack of any need to impose political order. In the inner chapters of the *Zhuang Zi* the greatest sages often refuse to serve in government, while the great second chapter, 'Discussion on Making All Things Equal', satirises the idea that hierarchical rule is natural:

> The hundred joints, the nine openings, the six organs, all come together and exist here [as my body]. But which part should I feel closest to? I should delight in all parts, you say? But there must be one I ought to favor more. If not, are they all of them mere servants? But if they are all servants, then how can they keep order among themselves? Or do they take turns being lord and servant? It would seem as though there must be some True Lord among them. But whether I succeed in discovering his identity or not, neither adds to nor detracts from his truth.[34]

Further, in the (inner) chapter seven, Zhuang Zi suggests the disaster that will follow from artificial attempts to impose order:

> Shu ['Brief', the emperor of the south Sea] and Hu ['Sudden' – the emperor of the north Sea] from time to time came together for a meeting in the territory of Hun-tun ['Chaos', or 'primordial unity'], and Hun-tun treated them very generously. Shu and Hu discussed how they could repay his kindness. 'All men', they said, 'have seven openings so they can see, hear, eat, and breathe. But Hun-tun alone doesn't have any. Let's try boring him some!'
> Every day they bored another hole, and on the seventh day Hun-tun died.[35]

Clearly, if in more gentle language than used by later Daoists, the inner *Zhuang Zi* chapters oppose the idea of rule as morally virtuous.

Likewise, the received DDJ often depicts the idea of morally virtuous rule as at best a step down from the ideal, as in chapter seventeen:

> With the most excellent rulers, their subjects only [barely] know that they are there,
> The next best are the rulers they love and praise,
> Next are the rulers they hold in awe,
> And the worst are the rulers they disparage.[36]

Given the Daoist admonition to (would-be) sages to rule by *wu-wei* (non-action or doing nothing) throughout the received DDJ, in addition to its denigration of laws and punishments, taxes, warfare, education, and virtually any other element of rule, one could argue that even the received DDJ is trying to subvert government by advising the ruler to emulate leaders of hunter-gather bands and thus remove the ruler's monopoly on the legitimate use of coercion, advice which would do away with the state as it is minimally defined by Max Weber.[37] Following Joseph Needham, one could argue that the authors of the inner chapters of the *Zhuang Zi* and the received DDJ may have lived early enough to have at least dim memories of surviving remnants of wild hunter-gatherer or semi-sedentary ways of life in the south of ancient China and thus opposed the increasing centralisation of power that began in the late Spring and Autumn (770–476 BCE) to the Warring States periods.[38] We know that Daoist thinkers often came from more recently settled or partially settled regions of China, such as the 'madman' Xiu Xing from the state of Chu who argued with Mencius, the great fourth century Confucian exponent of the doctrine of humane rule.[39] Indeed, the Guodian tomb is located within the historical boundaries of the state of Chu, which perhaps would place its ideas within this 'southern' tradition of Chinese political thought opposed to harsher types of rule. Before we return to that question below, we must first re-examine the Guodian text to see whether it indeed lacks anti-Confucian and anti-statist utopian language.

The Guodian texts re-examined

The questions of dating and authorship

In re-examining the claims that the Guodian texts point to an 'accommodationist' Daoism, one must first examine the issue of dating. Though it is currently the oldest known version of the text, whether or not all later editions of the DDJ were additions to the Guodian texts or whether there was a pre-existing oral and/or written tradition to all received or discovered versions of the DDJ is a matter of dispute. Even if one accepts the view of scholars who point to linguistic evidence to suggest that sections of the Guodian texts were more succinct and thus that later DDJ versions contained many emendations,[40] this does not mean that later authors of texts that entered into the received DDJ were starting wholly new traditions. Instead their texts could have been based on pre-existing utopian traditions, such as that of Shen Nung, which might have had a history predating the Guodian manuscripts.

Robert Henricks points out that the Guodian strips were discovered in the tomb in at least three bundles, which were copied separately in at least two different hands, probably from at least three other written sources. The complete text of the DDJ may have existed by 300 BCE in more than one version, and the common ancestor of all versions may have been written earlier in the fourth century.[41] The Guodian strips thus may be copies of copies and transcribed from versions of the text that date to 350 BCE or earlier.

Whether or not the idea of one man named Lao Zi as the author of the DDJ was a later invention, as Chinese intellectuals of the 1920s and 1930s believed and most contemporary western and Japanese scholars contend, or whether the DDJ really dates back to someone such as the sixth-century BCE legendary figure Lao Tan or Li Erh, certainly at a minimum the main principles of the received DDJ date to the Warring States period.[42]

Perhaps based on the traditional Chinese view of Lao Zi as the author of the DDJ, most contemporary Chinese scholars contend that the Guodian texts prove there was an already existing version of the DDJ much earlier than previously believed. Most western scholars, on the other hand, believe that the lack of many DDJ chapters in the Guodian texts and other linguistic evidence show that the complete DDJ was not yet in existence in 300 BCE.[43] While many western observers find the Chinese belief in an early DDJ as authored by Lao Zi to be based more on a conjectural 'act of faith' rather than hard evidence,[44] other western scholars are starting to come around to the Chinese position, including Edward Shaughnessy, who finds that Western views might also be faith based and premature based on the evidence at hand, and Robert Henricks,[45] who as we saw above is willing to consider that a complete version or versions of the DDJ may have existed as early as 300 BCE. Liu Xiaogan sees a possible third, compromise position: that much of the DDJ may have been composed after Confucius (sixth century BCE but before the historical Zhuang Zi (i.e. before the mid fourth century).[46] If so, that would put much of the DDJ much farther back than 200 BCE (i.e. in the early years of China's first empire), showing that much of the radical side of Daoism can be traced back farther in Chinese history than many observers previously believed.

Even if much of the DDJ dates far back into the Warring States period, critics of radical Daoism as original would still raise the questions noted above, which we will now consider successively, that is, the 'missing' (radical) chapters from the Guodian strips, the changes in what became chapter nineteen of the DDJ, and the question of the 'law of return'.

The 'missing' chapters from the Guodian texts

Despite the fact that some chapters and sections of the received DDJ are missing from the earlier Guodian texts, upon closer examination one can find even in the Guodian strips precursors of much of the later radical utopian argument. To take a crucial example, the concept of *wuwei*, non-action or doing nothing, still can be found in the Guodian texts, despite the lack of several DDJ chapters that focus on the concept. For example, in the Guodian version of what became chapter fifty-seven, the author has the perfect sage say the following:

> I am unconcerned with affairs, and the people on their own enjoy good fortune;
> I do nothing, and the people transform on their own . . .[47]

Besides *wuwei*, other *wu* forms such as *wuzhi*, literally 'not knowing', and *wuyu*, literally 'not desiring' (or 'unprincipled knowing' and 'objectless desire' respectively, as David Hall more clearly translates those terms[48]) exist in one form or another in the Guodian texts.[49] These terms were crucial in developing the Daoist ideal of rule by non-interference with the natural order, which Hall[50] regards as central to the philosophical anarchist vision of Daoism.

Likewise, despite the fact that the Guodian slips contain only about one third to two fifths of the received DDJ, in addition to the *wu* forms, the Guodian texts include other key concepts, such as *pu* (uncarved wood) and *si* (raw silk),[51] terms that related to advice to return to an 'original' simple and unrefined nature, thus pointing to a critique of overly refined methods of rule.

Especially if one accepts the argument of Liu Xiaogan that later versions of the DDJ mostly amount to first a 'linguistic assimilation' that may have amplified and intensified but not directly changed the meaning of the text, and second a 'conceptual focusing' that 'highlights key concepts but also strengthens consistency in language',[52] then one can argue that the core message of the later DDJ is contained in the Guodian strips. For example, Liu contends that concepts such as *wuwei* may be used less often and in less intense fashion in the Guodian texts, but they can still be found, just as the anti-Confucian questioning of rule by benevolence or morally virtuous leaders is still present if one looks more closely – which leads us back to the question of chapter nineteen.

The changes in chapter nineteen

Even if some terms and concepts of the received DDJ can be found in the Guodian texts, there is still the celebrated change regarding the lack of explicitly anti-Confucian language in what became chapter nineteen of the received DDJ. Even here, however, Liu Xiaogan's point applies about the received text of the DDJ only amplifying and not distorting the fundamental message in the Guodian text. As Liu says, 'in chapter nineteen in [later versions of the DDJ] neither the amendment of sentences nor criticism of Confucianism are sudden or incomprehensible. They do not distort the original thought of the bamboo versions.' For Liu the changes in chapter nineteen are 'special case[s] of conceptual focusing' that mostly 'amplify criticisms in the bamboo versions' and intensify the criticism without changing the essential meaning of the text.[53] This is especially true if one looks at the eighteenth chapter in the received DDJ, which was found intact in a separate bundle of Guodian strips. In the latter part of this chapter the anti-Confucian language survives, as follows:

> Therefore, when the Great Way is rejected, it is then that 'humanity'
> and 'righteousness' show up on the scene;
> When the six relations are not in harmony, it is then that we hear of
> 'filial piety' and 'compassion';
> And when the state is is chaos and disarray, it is then that there is praise for
> the 'upright officials'[54]

For Henricks, combining the sentiments in this paragraph with the advice in what became chapter nineteen to eliminate attempts to use knowledge and distinctions to morally transform the people, it is clear that even if this Guodian chapter is 'not yet "anti-Mencian"', that is, not explicitly opposed to that fourth-century philosopher's focus on humane rule, 'it is still very "anti-Confucian"', that is, against the idea of rulers trying to inculcate morality and compassion in the people.[55]

The 'law of return'

Though differences between the Guodian text and what became chapter thirty of the received DDJ are not as famous as the changes in what became chapter nineteen, the lack of a clear 'law of return' in the Guodian texts may be the biggest difference between the Guodian strips and the received DDJ. Again, this absence is important since anyone who wants to argue that a stateless utopia is the natural human condition has to explain how people could ever have fallen so far as to live under Confucian or Legalist-influenced governments.

In making the case for the continuity of the utopian Daoist tradition, one should first note that a law of return is implicit in the Guodian texts, since they still emphasise that ruling through inaction or unconcern with affairs is the best way for the sage to endure. Most scholars who have examined the Guodian version of what became chapter thirty emphasise that it is very likely that a punctuation error in the text should be corrected so that the final line reads, 'such deeds [i.e. those achieved by being modest and not desiring to use weapons] are good and endure'[56] or 'its affair tends to be prolonged' (qi shi hao chang).[57] In other words, one who rules by doing nothing will survive, clearly implying the opposite for those who fail to heed this warning. Thus again, the later, clearer versions of the DDJ which talk about those 'not being on the Way [coming] to an early end'[58] are merely examples, to borrow Liu Xiaogan's terminology, of 'intensifying' or 'focusing' concepts that can be found in the Guodian texts.[59]

Likewise, the anti-militarism of the received DDJ is present in the Guodian text with or without an explicit law of return, as in the likely suggestion of what became chapter thirty-one that 'weapons are instruments of ill omen'.[60] Henricks finds that the key characters found in later texts contained what the missing characters in the strips must have said, which in any case is consistent with the Guodian version of what became the opening lines of chapter thirty:

> One who uses the Way to assist the ruler of men
> Does not desire to use weapons to force his way through the land.[61]

Indeed, Shaughnessy speculates that the separation of the two chapters in the Guodian text may have been due to a misplaced bamboo strip (which would not be hard to imagine given the chaotic state in which the strips were first found in the tomb). This strip may have in fact contained the more direct language 'where troops are based brambles will grow', a clear example of the law of return which might have later been moved to a different place in the received version of the DDJ.[62]

The radical utopian vision of the DDJ

To relate this technical debate among specialists on ancient China to the point of trying to find the genesis of the radical utopia in the Guodian texts, we should conclude this section by examining the main point in the DDJ shared by all philosophical anarchists who present a utopian vision of what society would look like without government, namely that humans can find morality on their own, that is, can find the link between individual freedom and community without the need of outside intervention. In western anarchism that point is made most clearly and consistently in the works of Peter Kropotkin, who asserts that 'mutual aid' is the natural and voluntary method humans have always used in order to survive, as opposed to the more hierarchical concept of 'charity' projected by those trying to justify rule of some over others.[63] Similarly, Leo Tolstoy argues that the spirit of love as expressed by Jesus in the Sermon on the Mount points to a voluntary process where individuals see the link to each other inside their own hearts, as opposed to orthodox Christian doctrines which preach the need for sinful humans to be saved from without.[64] If such ideas are indeed at the core of all philosophical anarchism, then the Guodian strips contain the same message. That message is for the (would-be) sage to let go, not to direct the people, and let things take care of themselves. The Guodian version of what became the latter part of chapter sixty-four of the received DDJ contains this message most clearly, while also containing the germ of the law of return:

> Those who act on it ruin it,
> Those who hold on to it lose it.
> Therefore the Sage does nothing, and as a result he has no disasters;
> He holds on to nothing, and as a result he loses nothing.
>
> The rule to follow in approaching all matters, is –
> If you're as careful at the end as you were at the beginning
> You will have no disasters.
> The Sage desires not to desire and places no value on goods that are hard to obtain.
> He teaches without teaching, and backs away from matters in which the masses go to excess.
>
> As a result, the Sage is able to help the ten thousand things to be what they are in themselves, and yet he cannot do it.[65]

This Guodian chapter especially contains both the idea of opposing 'charity' and a version of the law of return. If the sage does nothing, the people will eventually find their true nature. They may stray from the Way, in which case the sage, like a tribal elder but not a ruler possessing the power of coercion, would back away from them and remove his approval, but on their own they would return to the Way, that is, to the natural morality which is contained in all of us. That trust in people to rule themselves is the heart of the utopian vision of anarchism, and at root, one could argue, that belief is still contained in the Guodian strips.

Conclusion: the Guodian texts and the state of Chu

Why then, if the core utopian message remains in the Guodian texts was the man who owned the texts, and perhaps those who first wrote and transcribed them, so seemingly willing to embrace the idea of humane rule? To answer this question, it may be useful to look at who was buried in the tomb where the strips were found. The owner of the Guodian strips may have been a relatively high-ranking, Confucian-influenced teacher of the heir apparent to the ruler of the state of Chu.[66]

The state of Chu was an important southern state during the Warring States period, famous among other things for some of the most legendary 'madmen', hermits and poets who perhaps based their anti-statist ideas on earlier, pre-sedentary traditions.[67] The idea of Daoism as part of China's 'southern' tradition, more apart from and sceptical of official life, has a long history.[68] In other words, it may be that even the Confucian tradition in Chu was affected by Daoism. Li Cunshan, for example, points out that some of the other texts unearthed at the Guodian tomb were examples of a southern form of Confucianism very much influenced by Daoism.[69]

Thus it may not be so much that Confucianism tamed Daoism in this time and place but that Daoism affected Confucianism, for example in leading it to oppose 'artificial' filiality and to favour ruling more by *wuwei*, inaction or doing nothing. Others similarly have argued that the Guodian texts demonstrate that early Confucianism was more than a dispassionate elitism and was instead influenced by Daoism to put more stress on human feelings (*xing*).[70]

Thus one could easily speculate that in choosing which parts of what became the DDJ to recopy for the use of tutoring his pupil, the owner of the Guodian strips may have selected sayings that backed up his own views and would best aid his goal of influencing his student to rule less harshly once he succeeded to the throne.[71] The teacher could not be openly anti-statist but only gently suggestive of less harsh doctrines of rule, a goal perhaps of southern Chinese intellectuals who saw such doctrines as based on dangerous 'northern' traditions that were starting to take over the Chinese world.

The view that Confucian intellectuals in the period of the Guodian texts and later were trying to convince their pupils to accept less interventionist forms of rule while preserving their own role as advisors perhaps resonates with Roger Ames' view of the later Daoist text, the *Huainanzi*. Later Daoists in times of more centralised order in the early imperial era of the Qin and Han dynasties (ca. third to second centuries) may have interpreted Daoism as supporting the principle of rule at the same time that they were trying to subvert rule in practice.[72] Whether they succeeded in this double game or in the end helped more to legitimise the new imperial forms of rule of course would depend on one's own underlying political perspective.

That Confucian scholars even before the time of Mencius were trying to promote a 'humane rule' doctrine that would mitigate authoritarian rule, and thus that Confucianism is at root not dictatorial or 'feudal', is an important part of more contemporary Chinese intellectual discourse. The idea that Confucianism can be reconciled with constitutional monarchy and even democracy was a crucial part of the later Chinese 'Hundred Days' reforms of 1898. The idea of Confucianism as a pro-democratic doctrine can be found in the works of 'liberal' Chinese intellectuals from the 1920s and 1930s up to contemporary philosophers such as Tu Wei-ming, who has explicitly focused on the Guodian manuscripts as showing that there is a long history in China of limits to autocratic rule.[73]

A radical Daoist, on the other hand, might point out the remaining danger that any doctrine of humane or democratic rule could subvert true equality and freedom. The Daoist might point to the potential for intellectuals to use such humane rule doctrines to satisfy themselves that they are not responsible for harsher forms of rule, even as their acquiescence in the principle of rule not only preserves their elite status but helps to legitimate the state in general.

In any event, in times of disorder in China, when fighting between rival states intensified and rule became increasingly more oppressive, some intellectuals started to make more directly radical statements based on the utopian anarchist side of Daoism. This essay argues that these more direct statements are not distortions of the original message represented by the Guodian texts but are instead a more explicit statement of Daoist anti-statist impulses that always exist for many people. In times when the state's rule becomes more oppressive and more obviously for the benefit of rulers rather than ruled – for example, during times when states swallow each other up in war and become increasingly centralised – earlier, more gentle tendencies can often evolve into more blatant anti-statist doctrines. In times of disorder, with constant warfare, pestilence, disease, and famine, perhaps at least some intellectuals who feel they have nothing to lose in a situation when their lives are under constant threat anyway are more likely to return to Daoism and bring out its utopian anarchistic tendencies.

Notes

I would like to thank Anita Andrew, Ed Friedman, Daniel Youd, Roger Ames, Ruth Kinna, and Laurence Davis for their comments and criticism. I would also like to thank my students at Beloit College for their patience and inspiration.

 1 Many China scholars argue that the idea of philosophical versus religious Daoism, not to mention the very idea of clearly delineated schools of 'Daoist', 'Confucian', and Legalist' thought, was a much later idea in Chinese history that later scholars projected back to earlier periods. Nevertheless, this author would contend that the *Daodejing*, including the Guodian partial version, contains similar ideas to those in texts such as the *Zhuang Zi* and later works, ideas which can be grouped together and contrasted with ideas in texts that later became part of imperial ruling ideology. Thus for the purposes of this essay I use the terms 'Daoist', 'Confucian', and 'Legalist' to denote those contrasting ideas.
 2 See J. Rapp, 'Daoism and Anarchism Reconsidered', *Anarchist Studies*, 6:2 (1998), 123–51 and J. Rapp, 'Utopian, Anti-utopian and Dystopian Ideas in Philosophical Daoism', *Journal of Comparative Asian Development*, 2:2 (2003), 211–31.
 3 Space limitations preclude a fuller discussion, but suffice it to say that the terms 'radical utopian' or 'utopian anarchist' in this essay refer to the suspicion shared by philosophical Daoists and western anarchists that other utopias promote ideal governments, though Daoists and western anarchists present their own vision of an ideal (stateless) society. On anarchists' ambivalent attitude towards utopian thought see G. Woodcock, *Anarchism: A History of Libertarian Ideas and Movements*, pp. 23–4; S. Gemie, 'Fourier and the Politics of Utopia', *University of Glamorgan Occassional Papers in Humanities & Social Sciences*, p. 3; and Rapp, 'Utopian, Anti-utopian and Dystopian Ideas', 211–12.
 4 See R. Henricks, *Lao Tzu's Tao Te Ching: A Translation of the Startling New Documents Found at Guodian*, p. 22. For the original transcription of the strips, see Hubeisheng Jingmenshi bowuguan, (ed.), *Guodian Chu mu zhu jian*.
 5 See Tu Wei-ming, quoted in A. Shen, 'Ancient Script Rewrites History', *Harvard College Gazette* (March 2001), 8.
 6 U. Le Guin, with the collaboration of J. P. Seaton, *Lao Tzu's Tao Te Ching: A Book about the Way and the Power of the Way*, pp. 100–1.
 7 See J. Needham, *Science and Civilisation in China*, Vol. 2, 86–9, 121–32; J. Rapp, 'Utopian, Anti-utopian and Dystopian Ideas', 213–14.
 8 R. Ames and D. Hall, *Dao De Jing: Making This Life Significant: A Philosophical Translation*, p. 151.
 9 Rapp, 'Utopian, Anti-utopian and Dystopian Ideas', 213, 223–4.
10 A. Waley, *The Way and Its Power: A Study of the Tao Te Ching and Its Place in Chinese Thought*, p. 145.
11 *Ibid.* pp. 189–90.
12 Henricks, *Lao Tzu's Tao Te Ching*, p. 12.
13 *Ibid.* pp. 13, 29.
14 See, for example, Pang Pu, 'Gu mu xin zhi – Mandu Guodian Chu Mu' (New Information from an Old Tomb: Reading the Guodian Bamboo Ships), 7–12, translated in C. Defoort and Xing Wen, 'Guodian, Part I', *Contemporary Chinese Thought*, 32:1 (2000), 46–9.

15 Henricks, *Lao Tzu's Tao Te Ching*, p. 108.
16 Translated in A. C. Graham, *Disputers of the Tao Philosophical Argument in Ancient China*, p. 132; also see Ames and Hall, *Dao De Jing*, pp. 160–2.
17 For the idea of 'return' in the DDJ, see for example Ames and Hall, *Dao De Jing*, pp. 27–9.
18 Waley, *The Way and Its Power*, p. 209.
19 Rapp, 'Utopian, Anti-utopian and Dystopian Ideas', 222.
20 Henricks, *Lao Tzu's Tao Te Ching*, pp. 15, 36–7. Emphasis Hendricks' for the lines missing from the Guodian.
21 See for example, W. Boltz, 'The Fourth-Century B.C. Guodian Manuscripts from Chuu and the Composition of the *Laotzyy*', *Journal of the American Oriental Society*, 119:4 (1999), 594.
22 Argued in Rapp, 'Utopian, Anti-utopian and Dystopian Ideas'.
23 Argued in Rapp, 'Daoism and Anarchism Reconsidered', 135–47.
24 D. Holzman, trans., *Poetry and Politics: The Life and Times of Juan Chi (AD 210–263)*, p. 195. Emphasis added. See also E. Balazs, *Chinese Civilization and Bureaucracy: Variations on a Theme*, trans. M. H. Wright, Arthur F. Wright (ed.), p. 238, and W. Bauer, *China and the Search for Happiness*, trans. Michael Shaw, pp. 135–7.
25 Holzman, trans., *Poetry and Politics*, p. 195.
26 Balazs, trans., *Chinese Civilization and Bureaucracy*, p. 243.
27 Bauer, trans., *China and the Search for Happiness*, p. 139.
28 Liu Xiaogan, *Classifying the Zhuangzi Chapters*; Graham, *Disputers of the Tao*, pp. 197–9.
29 B. Watson, trans., *The Complete Works of Chuang Tzu*, p. 112.
30 *Ibid.* p. 110.
31 *Ibid.* p. 105.
32 Rapp, 'Utopian, Anti-utopian and Dystopian Ideas', 216.
33 Graham, *Disputers of the Tao*, pp. 64–74.
34 Watson, trans., *The Complete Works of Chuang Tzu*, p. 38.
35 *Ibid.* p. 97.
36 Henricks, *Lao Tzu's Tao Te Ching*, p. 112. Henricks finds the last phrase largely intact in the Guodian version, if combined with the next chapter.
37 Rapp, 'Daoism and Anarchism Reconsidered', 127–31.
38 Needham, *Science and Civilisation*, pp. 100–32.
39 Graham, *Disputers of the Tao*, pp. 70–2.
40 See Li Cunshan, 'Cong Guodian Chu jian kan zaoqi Dao Ru guanxi' (Early Daoist and Confucian Relations as Seen from the *Guodian Chu* Slips), *Zhongguo zhexue* (Chinese Philosophy), 20 (1999), 199, trans. Defoort and Xing, 'Guodian, Part II', p. 82.
41 Henricks, *Lao Tzu's Tao Te Ching*, pp. 21–2.
42 For a summary of the 'doubting of antiquity' debate in the DDJ, see E. Shaughnessy, 'The Guodian Manuscripts and Their Place in Twentieth-Century Historiography on the "Laozi"', *Harvard Journal of Asiatic Studies*, 65:2 (2005), 417–57, 417–28, 433–44.
43 Shaughnessy, 'The Guodian Manuscripts', 445; also see S. Allan and C. Williams (eds), *The Guodian Laozi: Proceedings of the International Conference, Dartmouth College, May 1998*, pp. 142–6.
44 Boltz, 'The Fourth-Century B.C. Guodian Manuscripts', 594.

45 Shaughnessy, 'The Guodian Manuscripts', 447–8; Henricks, *Lao Tzu's Tao Te Ching*, pp. 21–2.
46 Liu Xiaogan, 'From Bamboo Slips to Received Versions': Common Features in the Transformation of the Laozi', *Harvard Journal of Asiatic Studies*, 43:2 (2003), 340.
47 Henricks, *Lao Tzu's Tao Te Ching*, p. 68.
48 D. Hall, 'The Metaphysics of Anarchism', *Journal of Chinese Philosophy*, 10 (1983), 59.
49 See Ames and Hall, *Dao De Jing*, pp. 48–53; Liu, 'From Bamboo Slips to Received Versions', 363–8, and D. Hall and R. Ames, *Thinking from the Han: Self, Truth, and Transcendence in Chinese and Western Culture*, pp. 45–58.
50 Hall, 'The Metaphysics of Anarchism', *passim*.
51 Henricks, *Lao Tzu's Tao Te Ching*, p. 17.
52 Liu, 'From Bamboo Slips to Received Versions', 339.
53 *Ibid*. 373.
54 Henricks, *Lao Tzu's Tao Te Ching*, p. 112.
55 *Ibid*. p. 15.
56 *Ibid*. p. 36.
57 Shaughnessy, 'The Guodian Manuscripts', 453–4.
58 *Ibid*. p. 453.
59 Liu, 'From Bamboo Slips to Received Versions', 339.
60 Henricks, *Lao Tzu's Tao Te Ching*, pp. 117–18.
61 *Ibid*. p. 36.
62 Shaugnessy, 'The Guodian Manuscripts', 455–6.
63 P. Kropotkin, *Mutual Aid: A Factor in Human Evolution*.
64 L. Tolstoy, *The Kingdom of God is Within You: Christianity Not as a Mystic Religion but as a New Theory of Life*.
65 Henricks, *Lao Tzu's Tao Te Ching*, p. 42.
66 *Ibid*. pp. 4–5; also see Liu Zuxin, 'An Overview of Tomb Number One at Jingmen Guodian', in Allan and Williams, *The Guodian Laozi*, p. 32; and Jiang Guanghui, 'Guodian Chu jian yu zaoqi ruxue' (The *Guodian Chu* Slips and Early Confucianism) *Zhongguo zhexue* (Chinese Philosophy), 20 (1999), pp. 81–92, trans. Defoort and Xing, 'Guodian, Part II', pp. 6–38.
67 Needham, *Science and Civilisation*, pp. 100–32.
68 See Watson, introduction to *The Complete Works of Chuang Tzu* for the application of this idea to the *Zhuang Zi*. For the application of China's north–south divide to the contemporary era, see E. Friedman, 'China's North–South Split and the Forces of Disintegration', in *National Identity and Democratic Prospects in Socialist China*, pp. 77–86.
69 Li, 'Cong Guodian Chu jian kan zaoqi Dao Ru guanxi', 87–90.
70 For example, see Tu Wei-ming cited in Shen, 'Ancient Script Rewrites History'; also see Pang Pu, 'Kong Men zhi jian – Guodian Chu jian zhong de rujia xinxingshuo' (From Confucius to Mencius: The Confucian Theory of Mind and Nature in the Guodian Chu Slips), *Zhongguo zhexue* (Chinese Philosophy) 20 (1999), 22–35, trans. Defoort and Xing, 'Guodian, Part II', pp. 39–54.
71 This argument leaves aside the question of whether the robbers who first broke open the tomb and scattered its contents made off with any of the strips.

72   R. Ames, *The Art of Rulership: A Study in Ancient Chinese Political Thought*.
73   Tu, quoted in Shen, 'Ancient Script Rewrites History'.

References

Allan, S. and C. Williams (eds), *The Guodian Laozi: Proceedings of the Inter-national Conference, Dartmouth College, May 1998* (Berkeley: Institute of East Asian Studies, University of California, 2000).

Ames, R., *The Art of Rulership: A Study in Ancient Chinese Political Thought* (Honolulu: University of Hawaii Press, 1983).

——and D. Hall, (trans. and commentary), *Dao De Jing: Making This Life Signifi-cant: A Philosophical Translation* (New York: Ballantine Books, 2003).

Balazs, E., *Chinese Civilization and Bureaucracy: Variations on a Theme*, trans. M. H. Wright, Arthur F. Wright (ed.), (New Haven: Yale University Press, 1964).

Bauer, W., *China and the Search for Happiness*, trans. Michael Shaw (New York: Seabury Press, 1976).

Boltz, W., 'The Fourth-Century B.C. Guodian Manuscripts from Chuu and the Composition of the *Laotzyy*', *Journal of the American Oriental Society*, 119:4 (1999), 590–608.

Defoort, C. and Xing Wen (ed. and trans.), 'Guodian, Parts I and II', *Contemporary Chinese Thought* 32:1 (2000) and 32:2 (2001).

Friedman, E., 'China's North–South Split and the Forces of Disintegration', in *National Identity and Democratic Prospects in Socialist China* (Armonk, NY: M. E. Sharpe, 1999), pp. 77–86.

Gemie, S., 'Fourier and the Politics of Utopia', *University of Glamorgan Occasional Papers in Humanities & Social Sciences*, Prifysgol Morgannwg (Wales: University of Glamorgan, 1995).

Graham, A. C., *Disputers of the Tao: Philosophical Argument in Ancient China* (LaSalle, IL: Open Court Publishing, 1989).

Hall, D., 'The Metaphysics of Anarchism', *Journal of Chinese Philosophy*, 10 (1983), 49–63.

——and R. Ames, *Thinking from the Han: Self, Truth, and Transcendence in Chinese and Western Culture* (Albany: State University of New York Press, 1998).

Henricks, R., *Lao-Tzu Te-Tao Ching: A New Translation Based on the Recently Discovered Ma-wang-tui Texts* (New York: Ballantyne Books, 1989).

——*Lao Tzu's Tao Te Ching: A Translation of the Startling New Documents Found at Guodian* (New York: Columbia University Press, 2000).

Holzman, D., *Poetry and Politics: The Life and Times of Juan Chi (AD 210–263)* (Cambridge: Cambridge University Press, 1976).

Hubeisheng Jingmenshi bowuguan (Hubei Province Jingmen City Museum) (ed.), *Guodian Chu mu zhu jian* (Beijing: Wenwu chubanshe, 1998).

Jiang Guanghui, 'Guodian Chu jian yu zaoqi ruxue' (The *Guodian Chu* Slips and Early Confucianism), *Zhongguo zhexue* (Chinese Philosophy) 20 (1999), 81–92, trans. Defoort and Xing, 'Guodian, Part II', pp. 6–38.

Kropotkin, P., *Mutual Aid: A Factor in Human Evolution* (London: W. Heinemann, 1914). Reprint edition: New York: New York University Press, 1972).

Le Guin, U., with the collaboration of J. P. Seaton, *Lao Tzu's Tao Te Ching: A Book about the Way and the Power of the Way* (Boston and London: Shambala Publications, Inc., 1997).

Li Cunshan, 'Cong Guodian Chu jian kan zaoqi Dao Ru guanxi' (Early Daoist and Confucian Relations as Seen from the *Guodian Chu* Slips), *Zhongguo zhexue* (Chinese Philosophy) 20 (1999), 187–203, trans. Defoort and Xing, 'Guodian, Part II', pp. 68–90.

Liu Xiaogan, *Classifying the Zhuangzi Chapters* (Ann Arbor, Michigan: University of Michigan, Center for Chinese Studies, 1994).

——'From Bamboo Slips to Received Versions: Common Features in the Transformation of the Laozi', *Harvard Journal of Asiatic Studies*, 43:2 (2003), 337–82.

Liu Zuxin, 'An Overview of Tomb Number One at Jingmen Guodian', in Allan and Williams, *The Guodian Laozi*, pp. 23–32.

Needham, J., *Science and Civilisation in China*, Vol. 2 (Cambridge: Cambridge University Press, 1956).

Pang Pu, 'Kong Men zhi jian – Guodian Chu jian zhong de rujia xinxingshuo' (From Confucius to Mencius: The Confucian Theory of Mind and Nature in the Guodian Chu Slips), *Zhongguo zhexue* (Chinese Philosophy), 20 (1999), 22–35, trans. Defoort and Xing, 'Guodian Part II', pp. 39–54.

——'Gu mu xin zhi – mandu Guodian Chu mu' (New Information from an Old Tomb: Reading the Guodian Bamboo Strips), *Zhongguo zhexue* (Chinese Philosophy), 20 (1999), 7–12, trans. Defoort and Xing, 'Guodian Part I', pp. 43–9.

Rapp, J., 'Daoism and Anarchism Reconsidered', *Anarchist Studies*, 6:2 (1998), 123–51.

——'Utopian, Anti-utopian and Dystopian Ideas in Philosophical Daoism', *Journal of Comparative Asian Development*, 2:2 (2003), 211–31.

Roberts, M. (trans. and commentary), *Lao Zi Dao De Jing: The Book of The Way* (Berkeley: California University Press, 2001).

Shaughnessy, E., 'The Guodian Manuscripts and Their Place in Twentieth-Century Historiography on the "Laozi" ', *Harvard Journal of Asiatic Studies*, 65:2 (2005), 417–57.

Shen, A., 'Ancient Script Rewrites History', *Harvard College Gazette* (March 2001), 8.

Tolstoy, L., *The Kingdom of God is Within You: Christianity Not as a Mystic Religion but as a New Theory of Life*, trans. C. Garnett (New York: Cassell, 1894. Reprint edition: Lincoln, Nebraska: University of Nebraska Press, 1984).

Waley, A., *The Way and Its Power: A Study of the Tao Te Ching and Its Place in Chinese Thought* (New York: Grove Press, 1935).

Watson, B., (trans. and commentary), *The Complete Works of Chuang Tzu* (New York: Columbia University Press, 1970).

Woodcock, G., *Anarchism: A History of Libertarian Ideas and Movements* (New York: The New American Library, 1962).

3 Peter G. Stillman

Diderot's *Supplément au voyage de Bougainville*: steps towards an anarchist utopia

Introduction

Denis Diderot's *Supplément au voyage de Bougainville*[1] is a brief, complex, and enigmatic text. Diderot wrote it in response to Louis-Antoine de Bougainville's straightforward account of his circumnavigation of the globe from 1767 to 1769, published in 1771. Public attention to his voyage focused on his time in Tahiti, which members of the expedition called 'the only corner of the earth where men live without vices, prejudices, want, and dissension'.[2] Diderot wrote his *Supplément* for his friend Melchior Grimm's *Correspondance littéraire*, a manuscript periodical, where it appeared in 1773 and 1774. Diderot revised it around 1780, and the text, lacking the 1780s revisions, was finally published posthumously in 1796 and reprinted in all the major editions of Diderot's works in the nineteenth century.[3]

The *Supplément*'s title announces that its text is not complete within itself but is a supplement to another book, Bougainville's *Voyage* (and Diderot's *Supplément* contains material from a purported 'Supplement' by Bougainville). The subtitle promises a dialogue on a general topic not directly related to travel reports: 'the inappropriateness of attaching moral ideas to physical actions that do not accord with them'; and the epigraph from Horace's *Satires* includes a reference to nature as a standard. Although the book is usually reprinted as an independent work, it is also the third of a trio of *contes* Diderot wrote in the early 1770s and it refers to characters in the other two stories.[4] The three stories explore the relation of Christian morality, public opinion, and individual values and (especially sexual) behaviour. The *Supplément*'s form of presentation varies: dialogues between two French interlocutors (named A and B); a Tahitian leader's speech ('The Old Man's Farewell'); and conversations between a French chaplain and Orou, another Tahitian (both the speech and the conversation are purportedly drawn from Bougainville's supplement to his *Voyage*). In his revision of 1780, Diderot interpolated a story about Polly Baker (a New England prostitute).[5] As in much of Diderot's fiction, his authorial (or even editorial) voice is not obvious.

The *Supplément* is a singular work. Its brevity, allusiveness, lack of authorial voice, and diversity of style make it very different from Diderot's modernist monument, *The Encyclopédie*. Its provocative and imaginative questioning of state, authority, religion, and morality puts it at odds with some of Diderot's famous projects, such as his involvement with enlightened despotism as advisor to Catherine the Great of Russia[6] and his advocacy, with Mercier de la Rivière, of a regime of experts.

It also seems at odds with the dominant tendencies of early modern utopias. Following the pattern set by Thomas More's *Utopia* (1516), many early modern utopias propose strong central governments that maintain order, establish laws, punish swiftly and (at least for a second offence) severely, and mandate a strict morality for a society that is developed and closed, with little room for change. All citizens of Utopia believe in some higher being, and Hythloday thinks they are ripe for conversion to Christianity. Although property is shared, hierarchies of age, gender, and political or religious status exist.

Tomasso Campanella's *City of the Sun* replicates many attributes of Utopia, although the hierarchies are more pronounced (and the hierarchy of knowledge is carved into the concentric walls of the city) and the religion not obviously Christian. Offences against morality are, as with More, punished sharply; for women to dress provocatively (such as wearing cosmetics) is a capital offence. Francis Bacon's *New Atlantis* is ruled by scientists, who use religious pomp and ceremony for patriotic purposes, such as a parade celebrating the arrival of a Father of Salomon's House, and who stress family values, including the authority of the husband and deference by wife and children, as symbolised by the 'Feast of the Family'.

Much early modern French political thought from Jean Bodin's *Six Books of the Commonwealth* (1576) into Diderot's century also emphasises the importance or centrality of the state. In *The Spirit of the Laws* (1748) Montesquieu discusses legitimate forms of rule. Voltaire admires Frederick the Great of Prussia as a model for government. Rousseau is more various. When he looks to primitive times, he can imagine a society without a state: the idyllic 'patriarchal and rustic life, man's first life', as human beings emerge from Rousseau's state of nature into simple society, 'is the most peaceful, the most natural, and the sweetest life for anyone who does not have a corrupt heart'.[7] Otherwise, Rousseau's good small societies, like Clarens (in *Julie*), assume the continued existence of the state; and his famous and complex *Social Contract* can readily be interpreted as statist: the general will can 'force [one] to be free' in a democratic despotism.

Although much early modern French utopian thought follows the tendencies of More, Campanella, and Bacon, some authors do criticise state authority, hierarchy, religion, and moral restrictions. For instance, François Rabelais advocates the rule of philosopher-kings like Gargantua but has him rule with tolerance; the highly structured Abbey of Thélème has strict entry requirements but its motto is 'do as you will'; and Rabelais's works as a whole contain a carnivalesque spirit that upsets any current order, encourages the sensuous, and allows diverse individual expression and action.[8]

Difference and sensuousness are also advocated in a later and less well-known satirical utopia, Gabriel de Foigny's *Southern Land, Known*. Foigny's traveller Jacques Sadeur visits the Australians, who are hermaphrodites and 'rational beings' 'exempt . . . from passions', and who inhabit what is at first glance a utopia.[9] But, as he gradually learns, many Australian practices are not utopian. They are intolerant towards others who are unlike themselves, for instance killing their babies who are born with only one sex. They refuse to talk about many of their own practices and threaten Sadeur with death when he asks about their nudity, copulation, procreation, or religion. They are ferocious in war: after capturing an enemy city, 'no one, of any age or condition, was spared'.[10] Their secrecy about procreation is so extreme that they threaten to kill Sadeur when he gets a (visible) erection. Foigny's satirical criticisms of the Australians suggest strongly the need for individual expression, sensuality, openness to difference, communication, and restraint on violence by the state.

A famous dystopian and satirical epistolary travel tale, Montesquieu's *Persian Letters* criticises despotic rule, French religious and political institutions, and French manners and morals – all told in letters written home by the travelling Persian sultan Usbek and his friend Rica. Montesquieu imagines how others could view France; and he respects the manners and knowledge of another culture by making many of Usbek's and Rica's letters insightful, urbane, and humane. Montesquieu structures his book carefully; the letters critical of France make up the predominant portion of the book, and then at the end (and out of chronological order) a series of letters between Usbek, his chief eunuch, and his wives describes the intolerant and intolerable despotism of the seraglio, which corrupts all involved with it, truncating their emotions, passions, and sexual behaviours and leading Usbek to advocate violence against any wife who is disobedient.

Diderot's *Supplément* builds on the strands of French early modern utopian thought that are at odds with the predominant themes of early modern utopian thought generally since More and of early modern French political thought. What Rabelais, Foigny, and Montesquieu suggest in some aspects of their work, Diderot develops rather more fully in his *Supplément*.

Tahiti as apparent anarchist utopia

In the first sections of the *Supplément* Diderot presents Tahiti as a sort of natural if primitive utopia. As Diderot's interlocutors converse, B praises Tahiti and tells a sceptical A that 'you wouldn't doubt Bougainville's sincerity if you know the supplement to his Voyage'[11] in which the Old Man, a respected Tahitian elder,[12] gives a long speech extolling Tahiti's way of life. The Tahitians have limited needs and they all work together to satisfy those needs. Living a simple life and working, they are healthy and strong. Without money or private property, they share, mutually aid each other, and do not exclude any from the benefits of the society – and their sharing extends to sex also.[13]

But Diderot calls into question the Old Man's report and the readers' first impressions. In subsequent sections, Tahiti is presented as much less idyllic (and less utopian and anarchist) than the Old Man says. Although without a government, its seemingly free and open sexual behaviour is, according to Orou,[14] encouraged by strong social norms 'to produce children'. Although French prohibitions about sex are much more restrictive than Tahiti's, the island does prohibit sex by women who are menstruating, pregnant, or sterile (post-menopausal or otherwise) and by boys or girls who have not yet undergone the coming-of-age ceremony.[15] Women are exiled or sent into slavery; girls are grounded, to use contemporary American parlance; and boys' parents are reprimanded.[16] Although Orou dismisses the importance of these penalties, he does insist that Tahitian morals are 'actually improved' by tying and identifying 'private and public gain with the growth of population'. Lacking an overt government, Tahiti's rules of sexual behaviour and norms for reproduction have replaced government.

Moreover, the *Supplément* raises the question throughout whether a primitive utopia has any relevance to Europeans, and A explicitly asks the question near the end of the text: 'what useful consequences can be drawn from the manners and strange customs of these uncivilised people?'[17] The Tahitians lead such a simple life and pursue such unaffected natural needs that it is difficult to imagine Europeans who wish to or can imitate them. Whereas Tahitians by and large must come to grips with their relatively uncomplicated needs, the French must confront complex and contradictory natural and social needs. What might seem to be a utopia (or an ideal state of nature) – Tahiti as described by the Old Man – turns out, then, on further examination to be a flawed or inadequate utopia, which in any case civilised Europe could not imitate.

Although Tahiti is not unambiguously a utopia and France is far from one, nonetheless the *Supplément* can be read as an anarchist utopian text. It is a utopian text because, in the contrasts and interactions of Tahiti and France (as well as with the other events and the conversations in the text), the reader can discover important principles and practices constitutive of a utopia. Some important utopian texts are structured so that their utopia is to be found not in any one society that is presented in the text but somewhere in-between or in the interaction or the comparison of the societies.[18] In Rabelais's *Book Four*, Pantagruel with some comrades boards a ship, the *Thalamège*, and like a latterday Odysseus seeking not his homecoming but the holy bottle of Bacbuc, he visits many islands. But neither the community of the ship nor any one of the many one-dimensional and insular societies they visit suffices as a utopia by itself; in the interactions of each society with the sailors the reader learns more about what constitutes a good society. To skip forward centuries, Aldous Huxley in *Brave New World* seems to present only Mustafa Mond's technological dystopia or John the Savage's miserly nature as alternatives, but, as Huxley wrote in his 1946 Foreword, between the two lies 'the possibility of sanity';[19] and Ursula Le Guin in *The Dispossessed* presents neither Urras nor Anarres as unambiguous utopias but suggests that the reader can discover utopia (ambiguous or not) from their interrelations.[20]

The *Supplément* is anarchist because it criticises the French state and proposes alternate principles and practices compatible with or constitutive of strands of later anarchist thought.[21] In its description of the interactions among Tahitians and French, it criticises French imperialism, restrictive laws, and violence – and the state that condones and encourages them. It suggests a lessening of the scope and intensity of the state, religious commandments, and the state's and religion's laws. And it proposes principles and practices that could help move a society towards the elimination of domination, hierarchy, and coercion. Diderot suggests that reciprocity, hospitality, and generosity – within a context of open communication seeking understanding – can help constitute an egalitarian, open, non-oppressive, and non-hierarchical society. So Diderot's book presents some anarchist principles as well as suggesting how even civilised countries like France might make some moves towards a society that would be more anarchist, more free – and more like an anarchist utopia.

The critique of state, authority, and laws

Throughout the *Supplément* are discussions and criticisms of authorities and their rules: the political, religious, and social laws, backed by governmental force and public opinion, that make life difficult, conflictual, and repressed for the French, and whose relative absence in Tahiti makes life there simpler, closer to nature, and more happy. For Diderot, the French (and, as the Polly Baker episode suggests, Americans too) have developed authorities and rules that in many ways are at odds with nature and human desires, feelings, and thoughts.

Bougainville's voyage was undertaken in part to restore French confidence after its losses in the Seven Years' War, and he was charged not only with mapping places hitherto unknown to Europeans but also with claiming any unclaimed lands. So, upon landing in Tahiti, he claimed it for France. His sailors gratefully received the sexual advances and other favours of the Tahitians, but at the same time rigorously (and if necessary violently) enforced their rights to their own trinkets, clothing, and other property. The French imposed on Tahitians, who knew only common property, the French idea of exclusive private property.[22] As Diderot has the Old Man castigate the French, '[the Tahitian] offered you his fruits, his wife, his daughter, his hut, and you killed him for a handful of beads which he took without asking'.[23] The French will return, he prophesises to his people, 'to enslave you, slaughter you, or make you captive to their follies and vices. One day you will be subject to them, as corrupt, vile and miserable as they are.'[24] French colonisation, based on French superiority in firearms and force, is, Diderot suggests, illegitimate, whether used to colonise Tahiti or protect (French definitions of) property.[25]

Diderot's wickedly gleeful critique of the French catholic religious authorities and their rules permeates the text. The Old Man sees that the French impose their religious strictures to oppress the Tahitians, who 'follow the pure instincts of nature'.[26] Orou extends the critique of religious rules and the contrast with the Tahitians. After listening to the chaplain describe French rules about sex, he states, 'I find these strange precepts contrary to Nature, an offence against reason, certain to breed crime and bound to exasperate' the god that established them.[27] 'What could seem more ridiculous', he continues, 'than a precept which forbids any change of our affections' and requires life-long constancy in a world marked by change and flux. Orou finds equally surprising the abstinence from sex and work of men and women of the cloth.[28] The Polly Baker story, extending the critique of civilised society to America, displays church-based strictures adopted by the government and used to oppress women.

French political and religious rules place intolerable demands on the inhabitants of France. Diderot has Orou argue that a Frenchman has to answer to three masters – the church, the state, and himself – and the disparate despotisms of church and state (not to mention their rules that contradict the citizen's natural being) place the citizen in impossible conflicts: 'You'll come to despise all three of them, and you'll be neither a man, nor a citizen, nor a true believer. You'll be nothing. You'll be out of favour with each form of authority, at odds with yourself.'[29] And French citizens must follow French property rules: whereas the Tahitians' common property allows everyone to satisfy needs at a moderate level and peacefully among themselves, French exclusionary private property, backed by the threat of violence, leads to conflict over the satisfaction of needs, fighting, and death.

Anarchist utopian principles and practices

Lessen the scope of authority

Diderot proposes alternatives to laws and morals established by state and church and enforced, ultimately, by violence. After exploring a plurality of meanings for nature as a goal or standard, he thinks in terms of conditions that are more natural than France's as a norm by which to judge French (and American) family laws and other laws. He insists on individual consent for each undertaking. His theorising focuses on human desires and human happiness.

Diderot does not look to nature as the obvious, univocal alternative norm from which to construct a civilisation. Rather, Diderot engages in a careful and highly nuanced analysis of nature. He does not imagine a nature–civilisation dichotomy or binary, as in Bougainville's book or the popular imagination; insistently asking what is natural, Diderot sees nature not as a single stage but as a development of stages in the youth of mankind. So no single condition can be called 'the' state of nature (and so no single social or political order can be automatically read off from a discussion of the state of nature).[30] Indeed, nature seems to be used as a standard by which to judge a society's existing laws and rules, but not necessarily as a goal that a society can try to attain. Diderot's epigraph from Horace's *Satires* is indicative: 'how much better, and how different . . . is the course prompted by Nature, rich in her own resources. If you would only make proper use of them, and not confuse what should be avoided with what is desirable!'[31] Nature and her resources cannot be used to construct a society, but they can be used to determine what to avoid or to minimise – although, again, there are a plurality of 'natures' which may suggest differing judgements. And, as small Lancer's Island, with its natural society, overpopulation, and possible cannibalism warns,[32] sometimes the natural is not even a desirable norm. So, keeping in mind the complexity and occasional ambiguity of nature as a standard, for Diderot all laws and regulations that unnecessarily conflict with nature should be criticised, re-evaluated, and perhaps abandoned.

Diderot's extensive critique of the French family (indeed of the Christian or European family) shows that family laws and practices especially need to be reformed because they so unnecessarily conflict with nature. Human affection cannot be kept constant over a life-time; roles and responsibilities in the family are so rigidly structured that individuals must be forced into them; the 'tyranny of man' in unbreakable marriage has transformed women into property; and children, who add 'to the wealth of the nation as a whole, more often and more certainly' add to the impoverishment of its family.[33] Loosening legal restrictions and social rigidities – in a direction more accepting of the existence and changeableness of human desires – could drastically affect the happiness of the society and free the individual from superfluous restrictions.

Diderot also re-examines the relation of the individual to political authority. Although much of his general political writing makes him sound like a typical state-of-nature theorist, arguing that the consent of the people to the state makes the state legitimate as long as it continues and without the right of revolution,[34] Diderot suggests that in Tahiti authority is not based on any historical or hypothetical consent but requires the active, stated consent of the party at issue. When Orou offers the hospitable use of his wife or daughters to the chaplain, he justifies his action very carefully (and in language suited to western political philosophy). At first, he sounds like the traditional paterfamilias: 'They're mine, and I'm offering them to you.' But then he acknowledges that every member of his family is an independent actor: 'They are their own as well and give themselves up to you freely . . . I am in no way exceeding my authority, and you may be sure that I know and respect the rights of individuals.'[35] The youngest daughter Thia then shows her own independent agency: grasping the chaplain's knees, she implores him to go to bed with her, which she wishes. In other words, in this instance the father's authority extends only in so far as he is requesting of his daughter something that his daughter herself actively requests. A similar co-assertion happens at the end of the Old Man's speech. As the French are leaving, he ends his speech with the words: 'And you, inhabitants of Tahiti, go back to your huts . . .'.[36] The Tahitians do so immediately; but their actions, too, are not obedience to authority so much as they are the affirmation by each to do what the Old Man said.

Social contract theory moves easily from the state of nature, where the original contractual consent is explicit, to an established state and laws, where a citizen must obey a law that he thinks misguided, dangerous, or dubious, because (or even if) the citizen has (only) implicitly consented to his government. Diderot's own 'Authorité Politique', like many other contract writings, allows implicit consent, or consent given long ago, to all the legal actions of the governing authority. In the Supplément, however, Diderot overturns that statist move by showing that, on Tahiti, those with claims to authority can assert those claims effectively only when the other affected individuals explicitly assert each and every one of those same claims with them. In a sense, a statement by an authority in Tahiti becomes effective only when the affected individual actively asserts the same statement. On Tahiti, on some issues at least, the people practise anarchy.

Diderot makes other important arguments that help transform the focus of utopian thinking in ways that make possible anarchist utopias. In the Supplément Diderot does not engage in an extensive discussion or critique of government in the manner of English early modern utopians like More; and his critique of religion, while it has a few amusing theological points, is more directed at damage done by Christian morality. So Diderot is moving utopian thought from a focus on the structure and functions of government – a focus that, of course, precludes anarchy – to a concern with human happiness within a context of human freedom and utility – which opens up the scope of utopian thought, displaces the primacy of government, and makes it possible to think of *anarchist* utopias.

And in his emphasis on human happiness Diderot treats, among other matters, human desires and their satisfaction, especially human sexual desires. Other political and economic philosophers who begin with human beings as desiring beings frequently stop their theorising at the bedroom door; like Hobbes or Smith, the desires and passions they focus on are 'public' passions – that are manifest in the political or economic sphere, that involve the satisfaction of the needs for food, clothing, and shelter, and that lead to laws. For Diderot, the full range of human desires is a valid and valued dimension of utopian thinking.

Reciprocity, hospitality, generosity, and communication

Diderot also proposes a set of legitimate social interactions that permit human beings to act freely and without government or religion. Reciprocity is one. The French undertake a set of actions on the Tahitians – their imperialism – which they would not allow the Tahitians to do to them. The French actions are reprehensible; and the French could see them as reprehensible if they could but look at their actions from the Tahitian perspective, as the Old Man does (and as the Old Man enables readers, including French readers, to do).[37] The Old Man, noting the Tahitian refusal to try to enslave the French, asserts that Tahitians recognise that Tahitian and French 'are both children of Nature . . . We respected our own image in you.'[38] For the Old Man, the Tahitians act on a principle of mutual recognition of the other. That principle precludes slavery, violence, and colonialism, and encourages interactions that are egalitarian and mutual.

A second set of legitimate social interactions has to do with hospitality and the relations of host and guest.[39] As the Old Man says, the Tahitians understand their 'obligations as hosts'.[40] They offer all that they have – food, shelter, and sex – to the French, who land there for their enjoyment and to satisfy their needs as needy travellers. But the French do not play the part of guests well, acting as badly as Penelope's suitors in Homer's *Odyssey*. Equally, the Tahitian Aotourou, transported to France, is not a good guest when he attempts to sleep with every French woman he meets – although he may not realise that the French are not offering him the women as sexual partners. The chaplain – 'But my religion! My holy orders!'[41] – is at first a poor guest, refusing the host's offer of the four women in his household, until Thia's words (and body) finally entice him into bed. Finally, and like a good guest, 'out of courtesy he granted the fourth night [in bed] to the wife of his host'.[42]

Although Orou may push the chaplain more than a gentle host should, the Tahitians offer their guests gracious hospitality. But, except for the chaplain finally, the guests in the *Supplément* do not respond as guests should act: they should receive the hospitality of the hosts, accept their norms and practices, and only do further what the hosts invite.

The third important principle of social interaction, related to hospitality but worthy of consideration in its own right, is generosity. Both host and guest need to be generous, of course, but generosity as a principle of human interaction goes beyond the guest–host relation. The *Supplément* presents the reader with a few instances of generosity to suggest how it ameliorates human relations and counters the effect of human (narrow) self-interest in society. For instance, when Orou and the chaplain are sparring about sexual relations in Tahiti and in France, the chaplain suggests that women who are not good-looking – 'on whom Nature has not smiled' – are overlooked by Tahitian men. Orou's response is quick: 'Your remark convinces me that you don't have a high opinion of the generosity of our young people.'[43]

What Orou later labels the 'self-interest' of a Tahitian already includes generosity. Because for Orou the Tahitian self is so bound up in the good of others close to him, he pursues their well-being as his own.[44] Indeed, when Orou is trying to convince the chaplain to sleep with his daughters, he uses the language of charity and generosity: 'wouldn't the pleasure of doing a good deed, of assuring that one of my daughters was honoured among her companions and sisters – wouldn't that suffice for you? Be generous.'[45] Thia too asks that she be granted 'this favour', not only for her sake but to make her family happy.[46] Generosity begets generosity, and finally even the chaplain joins the cycle. In short, generosity helps bind people together because it moderates individuals' pursuit of what seems best for only themselves regardless of its effects on others by leading them to think of others; at the same time the recipients of the generosity become more fully participants in social interactions.

Pervading the *Supplément* is the theme of using communication to learn about one's own assumptions, to discover the other's way of life, and to attempt to come to understandings and actions that can generate a better world for oneself and those with whom one interacts. Throughout the time in which the book takes place, A and B are constantly talking with each other. B, who knows more about Bougainville's trip, takes a lead role in much of the discussion, but A gets in some good lines, and by the end they are talking in harmony with each other because each has learned from their discussions and each wishes to learn more.

Indeed, A and B are transformed. Before reading Bougainville's writings, B thought that in no other place 'could one be as happy as at home';[47] before talking with B, A attributed only noble motives to the French sailors. By the end, A and B are able to see France differently. The perspectives from Tahiti – what the Old Man and Orou 'tell' them about Tahiti – in confluence with the Polly Baker story give A and B insights into the costs to human happiness and freedom of European attitudes and practices as well as the knowledge that human interactions *can* take place differently. In a way, through the conversation, reading, and learning that have gone on, A and B have left their quiet complacency with their home, France, and their own narrowly circumscribed worlds, and have broadened their horizons. They do not always agree; but they see disagreement as the opportunity to engage in reasoned discourse: a discourse in which the goal of each is not primarily to defeat the other by sharp debating techniques, but rather to present one's ideas, to listen to others', to try to distil the most accurate assessment from those various points of view and then to move on to further ideas, further interaction, and further learning – an open conversation free from constraints of power, hierarchy, and arbitrary authority on the part of the participants. A and B have entered in their own way into the eighteenth-century culture of criticism, where they are able to question, analyse, and interpret information, ideas, and actions, think about them without complacency, and come up with further ideas and actions.

A and B at the end, indeed, decide that their own conversations, their own learning and critique, are inadequate. They have 'listened' to the Old Man and Orou on Tahiti and on women in Tahiti; they have heard the Polly Baker story; and they have thought about the women characters in Diderot's other two *contes*.[48] But they have discovered, in that process, that to learn about Tahiti (and France) it helps to listen to Tahitians; and so, at the end of the *Supplément*, when A and B start to talk about the role of women in French society, they recognise the importance of talking with women. They come to that conclusion by beginning with sexist clichés that are as narrow as their cultural chauvinism at their conversation's opening:[49] whether A and B will be free after dinner 'depends upon the women', who presumably structure A's and B's social lives. 'Always it's women; you can scarcely take a step without running into them.'[50] A then suggests reading them Orou's conversation with the chaplain – and the possibility for conversation, interaction, and mutual learning is set.

But Diderot also warns that conversations with the subaltern, with different cultures, and with those occupying different roles in one's own culture are always fraught with possibilities of misunderstanding that are difficult to overcome. Problems of translation, dissembling, and fabrication can misdirect or derail communication. A frequently notes the problem of understanding someone in a different language, even in translation,[51] and Orou, who has lived all his life in Tahiti, sometimes speaks the language of western political thought through the translator. Especially the subaltern may dissemble or speak with caution: at the end of the text, when A and B decide to talk with the women about Orou's conversation, B asks A what they will think of Orou's words, and A, in the last line of the book, responds that what they think is 'probably the opposite of what they say'.[52] Of course, to survive in French society, women need to be very careful with their words,[53] as do subordinates in any society. Stories may be fabricated. A seems worried that the Polly Baker story is invented, and is assured when B says that it is true.[54] But Diderot, who has concocted so much in a book that claims to be a supplement to Bougainville's reports, suggests to the reader that the issue of fabrication (whether something is true or false) is less important than the question of verisimilitude (whether a story is close enough to being an accurate representation so that it can give the reader important insights into human beings, behaviour, and culture).

Diderot's meta-textual anarchy

The structure of the *Supplément* fits – or, it could equally be said, proposes – a kind of learning, conversational, critical model in which no set hierarchy exists among different forms of literature or among the various presentations by authors and characters. The book is an amalgam of different genres, in which linear links are lacking and into which, a reader can imagine, Diderot could well insert another section, as different from what is currently in the text as the Polly Baker digression is different from the rest of the text. The forms cascade in no apparent or necessary order: dialogue by the main characters; reading of Bougainville's *Voyages* and of the supplements to it; the Old Man's speech and Orou's conversation with the chaplain; dialogue interspersed; the Polly Baker story; more of Orou's conversation; and finally, an extensive dialogue of A and B in which they reflect on what they've just read, heard, and talked about and then decide they need to go on: having explored Tahiti they now need to explore the role of women in their own society. No one form – dialogue, book (Bougainville's *Voyage* and its fictitious supplement),[55] speech, journalistic report – has a priority over the others; all the forms exist and ask to be combined into a whole. Just as in everyday experience everyone confronts a variety of ways of learning and knowing – stories, direct experience, conversation, reading of books or newspapers – so too Diderot amalgamates elements into his text.

There is, indeed, a kind of exuberant anarchy in this process. No firm authority exists in the text: Diderot's own voice is absent; there seems no overarching authorial demand that one genre, one episode, or one character be accorded place of honour as *the* authorised source for interpretation and understanding; and a reader attuned to Diderot's style could well imagine that readers could (may? should?) insert their own stories, and draw their own further conclusions (a process perhaps fitted for a postmodern reader to conceive). To be sure, the open ending – A and B are going to talk with the women – invites the reader to pursue further conversations as well, and to go beyond the confines of Diderot's own text into conversations that Diderot himself does not chart. Diderot in his text abnegates as much as possible the authority role of the author and suggests a mode of composition fit for anarchy.

So the reader can – rather, to understand the reader must – play an active role, incited by Diderot, but always incited also to go beyond Diderot's text. The reader cannot be passive but must piece together an interpretation of the amalgamated elements, ask what other experiences and ideas need to be brought to bear, and discover what further questions could be asked. Because the text ends with the question of women in society, Diderot invites the reader, like A and B, to explore further the question of women: to do so raises the possibility of having to overturn the male-oriented statements that run through the *Supplément* (most of the time, men share women in Tahiti, not vice-versa) and thus, in a sense, re-write Diderot's book; and it raises the possibility that the reader will see the issue of the relation between men and women as a (or the) key question for human interaction – a very different question from the issues of state power, imperialism, and colonisation with which the book starts, although certainly a question that has important bearings on state power. Diderot invites, and the reader needs to be an active participant in the anarchical style.

Radical ideas, hesitant theory, and halting practice

Diderot seems willing if not eager to moderate, reform, or eliminate many superfluous rules and regulations. He flirts with a radical loosening of family law and a radical (indeed anarchist) re-working of social contract theory. He suggests many principles and practices that are compatible with or make possible anarchist utopias. He nonetheless did not publish the *Supplément* and did not take any extensive overt action based on its conclusions. The discussion between A and B near the end of the *Supplément* certainly suggests a kind of moderated reformism. B argues:

> We must speak out against senseless laws until they're reformed and, in the meanwhile, abide by them. Anyone who on the strength of his own personal authority violates a bad law thereby authorises everyone else to violate the good. Less harm is suffered in being mad among madmen than in being wise on one's own. We should both tell ourselves and cry out incessantly that shame, punishment and dishonour have been administered for actions quite innocent in themselves; but let's not perform such actions ourselves, because shame, punishment and dishonour are the worst evils of all. Let's follow the good chaplain's example and be monks in France and savages in Tahiti.[56]

Referring only to the last point, A chimes in: 'Wear the costume of the country you visit, but keep your own clothes for the journey home.'[57]

Perhaps here as in his other fictional writings Diderot was radical in his theories and cautious in his practice. Perhaps he felt the ethical relativism of B's and A's comments, and found it easy therefore to criticise France (by, for example, putting on the savage's costume as he writes the *Supplément*) but more difficult to reconstruct it. Perhaps too he thought so many Frenchmen to be so uneducated that, whether as a matter of élitism or sociological analysis, he thought any kind of actively participatory mode of life not yet possible in France. In addition, the French throne censored writings: Diderot himself was criticised for omitting mention of God in his 'Authorité Politique' article and had to include an errata sheet in which he stated that 'we never claimed that the authority of princes did not come from God'.[58] It also imprisoned authors (as Diderot was himself imprisoned). In the face of such censorship and imprisonment, the stance that B asserts – to obey, speak out against, and seek to reform bad laws – may be the most radical public stance that is prudent.

Diderot's caution may also stem from a theoretical difficulty. Diderot seems to suggest – or seems to be able to conceive – that only relatively primitive countries, whose inhabitants have simple needs, can go without laws. The French, on the other hand, have natural needs and also complex, corrupt, civilised needs. So it is almost impossible to imagine them as living by natural instinct or following a principle of unified public and private utility. Because Diderot envisions the process of civilising as one of maturing and aging, he tends to see it as unilinear and non-reversible; the French cannot 'go back' or become youthful again. His theoretical difficulty is particularly ironic because part of the *Supplément*'s power derives from Diderot not placing Tahiti and France in binary opposition; Tahiti can speak to (and be used to criticise) France because the French are, like the Tahitians, natural beings with natural needs. In other words, using Tahiti to criticise France has power and effectiveness precisely because France is partly like Tahiti. But when Diderot moves from criticism to construction, then the civilised complexity and corruption of France make transformation difficult to imagine (and French repressive absolutism makes it difficult to undertake partial transformations that would make social and political change less difficult to imagine).[59]

Nonetheless, and regardless of the problems posed by the extent of civilised corruption in France, Diderot in the *Supplément* raises and pursues a series of important political issues. Contrary to the reliance on authority of so many early modern utopians and political philosophers (and so much early modern political practice), he questions and challenges those authorities and the force that upholds them. By portraying or suggesting human interactions different from ones that rely on authority and violence, Diderot takes some important steps towards an anarchist utopia.

Notes

I wish to thank the Research Committee and the Dean of the Faculty at Vassar College for their generous financial assistance, the Utopian Studies Society for their hospitality in hosting a conference during which an earlier draft of this essay was presented, and Laurence Davis and Ruth Kinna for their insightful communications with me as they read drafts and helped develop ideas.

1 I use the edition on pp. 35–75 of D. Diderot, *Political Writings*, J. H. Mason and R. Wokler (eds). Citations consist of the section number in Roman numerals (for those using different editions with five sections; those with four sections should elide III and IV into III, and change V into IV) and the page number in Arabic. I have checked the Mason and Wokler edition against the excellent critical French edition, D. Diderot, *Supplément au Voyage de Bougainville*, H. Dieckmann (ed.).

   The *Supplément* is but one of many works Diderot wrote during his lifetime (1713–84) as a leading French Enlightenment thinker. His most famous undertaking was editing the *Encyclopédie*, a twenty-eight volume work that appeared between 1751 and 1772. It manifests a quest for knowledge about all human undertakings, including sciences, arts, and crafts, and expresses the goals of spreading knowledge and changing the way people think. As he wrote, in an encyclopedia 'everything must be examined, everything investigated, without hesitation or exception' (Diderot, *Political Writings*, p. 25). In addition to his work on the *Encyclopédie*, Diderot wrote many essays, letters, and fictional works.

2 For selections, see Dieckmann, 'Appendice', to his edition of Diderot, *Supplément*, esp. pp. 75 and 82.

3 See Dieckmann, Introduction, pp. xxvi and xi n. 1, where he also comments that the published versions differed in some details (perhaps because derived from different manuscripts).

4 Diderot, *Political Writings* V, p. 74.

5 Polly Baker was seduced, impregnated, and abandoned by her fiancé; destitute, she turned to prostitution and bore four more illegitimate children. Punished with fines and jail, in this episode she finally prevails on her judges not to punish her and on her former fiancé, now a rich magistrate and merchant, to marry her. Only one manuscript of the *Supplément*, in St Petersburg, contains the story; discovered in 1912, it was published for the first time in 1935 by Gilbert Chinard in his edition of the *Supplément*. Because the readers at the end of the eighteenth and throughout the nineteenth centuries did not know the Polly Baker story as a part of the text, I use it only as supplementary evidence in this chapter.

6 Diderot does repudiate Catherine's programme in his *Observations sur le Nakaz* (Diderot, *Political Writings*, pp. 81–164).

7 Although the lengthier description is in *The Second Discourse* at the beginning of Part II, the quotation is from J.-J. Rousseau, *Émile*, Bk V, p. 474.

8 Rabelais describes Gargantua's education and rule throughout *Gargantua* [Book I], and the Abbey in chaps 52-7 of F. Rabelais, *Oeuvres complètes*; for the carnivalesque, see famously M. Bakhtin, *Rabelais and His World*.

 9 G. de Foigny, *The Southern Land, Known*, p. 78. Indeed, at first glance Foigny's
    Australia is an anarchist utopia: the Australians believe that freedom – no
    subservience, no serving others – is the 'essence' of man and that 'the very word
    commandment is odious' (*ibid*. pp. 60–1). But their restrictions on Sadeur's
    questioning belie their freedoms, and when Foigny describes their effective
    military as anarchist – 'without any leader, without orders, and without even
    speaking', with 'reason alone', they 'fall in with . . . prefect agreement' and
    attack successfully (*ibid*. pp. 110–11) – his satire must hit almost every reader.
    Foigny's utopia is like Swift's land of the Houyhnhnms: an apparent utopia,
    run by rational beings who, being perfect, see others as impure or defective and
    so can oppress and kill (or discuss killing) the others.
10 *Ibid*. p. 117.
11 Diderot, *Political Writings* I, p. 41.
12 *Ibid*. II, pp. 41–5.
13 *Ibid*. I, pp. 39–40.
14 *Ibid*. III, esp. pp. 54–5.
15 Compulsory heteronormativity reigns; unmentioned, homosexuality is presum-
    ably prohibited by the norms advocating producing children.
16 Diderot, *Political Writings* IV, p. 62.
17 *Ibid*. V, p. 66.
18 In addition, many utopian texts present a plurality of different, imagined socie-
    ties (or utopias) that allow their readers to compare ideals and reflect on what
    constitutes a good society. In *Utopia* (Book One) Thomas More has Hythloday
    praise not only Utopia but also the lands of the Polylerites, the Macarians, and
    the Achorians. One reason to consider Diderot's *Supplément* a utopian text is
    that it employs this utopian technique with such gusto, presenting as utopias
    the Old Man's Tahiti, Orou's Tahiti, France according to A at the beginning
    (I, p. 40), and the communicative, mutually respectful, and educative com-
    munity between A and B.
19 See Aldous Huxley, *Brave New World*, Foreword to the 1946 edition.
20 This theme pervades L. Davis and P. Stillman (eds), *The New Utopian Politics
    of Ursula K. Le Guin's The Dispossessed*.
21 J. P. Clark argues that, while the definition of anarchism begins with opposition
    to domination, hierarchical organisation, and exploitation, much of the power,
    interest, and diversity of anarchism lies in the various practices and ideals
    anarchists suggest as means to realise their goals. Following Clark's lead,
    I discuss first Diderot's criticisms of rule and violence and then the specific
    practices and principles he proposes that can lead to a more anarchistic – non-
    coercive, nonauthoritarian, and without domination – society. See J. P. Clark,
    'What is Anarchism?', in J. Roland Pennock and John W. Chapman (eds),
    Anarchism, pp. 3–28, esp. pp. 13–14.
22 Diderot, *Political Writings* II, p. 42.
23 *Ibid*. II, p. 44.
24 *Ibid*. II, pp. 41–2.
25 In the sections he wrote in Abbé Reynal's *Histoire des deux Indes*, Diderot
    lays out explicitly his attitude towards colonisation. Only an uninhabited
    and deserted country may be appropriated as a colony, and a partly deserted
    country can be appropriated, in its deserted part only, and then only by occupy-

ing it and labouring there, to assure that it becomes inhabited. 'If it is fully inhabited I can lay legitimate claim only to hospitality and assistance which one man owes another . . . If I demand more, I become a thief and a murderer' (Diderot, *Political Writings*, pp. 175–7). The *Supplément* presents fictionally the last part of the *Histoire*'s theoretical argument.

26 Diderot, *Political Writings* II, p. 42.

27 *Ibid.* III, p. 50.

28 *Ibid.* IV, pp. 64–5.

29 *Ibid.* III, p. 51.

30 Diderot contrasts sharply with Hobbes and Locke, who each (in his own way) constructs a single state of nature in order to present the only social contract and political society that can follow from that state of nature.

31 Diderot, *Political Writings*, Epigraph, p. 35.

32 *Ibid.* I, p. 38.

33 *Ibid.* pp. 70–1. Dieckmann, 'Introduction', pp. xxxv–lxxv, treats extensively the conflict between (religious) sexual morality and natural sexual practices, topics Diderot also touches on in the two *contes* that go with the *Supplément* (V, p. 74). Radically re-evaluating childhood, Diderot imagines a Tahitian society where children are valued and valuable, and thus where any dissolution of parental affections (e.g. separation, divorce) is not troubled by fear of childcare burdens.

34 See 'Authorité Politique' (Diderot, *Political Writings*, pp. 6–11). Diderot states that against an 'unjust, ambitious and violent king' the only 'legitimate redress' for the people is to calm him by their submission and assuage God by prayers (*ibid.* pp. 10–11). Given governmental censorship of the *Encyclopédie*, his argument here may be primarily prudential.

35 Diderot, *Political Writings* III, p. 48.

36 *Ibid.* II, p. 45.

37 Diderot here follows Montesquieu's technique in the *Persian Letters*, where Usbek's criticisms of French life allow even French readers to see and understand their society's deficiencies.

38 Diderot, *Political Writings* II, pp. 42–3.

39 I am indebted here to an excellent treatment of hospitality in Diderot: Jimmy Casas Klausen, 'Of Hobbes and Hospitality in Diderot's *Supplement to the Voyage of Bougainville*', *Polity* 27:2 (2005).

40 Diderot, *Political Writings* II, p. 45.

41 *Ibid.* III, p. 48.

42 *Ibid.* IV, p. 65.

43 *Ibid.* IV, p. 62.

44 *Ibid.* IV, p. 63.

45 *Ibid.* III, p. 48.

46 *Ibid.*

47 *Ibid.* I, p. 40.

48 Diderot reports the words (in translation) of the Old Man and of Orou in conversation with the chaplain, and in telling the story of Polly Baker Diderot also reports some of her words. They do not speak only as the other in the reports of the superior. Diderot gives voice to the voiceless; the subaltern speak, and they speak for themselves.

49 Diderot, *Political Writings* I, p. 40.
50 *Ibid.* V, p. 75.
51 *Ibid.* I, p. 41; II, p. 46; V, p. 66.
52 *Ibid.* V, p. 75.
53 *Ibid.* V, p. 74.
54 *Ibid.* III, p. 59.
55 *Ibid.* I, p. 41.
56 *Ibid.* V, p. 74.
57 *Ibid.*
58 Diderot, *Political Writings*, pp. 11–12.
59 Indeed, Clark ('What is Anarchism?', p. 13) sees 'a strategy for change' as important for a full anarchist position, and Diderot seems to have found it impossible to imagine how to replace 'violent and coercive institutions by voluntary and libertarian ones' in the France in which he lived. Lacking the possibility of anarchist practice, Diderot could not articulate the possibilities of a transition to a noncoercive, nonauthoritarian condition.

References

Bakhtin, M., *Rabelais and His World* (Cambridge, Mass.: The M.I.T. Press, 1968).

Clark, J. P., 'What is Anarchism?', in J. Roland Pennock and John W. Chapman (eds), *Anarchism* (NOMOS XIX; New York: New York University Press, 1978).

Davis, L. and P. Stillman (eds), *The New Utopian Politics of Ursula K. Le Guin's The Dispossessed* (Lanham, Md.: Lexington Books, 2005).

de Foigny, G., *The Southern Land, Known* (Syracuse, NY: Syracuse University Press, 1993).

Diderot, D., *Supplément au Voyage de Bougainville*, ed. G. Chinard (Baltimore, Md.: The Johns Hopkins University Press, 1935).

——*Supplément au Voyage de Bougainville*, ed. H. Dieckmann (Genève: Droz, 1955).

——*Political Writings*, ed. J. H. Mason and R. Wokler (Cambridge: Cambridge University Press, 1992).

Huxley, A., *Brave New World* (New York: Harper & Row, 1946).

Klausen, J. C., 'Of Hobbes and Hospitality in Diderot's *Supplement to the Voyage of Bougainville*', *Polity*, 27:2 (2005), 167–92.

Rabelais, F., *Oeuvres complètes* (Paris: Gallimard, 1955).

Rousseau, J.-J., *Émile*, ed. Allan Bloom (New York: Basic, 1979).

PART III

Anti-capitalism and the anarchist utopian literary imagination

Everyone an artist: art, labour, anarchy, and utopia

We live in a time when the idea of utopia is almost universally denigrated. To be utopian, according to this commonplace view, is to be hopelessly impractical, or dangerously idealistic, or both. In the wake of the night-marish horrors of the twentieth century, with its totalitarianisms and geno-cides, who any longer can believe in utopia?

To some extent, these understandings of utopia have merit. Insofar as utopia is equated with the quest for perfection, then it appears to invite the charge that it functions merely as harmless escape or dangerous illusion.[1]

And yet, such critical accounts do not tell the whole story of utopia. The critics focus only on those aspects of the utopian tradition associated with the quest for perfection in some impossible future. They curiously omit those elements associated with the encouragement of greater imaginative awareness of neglected or suppressed possibilities for qualitatively better forms of living latent in the present. In this essay I will consider one such ostensibly anti-perfectionist form of utopianism: namely, the anarchist or libertarian socialist literary utopia from the late nineteenth century to the present day.

The anarchist scholar of utopia Marie Louise Berneri nicely suggests some of the distinctive features of the anti-authoritarian utopian tradition as a whole in the concluding lines of her book *Journey through Utopia*:

> The authoritarian utopias of the nineteenth century are chiefly responsible for the anti-utopian attitude prevalent among intellectuals to-day. But utopias have not always described regimented societies, centralised states and nations of robots. Diderot's *Tahiti* or Morris's *Nowhere* gave us utopias where men were free from both physical and moral compulsion, where they worked not out of necessity or a sense of duty but because they found work a pleasurable activity, where love knew no laws and where every man was an artist.[2]

To be sure, neither Diderot nor Morris conceived their work as part of an 'anarchist' utopian tradition. It is thus perhaps advisable to follow the example of the historian of anarchism Peter Marshall when he refers to

them as 'libertarian' writers who have played an important part in the
history of anarchism, in Diderot's case as a 'forerunner of anarchism' and
in Morris's case as part of its 'extended family'.[3] Bearing this subtle but
important distinction in mind, I wish to focus in this paper on one relatively
neglected but I believe highly significant aspect of the libertarian utopian
tradition highlighted in the final part of the Berneri quotation above:
namely, the ideal of 'every man . . . an artist', or as I would re-formulate
the idea to take account of *both* halves of the human race, everyone an
artist. I intend to do so by considering it in relation to another idea in the
above quotation, that of pleasurable labour. My primary aim in undertaking
these conceptual tasks is to draw out what I take to be one of the most
compelling and vibrant *political* functions of the libertarian utopian tradition in the modern world. I refer, more specifically, to the ways in which it
may function as a counter-cultural challenge to the currently dominant,
capitalist form of archist ideology and practice by opposing to it an anarchist or libertarian socialist utopian alternative distinguished by the qualities of self-direction, free expression, and creativity associated with artistic,
non zero-sum, and nature-friendly labour.

I develop this analysis by means of a quite focused consideration of
relevant politically oriented fiction and essays by three anarchist or libertarian socialist[4] artists who attempted to formulate self-consciously utopian
visions of a world in which the arts might flourish: William Morris (1834–
1896), Oscar Wilde (1854–1900), and Ursula K. Le Guin (1929–). Foremost among the many reasons why I have chosen to focus on these particular
writers is that (as I will demonstrate by means of detailed textual analysis)
all three strove to imagine post-capitalist, non-coercive societies in which
artistic creation would replace profit-driven economy as the fundamental
aim of social life, yet they did so from revealingly different perspectives
about the nature and social functions of art. A careful comparative analysis
of these different perspectives may, I suggest, help to illuminate the genealo-
gies of – and hence potential alternatives to – some particularly dogmatic
and destructive ongoing ideological debates in the areas of cultural politics,
ecology and the politics of work and technology, and anarchist and utopian
studies. More to the point politically, it is intended as a contribution to
the revolutionary project of constructing a sustainable anarchist utopian
counter-cultural challenge to the capitalist form of archist domination that
has so disfigured our world and the lives of all those who inhabit it.

The plan for the chapter is as follows. First, I will systematically reconstruct, analyse, and contrast the utopian visions of artistic community
animating the work of Morris and Wilde. I will then conclude by arguing
that Le Guin's *The Dispossessed* draws what are opposing positions in the
work of Morris and Wilde into creative dialogue, and in so doing redeems
the promise of anarcho-socialist revolution held out by her nineteenth-
century utopian predecessors.

The craft utopia of William Morris

William Morris's most original and lasting contributions to political thought were his critique of useless toil under capitalism and his utopian vision of a world in which all forms of labour, even the commonest, might be made attractive. These contributions are inextricably linked insofar as Morris believed that only with the historical evolution of specifically capitalist institutions was a wedge driven between art and work. As capitalism has grown the wedge has deepened, with the result that most people are now surrounded by ugliness and work and live in pain. The situation will be reversed, he claimed, only when artificial obstacles to pleasurable labour distinctive to market-engulfed capitalist societies are removed, and all have the opportunity to make their innate senses of beauty an integral part of their lives.

Morris developed his vision of a society in which work and art – and nature – blend harmoniously in a range of utopian writings, the best known of which is his socialist romance *News from Nowhere* (1891). A moneyless and stateless craft utopia, perhaps the most radically utopian feature of Nowhere is that all the work done in it is pleasurable, either because of the hope of social honour with which the work is done, which causes pleasurable excitement even when the work itself is not pleasant; or because it has grown into a pleasurable habit, as in the case of mechanical work; or most importantly of all, because everybody is an artist insofar as they are able to take some conscious sensuous pleasure in the work itself.

We first encounter this aspect of the tale in chapter two, when a casual remark by an inhabitant of future London alerts the reader to a recurring feature of the romance: namely, detailed descriptions of physical objects that suggest the loving artistic care lavished on them by the multi-skilled craftspeople who populate Nowhere. Considered as a whole, these details depict an alluring and compelling vision of a society infused with art. It is not 'art' as we know it, however – the prerogative of isolated and mysteriously inspired beings detached from the workaday world of ordinary people – but the living popular art produced by those able to take pleasure in their daily work.

Following his Oxford mentor John Ruskin, Morris understood art in very broad terms as 'man's[5] expression of his joy in labour'.[6] Understood in this way, art extended well beyond 'those matters which are consciously works of art', to encompass not only 'painting and sculpture, and architecture, but the shapes and colours of all household goods, nay, even the arrangement of the fields for tillage and pasture, the management of towns and of our highways of all kinds; in a word . . . the aspect of all the externals of our life'.[7] Artists, in turn, were simply those who were committed to standards of excellence in their daily work: 'what is an artist but a workman who is determined that, whatever else happens, his work shall be excellent?'[8]

Such definitional claims of course beg the question of why Morris's vision of art could not easily be realised in late Victorian England, or indeed in our own contemporary world. If standards of workmanship are the key to artistic production, then why can't such standards be encouraged within the framework of existing industrial capitalist societies? In fact, this same question bedevilled Morris at a quite personal level for many years. In the early 1860s, he and some friends established a business that proposed to undertake quality handiwork in various forms of decoration. By the 1870s, the firm had grown considerably and was generally regarded as a success, not only in purely commercial terms but as a trend setter among the so-called 'cultivated' (i.e. wealthy) elite. However, Morris himself was dissatisfied. He explained the reasons for this dissatisfaction in a letter written in 1883 to his socialist friend Andreas Scheu:

> In spite of all the success I have had, I have not failed to be conscious that the art I have been helping to produce would fall with the death of a few of us who really care about it, that a reform in art which is founded on individualism must perish with the individuals who have set it going. Both my historical studies and my practical conflict with the philistinism of modern society have *forced* on me the conviction that art cannot have a real life and growth under the present system of commercialism and profit-mongering.[9]

Deeply egalitarian by temperament, and painfully aware of the depths into which art had fallen since commercial society divorced it from authentic popular tradition, Morris could not be content with art for a few. He demanded instead an *'art which is to be made by the people and for the people, as a happiness to the maker and the user'*,[10] and it was his passionate desire for the satisfaction of this egalitarian artistic and altruistic craving that ultimately propelled him across 'the river of fire'[11] to become a revolutionary socialist.

From Morris's perspective, piecemeal reforms of capitalism divorced from a larger revolutionary strategy to overthrow it altogether would be ineffectual and even counterproductive, insofar as the imperative of the quest for ever-greater profit is one of its constitutive defining features. And while it is quite true that his conception of revolutionary strategy evolved in response to changing historical circumstances, he never wavered in his studied conviction that the system of organising labour for individual profit is unsustainable, and that, as he once put it, 'the whole people have now got to choose' between 'the confusion resulting from the break up of that system' and the determination to organise labour instead for 'the livelihood of the community'.[12] In either case the transition to a post-capitalist world would be fraught with difficulties, the former associated with social breakdown and ecological collapse, and the latter with the violent resistance likely to be mounted by those with a strong vested interest in maintaining the status quo. Only the second choice, however, offered a plausible hope of a sustainable alternative way of life based on cooperation rather than perpetual war.

Morris's utopian speculations on post-capitalist forms of artistic labour may be understood within this context as a means of stimulating an urgently necessary democratic dialogue about the relationship between art, work, nature, and society. Unlike so many other utopian writers, Morris did not attempt to prescribe in law-like detail how people ought to live their lives. Rather, he developed a new, chastened, and anti-perfectionist style of utopian writing that was neither prescriptive nor prophetic but heuristic. It was a style, in other words, meant to help awaken ordinary people's latent hopes and desires for a radically egalitarian, cooperative, and creative form of life; provoke them to reflect on, and discuss and debate collectively, the rationality of such hopes and desires; and give them the courage and confidence necessary to strive for the studied convictions that emerged from this process of constructive imagination, reflection, and democratic dialogue. As Morris himself put the point, 'Education towards Revolution seems to me to express in three words what our policy should be; towards that New Birth of Society which we know must come, and which, therefore, we must strive to help forward so that it may come with as little confusion and suffering as may be'.[13] Towards this end, he not only contributed hundreds of intelligent and accessible articles to a journal (the *Commonweal*) whose primary audience was the British working classes. He also (as Salmon observes) between 1883 and 1890 addressed more than 1000 political and artistic gatherings, and was heard in person by as many as 250,000 people.[14]

In those of his publications that explore the possible forms of art and work in the new society, Morris articulates a number of imaginative 'hints' as to how they might be reconnected and thus transformed such that all working people would be artists and creators able to take an intelligent interest in their labour. In *News from Nowhere*, for example, he depicts a society organised around artisan production, with its emphasis on individual initiative, responsibility, and self-imposed timescales and rhythms set in an environment of spontaneous co-operation. In this profoundly democratic society, people are free to decide for themselves what they need and want, balancing those desires against how much work they want to do.[15] In stark contrast to our own world, where most of the work done is useless toil in the service of commerce or social control, in Nowhere everyone takes tremendous pleasure in creating things that are both beautiful and useful to others. Refined machine tools are used to relieve people of irksome labour but otherwise are done without. As a result, technology has lost its destructive dynamism and humanity neither conquers nature nor is conquered by it. The denizens of Nowhere have recovered a strong sense of place rooted in the land, and their community life is bound together by the natural order of work rather than the coercive powers of the state.

Morris's critics have replied dismissively that this utopian vision is sheer romanticism, an anachronistic throwback to the pre-industrial era and the non-market economies of 'primitive' societies. And even otherwise far more sympathetic fellow socialists have responded with scepticism to the notion that it is possible to have both the abundance of material goods made available by the ruthless productive methods of the global market economy and the transformation in the nature of work facilitated by its abolition. My own considered view is that Morris may have the proverbial last laugh, if one can speak of laughter when considering the revolutionary political implications of the current global ecological crisis.

In the first place, while it is true that Morris's largely craft utopian vision of creative and artistic work would entail a significant slowing of the present dynamism of technical advance, it does not necessarily follow that this vision is thus (as H. G. Wells and George Orwell, among others, believed) doomed to remain an unrealised dream. C. Douglas Lummis's comments in this regard are apt:

> Some may object that it is futile at this late date to lament the passing of the preindustrial craft worker. Industrialism is here, and 'You can't turn back the clock'. What a poor analogy this old saw is: in fact, you can turn back clocks: they have handles for doing just that. What you cannot do is make the past itself happen again: the events cannot be repeated, and the people are gone. But the things known by the people in the past can be known by us as well. As if I couldn't break a walnut with a hammer, wear cloth of woven wool, or drink water from a clay cup because these are neolithic technologies![16]

Second, as Ruth Kinna has pointed out, Morris freely acknowledged that material goods would not be produced in any great abundance in a society infused with art. Because such goods would be individually crafted and vested with meaning, they would only be available in limited quantities. However, Morris believed that this fall in supply would be more than offset by the skill and thoughtful attention lavished on available wares, as well as by the resulting improvements in their durability. Moreover, as artists rather than mere consumers people would develop a love for well-crafted products, and would be less likely to become bored with their possessions.[17] As Old Hammond explains in News from Nowhere: 'The wares which we make are made because they are needed . . . So that whatever is made is good, and thoroughly fit for its purpose'.[18]

Third, Morris's revolutionary romantic[19] response to industrialism is not only compatible with, but is both validated by and has been a direct and important influence on, the rapidly growing radical ecological movements and counter-cultural communal experiments found in even the most industrialised nations. The similarities are striking, among them the shared commitment to a decentralised, low-growth, and ecologically sustainable economy; the considered belief that such an economy would provide more profound forms of fulfilment (in terms of sociality, mutuality, rewarding work, cleaner air and water, greater self-reliance, harmony with nature, social peace, etc.) than its consumerist counterpart; the distinction made between needs and wants in persuading people of the value of fundamental social change; a thorough re-rethinking of the nature and value of work; ambivalence about modern technology; and a recognition of the importance of culture in radical political strategies for eco-friendly social reconstruction. To be sure, there are differences as well, most notably the wealth of rigorous scientific evidence now available to support the sort of post-industrial ecological ideas which Morris articulated over a century ago in more poetic fashion. Nevertheless, Morris remains an abiding influence on contemporary ecologism, both in its strictly eco-socialist variants and otherwise.[20]

Among recent ecological works that both draw upon and creatively develop Morris's ideas in a way that turns the tables on his unlimited economic growth-oriented critics, Keekok Lee's *Social Philosophy and Ecological Scarcity* is one of the most notable. According to Lee, a civilisation based on the promise of an inexhaustible supply of material goods – and one that consequently urges as the criteria of the 'good society' and the 'good life' ever-expanding economic growth, ever-increasing possession and consumption of external material things – is both unsustainable and morally bankrupt. In opposition to the blind alley of the consumerist society and its associated morality of consumption, Lee proposes as an alternative what she refers to as an 'artistic morality' based on an 'artistic mode of production'. Like Morris, she understands the terms 'art' and 'the artist' in a very broad sense. Like Morris as well, she links art and labour in such a way that both concepts are radically transformed. Rejecting what she refers to as the 'cornucopic' version of socialism propounded by Marx on the grounds that it is incompatible with thermodynamic and ecological reality, she turns instead to Fourier and Morris in order to develop an 'ascetic or frugal' model of socialism that unambiguously rejects both the instrumental view of work as a curse and the ruthless exploitation of nature to meet ever-increasing needs. Morris is so important, she suggests, primarily because with him the artistic mode of production acquires an aesthetic dimension.[21]

Interestingly, however, unlike Morris she explicitly draws a distinction between the aesthetic and ethical dimensions of artistic labour even as she recognises their interconnection. For Lee, the defining characteristics of the artistic mode of production are both aesthetic and ethical. They are aesthetic insofar as: first, there are no external ends to which the activity is subordinated, such as reward, fame, honour, and so on; second, the artist strives to create an object which is dictated by the laws of art peculiar to the object; and third, artist and material are part of a single process of production so that interaction between the two is not a means to an externally imposed end, but is simply a part of the activity which is the artist's end. They are ethical and social as well insofar as '*qua* artist' she or he need not look upon others as hostile rivals and competitors but as mutually inspiring; and the activity performed enables the individual to dedicate her- or himself to something larger than purely private ends, 'to an ideal or movement which one is helping to sustain and enrich'. In this way, Lee concludes, 'conflict between individual and social demands may become muted and less polarised'.[22]

This point is interesting because it highlights a feature of Morris's craft utopian vision that in my opinion ought to be more carefully and critically scrutinised. As the commentary from Lee's work just quoted makes clear, she imagines that the transition to an artistic mode of production would reduce the conflict between individual and social demands. She does not suppose that it would eliminate entirely all lasting public disagreement about fundamental matters of principle. Morris, by contrast, supposes precisely this. Consider, for example, the following passage from a book he authored jointly with the socialist philosopher E. Belfort Bax:

> As regards the future form of the moral consciousness, we may safely predict that it will be in a sense a return on a higher level to the ethics of the older world, with the difference that the limitation of scope to the kinship group in its narrower sense, which was one of the causes of the dissolution of ancient society, will disappear, and the identification with social interests will be so complete that any divorce between the two will be inconceivable to the average man.[23]

The ethics of the older world to which Morris and Bax refer are the ethics of the tribal societies that predated the development of ancient Greek civilisation. Unlike them, the ethics of a future communist society would be both conscious and universal, with a socialist love of humanity dialectically subsuming both kinship ethics and the world's major religions:

> When this beggarly period has been supplanted by one in which Socialism is realized, will not the system of morality, the theory of life, be all-embracing, and can it be other than the Socialistic theory? . . . No separate system of ethics will then be needed; there will be no protest needed against the theory of life which will then be commonly held, we shall only have to guard the freedom which we have won.[24]

In short, Morris appears to believe that the individual and the social will cease to conflict in any enduring and fundamental way in communist society because the individual will realise her- or himself in social perfection.[25]

This perfectionist conception of social ethics – an anomaly, it should be said, in Morris's otherwise remarkably anti-perfectionist utopian output – in turn influences his aesthetic ideas. Art may be for Morris man's expression of pleasure in his labour, but only when that pleasure is derived from serving what one takes to be the needs of others. Only when art is 'social'

and 'organic'; only when the individual subordinates his freedom of hand
and mind to the 'co-operative harmony' of the community; only when the
artist produces goods for 'use', subject to the 'demands of the public', rather
than succumbing to the 'affectation and effeminacy' of 'the production of
beauty for beauty's sake'; only then, according to Morris, will art take up
where it left off with the decline of the Middle Ages.[26] Only when people
work and live for others, in other words, will art flourish once again.

The difficulty with this line of reasoning has been nicely articulated by
even so convinced an advocate of a new ethic of work as David Meakin.
If, as Meakin remarks, a balanced view of the ideal relationship between
work and art entails on the one hand freeing work as far as possible from
the rule of mechanical efficiency, while on the other hand seeing art in its
potential relationship with purposive social activity, then we must acknowledge that this is a delicate balance indeed. As he goes on to observe, no one
could deny the impoverishment that would result from restricting art to the
decorative arts and crafts, or from applying too rigorously or unimagina-
tively the criterion of social usefulness.[27]

Is this criticism applicable to Morris's utopian writing? Judging by the
passages just quoted from his writings on art and society, I believe that
to a certain extent it is. Consider as additional evidence the depiction of
literature and book learning in News from Nowhere. To cite but one relevant example, in chapter twenty-two we encounter the 'grumbler', a
socially maladjusted elderly man who persistently laments the loss of the
'splendid works of imagination and intellect' produced in past times. In
response his granddaughter Clara exclaims exasperatedly, 'Books, books!
Always books, grandfather! When will you understand that after all it is
the world we live in which interests us; the world of which we are a part,
and which we can never love too much?'[28] The reason for this exasperation
soon becomes clear. Clara is reacting vehemently against what we are
encouraged to regard as the class-deformed expressions of a malignant
culture that is deeply alienated from nature and the body and cut off from
everyday life.

Understandable as Clara's reaction may be, it does not follow that all
the artistic products of that culture ought to be tarred with the same brush,
or that even the most socially insensitive of them might not have other
redeeming qualities. Nor does it follow that what is now unfortunately
commonly referred to as 'high art' (literature, music, dance, theatre, painting, sculpture, etc.) ought to be consigned in a more egalitarian and democratic future to a subordinate status comparable to that now reserved for
the decorative arts. Yet that is precisely what occurs in fictional form in
Morris's News from Nowhere,[29] which at times reads like a kind of tolerant
and good-humoured 'revenge'[30] against the injustices and inequalities of
nineteenth-century Britain. To be sure, there are no formal controls on
aesthetic expression such as may be found in Plato's Republic and so many

subsequent archist utopias. Nevertheless, introspective, visionary, avant-garde, or critical aesthetes and intellectuals are a rarity in Morris's craft utopia, a breed apart tolerated rather than encouraged in a thoroughly socialised world in which artistic activity is judged primarily by the gender-coded 'manly' criterion of social usefulness.

The artist's utopia of Oscar Wilde

By way of a corrective to this perhaps too pronounced functionalist tendency in Morris's writing, it may be helpful to turn briefly to the writing of another artist who imagined an anarchist or libertarian socialist utopia in exactly the same year (1891) that *News from Nowhere* was published in book form. In many ways, the utopian vision of a society infused with art that is articulated in Oscar Wilde's classic essay *The Soul of Man under Socialism* is strikingly similar to Morris's.[31] Like Morris, Wilde conceives his utopian vision in quite radical terms as an expression of a root-and-branch repudiation of capitalist society. He suggests that charity and other palliative measures do more harm than good by preventing people from realising the full horrors of the system of private property, and advocates the reconstruction of society on such a basis that poverty would be impossible. He does so, moreover, from a distinctively socialist perspective insofar as he believes that private property and the wage-based society must be abolished in order to make way for a community in which all will share in the general prosperity and happiness. Like Morris as well, he unambiguously rejects authoritarian socialism in favour of a libertarian variant. He emphasises the values of freedom from any form of government and from compulsion in work, and links these notions to an ideal of universal individual self-realisation associated with the diffusion of art into all aspects of life.

Where Morris and Wilde differ most clearly is the latter's much more emphatically individualistic conception of art. This point is apparent from the very first page of Wilde's *The Soul of Man under Socialism*, which opens with a perspective on altruism diametrically opposed to that implicit in Morris's work: 'The chief advantage that would result from the establishment of Socialism is, undoubtedly, the fact that Socialism would relieve us from that sordid necessity of living for others which, in the present condition of things, presses so hardly upon almost everybody.'[32] For both Morris and Wilde, one of the reasons why capitalism ought to be opposed is because it stifles the artistic impulses latent in all human beings. Each means something very different from the other, however, when he uses the term 'artistic'. For Morris, the paradigm case of an artistic community is the medieval guild. He admires in particular the paternalistic moral force that the guild ideally exercised over its members – its power in fairly apportioning the work at hand, in distributing the rewards of labour, in checking competition, in ensuring production for use and not profit, and in maintaining a standard of value. For Wilde, by contrast, the exercise of paternalistic moral force in the realm of artistic production would be a prime example of that 'sordid necessity of living for others' which has spoiled so many lives. The artistic impulse is not something that responds to the 'clamorous claims of others' and has nothing to do with the fact that other people want what they want. Rather, it emerges naturally from a mature and self-expressive personality. In the present stunted and stifling condition of society, he believes, the expression of artistic personality is confined to the work of a few highly gifted and materially privileged individuals who succeed in isolating themselves from the demands of the public. In a libertarian socialist or anarchist society in which the ordinary daily work of the world is done by machines, wealth is distributed equitably, and people have developed an unselfish respect for the individual autonomy and creativity of others, everybody would have the opportunity to express him- or herself in an artistic manner.

Unlike Morris, Wilde is in his discussion of art particularly sensitive to the danger of what John Stuart Mill famously referred to in his essay *On Liberty* as a 'tyranny of the majority'. According to Mill, those who wish to protect individual liberty must be vigilant against more than just the tyranny of the magistrate. They must guard as well against 'the tyranny of the prevailing opinion and feeling; against the tendency of society to impose, by other means than civil penalties, its own ideas and practices as rules of conduct on those who dissent from them; to fetter the development, and, if possible, prevent the formation, of any individuality not in harmony with its ways, and compel all characters to fashion themselves upon the model of its own'.[33] Wilde articulates a similar point in *The Soul of Man*, though of course in his own inimitably epigrammatic way, and with particular reference to the sphere of art. Specifically, he suggests that while tremendous progress has been made over time in limiting social interference with the individualism of speculative forms of thought such as science and philosophy, the attempt to interfere with the individualism of imaginative art persists in quite an aggressive and brutalising way. As evidence for this proposition, he cites the damage done to the English novel and the dramatic arts by the exercise of popular authority. More specifically, he observes that any attempt to extend the subject-matter of art has provoked a fearful reaction on the part of the public, who regard such artistic innovation as a disturbing form of individualism. And they are right to do so, for 'art is the most intense mode of Individualism that the world has known'.[34] 'Art is Individualism', in fact, and 'therein lies its immense value. For what it seeks to disturb is monotony of type, slavery of custom, tyranny of habit, and the reduction of man to the level of a machine'.[35] In other words, far more so than Morris, Wilde acknowledges a positive role for the socially disruptive individualistic dimension of art. If for Morris this anarchic aspect of art is nothing more than a symptom of its degeneration under capitalism that will disappear with the re-unification of art and labour under socialism, for Wilde it is a sign of social vitality and an essential safeguard against the ever-present threat of social conformity and stagnation posed by popular authority masquerading as guardian of the peace.

Critics of Wilde's conception of art in *The Soul of Man* have labelled it 'elitist' or 'aristocratic', and there is some truth in this charge, though not to the extent and in the way that most of them assume. For example, it is frequently claimed that his utopian vision of a society composed of artistic individuals engaged in 'cultivated leisure' reflects his own belief in a slothful or hedonistic mode of life based primarily on self-development through commodity consumption. However, the evidence of the text suggests otherwise. While Wilde does indeed speculate at one point in the essay that 'cultivated leisure . . . , and not labour, is the aim of man',[36] the passage in question ought to be interpreted in context, for Wilde makes it very clear only a few sentences earlier that by 'labour' he means in this particular instance 'all unintellectual labour, all monotonous, dull labour, all labour that deals with dreadful things, and involves unpleasant conditions'.[37] In addition, in the remainder of the sentence quoted above, he imagines a wide variety of non-consumerist ways in which individuals emancipated from the tyranny of want might make use of their new-found freedom: 'while Humanity will be amusing itself, or enjoying cultivated leisure – which, and not labour, is the aim of man – or making beautiful things, or reading beautiful things, or simply contemplating the world with admiration and delight, machinery will be doing all the necessary and unpleasant work'.[38] In short, like Morris, Wilde envisages in *The Soul of Man* an exceptionally creative, imaginative, beautiful, and joyful way of life very different from what passes for 'the good life' in contemporary consumerist societies.

It is also frequently claimed that Wilde's conception of artistic individualism in the essay is elitist insofar as it can only possibly be realised by a few. Interestingly, however, Wilde himself does not draw such a conclusion. To the contrary, he refers to 'the great actual Individualism latent and potential in mankind generally',[39] an individualism that has been corrupted by political and economic power in hitherto existing societies, but which in a truly non-authoritarian society would blossom as naturally and simply as a flower. And when it does, he speculates, it will be infinitely varied, because 'there are as many perfections as there are imperfect men'.[40]

In what sense, then, may Wilde's utopian vision be characterised as elitist? In order to answer this question in a fair and balanced fashion, it may be helpful to recall briefly why and in what ways Morris believed that art ought to be democratised. For Morris, one of the most distressing features of modern life was the wedge driven between art and labour by the historical triumph of capitalism. He demanded a revolutionary change in the basis of society that would lead to a world in which work and art – and nature – blend harmoniously. This harmony is made possible by the fact that work is no longer a curse entailing the ruthless exploitation of nature to meet ever-increasing human needs. Instead it has become a source of joy, an infinitely rewarding cooperative endeavour in which all contribute voluntarily and usefully to the support of the community as a whole. It is also a well-spring of living popular art insofar as people no longer driven desperately to painful and terrible overwork are apt to crave beauty in their lives, and to begin to learn once again how to ornament their creations by emulating the products of nature.

For Wilde, by contrast, artistic beauty and social usefully labour must be firmly separated. The former is the purely individualistic product of a unique temperament. The latter is the responsibility of the state, which in Wilde's utopia is to be constituted as a non-governing voluntary association that organises labour and manufactures and distributes necessary commodities. Any attempt to bridge this divide between individualistic art and social labour will surely lead to the loss of both: 'Now, I have said that the community by means of organisation of machinery will supply the useful things, and that the beautiful things will be made by the individual. This is not merely necessary, but it is the only possible way by which we can get either the one or the other'.[41] The reason why this is so, according to Wilde, is that an individual who has to make things for the use of others, and with reference to their wants and wishes, does not work with interest, and consequently cannot put into his work what is best in him. Conversely, the moment an artist takes notice of what other people want, and tries to supply the demand, 'he ceases to be an artist, and becomes a dull or an amusing craftsman, an honest or a dishonest tradesman'.[42]

The difficulty with this line of reasoning is that it is premised on precisely those capitalist-era, class-based distinctions between intellectual and manual labour, socially respected artists and socially reviled craftsmen, that in a socialist society would presumably be obsolete. It is difficult to conceive how a socialist society could maintain such hierarchical, status-oriented distinctions and still be recognisably socialist. One possible reply to this conundrum might be that while the distinctions themselves would linger on they would cease to have any practical meaning because machines would do all the utilitarian work necessary to sustain civilisation. But this reply in turn raises more questions than it answers. Specifically, it elides all of the profoundly challenging questions hinted at or implied by Morris about the wisdom of embracing a machine-based civilisation. For example, who will design, control, and operate the machines in Wilde's technocratic utopia? Would members of the general population be expected to volunteer to undertake such tasks on a temporary basis? If so, why would they do so, knowing that not only would no social honour accrue to their altruistic behaviour, but that they would on the contrary be regarded derisively as dull or amusing craftsmen? And if, as might be expected in such circumstances, the necessary volunteers did not come forward, would 'the state' in Wilde's utopia be composed of a permanent sub-class of non-artists whose aim in life was to secure the material pre-conditions for the free individual development of others? Finally, even granting the very remote possibility that technology might be developed by self-regarding, scientifically oriented individuals to such an extent and in such a way that it was entirely non-exploitative and largely self-operating, what impact would this elaborate technology have on the environment and on humanity's relationship with nature? Would nature continue to be regarded, as it is now, merely as a disposable resource for human consumption?

Such difficulties and lacunae notwithstanding, Wilde's exceptionally intelligent and engaging essay raises some profoundly challenging questions of its own about the nature and social functions of art. For example, is art social primarily because it stands opposed to society as an autonomous entity unconstrained by conventional social norms? Or is it social in the radically democratic, popular, and labour-oriented sense suggested by Morris? Can it be both, and, if so, to what extent are these ideas necessarily in tension with one another?

The heart of the matter, I contend, is that Morris and Wilde each glimpse a fragment of a larger truth about the relationship between art and society. As John Stuart Mill observed in his essay *On Liberty*, truth, in the great practical concerns of life, is primarily a question of the reconciling and combining of opposites. Truth in this sense is not the unitary phenomenon so many monistic thinkers have supposed it to be, but a multifaceted affair that eludes easy classification by those who view only one side of it. In what follows I will argue that both Morris and Wilde are right in part, and that what is now needed in the way of a sustainable counter-cultural challenge to capitalism is an anarchist utopian cultural politics that balances individual and society in a way that simultaneously protects the autonomy of art and firmly rejects the assumption that it must be something precious and elitist maintained by the joyless labour of an enslaved majority. I intend to make this argument not abstractly but in the context of a close textual reading of Ursula K. Le Guin's *The Dispossessed*.

Art and anarchy in Le Guin's *The Dispossessed*

In many ways, the utopian societies depicted in Morris's *News from Nowhere* and Le Guin's *The Dispossessed* are strikingly similar.[43] Both are based on a profoundly ecological understanding of the world not as some sort of machine, but as a vast and complexly interdependent organism. Both have abolished the profit-oriented institutions of their ruthlessly competitive and violent capitalist forebears, and organised social life instead according to the principle of from each according to his or her initiative and ability, to each according to his or her needs. Both have opted for a pace of technological growth much slower than that of profit-driven societies, but without regressing to pre-technological tribalism. Both wholeheartedly respect the values of free individual choice and personal responsibility, and are committed to the idea that people flourish best without imposed authority and external coercion. Both are decentralised, composed of small, dispersed communities that are self-regulating and self-governing. Both make space for misfits. Both are deeply committed to the ideals of equality and mutual aid, and strive for a condition in which human beings are at peace with themselves and their environment. Both originate in revolution and acknowledge the enduring reality of human suffering.

Both are also premised on the belief that people free to choose what work they wish to do when they wish to do it will engage in creative pursuits that contribute to social and individual well being. In *The Dispossessed*, this philosophy is encapsulated in the words of Laia Odo, the revolutionary anarcho-syndicalist thinker whose writings inspired the anarchist utopian settlement on Anarres:

> A child free from the guilt of ownership and the burden of economic competition will grow up with the will to do what needs doing and the capacity for joy in doing it. It is useless work that darkens the heart. The delight of the nursing mother, of the scholar, of the successful hunter, of the good cook, of the skillful maker, of anyone doing needed work and doing it well – this durable joy is perhaps the deepest source of human affection, and of sociality as a whole.[44]

In keeping with Odo's teachings about the natural and durable joy of doing needed work and doing it well, Pravic, the language of Anarres, employs the same word for both work and play (a different word is used to express the idea of drudgery). Those of Le Guin's readers acculturated in modern capitalist societies may, of course, be somewhat sceptical about such a conflation of terms. In our world, work and play are generally regarded as antonyms. The former is associated with the economic compulsion to 'earn a living' and the latter with simple idleness or 'leisure pursuits' (pithily defined by Bob Black as 'nonwork for the sake of work', and more wittily as 'time spent recovering from work and in the frenzied but hopeless attempt to forget about work'[45]). In Anarresti society, by contrast, there is no economic compulsion to work because everybody simply takes what material goods they need from the communal stores. An entirely voluntary activity free of coercively imposed external restriction, work is no longer a curse but instead a form of play integrally associated with sociability, festivity, and joyful artistic creation.

Like Morris, Le Guin does not simply tell her readers that this is the case. Rather, she conveys in imaginative and persuasive detail the quotidian drama of people in such a society going about their ordinary business. In chapter four, for example, we accompany Shevek, the novel's main character, as he explores for the very first time the town of Abbenay in which he will subsequently complete the bulk of his groundbreaking life's work in temporal physics. With him we marvel at its deep green fields and wide clean streets fronted almost exclusively by low-rise buildings (the only exceptions being the 'strong, spare towers' of the wind turbines). We experience its hustle and bustle, with people everywhere engaged in activity of some kind or another, and pass through the open squares that constitute its working heart. As we do so, several features of working life on Anarres stand out immediately by virtue of their stark contrast with what one might find in our own towns and cities.

First and perhaps most startlingly, all the varied work being done is out in the open and plainly visible. Whereas in modern capitalist societies productive activity is generally hidden away behind walls (as it is in the novel in the archist capitalist state of A-Io), and 'salespeople' in a bewildering array of glass-fronted shops have no relation to the items they are selling but that of possession, on Anarres all working life is open to the eye and to the hand. Workshops and factories front on squares or open yards, and their doors are left open. As a result, when Shevek passes a glassworks he notices a workman 'dipping up a great molten blob as casually as a cook serves soup'.[46] Proceeding past a busy yard where foamstone is cast for construction, he observes the gang foreman, 'a big woman in a smock white with dust . . . supervising the pouring of a cast with a loud and splendid flow of language';[47] shortly thereafter, he is overwhelmed by the blast of steam and conversation emanating from the wide-open doors of a laundry.

Second, having eliminated all the unproductive work that in capitalist societies serves no other purpose than commerce or social control, the typical Anarresti working day is much shorter than our own. In chapter four we know this to be the case when Shevek's mother indignantly remarks of a shockingly understaffed medical clinic, 'some of these aides and doctors are working eight hours a day!'[48] The point is confirmed in chapter six when we learn that most Anarresti work five to seven hours a day, with two to four days off every ten days.

Third, everybody shares in the necessary drudgery work. Typically, such work is organised by means of a rotational system in which people are expected to volunteer every ten days or so for communal tasks. Nobody is compelled to do so, but in practice few fail to make themselves available. In part this is because the process has become a social routine. In part as well it is due to the deeply ingrained spirit of mutual aid that so noticeably distinguishes Anarresti society from its capitalist counterpart on the neighbouring world of Urras. No doubt some of Le Guin's more capitalist-minded readers will find this aspect of the narrative unpersuasive. Perhaps anticipating precisely such a reaction, Le Guin plots a scene in which in the course of a private dinner at the home of one of his Urrasti hosts Shevek is asked why his fellow anarchists do communal dirty work at all if it is organised on an entirely voluntary basis. His answer suggests a wide range of plausible motivations: the fact that the work is done together, the desire for a challenge or for variety of labour, the opportunity it presents to show off, the need to gain the respect of one's fellows, and, perhaps most importantly of all, the recognition of the lasting pleasure that comes from doing needed work and doing it well. Having thus satisfied his host's curiosity, Shevek proceeds quite innocently to ask him who does the dirty work on Urras: 'I never see it being done. It's strange. Who does it? . . . Are they paid more?' The deeply unsettling implications of the reply – 'For dangerous work, sometimes. For merely menial tasks, no. Less' – are made plainly and devastatingly apparent in the poignant exchange that follows:

> 'Why do they do them, then?' 'Because low pay is better than no pay,' Oiie said, and the bitterness in his voice was quite clear. His wife began speaking nervously to change the subject, but he went on, 'My grandfather was a janitor. Scrubbed floors and changed dirty sheets in a hotel for fifty years. Ten hours a day, six days a week. He did it so that he and his family could eat.'[49]

Fourth, as in *News from Nowhere*, craftspeople express pride and joy in their labour by means of the decorative arts. In the textile district briefly described in chapter four, for example, the centre of each square is planted with poles strung from top to bottom with banners and pennants 'proudly proclaiming' the local dyer's art in all its varied colours. Further on, Shevek notices a wiremaker's shopfront 'cheerfully and ornately' decorated with patterns of vines worked in painted wire.[50] In fact, as we discover later on in the novel, these expressions of craft pleasure are in part the product of an educational system that trains all Anarresti in the practice of the arts from a very young age. Because no distinction is drawn on Anarres between the arts and the crafts – and everyone receives as a matter of course practical training in singing, metrics, dance, the use of brush, chisel, knife, lathe, and so on[51] – art is generally regarded 'not as having a place in life, but as being a basic technique of life, like speech'.[52] In short, art suffuses Anarresti society, and everyone is a creative artist in the practical and popular sense of the term suggested by Morris.

At a much deeper philosophical and cultural level, Anarresti society is also an artistic community insofar as individual autonomy and wilfulness are generally expressed not in the form of domination and control, but as creativity conceived as the expression of artistic beauty. As a result, the destructive conflict between individual and society endemic to capitalist societies has been significantly diminished. People generally assume that others will be helpful and so tend to trust them. Such trust is not absolute or unconditional, and hence may be withdrawn if abused. Nevertheless, the anarchist inhabitants of Anarres tend by and large to recognise that their unique society, and the individual flourishing it makes possible, are dependent on a high degree of voluntary cooperation ultimately rooted in enlightened self-interest.[53]

Yet for all their accomplishments the Anarresti have not succeeded in eliminating entirely the conflict between individual and society. Moreover, Le Guin suggests paradoxically, this apparent failing is also a blessing, insofar as the realisation of the perfectionist ideal of complete harmony between the two would entail the death of individual liberty and the diversity, novelty, creativity, and vibrant life it makes possible. Like Wilde in this respect, and unlike Morris, Le Guin acknowledges a prominent and enduring place in her utopian vision for a socially disruptive form of individual assertiveness. In fact, it is fair to say that her representation of this disruptive assertiveness in the narrative of Shevek's progressive rebellion against the creeping conformity and stagnation of Anarresti society constitutes the main dramatic action of the novel.

In order to understand the nature of Shevek's rebellion, and so appreciate its significance for the simultaneously communistic and individualistic counter-cultural politics of the novel, it is necessary first to identify clearly and precisely what it is he is rebelling against. Why, in other words, does he become a rebel in utopia? Consider by way of an answer to this question the character of Tirin.

A relatively minor character in terms of the direct attention devoted to him in the novel, we first encounter Tirin as a young boy. The opening scene in which he appears, involving a cruel game played by a group of eleven-year-old Anarresti boys perversely fascinated by the archist concept of a 'prison', makes it clear that he has an unusually well-developed imagination and a pointedly satirical, play-acting streak in his personality. The next scene in which he features prominently suggests that he is endowed with a critical, questioning mind as well. In conversation with three other boys, one of whom is Shevek and another their mutual friend Bedap, Tirin raises some rather sharp questions about a school-sanctioned propaganda film depicting the evils of life on Urras. Interestingly in light of subsequent events in the novel, Tirin and Shevek find themselves on opposite sides of the ensuing debate, with Tirin imagining the liberatory impact on his world of a journey to Urras undertaken by an Anarresti and Shevek stubbornly resisting the idea. Shevek's protestations notwithstanding, Tirin's critical arrow finds its mark deep in his psyche, prompting the novel's omniscient narrator to make the following telling observation: 'But at this point the pleasure of the argument ceased for Shevek . . . He was disturbed.'[54]

Tirin proves to be a disturbing influence yet again years later, when in the course of a heated conversation with Bedap Shevek learns that their mutual friend had been admitted to an asylum in a remote part of Anarres. According to Bedap, the admission was one of a series of 'punishments' inflicted on Tirin for the 'crime' of composing and performing a play that his compatriots interpreted as a threat to the reigning social orthodoxies.

Shevek, for his part, once again initially resists the implication that his society has fallen short of its anarchist utopian ideal. However, he soon finds himself questioning this interpretation of events when he meets an artist friend of Bedap, a composer named Salas. Like Tirin, Salas suffers as a result of his artistic unorthodoxy. Specifically, because the pieces he writes are regarded as insufficiently 'harmonious' by the members of the Music Syndicate, he sees no alternative but to opt instead for a series of postings in unskilled labour. One of these postings is to a canal-digging crew, prompting Bedap to remark sarcastically to Shevek that 'Canal digging is important, you know; music's mere decoration. The circle has come right back around to the most vile kind of profiteering utilitarianism. The complexity, the vitality, the freedom of invention and initiative that was the center of the Odonian ideal, we've thrown it all away.'[55]

Ultimately, Shevek too comes to adopt a more critical perspective on his home world. But he does not condemn it absolutely. Rather, in contrast to Bedap, he comes to the conclusion that for all its manifest failures to live up to its high Odonian ideals, Anarres still holds out a promise of something very good and noble that might yet be redeemed by constructive revolutionary action. Pursuing this line of thought in conversation with Takver in chapter ten of the novel, Shevek articulates a balanced position on the proper relationship between individual and society that combines some of the most important insights of both Morris and Wilde.

On the one hand, like Morris he emphasises the value of mutuality and community in facing necessity. More specifically, he embraces the Odonian ideal of an organic community in which all share equally the inescapable burdens of life. On the other hand, like Wilde he is alert to the dangers of a tyranny of the majority, and hence also to the value of protecting individual autonomy even and perhaps especially when it conflicts with prevailing social norms. Indeed, his thoughts in this regard are occasioned by his recollection of the example of Tirin, whom he refers to approvingly as 'a born artist. Not a craftsman – a creator. An inventor-destroyer, the kind who's got to turn everything upside down and inside out. A satirist, a man who praises through rage.'[56] Like Wilde in this respect, and unlike most of his fellow Anarresti, Shevek distinguishes between artists and craftspeople. Moreover, he does so to emphasise the positive individualistic and anarchic function of art as a means of disrupting slavery of custom, tyranny of habit, hypocritical moralism, fear of social ostracism, fear of being different, fear in short of being free. However, unlike in Wilde's essay *The Soul of Man*, the distinctions Shevek draws in *The Dispossessed* between art and craft and artist and community have no elitist connotations, inasmuch as they are conceived within the context of an emphatically cooperative utopian vision in which individual and society are inextricably linked. As Shevek muses to himself at a pivotal point in the novel, 'With the myth of the State out of the way, the real mutuality and reciprocity of society and individual became clear. Sacrifice might be demanded of the individual, but never compromise: for though only the society could give security and stability, only the individual, the person, had the power of moral choice – the power of change, the essential function of life.'[57]

Taking this philosophy to heart, Shevek makes a brave decision. He resolves to fulfil his proper function in the social organism by becoming an anarchist revolutionary in an anarchist utopian society conceived as a permanent revolution. In so doing, he takes the first tentative step towards an increasingly public and political life that culminates in his groundbreaking journey to Urras and his momentous scientific breakthrough. He also begins a distinctive revolutionary journey that illuminates a road not yet taken in the continuing struggle on our own world to create a decent and sustainable alternative to capitalism.

Conclusion

From the perspective of those who inhabit market-engulfed societies, the revolutionary romantic aspiration to transform social life in such a way that everyone would be an artist may well appear to be an impossible dream. Yet it is a dream that inspired the artistic and political imaginations of some of the most brilliant utopian writers of the past two centuries, among them William Morris, Oscar Wilde, and Ursula K. Le Guin. Each in his or her own way, Morris, Wilde, and Le Guin strove to imagine post-capitalist, non-coercive societies in which artistic creation would replace profit-driven economy as the fundamental aim of social life, yet they did so from revealingly different perspectives about the nature and social functions of art. Morris the socialist craftsman believed that art should be radically democratised, and that it ought to serve the social function of making common labour a source of pleasure and joy. Wilde the dramatic artist and art critic believed on the contrary that art should be insulated from democracy, free to grow autonomously in a highly individualistic society characterised by a far greater degree of material equality and respect for individual difference than our own. Le Guin the Daoist literary artist arrived at her own accord at a position somewhere between the two, acknowledging that art is inextricably bound up with society and ought to be democratised to a far greater degree than it is today, yet also remaining acutely aware of the dangers of reducing art to its social function and hence neglecting the individual springs of both artistic and social vitality.

True to both her novelistic craft and her anarchist political convictions, Le Guin succeeds in embodying in *The Dispossessed* an extraordinarily imaginative and sophisticated utopian vision that draws the two apparently opposing perspectives outlined above into creative dialogue. Just as Shevek persistently strives 'not to deny one reality at the expense of the other, but to include and connect', so too Le Guin strives in her writing to balance individual and society in a way that both protects the autonomy of art and reminds us that it needn't be something precious and elitist maintained by the joyless labour of an enslaved majority. And just as Shevek ultimately succeeds in renewing the revolutionary promise of the utopian vision articulated in his world's past by Laia Odo, so too with *The Dispossessed* Le Guin succeeds in renewing the revolutionary promise of the utopian visions articulated in her world's past by Morris and Wilde.

She does so in at least two respects. First, she dramatises everyday life in an anarchist communist society in such a way as to render believable and appealing the revolutionary romantic ideal of everyone an artist. Second, she links this utopian vision to a simultaneously individualistic and communistic model of revolutionary change memorably encapsulated in the words of Odo: 'The Revolution is in the individual spirit, or it is nowhere. It is for all, or it is nothing. If it is seen as having any end, it will never truly begin.'[58] In both respects, Le Guin's *The Dispossessed* continues to speak powerfully and directly to those of us unwilling to acquiesce to the prevailing consensus that capitalism is the terminus of history and art and labour must be forever rigidly divided.

Notes

My thanks to Ruth Kinna and Peter Stillman for their helpful comments on an earlier version of this chapter.

1 For more extensive discussion of this point see my article 'Isaiah Berlin, William Morris, and the Politics of Utopia', *Critical Review of International Social and Political Philosophy*, 3:2–3 (2000), 56–86. See also Ursula K. Le Guin's important essay, 'A Non-Euclidean View of California as a Cold Place to Be', in her *Dancing at the Edge of the World: Thoughts on Words, Women, Places*, pp. 80–100.

2 M. L. Berneri, *Journey through Utopia*, p. 317.

3 See P. Marshall, *Demanding the Impossible*, pp. xiii–xiv, 118–21, 171–5, 639–42. Like Marshall, I believe that ideological borders are somewhat porous (particularly so, it should be noted, in late Victorian Britain, when anarchist and socialist ideas tended to overlap much more than they do today), and so I wish to avoid belabouring the vexed question of whether or not Morris was an anarchist. My aim in this chapter is much less ideologically contentious. I simply intend to consider the relevance of Morris's ideas in a quite specific intellectual context (namely, the conceptual space in which art, labour, anarchy, and utopia intersect) in which it has hitherto been largely neglected.

4 The latter term applies uncontroversially to Morris, while the former applies relatively uncontroversially to Wilde and Le Guin, both of whom have explicitly associated themselves with anarchism. Wilde, for example, once remarked, 'I think I am rather more than a Socialist. I am something of an Anarchist, I believe; but, of course, the dynamite policy is very absurd indeed' (quoted in

K. Beckson, *I Can Resist Everything Except Temptation*, p. 168). And while Le Guin has recently observed that she feels 'unworthy' of adopting the label given her far greater interest in writing than in political activism (though of course much of her writing is eminently political, and thus may itself be understood as a form of generously open-ended artistic political activism), she also notes that in its 'pacifist, not violent' form anarchism is 'the only mode of political thinking' that she 'feels at home with'. ('Ursula Le Guin on Anarchism, Writing', interview posted to Infoshop News on 19 March 2008). She has also repeatedly referred to *The Dispossessed* as her anarchist novel, most recently in L. Davis and P. Stillman (eds), *The New Utopian Politics of Ursula K. Le Guin's The Dispossessed*, p. 308.

5   Morris consistently tends to conceive socialist creativity and aesthetic expression as *manly* self-realisation through communal labour. To this extent, his socialist aesthetic seems to imply a sharply gender-coded, exclusively masculine model of individuation, and ought to be criticised accordingly. On the gender coding of Morris's utopian writing, see C. Lesjak, *Working Fictions*, pp. 173–4; R. Livesey, 'Morris, Carpenter, Wilde, and the Political Aesthetics of Labor', pp. 601–16; J. Marsh, 'Concerning Love', pp. 107–25; and R. Levitas, 'Utopian Fictions and Political Theories', pp. 81–99.

6   W. Morris, 'Art Under Plutocracy', in A. L. Morton (ed.), *Political Writings of William Morris*, p. 67 (subsequent references: Morton (ed.), *PW*).

7   *Ibid.* p. 58.

8   W. Morris, 'The Lesser Arts', in Morton (ed.), *PW*, p. 51.

9   Quoted in E. P. Thompson, *William Morris*, p. 98.

10 W. Morris, 'The Art of the People', in G. D. H. Cole (ed.), *William Morris: Stories in Prose, Stories in Verse, Shorter Poems, Lectures and Essays*, p. 535 (subsequent references: Cole (ed.) *Stories in Prose*). Emphasis in original.

11 See Thompson, *William Morris*, ch. 7.

12 W. Morris, 'How We Live and How We Might Live', in Morton (ed.), *PW*, p. 157.

13 W. Morris, N. Salmon (ed.), *Political Writings: Contributions to Justice and Commonweal 1883–1890*, p. 126.

14 Dialogic in its dynamic and popular mode of delivery and publication, Morris's utopianism is also dialogic in its pluralistic and inclusive approach to alternative radical visions. The open, constructive, and dialogic cast of Morris's mind is particularly evident on the few occasions when he reflects about the nature and purposes of utopia. Consider, for example, his remarks in a June 1889 *Commonweal* review of Edward Bellamy's utopian fiction *Looking Backward*. According to Morris, 'the only safe way of reading a utopia is to consider it as the expression of the temperament of its author' (N. Salmon (ed.), 1994, p. 420). Those who read them as 'conclusive statements of facts and rules of action' ignore their necessary partiality. Utopias, he explains further in this review and elsewhere, are necessarily partial for at least two reasons. First, individual tempers differ, and what is a dream to one person may be a nightmare to another. Second, the dreams of any utopian author are conditioned by, and responsive to, the historical circumstances in which he or she lives. As Morris and Bax put the matter in their jointly authored *Socialism: Its Growth and Outcome*, 'no man can really think himself out of his own

days . . . his palace of days to come can [therefore] only be constructed by the aspirations forced on him by his present surroundings, and from his dreams of the life of the past, which themselves cannot fail to be more or less unsubstantial imaginings' (W. Morris and E. B. Bax, *Socialism: Its Growth and Outcome*, pp. 17–18). As these remarks make abundantly clear, Morris was well aware of the limitations of the perfectionist utopian tradition. Crucially, however, rather than abandon utopianism altogether, he embraces it in a chastened and anti-perfectionist but paradoxically *more* revolutionary form.

15   C. D. Lummis, *Radical Democracy*, ch. 3.

16   *Ibid.* p. 103.

17   R. Kinna, *William Morris: The Art of Socialism*, pp. 51–2.

18   Morris, *News from Nowhere*, in Cole (ed.), *Stories in Prose*, p. 90.

19   For more on the revolutionary romantic tradition, see Max Blechman's excellent collection of essays, *Revolutionary Romanticism*. On the subject of Morris and the revolutionary romantic tradition in England, see also S. Pierson, *Marxism and the Origins of British Socialism*, and Thompson, *William Morris*.

20   See, for example, B. Macdonald, 'William Morris and the Vision of Ecosocialism', *Contemporary Justice Review*, 7:3 (2004), 287–304; P. O'Sullivan, 'The Ending of the Journey' in S. Coleman and P. O'Sullivan (eds), *William Morris and News from Nowhere*, pp. 169–81; A. Dobson, *Green Political Thought*, pp. 187–8; M. de Geus, *Ecological Utopias*, ch. 6; and M. Bookchin, *The Ecology of Freedom*, pp. 9, 75, 431.

21   K. Lee, *Social Philosophy and Ecological Scarcity*, pp. 274–5.

22   *Ibid.* pp. 223–4.

23   Morris and Bax, *Socialism*, p. 298.

24   M. Morris (ed.), *William Morris: Artist, Writer, Socialist*, Vol. II, p. 302.

25   In Morris's utopian imagination the denizens of a fully realised socialist society may differ in their opinions about public policy issues, and indeed differ to such an extent that a democratic vote is necessary to settle the dispute, but their disagreements will not and could not possibly concern fundamental matters of value. As Hammond explains to Guest in *News from Nowhere*, 'Amongst us, our differences concern matters of business, and passing events as to them, and could not divide men permanently. As a rule, the immediate outcome shows which opinion on a given subject is the right one; it is a matter of fact, not of speculation' (Morris, *News from Nowhere*, in Cole (ed.), *Stories in Prose*, p. 81).

26   W. Morris, in G. Zabel (ed.), *Art and Society*, pp. 120, 145, 110, 132.

27   D. Meakin, *Man and Work*, pp. 139–40.

28   Morris, *News from Nowhere*, in Cole (ed.), *Stories in Prose*, p. 140.

29   Though architecture is prized because it is a cooperative and socially 'useful' art. See the relevant comments by Morris quoted in D. D. Egbert, *Social Radicalism and the Arts*, p. 450.

30   Morris, *News from Nowhere*, in Cole (ed.), *Stories in Prose*, p. 19.

31   I do not have sufficient space in this essay to fit the writers discussed into a more historical frame. It is nevertheless worth noting that although the existing evidence is inconclusive, Wilde very likely read Morris's *News from Nowhere* when it appeared serially in *The Commonweal* magazine between January and October 1890, and thus was well aware of its contents as he composed

his own utopian essay. Like Morris, he was also influenced by the work of John Ruskin.

32 O. Wilde, *The Soul of Man under Socialism*, in I. Murray (ed.), *Oscar Wilde*, p. 1 (subsequent references: Wilde, *SOM*).

33 J. S. Mill, *On Liberty*, in J. Robson (ed.), *John Stuart Mill*, p. 7.

34 Wilde, *SOM*, p. 17.

35 *Ibid.* p. 19.

36 *Ibid.* p. 16.

37 *Ibid.* p. 15.

38 *Ibid.* p. 16.

39 *Ibid.* p. 7.

40 *Ibid.* p. 12.

41 *Ibid.* p. 16.

42 *Ibid.* p. 17.

43 For a rare comparison of the two utopias, see I. Tod, 'An Epoch of Change, William Morris and Ursula Le Guin'. Interestingly, Le Guin had read Morris before she began writing *The Dispossessed* (see U. K. Le Guin, 'Science Fiction and Mrs. Brown', p. 25), but was much more strongly influenced by Morris's anarchist contemporary Peter Kropotkin and her own anarchist contemporary Paul Goodman. Like Wilde, she was also very much influenced by the writings of Lao Tzu. For more on these and other intellectual influences see Philip E. Smith's essay 'Unbuilding Walls' and Le Guin's introduction to her short story 'The Day Before the Revolution'.

44 U. K. Le Guin, *The Dispossessed*, p. 247 (subsequent references: Le Guin, *TD*).

45 See B. Black, 'The Abolition of Work', in H. J. Ehrlich (ed.), *Reinventing Anarchy, Again*, p. 237.

46 Le Guin, *TD*, p. 99.

47 *Ibid.*

48 *Ibid.* p. 121.

49 *Ibid.* p. 151.

50 *Ibid.* p. 99.

51 The school curriculum also typically includes farming, carpentry, sewage reclamation, printing, plumbing, roadmending, playwriting, and 'all the other occupations' of the adult community. *Ibid.* p. 148.

52 *Ibid.* p. 156.

53 See D. Sabia, 'Individual and Community in Le Guin's *The Dispossessed*', in Davis and Stillman (eds), *The New Utopian Politics*.

54 Le Guin, *TD*, p. 44.

55 *Ibid.* pp. 175–6. As in Morris's *Nowhere*, Anarresti painting and sculpture serve largely as elements of architecture and town planning. Poetry and story telling tend to be ephemeral, and are generally linked with song and dancing. Of all the arts of words, only the theatre is ever thought of as a thing complete in itself. But as Tirin's experience demonstrates, it is accorded this privileged status only so long as it conforms to prevailing social norms.

56 *Ibid.* p. 328.

57 *Ibid.* p. 333. Shevek is presumably referring to 'compromise' of an individual's personal integrity or fundamental humanity.

58 *Ibid.* p. 359.

References

Beckson, K., *I Can Resist Everything Except Temptation: And Other Quotations from Oscar Wilde* (New York: Columbia University Press, 1996).

Berneri, M. L., *Journey through Utopia* (London: Freedom Press, 1982 [1950]).

Black, B., 'The Abolition of Work', in H. J. Ehrlich (ed.), *Reinventing Anarchy, Again* (Edinburgh and San Francisco: AK Press, 1996), pp. 236–50.

Blechman, M., (ed.), *Revolutionary Romanticism* (San Francisco: City Lights Books, 1999).

Bookchin, M., *The Ecology of Freedom: The Emergence and Dissolution of Hierarchy* (Oakland, CA and Edinburgh: AK Press, 2005 [1982]).

Cole, G. D. H., (ed.), *William Morris: Stories in Prose, Stories in Verse, Shorter Poems, Lectures and Essays* (London: Nonesuch Press, 1948 [1934]).

Davis, L., 'Isaiah Berlin, William Morris, and the Politics of Utopia', *Critical Review of International Social and Political Philosophy*, 3:2–3 (2000), 56–86.

——and P. Stillman, (eds), *The New Utopian Politics of Ursula K. Le Guin's The Dispossessed* (Lanham, MD: Lexington Books, 2005).

De Geus, M., *Ecological Utopias: Envisioning the Sustainable Society* (Utrecht: International Books, 1999).

Dobson, A., *Green Political Thought* (London and New York: Routledge, 2000 [1990]).

Egbert, D. D., *Social Radicalism and the Arts: Western Europe* (New York: Alfred A. Knopf, 1970).

Kinna, R., *William Morris: The Art of Socialism* (Cardiff: University of Wales Press, 2000).

Le Guin, U. K., 'Science Fiction and Mrs. Brown', in P. Nicholls (ed.), *Science Fiction at Large* (London: Gollancz, 1976).

——'A Non-Euclidean View of California as a Cold Place to Be', in U. K. Le Guin, *Dancing at the Edge of the World: Thoughts on Words, Women, Places* (New York: Grove Press, 1989).

——'The Day Before the Revolution', in U. K. Le Guin, *The Wind's Twelve Quarters* (New York: HarperCollins, 1991 [1975]).

——*The Dispossessed: An Ambiguous Utopia* (New York: HarperCollins, 2001 [1974]).

——'A Response, by Ansible, from Tau Ceti', in L. Davis and P. Stillman (eds), *The New Utopian Politics of Ursula K. Le Guin's The Dispossessed* (Lanham, MD: Lexington Books, 2005).

——'Ursula Le Guin on Anarchism, Writing', interview with the author posted to Infoshop News (2008) www.infoshop.org/inews/article.php?story=20080319181 05998, accessed 7 April 2008.

Lee, K., *Social Philosophy and Ecological Scarcity* (London and New York: Routledge, 1989).

Lesjak, C., *Working Fictions: A Genealogy of the Victorian Novel* (Durham and London: Duke University Press, 2006).

Levitas, R., 'Utopian Fictions and Political Theories: Domestic Labour in the Work of Edward Bellamy, Charlotte Perkins Gilman and William Morris', in V. Gough and J. Rudd (eds), *A Very Different Story: Studies on the Fiction of Charlotte Perkins Gilman* (Liverpool: Liverpool University Press, 1998), pp. 81–99.

Livesey, R., 'Morris, Carpenter, Wilde, and the Political Aesthetics of Labor', *Victorian Literature and Culture*, 32:2 (2004), 601–16.

Lummis, C. D., *Radical Democracy* (New York: Cornell University Press, 1997).

Macdonald, B., 'William Morris and the Vision of Ecosocialism', *Contemporary Justice Review*, 7:3 (2004), 287–304.

Marsh, J., 'Concerning Love: *News from Nowhere* and Gender', in S. Coleman and P. O'Sullivan (eds), *William Morris and News from Nowhere: A Vision for Our Time* (Devon: Green Books, 1990), pp. 107–25.

Marshall, P., *Demanding the Impossible* (London: Fontana Press, 1993).

Meakin, D., *Man and Work: Literature and Culture in Industrial Society* (London: Methuen, 1976).

Mill, J. S., *On Liberty* (1859), reprinted in J. Robson (ed.), *John Stuart Mill: A Selection of his Works* (Indianapolis: Bobbs-Merrill, 1966).

Morris, W., *William Morris: Artist, Writer, Socialist*, (ed.) M. Morris, Vol. II (Oxford: Basil Blackwell, 1936).

——*Political Writings: Contributions to Justice and Commonweal 1883–1890*, (ed.) Nicholas Salmon (Bristol: Thoemmes, 1994).

——and E. B. Bax, *Socialism: Its Growth and Outcome* (London: Swann Sonnenschein, 1893).

Morton, A. L., (ed.), *Political Writings of William Morris* (London: Lawrence and Wishart, 1979 [1973]).

O'Sullivan, P., 'The Ending of the Journey: William Morris, *News from Nowhere*, and Ecology', in S. Coleman and P. O'Sullivan (eds), *William Morris and News from Nowhere: A Vision for Our Time* (Devon: Green Books, 1990), pp. 169–81.

Pierson, S., *Marxism and the Origins of British Socialism: The Struggle for a New Consciousness* (Ithaca and London: Cornell University Press, 1973).

Sabia, D., 'Individual and Community in Le Guin's *The Dispossessed*', in L. Davis and P. Stillman (eds), *The New Utopian Politics of Ursula K. Le Guin's* The Dispossessed (Lanham, MD: Lexington Books, 2005), pp. 111–28.

Smith, P., II, 'Unbuilding Walls: Human Nature and the Nature of Evolutionary and Political Theory in *The Dispossessed*', in J. Olander and M. Greenberg (eds), *Ursula K. Le Guin* (New York: Taplinger, 1979).

Thompson, E. P., *William Morris: Romantic to Revolutionary* (New York: Pantheon Books, 1976 [1955]).

Tod, I., 'An Epoch of Change, William Morris and Ursula Le Guin', in the Institute of Contemporary Arts exhibition volume, *William Morris Today* (London: Journeyman Press, 1984), pp. 141–5.

Wilde, O., *The Soul of Man under Socialism* (1891), reprinted in I. Murray (ed.), *Oscar Wilde: The Soul of Man and Prison Writings* (Oxford: Oxford University Press, 1991).

Zabel, G., (ed.), *Art and Society: Lectures and Essays by William Morris* (Boston: George's Hill, 1993).

Anarchist powers: B. Traven, Pierre Clastres, and the question of utopia

'In the anarchist dictionary', Harold Barclay writes, 'power, authority and domination are critical terms'. Yet, as Barclay's writing illustrates, anarchist definitions of power are not uniform. Through an anthropological analysis of the meaning of social power and its relation to anarchist politics, Barclay challenges the sole identification of power with domination, which he attributes to anarchist figures such as Mikhail Bakunin and Rudolf Rocker, and posits in addition the existence of 'power in equality or mutuality'.[1] By raising the possibility that power defines the non-hierarchical project of anarchism, Barclay orients anarchist discussions of power away from monolithic conceptions and suggests productive lines of inquiry in anarchist research. In this essay I seek to extend Barclay's reflections on power through a discussion of B. Traven's *Treasure of the Sierra Madre* (1927) and the following anthropological writings by Pierre Clastres: *Chronicle of the Guayaki Indians* (1972), *Society Against the State* (1974), and *Archaeology of Violence* (1980). The writing of Traven and Clastres constitutes a significant and distinctive tendency in anarchist thought because it evokes the immanence of power to social life in ways that share and complicate Barclay's articulation of a non-hierarchical form of power. Further, these authors' emphasis on immanent social power is reinforced by the fact that they write anthropological and fictional texts rather than abstract political theory. In other words, the generic features of Clastres' anthropology and, even more so, Traven's novels facilitate an emphasis on power formations that cannot be abstracted from immanent social milieus. Both Traven and Clastres explore anarchist politics in cultural texts that are heavily reliant on portrayals of the indigenous people of Latin America – Traven's novels often depict Mexican Indians and Clastres writes about the Ache or Guayaki and Tupi-Guarani of South America. Each author struggles to nullify the ethnocentrism that inevitably haunts western representations of nonwestern cultures and yet insists that such cultures offer viable alternatives to both dominant political systems and conceptions of power that are tied solely to domination. The following material analyses

Clastres' theoretical concepts and then relates them to Traven's novel. Since Clastres' writings develop many of the primary notions that are also evident in Traven's narrative, such as exchange, primitivism, and historicism, it is productive to map the terms of Clastres' analysis before assessing Traven's concerns. The overall purpose of this essay is to recast the theoretical analysis of literature as a discussion of a strain of anarchist culture that cuts across disciplinary lines and offers multifaceted models of social power.

As Traven and Clastres investigate the nature of egalitarian power, they treat the question of utopia in ways that highlight significant differences between them. Each author subscribes to a dualistic model of transcendent and immanent utopia that resonates with the contemporary discourse in utopian studies.[2] On the one hand these authors depict in negative terms transcendent utopias that are restricted, rational, and idealistic and associated with escapism and domination. On the other hand Traven and Clastres celebrate immanent utopias that are open, dynamic, and linked to actual social practices. Despite these foundational similarities, Clastres treats the intersection of power and utopia in significantly less complex terms than Traven. Clastres' texts are characterised by an absolute distinction between societies with and without the state. For Clastres, the absence of coercive power (or the control of the behaviour of one individual or group by another) in societies without the state, such as those he studies, is associated with a dynamic and open utopianism that deters fixed, self-enclosed, and natural forms of social utopia. Contrastingly, Clastres identifies state-based societies of coercive power with the undifferentiated sociality of fixed and unchanging utopias. Since Traven fictionalises a range of social groupings that exist within the Mexican state in the early twentieth century, he does not appeal to the absolute distinction of Clastres' writing. Instead, Traven describes the emergence within the modern nation of social groups that exhibit Clastres' characteristics of societies without the state, the state's appropriation of aspects of societies without the state, and the possibility of a revolutionary state that is based on non-coercive power (or the capacity to realise autonomy, solidarity, and egalitarianism in social groups). All these tendencies are accompanied by utopian expressions that range from idealistic projections to practical struggles for egalitarianism. Also, Traven's concerns raise the possibility of cross-cultural alliances for immanent utopia that, in contrast to Clastres' restriction of non-coercive power to primitive societies, might include forces within state-based societies. While Traven adheres to Clastres' fundamental distinction between a dynamic utopianism of non-coercive power and a fixed utopianism that is ultimately complicit with the coercive power of the state, his complex fictional narrative re-inscribes these alternatives as tendencies within varied societies rather than attributes of utterly different social formations.

Clastres and primitivism: non-coercive power, exchange, and historicism

Pierre Clastres was a French anthropologist who conducted fieldwork among Ache Indians of Paraguay in the 1960s. Along with anthropological descriptions of Ache society, Clastres wrote extensive and controversial theoretical investigations into the nature of power in primitive society.[3] Even though his perspectives at times differ from the dualistic model of power in Barclay's anarchist anthropology, Clastres' writings on power and critiques of the state mean that he must be considered within anarchist traditions. His analysis of the role of the tribal chief constitutes the foundation of Clastres' theorisation of power and the point of most accord between him and Barclay. Clastres writes that the 'titular chief' has several unique functions in the tribe, including being a good orator, which he defines as the 'necessary conditions of power'. But the fact that the tribe is obliged to ignore the speech of the chief and is already aware of its content suggests to Clastres that oratory is a 'duty' laid upon the chief by the tribe.[4] The chief occupies the locus of power but does not exercise it. Since the chief's speech is, according to Clastres, the opposite of violence, it becomes an 'instrument of non-coercion' and an assurance that the chief and the institution of power will never coincide.[5] From such observations Clastres attacks the ethnocentrism of western anthropology's notions of power. He states that the first European conquerors of Indian America respected the 'genuine power' of the hierarchical Indian societies of Mexico and Peru, but regarded other Indian groups as being characterised either by the despotism of 'immediate social control' or an absence of the institutions of power that meant these groups could not be regarded as societies.[6] Clastres believes that such ideas remain evident in western anthropology and are predicated on the belief that power is always associated with violence and coercion. He counters such views by saying that primitive societies are permeated by power but lack separate political institutions. The political power that is immanent to social life in primitive societies is non-coercive and non-violent and thus represents an alternative formation of power to that propounded by western anthropology. In Clastres' analysis, power is contained within the social body of the tribe and is anti-coercive in that it limits the functions of the chief and maintains the egalitarian nature of the tribe. Unlike Barclay's theorisation of the egalitarian minimisation or diffusion of power as 'influence', a theorisation that regards power positively only in the sense that it is a diluted and mediated version of a negative conception of power, Clastres' view defines non-coercive power in wholly positive terms as the exercise of the capacity for collective living.[7]

Clastres argues that primitive societies lack 'social stratification and the authority of power' and that the power formations of primitive society serve to prevent the emergence of social divisions and inequality.[8] For Clastres, social hierarchy engenders the state as a political institution, which separates from and dominates society; in Barclay's terms, the state is able to exercise 'authority' because it is recognised as a 'legitimate' agent of coercive power.[9] Clastres states that primitive societies are wholly other to western societies because as societies without the state they ward off inequality and domination. Clastres frequently addresses the issue of how primitive society is aware of the form of power it seeks to prevent. He posits that primitive societies have an 'intuition' of dominatory power that is 'immediately subdued' by the 'social machines' of non-coercive power.[10] Clastres' references to intuitions and social machines are central to his understanding of power in primitive societies. He claims that the family and tribal chiefs and warrior groups in primitive societies exemplify a 'condition of possibility' of societies with social divisions and the state.[11] His discussion of a potential for dominatory power that remains latent in primitive society often appeals to the language of the unconscious. For example, he speaks of primitive societies as 'places where evil desire is repressed' and the 'subterranean forces' of domination are 'damm[ed]'.[12] While such psychological terminology reflects Clastres' indebtedness to the structural anthropology of Lévi-Strauss, other moments in Clastres' texts evoke social dynamics that are irreducible to individual or collective psychology. For Clastres, domination in primitive society is a 'sociological impossibility' not because of 'rigorous personal ethics' but because of social practices.[13] Both unconscious and social mechanisms of prevention are apparent in Clastres' description of primitive law. Whereas in societies with the state, writes Clastres, the discourse of law exists in a separate social sphere, law in primitive societies is literally written on the body through scarification. As 'an unforgettable memory' of something experienced 'ahead of time', scarification rituals seek to 'exorcise' power-as-domination by writing on the body.[14] The bodily text is therefore an expression of the immanent as opposed to separated power of society over the individual.

According to Clastres, the immanence of political power in primitive societies relies on the containment of economic factors. The analysis of economics is at the heart of Clastres' challenge to western anthropology. He counters the perception of primitive societies as subsistence economies that are unable to produce surplus resources and thus are mired in an unchanging pattern continually existing on the verge of starvation. He seeks to reverse anthropology's belief that a subsistence economy lacks political power and to argue that the economic dimension of primitive society is a function of non-coercive power. He believes that primitive societies are aware that economic surplus will lead to material inequality and thus to social division, domination, and the state. Since primitive societies could easily increase production, argues Clastres, their adherence to subsistence must be viewed as a strategy designed to prevent the manifestation of coercive power. The immanent conjunction of economics and power means, for Clastres, that the functions of the chief in the empty site of power are also matters of exchange. As well as stating that the chief receives less than he gives in these exchanges, Clastres posits that the chief's actions, as illustrated by his speech, negate reciprocity and are best understood as 'pure values' – gestures and utterances that cannot be viewed as interactions or communication because they are not directed toward others – rather than exchanged signs. Relations among Ache hunters also involve the conjunction of exchange and its negation. These hunters cannot eat the meat of animals they kill so they are necessarily reliant on exchanging food with each other. Such practices are political in that they enforce equality among 'men who neutralize each other'.[15] At the same time the hunters sing songs to themselves of their hunting exploits. These songs express the fantasy of non-participation in social exchange and thus, like the chief's speech, become values not signs. Acknowledging the influence of Marshall Sahlins on his work, Clastres concludes that primitive society is 'a society against economy'.[16] He criticises Lévi-Strauss' preoccupation with exchange structures and Marxist anthropology's reduction of primitive society to pre-capitalist economism. For Clastres, primitive society protests against economic exchange through non-reciprocal language and reduces it to a minimum to ensure that economics does not become an autonomous social sphere and to maintain non-coercive power relations.

Clastres accepts the minimal presence of economics in primitive societies but he insists upon an absolute rupture between such societies and the process of history. He claims that coercive power is 'the stamp of *historical societies*'.[17] For Clastres, social divisions, inequality, economic surplus, and coercive power all coalesce as the historical process in which societies with the state are caught. The core of western anthropology's ethnocentrism, writes Clastres, is its belief that primitive societies are 'embryonic' versions of modern western nations. He rails against such a view because he feels that it understands primitive societies in terms that are wholly alien to them. Such considerations often lead Clastres to dispense completely with paradigms of temporal transformation in his study of primitive societies. He relates that in his time among the Ache in 1963 the experiences he witnessed were identical to those noted by Father Pedro Lozano in his *History of the Conquest of Paraguay*, completed in 1768. In addition to suggesting that Ache society is characterised by a continuity that is devoid of historical change, he posits that primitive societies of varied times and places are tied together by the 'metahistorical bond' of having been untouched by history.[18] In his essay on Étienne de La Boétie, the sixteenth-century French writer who questioned the tyranny of voluntary servitude, Clastres argues that La Boétie's ability to ask fundamental questions about the nature of power in human societies and to conclude that societies defined by inequality are 'historical' is due to a 'trans-historical' methodology that Clastres defines as the 'smooth transition from History to logic'.[19] The promulgation of logic at the expense of empirical evidence causes Barclay to dispute the validity of Clastres' argument and describe it as 'strangely detached from the solid earth',[20] but, as well as adhering to La Boétie's logic, Clastres reads primitive society in terms of a 'diachronic' temporality into which the rejection of history is folded.[21] Just as, for example, he believes that La Boétie transcends historicism to identify the 'historical moment of the birth of History',[22] he states that 'Time became History' with the emergence of the state in primitive society.

The primitive and utopia in Clastres' writing

All the above considerations raise with some force the question of utopianism in Clastres' writing. Clastres' fondness for the term 'primitive' suggests that even if he does not regard the societies he describes as early forms of modern societies, he does imagine they are simpler, better, and more authentic ways of life. There is no doubt that Clastres believes that these societies have managed to avoid many of the negative aspects of state-based societies, but his emphasis on the openness and fluidity of primitive societies means that they never appear static or idealised. It may be tempting to think that Clastres enthuses about primitive societies because they are close to nature or non-technological, but these societies view coercive 'power as the very resurgence of nature' and consequently repudiate both nature and coercive power.[23] As Clastres reiterates, these societies embrace technological changes but employ them for the reduction of work not the increase of production. Rather than being self-enclosed natural groupings, primitive societies are, to Clastres, inter-related cultural entities. In his *Chronicle of the Guayaki Indians*, he describes the contemporary existence of the Ache as one where they are restricted to an area named 'White Stream', which is owned and governed by a cruel and exploitative Paraguayan landlord. The condition of the Ache is not therefore utopian in the sense of being pure and self-enclosed, but rather is connected to and in conflict with external social forces. The openness of primitive societies to the outside is addressed most fully by Clastres in his description of war as the primary disposition of such societies. Instead of viewing primitive societies in transcendent utopian terms as naturally peaceful, Clastres says their readiness for war is an immanent utopian 'machine of dispersion' that embodies 'the primitive logic of the centrifuge' and ensures the autonomy of the social group.[24] While the 'war machine' of primitive societies represents the urge toward independence, it also means that such societies are inherently oriented toward external groups. Further, Clastres is critical of the tendency toward social homogeneity. The philosophy of the Tupi-Guarani, according to Clastres, states that 'the One is Evil itself'. The war machine staves off oneness by sustaining differences among primitive societies. Autonomy is not therefore a principle of transcendent utopian self-enclosure but a tactic of differential independence. He says of the Tupi-Guarani that increases in demographic density resulted in the increased authority of chieftainships. In response to these developments, Tupi-Guarani prophets urged the society to leave everything behind and search for 'the Land Without Evil, the earthly paradise'.[25] Such a pursuit of idealised utopian space had tragic consequences because it was predicated on a principle of oneness and articulated through discourse that, unlike the chief's speech, was meant to be heard. The prophets' discourse reversed the power of the society over the chief, annulled autonomous and non-reciprocal speech, and engendered the social divisions and coercive power that it was originally designed to negate.

As I have already suggested, the issues developed in Clastres' texts enable us to map the perspectives on power and utopia in *Treasure of the Sierra Madre*. Moreover, Clastres' emphasis on the productivity of immanent non-coercive power, which represents the key distinction between his work and Barclay's adherence to influence-based ideas of power, is extended in Traven's novels. The theorisations of Clastres' anthropological discourse are rooted in social practices rather than political philosophy, but they nevertheless include accounts of immanent power that are abstracted from such practices.

Traven: the dynamics of social power and the status of utopia in the *Treasure of the Sierra Madre*

Contrastingly, Traven's fictional discourse wholly embeds treatments of power within narrative scenarios and only refers to political or social theories in highly ironic and cryptic terms. Traven's novels must therefore be regarded as examples of those aesthetic texts that describe anarchist or libertarian social experiences without venturing into the realm of political theory.[26] Along with the state-based social context of *Treasure*, such enhanced textual immanence ensures that issues of power and utopia in the novel never attain the dichotomous theoretical simplicity that we see in Clastres' writing. The obscurity surrounding Traven's biography underscores the immanent aspects of *Treasure* because it weakens any appeal beyond the fictional text for an understanding of Traven's views.[27] In the text, the narrative involves three destitute Americans, Dobbs, Howard, and Curtin, who reside in Tampico, Mexico in the aftermath of the Mexican Revolution. Under the guidance of the older and more experienced Howard, the three men successfully dig for gold in the Sierra Madre mountains. As the narrative proceeds, the interactions between the characters are increasingly strained by greed, competitiveness, and the urge for domination. Along with the tales of gold prospecting that the characters narrate to each other, the presence of Lacaud (another American), a group of bandits, government officials, and nearby Indian villagers complicate Traven's treatment of the dynamics of social power. With Lacaud left behind and Howard temporarily inhabiting an Indian village, Dobbs inevitably tries to kill Curtin and leaves him for dead with the gold. Yet Dobbs is robbed and killed by Mexican peasants who do not recognise the gold dust and throw it to the wind. Howard and Curtin are reunited and are able to laugh once they discover the fate of the gold.

The relation between Clastres and Traven is clear from the opening sequences of *Treasure*. Whereas Clastres theorises a society without the state, Traven writes about the coercive and non-coercive tendencies in a society that is ensconced in a newly formed state and bears the weight of centuries of state domination. Such a predicament means that non-coercive power in *Treasure* cannot attain the untainted status imagined by Clastres, but it also means that non-coercive power exhibits great resilience as it asserts itself within the space of the coercive state. The novel's opening sections also reveal that Traven shares Clastres' differentiation between transcendent and immanent utopia. At the outset of the narrative Traven evokes the flimsy Hotel Oso Negro in Tampico, which houses a diasporic global proletariat, as a form of immanent utopia. An 'unwritten law' prevents any man from bothering the women who stay at the hotel, the old men are 'freer here than in a private house', and the public visibility of the patio prevents theft. By insisting that the order at the hotel is due to immanent self-regulation rather than the authority of the police or the law, Traven presents a spatial system of non-coercive power that, as in Clastres' writing, is not based on human nature or personal ethics. But the immanent utopian elements ascribed to the hotel are countered by the influence of external capitalist economics. The inhabitants must of course leave the hotel to obtain money, and once Dobbs has begged for a few centavos he treats himself to a Chinese meal and enjoys giving orders to the waiter. Here, the externality of the economic sphere facilitates Dobbs' tendency toward domination. As he shifts from descriptions of the hotel to depictions of wider economic circumstances and the authority of the oil industry, Traven introduces critical references to transcendent utopianism. The presence of western trade and industry has caused the decline of Villa Cuauhtemoc, the 'ancient Indian principal village of this region', with the result that its citizens are considered 'primitive Indians'. Unlike Clastres' discussion of the immanent utopia of primitive societies, the concept of the primitive is a capitalist construction of the communities it has destroyed. Such a concept is a version of transcendent utopianism because it situates the Indian in a natural, essential, and other-worldly realm. References by Pat McCormick, the corrupt and coercive oil entrepreneur, to the 'paradise' of workers' collectivity further discredit the language of transcendent utopianism.[28] That Traven establishes the opposition between noncoercive power/immanent utopia and coercive power/transcendent utopia in these initial passages reflects the central importance of these conjunctions in the novel.

As the novel shifts toward an emphasis on gold, Traven complicates his perspective on immanent power and links transcendent utopianism to issues of history and exchange, which, as we have seen, are integral to Clastres' analysis. Dobbs and Curtin first get the idea to prospect for gold when they see the jewellery store, La Perla. Like the hotel, La Perla is a social machine of immanent legal power. Gold and jewellery are prominently on display, but they are not stolen because of the combination of spatial factors, such as the proximity of escape routes, and immediate forms of punishment that do not involve the legal institution. Here, the forms of immanent social power attributed by Clastres to societies without the state and associated with the hotel in Traven's novel have been appropriated within the process of capitalist inequality. Made unattainable and desirable by the spatial functioning of La Perla, gold is associated with transcendent utopianism. Similarly, Howard's description of the quest for gold as a 'blessed paradise' that creates a 'noble brotherhood' and the desire to be 'perfectly happy and healthy' reflects a transcendent utopian view that the events of the novel will discredit. Through Howard's tale of the Green Water Mine, in which Spanish monks refer to the Indian workers whom they exploit as 'the innocent children of the earth',[29] Traven also underscores the link between capitalist coercion and the transcendent utopianism of Indian primitivism. Further, the Green Water Mine narrative attaches Clastres' concepts of history and exchange to transcendent utopianism. The narrative describes how in the 1870s and thereafter American prospectors searched for the mine with varying degrees of success. The relentlessness of the miners' pursuit of the gold is due, Traven suggests, to Americans' restlessness and need for constant change, and such subjective characteristics are presented as being homologous with the movement of history that the tale narrates. In the terms we have used to describe Clastres' views on exchange, the miners' quest is predicated on the desire to transform gold, which exists in its natural state as a value, into a commodity-sign. As in Clastres' writing, Traven therefore shows how the principle of exchange and the process of history work together to further capitalist power and the coercion of the Indians that it involves. The Indians' destruction of the mine indicates that they do not regard gold as a commodity-sign and are not participants in capitalism's history of inequality. Their social environment is an immanent utopia that has no need for the transcendent utopian lure that gold represents.

Social power and leadership in immanent and transcendent utopias

Having established the functioning of immanent social mechanisms and the relation between transcendent utopia, exchange, and history, Traven's novel, like Clastres' texts, primarily assesses the possibility of social groups based on non-coercive power in terms of the function of the leader. In the Green Water Mine narrative, Howard states that Harry Tilton, one of his former associates, is 'made leader' during a futile search for the mine and is tortured and pursued by his frustrated partners. Here, Traven presents leadership as duty not authority. Listening to the tale, Dobbs feels a 'second person' arising within himself and Curtin says that gold bestows an 'imaginary' form of 'power' that must be 'recognised' to be realised. Such instances articulate a version of Clastres' ideas of immanent power in which state appropriation is manifested as inversion. The references to Tilton suggest that the mining community, like Clastres' primitive society, requires an apparent leader who nevertheless does not have the power to lead, and Curtin's comments on the social nature of power reconfigure Clastres' identification of the social machines of power. Moreover, Traven's figuration of the pursuit of gold as an unconscious desire for domination (the 'second person') is an inverse parallel to Clastres' description of an unconscious avoidance of coercive power in primitive societies. By creating such a framework for the narrative, Traven indicates that he is less interested in celebrating an ideal anarchist community than in exploring the various ways in which immanent social dynamics can be conducive to coercive and non-coercive power and in particular the role of the leader or chief. As the three miners prospect for gold, Howard is referred to as 'daddy' and 'godfather'. Dobbs and Curtin are wholly dependent on Howard's paternal leadership but Howard is also described as the weakest member of the group. Further, his power is a function of his weakness. In many respects, Traven portrays the group as an autonomous community that is devoid of coercive power because of the role of the weak leader. Their decision not to register their claim with the government, their development of their own language and lack of comparative reference to the external social world, and their 'primitive means' of mining enhance the suggestion that this is a primitive society without the state. By likening the fact that the group is united in the face of common obstacles to the galvanising effect of the threat of war upon communities, Traven shares Clastres' viewpoint that a military disposition sustains the autonomy and non-coerciveness of the immanent utopian social group. Yet this is a society that is embedded within the state, driven by the desires of capitalist inequality, and linked to the separate economic sphere (as illustrated by Curtin's regular trips to a nearby Indian store for supplies). As the characters change from penniless lumpenproletarians to 'three miserable proletarians' to property-owning members of the middle class,[30] they undergo the historical changes associated with unequal capitalist societies. The economic–historical tendency is occasionally stalled, as when Howard informs the others that it is not so easy to kill one's partner because of both the possibility of a gnawing conscience and the social fact of others' knowledge of such a deed; as in Clastres' writing, the immanent conjunction of unconscious monitoring and social machine is again invoked as that which might prevent the emergence of domination. Yet the fragility of non-coercive power is continually revealed in the threats and accusations made by the miners to each other. Also, in the face of the imminent breakdown of the group, Howard, unlike Clastres, appeals to the utopian quality of nature. Such an appeal makes clear that Howard speaks from a position within the society of the state, where the transcendent utopian qualities of nature and primitivism seem most attractive and authentic.

As the narrative proceeds the roles of Howard and Dobbs illustrate how the leader function of non-coercive power gives way to domination and coercive power. According to Clastres the chief in primitive society only exercises authority during times of war. Similarly, the sole occasion on which Howard directs the others occurs when they are attacked by a group of bandits. Yet this temporary strengthening of the leader function disturbs the delicate relationship between social power and the chief's empty site of power that, in Clastres' account, defines the society of non-coercive power. Soon after the bandits are scared away by the threat of federal officials, the mining group decides to destroy the mine and leave with the gold. Through this decision the characters undergo the process that transforms gold from what Clastres describes as value to the commodity-sign. As well as involving a heightened and irreversible turn toward the external sphere of capitalist economics, the group's decision represents a renunciation of the immanent utopianism of the social group and thus makes them vulnerable to coercive power. Specifically, Dobbs enacts the emergence of coercive power from the fear of it. Whereas in Clastres' writing a similar dynamic is associated with the Tupi-Guarani's desire to find a refuge from coercive power in the Land Without Evil, in *Treasure* such fear arises internally from the disturbance of the leader function. In paranoid fashion, Dobbs frequently accuses others of trying to dominate him, but it is only when Howard leaves the group that he becomes dominated by such sentiments. Without the preventative function of the empty site of power, the desire for coercive power goes unchecked. It is during the ensuing zero-sum game between Dobbs and Curtin that the former shoots the latter. Alone with the gold and the burros, Dobbs dreams transcendent utopian dreams as he eagerly pursues the 'promised land' of civilisation, law, and justice. The manifestation of coercive power is therefore accompanied by the attribution of transcendent utopianism to the state. But Dobbs' power does not last long as he is confronted and beheaded by a group of peasants. While the decapitation of Dobbs is a sudden and violent event in the text, it is an effective acephalous image that encapsulates the text's desire to decapitate the leader who has assumed the position of dominance. The image also serves as a contrast to the role of Howard. The cause of Howard's disappearance from the group is a request from Indian villagers to provide medical assistance to a young boy. Howard agrees to go with the villagers and convinces them that he has cured the boy. The villagers insist that Howard stay with them and, according to Howard, wish him to be their 'president' and 'entire legislature'. As a powerless leader under the control of the village, Howard represents the restoration of the leader function of non-coercive power within an immanent utopian social group. However, Howard's inhabitance of immanent utopia is subverted by the fact that Howard is a 'true American' who 'longed for a change'.[31] The 'Homeric laughter' he emits when he learns that the gold is lost is a Clastresian value that also regards gold as a value rather than a sign, but Howard's subjectivity remains the product of the society of history, inequality, and the state.

Social formations in state-based societies

In order to understand fully the significance of the narrative of the mining group it is necessary, Traven suggests, to consider the larger social context of the narrative as one in which the historical transformations of the state produce outlaw cultures that seem to be antithetical to the state but that exhibit those characteristics of the state noted by Clastres. In his narrative of Doña Maria de Rodriguez, Howard describes the era of the American and French Revolutions as one that witnessed the destabilisation of Spanish colonial authority in Mexico and the appearance throughout the country of 'gangs of bandits composed of escaped convicts, murderers at large, deserters from the army, and all sorts of soldiers of fortune and adventurers'. The context of Doña Maria's story is an allegory of the events of the novel, as the post-revolutionary situation in Mexico throws up much social disorder, including roaming bandits and disenfranchised peasants. While the bandits are enemies of the new state, their allegiance to 'King Jesus' indicates that they are the product of centuries of domination by the catholic church and Spanish colonialism. Rather than opposing a society with to a society without the state, Traven stages multiple confrontations between different versions of state-based societies. The social formation of the bandits who attack the mining group does share some of the characteristics of Clastres' society of non-coercive power. For example, the bandits have a leader who wears a golden palm hat and is referred to as 'chief' and 'captain', but he exerts 'little authority' and each bandit thinks 'his own advice should be followed by the others'. At this moment the leader seems to function as the powerless leader in Clastres' formulation of primitive societies, but Traven insists these are 'corrupted Indians' who are mired 'deep in subjection' to the principle of domination. In these comments Traven disrupts the apparent opposition between the state and the bandits. In the post-revolutionary context, writes Traven, various politicians use the exploits of bandits to further their own agendas. That the bandits who attack the gold prospectors masquerade as federal officials and formerly fought for the revolution further undermines the opposition between social groups. The description of the pursuit of the bandits by federal police as 'the fight of civilization against barbarism' and the evocation of the peasants who rob and kill Dobbs as the 'garbage of civilization' are both ironic comments because they suggest that civilisation and barbarism are interchangeable consequences of the state.[32] Such events indicate that the constructions of the Indian as the authentic or barbaric primitive are equally the reflections of state power. In other words, the idea of the barbaric Indian may appear to be an inversion of the transcendent utopian notion of the authentic Indian but in effect it continues such utopian logic. These contextualising events suggest that there is no exterior to state power in the novel and that any attempt to produce non-coercive power and immanent utopia must seek to work within and appropriate state power, much as the forms of state power appropriate factors that Clastres associated with societies without the state.

As the mining group's society of non-coercive power proves untenable in the context of economic inequality and the seeming alterity of the bandits is revealed as the expression of the past and present of state power, Traven, in the novel's final sections, assesses the possibility of achieving immanent utopia and non-coercive power within the state. In so doing he continues to address the function of the leader in terms that share Clastres' interest in the conjunction of the site of power and a culturally open version of utopia. Such interest is first evidenced through the storekeeper that Curtin visits for the mining group's necessary supplies. As well as being mayor in the village, the storekeeper is 'king, law, judge, and executioner all in one'.[33] In this instance, Traven fuses the principle of immanent legal and political power with the function of a chief who is also both an ordinary member of the Indian society and a civil official. The society can be viewed in immanent utopian terms because it is open, as evidenced by Curtin's presence, and yet is able to ward off the economic accumulation that, for Clastres, engenders history, the state, and coercive power. That the villagers refer to the misconceptions regarding subsistence economics that Clastres attributes to western anthropology's ethnocentrism suggests that the villagers are aware of and can strategically mention the form of economics they avoid.[34] As the novel reaches its conclusion, Traven's attempts to combine state power with non-coercive power and immanent utopia intensify. For example, a federal health commissioner from the new republican government, who works against the catholic church's domination and is assisted by Dobbs and the others, vaccinates Indian villagers and is presented as the embodiment of progressive modernisation. Traven includes such material because he wishes to provide positive images of the Mexican state and celebrate revolutionary history. But his anarchist opposition to state separation and domination and belief in the inherence of inequality to history mean that such formulations are highly ambivalent. The peasants who murder Dobbs are apprehended by Joaquin Escalona, the elected mayor of an Indian village. As the chief of a community that celebrates 'Independence Day', has an orchestra that plays 'national tunes', and is proud to be 'a recognized part of the republic and under an organized local government', he is Traven's most substantial version of a progressive state representative who is also the chief of an egalitarian society. But even though the mayor brings narrative resolution and occupies a central role in an immanent utopia, he represents the authority of the state and, as the Christian burial of the executed peasants indicates, religion. In order to militate against the identification of the mayor with state authority, Traven, in an unusually primitivist moment, describes the mayor as being of 'pure Indian race'.[35] In other words, Traven's desire to make anarchist non-coercive power compatible with the revolutionary state leads him to fall back on images of transcendent utopian primitivism and legitimise mayorial power via Indian authenticity. The turn toward transcendent utopia underscores the fragile nature of non-coercive power in the novel, but Traven's overriding point is that the impulse toward immanent utopia continues to surface and cannot be wholly quashed by the might of coercive state power.

Conclusion

The writing of Clastres and Traven indicates the extensive relevance of Harold Barclay's formulation of two forms of social power (domination and mutuality) within anarchist culture. Both these writers explore the possibility of countering power-as-domination through the social mechanism of collective non-coercive power. Also, they imagine this relation between two forms of power as one that involves issues of history, economics, primitivism, utopianism, and the role of the state. Yet unlike Barclay, Clastres and Traven imagine non-coercive power as a positive alternative to, rather than a mediated version of, coercive power. For Clastres, the non-coercive power of primitive societies is an immanent utopian machine that wards off the possibility of coercive power by preventing economic accumulation and the formation of politics as a separate social sphere (the state). The function of the chief assumes an important role in Clastres' writing because it is an empty version of the form of domination that primitive societies seek to exorcise. Clastres insists that primitive societies exist outside the process of history and must not be viewed as embryonic versions of western societies. As a result, he opposes the attribution of primitivism to the societies he describes and bemoans the transcendent utopianism of the quest for the Land Without Evil, which he believes led to the emergence of coercive power among the Tupi-Guarani. In *Treasure*, Traven articulates perspectives that are similar to those of Clastres, but instead of positing the radical separation of societies with and without the state he narrates their interpenetration. The interpenetration of social formations separated by Clastres means that non-coercive power is celebrated as an immanent utopian tendency that survives the appearance of the coercive state. Immanent social machines, such as the Hotel Oso Negro or the mining community, at times manifest utopian non-coercive power, but they can also become vehicles of domination and economic inequality. That all social groups in *Treasure* exist within and are defined by the state means that the critique of transcendent utopianism is more urgent and more frequent in Traven's novel than in Clastres' writing. Such circumstances lead Traven to imagine a form of collective Indian power in which the leader is also the representative of the revolutionary state and to invoke primitivist notions of Indian authenticity. In other words, Traven's novel at times gives way to the transcendent utopianism it consistently negates. Like Clastres' absolute distinction between societies with and without the state, Traven's appeal to Indian authenticity restricts utopianism to particular groups and blocks the openness and dynamism that are otherwise celebrated by these authors. As David Graeber argues, a radical insistence on ethnic difference subverts claims to universalism or humanism, but it can also engender an isolating logic of identity that is at times evident in the writing of Traven and Clastres.[36] For Graeber anarchist anthropology seeks to identify social practices in various ethnic groups and consider the possibility of their being transferred or extended to other social contexts. His references to the influence of the Chiapas resistance movement on the practices of anti-globalisation activism exemplify the kinds of immanent utopian extensions he has in mind. Graeber's writings are useful for discussions of anarchism and utopianism because they suggest that the limitations of Traven's and Clastres' commitment to immanent utopia might be overcome by seeking to establish non-coercive power through decentralised cross-cultural alliances.

Notes

1 Harold Barclay, 'Power: Some Anthropological Perspectives', *Anarchist Studies*, 13:2 (2005), 104–5.
2 The opposition between transcendent and immanent utopia is closely related to Ursula K. Le Guin's distinction between 'euclidean' and 'non-euclidean' utopias, the former being identified with rational, future-oriented planning and

the latter being figured as an 'interactive, rhythmic, and unstable process', a 'potential' that exists in some sense 'here-and-now' rather than in the future (U. Le Guin, 'A Non-euclidean View of California as a Cold Place To Be', in *Dancing on the Edge of the World: Thoughts on Words, Women, Places*, pp. 87, 91, 88, 81). The utopian theories of Carl Freedman, Ruth Levitas, and Tom Moylan, which are rooted to varying degrees in Ernst Bloch's distinction between 'abstract utopia' and 'concrete utopia' (E. Bloch, *The Principle of Hope*, p. 146), are also similar to the dualistic utopianism of Traven and Clastres because they prefer the concrete desire and struggle for egalitarianism over abstract utopian schemes.

3   There are two primary criticisms of Clastres' anthropology. Marcus Colchester argues that the 'ideological inclinations' of Clastres' ' "anarchist" anthropology' result in 'conclusions that cannot be substantiated' and 'preposterous' claims based on 'the merest scraps of data' (M. Colchester, 'Les Yanomami, sont-ils libres? Les utopias amazoniennes, une critique. A Look at French Anarchist Anthropology', *Journal of the Anthropological Society of Oxford*, 13:2 (1982), 147, 151, 155). In contrast, Bartholomew Dean believes that Clastres' *Chronicle of the Guayaki Indians* is an 'old-fashioned monograph' that reiterates the shameful 'primitivism' of anthropology's imperialist past. For Dean, 'the cumulative force of Clastres' ahistoricism, rhetorical romanticism, and museumification sadly obscures the ongoing challenges facing indigenous peoples like the Guayaki' (B. Dean, 'Critical Revision: Clastres' Chronicle and the Optic of Primitivism' *Anthropology Today*, 15:2 (1999), 9, 11, 10). Jon Abbink's response to Dean's criticisms, in which he notes that Clastres uses 'a rhetorical device of social criticism' to situate Guayaki experience within contemporary social and political exigencies (J. Abbink, 'Doing Justice to Clastres', *Anthropology Today*, 15:4 (1999), 21), exemplifies the anthropological defence of Clastres' work.

4   P. Clastres, *Society Against the State*, trans. R. Hurley in collaboration with A. Stein, pp. 29, 153.

5   P. Clastres, *Chronicle of the Guayaki Indians*, p. 107.

6   Clastres, *Society Against the State*, pp. 15, 21.

7   H. Barclay, *People without Government: An Anthropology of Anarchy*, p. 20.

8   Clastres, *Society Against the State*, p. 28.

9   Harold Barclay, *The State*, p. 18.

10 Clastres, *Society Against the State*, pp. 44, 45; P. Clastres, *Archaeology of Violence*, trans. J. Herman, p. 99.

11 Clastres, *Society Against the State*, p. 77.

12 Clastres, *Archaeology of Violence*, pp. 91, 100.

13 Clastres, *Chronicle of the Guayaki Indians*, p. 108.

14 Clastres, *Society Against the State*, p. 188.

15 *Ibid.* pp. 46, 120.

16 Clastres, *Archaeology of Violence*, p. 111. Much of Clastres' thinking on the economic dimension of primitive societies is influenced by Sahlins. In particular, Sahlins' conception of primitive societies as affluent entities that refuse economic accumulation is central to Clastres' thinking. However, Clastres disagrees with some of Sahlins' interpretations of politics in primitive societies and

finds him guilty of a 'continuist prejudice' for claiming that the function of the chief in 'Melanesian big-man systems' represents the kernel of political domination; *ibid*. pp. 116, 112.

17 Clastres, *Society Against the State*, p. 24.

18 *Ibid*. pp. 24, 16, 152.

19 Clastres, *Archaeology of Violence*, p. 94.

20 Barclay, *People without Government: an anthropology of anarchy*, p. 81.

21 Clastres, *Society Against the State*, pp. 76, 77. As mentioned at the outset of this essay, Harold Barclay espouses the principle of non-coercive power that is central to Clastres' anthropology. However, Barclay does not mention the importance of non-coercive power in Clastres' writing and is critical of Clastres' theoretical reliance on a form of logic that is not subject to an 'empirical test' (Barclay, *People without Government*, p. 81). One of the purposes of this essay is to overcome such an aporia and unite Barclay's account of anarchist power with Clastres' theoretical statements on non-coercive power.

22 Clastres, *Archaeology of Violence*, p. 94.

23 Clastres, *Society Against the State*, p. 44.

24 Clastres, *Archaeology of Violence*, pp. 167, 166.

25 Clastres, *Society Against the State*, pp. 171, 215.

26 There is much evidence that links Traven to anarchist politics. According to Wolfgang Essbach, the anarchist milieu of Ret Marut was influenced by a reading of Max Stirner, the nineteenth-century author of *The Ego and Its Own*, disseminated by Gustav Landauer. Unlike the version of Stirner as individualist associated with John Henry Mackay, argues Essbach, Landauer's interpretation emphasises 'the disintegration of the individual from within himself' (*sic.*) (W. Essbach, 'A Language Without a Master: Max Stirner's Influence on B. Traven', in *B. Traven: Life and Work*, p. 110). Essbach finds much evidence of the influence of Landauer's Stirnerite anarchism in many of Traven's writings. Additionally, Traven's sympathies for the anarcho-syndicalist union, the Industrial Workers of the World, are evident in his first two novels. Heidi Zogbaum observes that Traven's fiction articulates 'the anarchist dream of a self-governing peasant community' and can be viewed as 'an anarchist's handbook on how to make a successful revolution' (H. Zogbaum, *B. Traven: A Vision of Mexico*, pp. 30, 189).

27 For biographic information regarding the life of B. Traven, see Karl S. Guthke's *B. Traven: The Life Behind the Legends*.

28 B. Traven, *The Treasure of the Sierra Madre*, pp. 10, 23, 37.

29 *Ibid*. pp. 50, 52, 51, 55.

30 *Ibid*. pp. 65, 68, 82, 90, 77, 85.

31 *Ibid*. pp. 263, 307, 308, 297.

32 *Ibid*. pp. 200, 131, 159, 144, 163, 175, 264.

33 *Ibid*. p. 105.

34 In response to Lacaud's inquiries about gold and silver mines in the area, the villagers say that 'they can hardly make their living, and if they didn't put in a heap of extra work by braiding mats and baskets and making pottery to sell in far-off towns, they would have to live like savages, with nothing to cover the nakedness of their bodies' (Traven, *The Treasure of the Sierra Madre*, p. 107).

35 Traven, *The Treasure of the Sierra Madre*, p. 277. According to Zogbaum, *indigenismo* was an urban intellectual current borne of the Mexican Revolution that sought to celebrate the culture of indigenous Indians in Mexico (Zogbaum, *B. Traven: A Vision of Mexico*, p. 76). While Traven was a committed supporter of the revolution and Mexican nationalism, his espousal of *indigenismo*, writes Zogbaum, led him to conflate racial and social categories. Zogbaum states that the concept of the 'Indian' in Mexico referred to a set of cultural practices, but that Traven defines the 'Indian' in exclusively racial terms. In *Treasure*, Traven appeals to Indian racial integrity as a means of legitimising the authority of state officialdom.

36 Graeber makes the following comments about media representation of the Zapatistas in Chiapas: 'Rather than a band of local rebels with a vision of radical democratic transformation, they were immediately redefined as a band of Mayan Indians demanding indigenous autonomy. This is how the international media portrayed them; this is what was considered important about them from everyone from humanitarian organisations to Mexican bureaucrats to human rights monitors at the UN. As time went on, the Zapatistas – whose strategy has from the beginning been dependent on gaining allies in the international community – were increasingly forced to play the indigenous card as well, except when dealing with their most committed allies' (D. Graeber, *Fragments of an Anarchist Anthropology*, p. 104).

References

Abbink, J., 'Doing Justice to Clastres', *Anthropology Today*, 15:4 (1999), 21.

Barclay, H., *People without Government: An Anthropology of Anarchy* (London: Kahn and Averill, 1990).

——*The State* (London: Freedom, 2003).

——'Power: Some Anthropological Perspectives', *Anarchist Studies*, 13:2 (2005), 104–17.

Bloch, E., *The Principle of Hope*, trans. N. Plaice, S. Plaice and P. Knight (Cambridge, MA: MIT, 1986).

Clastres, P., *Society Against the State*, trans. Robert Hurley in collaboration with Abe Stein (New York: Zone, 1987).

——*Archaeology of Violence*, trans. Jeanine Herman (New York: Semiotext(e), 1994).

——*Chronicle of the Guayaki Indians*, trans. Paul Auster (New York: Zone, 1998).

Colchester, M., 'Les Yanomami, sont-ils libres? Les utopias amazoniennes, une critique. A Look at French Anarchist Anthropology', *Journal of the Anthropological Society of Oxford*, 13:2 (1982), 139–46.

Dean, B., 'Critical Revision: Clastres' Chronicle and the Optic of Primitivism', *Anthropology Today*, 15:2 (1999), 9–11.

Essbach, W., 'A Language Without a Master: Max Stirner's Influence on B. Traven', in E. Schürer and P. Jenkins (eds), *B. Traven: Life and Work* (University Park, PA: Pennsylvania State University Press, 1987).

Graeber, D., *Fragments of an Anarchist Anthropology* (Chicago: Prickly Paradigm, 2004).

Guthke, K. S., *B. Traven: The Life Behind the Legends*, trans. R. C. Sprung (Chicago: Lawrence Hill, 1991).

Le Guin, U., 'A Non-euclidean View of California as a Cold Place To Be', in *Dancing on the Edge of the World: Thoughts on Words, Women, Places* (New York: Grove, 1989).

Traven, B., *The Treasure of the Sierra Madre* (New York: Hill and Wang, 1963).

Zogbaum, H., *B. Traven: A Vision of Mexico* (Wilmington, DE: Scholarly Resources, 1992).

Utopia, anarchism and the political implications of emotions

In 1850, notable Argentine statesman Domingo Sarmiento proclaimed in his utopian treatise *Argirópolis* (1850) that by raising up cities and sowing them throughout 'our beautiful land' one would do away with those 'uncultivated provinces'.[1] Sarmiento's work set out to offer a political model upon which a post-revolutionary Latin America could be founded. As this passage indicates, he envisioned the city as the potential solution to the continent's socio-economic woes. Sarmiento's words were reflective of a wider cultural trend, as the city would indeed continue to occupy a privileged space within political and literary discourse throughout the nineteenth century and beyond.

One particular movement in which urban space figured prominently was anarchism. In the 1880s, European immigrants arriving in Argentina and other Latin American countries brought with them a wide array of new social ideas which found favourable reception in the context of a growing labouring class that through unions sought to win improvements in working conditions and subsequently achieve class emancipation.[2] With the arrival of Italians Errico Malatesta and Pietro Gori and Catalonian José Pratt in Buenos Aires during this period, anarchist thought began to acquire more strength, and under their influence anarchist groups soon surpassed other socialist organisations in number.

In the Latin American setting, utopianism occupied a central place within the gamut of anarchist ideas. Similar to earlier anarchist utopian thought, Latin American anarchist utopias combined the anarchist emphasis on opposition to coercive state authority with the utopian vision of reformulating social and economic life along more egalitarian lines. In this sense, anarchist utopias illustrate an important aspect of Latin American anarchist thought in general: not the absolute abolition of the established community *per se*, but rather its reformulation in the attempt to improve the working and living conditions of the working classes. Both contemporary scholars and activists of the period defined this variant of Latin American anarchism, one that was critical of the liberal state and at the same time cognisant of the need to perpetuate some form of politics 'after the Revolution', as 'constructivist'.[3] Anarchist utopias functioned as unique fictional spaces in which the critical function of anarchist ideology converged with the constructive role of the utopian theories of space initially outlined in the work of thinkers such as James Silk Buckingham, Charles Fourier, Ebenezer Howard and Robert Owen.

The present study will examine the emergence of these anarchist utopias in Latin America by focusing on a select group of texts: Pierre Quiroule's (pseudonym for Joaquin Alejo Falçonnet) trilogy *Sobre la ruta de la anarquía* (*On the Route to Anarchism*) (1912), *La ciudad anarquista americana* (*The American Anarchist City*) (1914) and *En la soñada tierra del ideal* (*In the Dreamt Land of the Ideal*) (1924); 'Locópolis', in *La ciudad de los locos* (*The City of the Mad*) (1914) by Juan José de Soiza Reilly; and 'Villautopía', the ideal city in the Mexican novelist Eduardo Urzaiz's *Eugenia*.[4] In contrast to Quiroule – who explicitly proclaimed himself an anarchist, published his novel with an anarchist press and was an active militant in Argentina – neither Soiza Reilly nor Urzaiz clearly identified as an anarchist. However, their texts display elements aligned with conventional understandings of anarchist ideas. In the case of Soiza Reilly this is clear: there is no government at all; the family as an institution has been abolished; there is free love; and men enjoy an absolute freedom. Urzaiz's novel displays many of the same aspects. There is a state, but it is one that cares for and looks after its citizens. It is the coercive state that anarchists would of course reject. In *Anarchism and Authority* (2007), Paul McLaughlin rightly identifies that it is scepticism towards rather than a wholesale rejection of authority that most accurately characterizes anarchism; to hold that the anarchist is inherently 'anti-statist' or anti-authority is an impoverished view.[5] Urzaiz's writing is consistent with this approach.

The utopianism of Quiroule, Soiza Reilly and Urzaiz also takes different forms. Quiroule identifies his texts as utopian and in the introduction to *La ciudad anarquista americana*, he dedicates the novel to those 'forgers' of the 'Ideal', the 'admirable utopia'. The content of *La ciudad anarquista americana* also reflects Quiroule's utopian orientation. The representation of the 'City de los Hijos del Sol' exhibits many of the most common utopian attributes: he locates his utopia in a remote place which is difficult to identify; there has been a social cleansing of the bourgeoisie through a weapon of mass destruction, the 'Vibraliber'; he sets forth a new set of rules and laws which differ from those held by capitalist rulers; and his society is portrayed as a much better place to live than the previous social models.[6] The models imagined by Soiza Reilly and Urzaiz are also better places and utopian in this sense, though Urzaiz's is perhaps most difficult to classify as a utopia and has dystopian elements. One could argue that Urzaiz's *Eugenia* resembles *Brave New World* and that, as John Carey argues of Huxley's work, 'it can be read as an ambivalent text, dystopian from one angle, utopian from another'.[7] Today, many of his ideas appear naive and perhaps disturbing. But in *Eugenia*, hunger, war and misery belong to the past and society has achieved a certain degree of sophistication thanks to technological progress and the improving role of government.

In all of these writings, the city emerges as the privileged space in which anarchist writers depict their imaginary communities, but it is an idea that contrasts to that explored by the sociologist Henri Lefebvre. In *Le droit à la ville* (1968), Lefebvre defines urban society as a social reality born in relation to its inhabitants.[8] The space that houses a society configures reality for individuals. Furthermore, in treating industrialised society and modern society as homologous, Lefebvre identifies the emergence of this space as a territory of contrasts and exclusions, in which the city assumes in itself an exclusive use and exchange 'value'.[9] Violent contrasts between the rich and poor, political confrontations and struggles between the powerful and the oppressed take place in the city, which serves as the ultimate arena for these conflicts. The urban spaces examined in the texts under consideration here serve as a staging ground for political discourse. However, the cities of Quiroule consciously attempt to set aside inter-class conflict and instead introduce an alternative ideal reality in the form of an anarchist utopia.

The first part of this study will consider Franco-Argentine Pierre Quiroule's utopian trilogy, pointing to his efforts to establish a new egalitarian social order in which class differences will be abolished.[10] The second part sets out to contrast Quiroule's model of society with those of Mexican writer Urzaiz and Argentine Soiza Reilly. Unlike the utopia formulated by Quiroule, the utopian cities of Urzaiz and Soiza Reilly unavoidably give rise to tensions either within the community (in the case of Soiza Reilly) or between individuals (in the case of Urzaiz), when the characters of the novels become *humanised* and their passions interfere with collective projects for social harmony. In these two texts, utopian ideals thus come into conflict with social desires – indeed, either one or the other ends up being destroyed – because these ideals do not provide for the expression of emotions which eventually flood into everyday social life.

In *Communes, Sociology and Society* (1976) the sociologist Philip Abrams argues that the profound commitment of collectively bonding into a utopian community comprises a powerful component of willing renunciation and self-denial of private interests in the name of more elevated, commonly shared objectives.[11] The hypothesis of this study is that, when this commitment is transgressed, communities lose their utopian component and can even disintegrate. As Abrams notes, the utopian community is established as a social entity, with strong ties and a distinctive identity, constructed in a real place, as a force separate from its members.[12] This explains the descriptive nature of the utopian genre, where characters are nominally emptied of their emotional content and expected to conform to their ideological functions. However, when individual passions (such as love, jealousy, selfishness, fear or hate) overshadow personal commitments to the collective unit, a potential danger emerges to threaten the viability of the utopian society.

The city as a space for transformation

The three texts by Quiroule under discussion form a triptych of utopias through which the author not only portrays the social structure and urban organisation of the society of the future, but also encourages fellow believers to formulate a plan to anticipate and resolve problems that may arise following revolution. In *Sobre la ruta de la anarquía* (1909) he describes a supposed social revolution that begins in France, inspired directly by the 1871 Paris Commune, and spreads to the rest of Europe. Here the city represents the space of destruction and violence against power as institutional repression. Destruction's cathartic violence enables the construction of a territory *ex nihilo*, where a new society is instituted. Yet Quiroule's social revolution survives only in Paris and its surrounding area; in the remaining European cities the much yearned for happiness rapidly dissipates. Writing the *semaine sanglante* out of his narrative, the Commune survives and perpetuates itself into the foreseeable future.[13] For this reason, France represents 'a most perfect harmony' and a 'Golden Age' where the discontented from other nations in *Sobre la ruta de la anarquía* immigrate 'toward that region of prosperity and liberty without equal'.[14] So concludes the text.

The first four chapters describe the beginning of a war between the majority of European countries, starting with the confrontation between England and Germany for hegemony over the world market. Socialist leaders' calls for a revolution are rapidly acted upon. Throughout the story it is unclear how a causal relation is established between trans-national war and the realisation of social utopia. Revolutionaries dismiss the official government's call for a return to order and proceed to liberate political prisoners, the majority of whom are working-class labourers.[15] The much-feared mob or crowd that served as the object of analysis for positivists of the time here assumes the role of historical agent, acting as the engine of the revolt. It is the 'revenge of the people' whose crimes never equal those committed coldly by bourgeois society. The 'pariahs' of the bourgeois patriciate become, through a process of transformation and transition, the executors of revolution. The city, for its part, becomes the central stage for their collision. The taking of the city is symbolic, although it may have real echoes; and, as Lefebvre signals in his discussion of the Paris Commune, we find ourselves confronting the return of the labourers who, once rejected and expelled towards the periphery, now turn back towards the urban centres 'in order to re-conquer the city, this spoil amongst spoils' and recover all the other rights of which they had been stripped or dispossessed.[16]

Aware of the importance of the city as the main arena where class struggle and future revolutions would take place, Quiroule chooses an urban setting to develop his narrative. Anchored in a new urban configuration, *Sobre la ruta de la anarquía* establishes the base for Quiroule's later anarchist utopias. It serves as a preamble to later works and represents their justification. It is indeed rooted in the fictional account in which utopia constitutes the space of the unknown and where urban centres form the axis of a new social order. Following this logic, the spatial representation of *La ciudad anarquista americana* (1914) can be read as a projection of this territory in full transformative ebullience once the 'work in progress' is complete and an urban utopia has materialised. The novel opens with the establishment of the 'Ciudad de los Hijos del Sol' (City of the Children of the Sun) which has been erected on the ruins of the 'bourgeois monarchy of El Dorado'.[17] Quiroule emphasises how the emancipated proletariat 'swept away' this regime in a 'revolutionary wave' which assured the end of capitalist dominance not only in this particular region but throughout much of the Americas.[18] Like *Sobre la ruta de la anarquía*, *La ciudad anarquista americana* depicts the achievement of the urban utopia, but now Quiroule has transferred this new social experiment to the other side of the Atlantic and social revolution now plays out in America.[19]

Of all the works in the trilogy, *La ciudad anarquista americana* represents the most complete form of utopia. In addition to offering the reader a large fold-out map of the anarchist city – complete with streets, avenues, buildings, plazas and gardens in a perfect urban balance – the description that appears in the work is as much discursive as it is totalising. According to Louis Marin, the totality and harmony of utopian description are derived from the textual form of representation: given that descriptive discourse constructs a representation in utopia, this discourse must be exhaustive and without residue.[20] And in organising and setting out the contours of the anarchist city in painstaking detail, Quiroule is responding to those who would dismiss anarchism as a purely critical and destructive force.[21] In Quiroule, we thus do not find a city devoid of coherence but rather *La ciudad anarquista americana* configures a discourse that elevates a work of 'true progress and civilization' whose objective consists in 'fashioning human happiness'.[22] Quiroule's narrative carefully distinguishes between 'Ciudad de los Hijos del Sol' and the modern industrialised urban space in that the former is green and airy, free of noise and pollution and of relatively small size where inhabitants experience an 'intimate and immediate contact with nature';[23] the latter, on the other hand, is presented as a 'colossal' degraded society, whose splendour has been 'amassed with the blood of the proletariat'.[24]

Further juxtaposition between the cities depicted in the first two books of Quiroule's trilogy illustrates a marked progression in his perception of revolutionary action in the course of merely two years. While the anarchist utopia in *Sobre la ruta de la anarquía* manifests itself in the French capital, *La ciudad anarquista americana* has denied revolutionary agency to European countries and has transferred this power to the New World. For Quiroule, America now represents the ideal territory for the constitution of an urban utopia as it functions as a virgin space in which corruption, hunger and misery are absent. *La ciudad anarquista americana* indeed reincarnates the early modern myth of America as a *vacuum domicilium* where Quiroule is able to found a new egalitarian society. Perhaps this shift away from Europe may be attributed in part to the heightened nationalist tensions on the continent which would culminate in the outbreak of the Great War the same year that *La ciudad anarquista americana* was published.

The nameless city depicted in the final book in Quiroule's trilogy, *En la soñada tierra del ideal*, exists in the distant future in relation to the earlier 'Ciudad de los Hijos del Sol' and provides Quiroule an opportunity to reconsider some of the most preoccupying issues from previous works. A major problem he attempts to resolve in this text is how to reconstruct the social apparatus once the preceding capitalist system has disappeared. Reconfiguring the post-revolutionary landscape hinges upon the confrontation between syndicalists and anarchists in which the former urge a wholesale embrace of the industrial city as the anchor for the post-revolutionary society, while the latter – the anarchists – attempt to integrate nature into this urban space. Similar to *La ciudad anarquista americana*, the anarchist city here represents a fusion of city and country in one communal entity where both are 'tied together by the same economic interests and intellectual needs'.[25] Quiroule develops this theme of combining the natural and human worlds at a symbolic level through the social relations cultivated in the narrative, particularly in the description of the sincere friendship between the three protagonists – Citis, Campaniola and Fructar. Their close relationship allegorically represents the synthesis of the city (Citis) and country (Campaniola), from whose fruit (Fructar) is born the 'land of the Ideal'.

The urban utopias presented in Quiroule's anarchist trilogy are exemplary, indeed illustrative, in that they offer a pragmatic staging of society. For Karl Mannheim a utopia is any idea conceived of in a transcendental manner, and one that changes the existing historic and social order in accordance with its own conceptions.[26] From this perspective, we can postulate that these urban utopian spaces do not change the established order in any direct fashion, although in their consummation (their very existence) they nevertheless manage to awaken our imaginations to better societies. And yet Quiroule's cities present an idealised or even crystallised picture in which the basic social problems that might otherwise have detracted from the beauty of these utopias are left aside. Besides the friendship between the main characters in the third novel, which functions only to emphasise an important ideological element of the anarchist utopia, basic human emotions – sexual desire, passion and so forth – are noticeably absent. In contrast, in the following group of anarchist utopias survival is much more difficult precisely because these spaces are humanised and characters possess and express a whole range of feelings towards themselves and others. In this flood of emotions, these anarchist utopias become untenable.

The city as a space for destruction

Juan José de Soiza Reilly's *La ciudad de los locos* (1914) recounts the story of Tartarín Moreira, an illustrious young man whose account begins in an asylum for the insane. His madness is the result of a failed science experiment and it is unexpectedly within the mental institution that the project of erecting a utopian city is initiated. Perched in a treetop, Tartarín calls out to his fellow patients, inviting them to escape to a solitary and enchanting region, where they can live as nomads and found the 'brilliant and wonderful Locópolis' (roughly translated as 'City of the Mad').[27] Here we encounter an operation similar to that found in the preceding anarchist utopias where a rupture occurs with respect to the previous order, and where a new society completely distinct from the previous system is erected atop the rubble of the old. Conceived of as the flipside of dominant societies (the normal, sane, oppressive and authoritarian), the foundations of a new society are established according to the principles of human desires and liberty – core values in the anarchist–utopian framework.[28]

After burning down the hospital, Tartarín guides the asylum residents to a forest at the edge of the sea where they erect the city of Locópolis. With madness as the regulating principle, its citizens enjoy complete freedom, in accordance with the proclaimed principles of anarchism. Shortly after the city's founding, Tartarín falls in love with a certain Luisa, a union that prompts some in Locópolis to re-evaluate their leader. Even if the people continue to believe that Tartarín is a quasi-divine immaterial being, they now assign him one defect, and on this basis he is similar to all men: 'he now believed in love'.[29] Love therefore serves to de-sacralise Tartarín and, as he remains the driving force behind Locópolis, this transformation is extended to the entire community.

In his ability and willingness to express and receive feeling, Tartarín differs markedly from the characters of Quiroule. And as long as his love can be translated into passion, it is a potentially destabilising sentiment. When friendship and love are expressed in Quiroule's trilogy, they are always domesticated, in that they are systematically channelled towards the political community that the characters inhabit, as they have already renounced their individual identity and committed themselves wholly to the political cause that sustains them. Locópolis, by contrast, displays the tension provoked by the young and beautiful Rosaura, whose amorous feelings for Tartarín drive her to toss a poisonous liquid in the face of Luisa, rendering her hideously disfigured. This saga of love, jealousy and revenge soon unleashes subsequent events, anticipating the destruction of the city and the conclusion of the narration. The utopia of the mad cannot be sustained because the emotions of its citizens have impeded its realisation (that is to say, there is no longer any seamless relationship between individual social interaction and the common good). The story thus concludes with the inhabitants of the city committing a collective mass suicide.

First published in 1919, Eduardo Urzaiz's futuristic *Eugenia* did not enjoy a wide circulation. The novel opens in the year 2118 in 'Villautopía' ('Utopiaville'), the capital of the 'Central American Subconfederation'. The two main characters, Ernesto and Celiana, are lovers at the beginning of the story. Ernesto is appointed to be the 'Official Reproducer of the Species,' a position that recognises his merits as a 'perfect man' but also requires him to engage in constant promiscuous sex with a great number of women who have also been selected as official 'reproducers'.[30] He willingly enters into an agreement with the state to produce a certain number of children for the community. Tension begins between Celiana and Ernesto after he has accepted his new role, as from that day forward the couple give up the sexual exclusivity they had previously maintained. Plagued by the agony of love, Celiana asks herself what right she has to completely 'monopolise the virgin heart of that boy'.[31]

As feelings are considered to be social constructions in Villautopía, the insertion of passions and their destructive power allow the reader to question the viability of this society. When Celiana feels jealousy, she immediately discredits such an emotive response, explaining that 'in the social state of her time jealousy was an anachronistic sentiment'.[32] Furthermore, she states that love in the present 'tends to liberate itself from atavistic chains of passion and jealousy'.[33] A potentially socially disruptive contradiction thus emerges. On the one hand, the new social order considers the passions as socially constructed; they are relegated to a distant archaic past and are no longer considered to possess social or political relevance. And yet, as the case of Celiana poignantly illustrates, the passions (specifically love and jealousy) do indeed continue to shape individual experience within utopian society. She regretfully believes that 'she was one of those beings still tied by hereditary chains to the pain of loving pathologically and abnormally'.[34] The individual renunciation for the totality that is the mark of utopian community thus carries a high cost.

This feeling of disenchantment and pain is prolonged throughout the story until the moment in which Ernesto meets Eugenia, who also has just been named an official 'reproducer,' and with whom he immediately falls in love. Their union, in fact, ratifies the triumph of the reproducer, since their fruit or progeny will mark the social evolution of the species and the improvement of the human race. In this case there is no destruction of utopian urban space. There is, on the other hand, a destruction of individualities: by the end of the story, Celiana has become a 'galvanised cadaver,' given that she has lost the only inspiration in her life: love.[35] The cost of renunciation and self-denial in relation to the existence and continuity of the utopian community is, as indicated by Abrams, the dissolution of the individual self.

Conclusion

Investigating the literary representation of urban space in the anarchist utopias of these authors brings to light two important points about early twentieth-century anarchist thought in Latin America. First, by comparing and contrasting the cities of Soiza Reilly and Urzaiz with those of Quiroule, it becomes apparent that in humanising their characters (as positive as this may seem at an emotional level), a sort of destruction ensues: in Soiza Reilly, it is the complete demise of Locópolis; in Urzaiz, it is of an individual member of the community, Celiana. In both *La ciudad de los locos* and *Eugenia*, love operates as a category that organises the interaction of characters in the narrative and eventually prevails over the anarchist social order. Therefore, unrequited or not, love and the passions not only exercise their demolishing power, but also outlive the communitarian forms in which they initially took form. While characters in Quiroule are not endowed with any particular emotional qualities and remain essentially uniform in disposition throughout his works, those inhabiting the texts of Soiza Reilly and Urzaiz express distinct personalities and desires. However, it is precisely this introduction of temperament into character development that undermines anarchist utopian individual–community relations.

Second, these Latin American anarchist utopias embody an intriguing and unresolved paradox. Throughout these works the New World is the space chosen to represent the ideal territory for the constitution of an urban utopia for, unlike Europe, it does not find itself tainted by vice. But, as noted above, if the Americas once again embody the myth of an uncontaminated virtuous space as they did in the early modern period, then the representation of these utopian spaces does not concretely exhibit any distinctively American attribute. While earlier Latin American utopias of the nineteenth century – notably Sarmiento's *Argirópolis* and Bolivar's utopian project for a wider Latin American federation – sought through their ideal spaces to give form to a shared cultural, political and economic identity from and for Latin Americans, these twentieth-century anarchist territories comprise a different identity. Similar to the cities and society portrayed, identity in these anarchist utopias is founded *ex nihilo*, without a past, without a memory and without a tradition. In other words, it is a Latin American utopia thoroughly *de-Americanised*.

The anarchist utopian cities of this study operate as visions of the future and propose an urban setting as a space for social transformation. Nevertheless, it is in those ideal spaces where the identity of subjects is distinctive and in which identity is de-coupled from its merely functional role that characters acquire a certain degree of verisimilitude much closer to the daily existence of the reader. It is these characters who open up a possibility of a reading that accounts for the future of imaginary cities in all its possible variants, posing unresolved problems that deserve to be constantly reviewed and reformulated.

Notes

I would like to thank Kenneth Loiselle for having read the text in its entirety. His poignant criticism and suggestions have been invaluable.

1 See D. Sarmiento, *Argirópolis*, p. 137, 173.
2 Ángel Cappelletti recounts that the '*first* popular movement (and more specifically working-class movement) that was produced in Argentina', as a result of the 'great European immigration', 'incipient industrialisation' and 'class consciousness' was 'anarchism, or, if you prefer, anarcho-syndicalism'. A. Cappelletti, *Hechos y figuras del anarquismo hispanoamericano*, pp. 9–10. See also F. Weinberg, *Dos utopías argentinas de principios de siglo*, pp. 15–16.
3 See L. Gómez Tovar, 'Geografía de lo imaginario', in L. Gómez Tovar, R. Gutiérrez and S. A. Vázquez (eds), *Utopías libertarias americanas: la ciudad anarquista americana de Pierre Quiroule*, p. 38.
4 Pierre Quiroule's (Alejo Falçonnet's) complete trilogy *La ciudad anarquista americana. Obra de construcción revolucionaria, con el plano de la ciudad libertaria*, *Sobre la ruta de la anarquía (Novela libertaria)* and *En la soñada tierra del ideal* can be found at the Internationaal Instituut voor Sociale Geschiedenis (IISG), Amsterdam. For the remaining texts, see Juan José de Soiza Reilly, *La ciudad de los locos (Aventuras de Tartarín Moreira)* and Eduardo Urzaiz, *Eugenia*.
5 Paul McLaughlin, *Anarchism and Authority: A Philosophical Introduction to Classical Anarchism*, pp. 29–33. In a similar vein, Frank Fernández has also noted that it is not political association *per se* that falls under anarchist criticism but rather certain forms of organisation: 'Over and over in the writings of Proudhon, Bakunin, Kropotkin, Rocker, Ward, Bookchin, et al., one finds not a rejection of organization, but rather a preoccupation with how society should be organized in accord with the anarchist principles of individual freedom and social justice ... [t]his is hardly a rejection of organization.' F. Fernández, *Cuban Anarchism: The History of a Movement*, trans. C. Bufe, p. 5. All of the authors under discussion in this essay indeed posit various forms of socio-political organisation, be they spontaneous forms of government

(Soiza Reilly), local oversight (Quiroule) or larger, more organised state bodies
(Urzaiz).

6   These familiar characteristics of utopia are discussed in the *International Ency-
    clopedia of the Social and Behavioral Sciences*, pp. 16123–7.
7   J. Carey, *The Faber Book of Utopias*, p. 448.
8   H. Lefebvre, *Le droit à la ville*, p. 1.
9   *Ibid.* pp. 2–3.
10 Born in Lyon in 1867, Quiroule immigrated as a child to Buenos Aires.
11 'Accordingly, the bonding of members of a utopian community is not a matter
    of conditional negotiation, exploration, tentative affirmation or withdrawal,
    but of strong and deep commitment, self-denial and renunciation in the name
    of higher purposes', P. Abrams, *Communes, Sociology and Society*, p. 36. I use
    this citation to signal the almost total absence of works that analyse the rep-
    resentation of emotions, affections and feelings in utopian communities and/or
    territories.
12 'Above all, the utopian community is one that has been established socially as
    "an entity" with strong boundaries and strong identity – in other words, it is
    a place that has become a thing, a social force separable from its members',
    ibid.
13 The *semaine sanglante* refers to the massacres of Communards after the fall of
    the Commune, which claimed an estimated 20,000 victims.
14 Quiroule, *Sobre la ruta de la anarquía*, p. 117.
15 *Ibid.* p. 51.
16 Lefebvre, *Le droit à la ville*, p. 18.
17 Quiroule, *La ciudad anarquista americana*, p. 19.
18 *Ibid.*
19 For Felix Weinberg Quiroule's conception of the city is completely novel and
    constitutes a clear anticipation of experiments that were undertaken during
    the twentieth century; Weinberg, *Dos utopías argentinas de principios de siglo*,
    p. 90. It proposes an urban plan in dialogue with the 'Garden City' concept
    elaborated by Ebenezer Howard in his book *To-morrow: A Peaceful Path to
    Social Reform* (1898). In this work, Howard advocates the establishment of
    autonomous communities in open spaces as an alternative to overcrowded
    and unhealthy urban working-class areas. While William Morris had already
    expressed the necessity of ending the era of big cities – whose unceasing over-
    crowding degrades their inhabitants – through the fusion of city and nature, it
    is Howard who established a poetics of what he called the marriage of city and
    country, or what for Quiroule constitutes a poeticising of human existence;
    ibid. p. 6.
20 L. Marin, *Utopiques: Jeux d'Espaces*, p. 79.
21 Quiroule, *La ciudad anarquista americana*, p. 17.
22 *Ibid.* p. 9.
23 *Ibid.* p. 14.
24 *Ibid.* p. 10.
25 Quiroule, *En la soñada tierra del ideal*, p. 18.
26 K. Mannheim, *Ideología y utopía, introducción a la sociología del conoci-
    miento*, p. 169.
27 Soiza Reilly, *La ciudad de los locos*, p. 79.

28 The emphasis on individual freedom can be seen in earlier landmark anarchist–utopian texts, notably *L'Humanisphère* (1857) of Jacques Déjacque, a French political figure operating in the United States. According to historian Luis Gómez Tovar, Déjacque exercised an influence on the anarchist movement in Latin America through the intermediary figure of journalist Sebastian Faure. In 1895, Faure began publication of the paper, *Le libertaire*, which echoed Déjacque's emphasis that individual happiness requires the absence of oppressive governmental or familial authority. See Gómez Tovar, 'Geografía de lo imaginario', pp. 30–1.

29 Soiza Reilly, *La ciudad de los locos*, pp. 123–4.

30 Urzaiz, *Eugenia*, pp. 15, 29.

31 *Ibid*. p. 66.

32 *Ibid*. p. 84.

33 *Ibid*. p. 100.

34 *Ibid*.

35 *Ibid*. p. 115.

References

Abrams, P., *Communes, Sociology and Society* (Cambridge: Cambridge University Press, 1976).

Cappelletti, A., *Hechos y figuras del anarquismo hispanoamericano* (Madrid: Ediciones Madre Tierra, 1990).

Carey, J., *The Faber Book of Utopias* (London: Faber and Faber, 1999).

Cazes, B., 'Utopias: Social', in Neil J. Smelser and Paul B. Baltes (eds), *International Encyclopedia of the Social and Behavioral Sciences* (Amsterdam and New York: Elsevier, 2001).

Choay, F., *L'urbanisme, utopies et réalités* (Paris: Editions du Seuil, 2001).

Déjacque, J., *Question révolutionnaire. L'Humanisphère. A bas les chefs. La libération des Noirs américains* (Paris: Éditions Champ Libre, 1971).

Fernández, F., *Cuban Anarchism: The History of a Movement*, trans. C. Bufe (Tucson, Arizona: Sharp Press, 2001).

García Cantú, G., *Utopías mexicanas* (México D.F.: Era, 1963).

Gómez Tovar, L., 'Geografía de lo imaginario,' in L. Gómez Tovar, R. Gutiérrez and S. A. Vázquez (eds), *Utopías libertarias americanas: la ciudad anarquista americana de Pierre Quiroule* (Madrid: Tueros/Fundación Salvador Seguí, 1991).

Howard, E., *To-Morrow: A Peaceful Path to Real Reform* (London and New York: Routledge, 2003).

Joll, J., *The Origins of the First World War* (New York: Pearson Longman, 2006).

Lefebvre, H., *Le droit à la ville* (Paris: Anthropos, 1968).

Mannheim, K., *Ideología y utopía, introducción a la sociología del conocimiento* (México: Fondo de Cultura Económica, 1941).

Marin, L., *Utopiques: Jeux d'Espaces* (Paris: Les Éditions de Minuit, 1973).

McLaughlin, Paul., *Anarchism and Authority: A Philosophical Introduction to Classical Anarchism* (Aldershot, England and Burlington, VT: Ashgate, 2007).

Quiroule, P. (Alejo Falçonnet), *Sobre la ruta de la anarquía (Novela libertaria)* (Buenos Aires: Bautista Fueyo, 1912).

——*La ciudad anarquista americana. Obra de construcción revolucionaria, con el plano de la ciudad libertaria* (Buenos Aires: 'La Protesta', 1914).

——*En la soñada tierra del ideal* (Buenos Aires: Bautista Fueyo, 1924).

Sarmiento, D., *Argirópolis* (Buenos Aires: 'La Cultura argentina', 1916).

Soiza Reilly, J. J. de, *La ciudad de los locos (Aventuras de Tartarín Moreira)* (Barcelona: Casa Editorial Maucci, 1914).

Urzaiz, E., *Eugenia* (México D.F.: Premiá Editora, 1982).

Weinberg, F., *Dos utopías argentinas de principios de siglo* (Buenos Aires: Solar/ Hachette, 1976).

Anarchy in the archives: notes from the ruins of Sydney and Melbourne

Long before the arrival of anarchist writings in Australia in the 1880s, settlers on the continent were already producing utopias in the anarchist spirit. Perhaps it is anarchism's mediation of the needs of the individual and society that appealed to early colonists who, despite their individualist bush ethos, would not have survived the harsh natural and economic environment without the help of their mates. It is difficult to separate the proto-anarchist tendencies of these utopias from their broader anti-colonial sentiments. As Annegret Maack has shown, early Australian utopias exhibited a degree of hostility toward the state arising from a more general anti-imperialism, from the 'decay of nations' predicted in Robert Williams's *Eureka* (1837), to Robert Desborough's *State Contentment* (1870), which describes a valley outside of Melbourne where the people are 'free from those narrow-minded prejudices that distinguish nationalities', and in which '[a]ll human beings have equal rights, women as well as men; aristocracy and monarchy are abolished; [and] there is no private property'.[1]

Melbourne boasts a rich local history of utopian radicals who expressed a more sophisticated understanding of the imbrications of colonialism and state rule, but it is a history that is largely unwritten, fragmented and dispersed. The archives of the State Library of Victoria contain boxes of all but forgotten anarchist tracts, letters and works of fiction advocating social change on behalf of the impoverished workers of Australia's first colonial century, and depicting the repeated destruction of Sydney and Melbourne by rioting mobs. These dystopian visions of the antipodean metropolis under siege were in part influenced by imported examples, most notably Edward Bellamy's *Looking Backward* (1888), William Morris's *News from Nowhere* (1890) and Ignatius Donnelly's apocalyptic *Caesar's Column* (1890), as John Docker has shown.[2] But the imagined destruction of the antipodean metropolis was also a reaction to the local discourse of urban planning that grew out of discussions of slum clearance in Sydney in 1870 and spread quickly to Melbourne, before merging in the 1890s with federalist plans for wide-scale centralisation and urban redesign. At a time when local space was being reconfigured to fit the contours of a brand new nation, many writers were imagining alternative futures for Australia's metropolises, futures that were post-colonial, post-capitalist, anti-statist – and soon forgotten.

Australia's urban development in the late nineteenth century is typically described as an inexorable march from colonial rule toward federalism, but in fact the nation emerged through a dialectic with these socialist and anarchist alternatives. Most histories fail to record that, in the 1890s, members of the Melbourne Anarchist Club (MAC) and the Australian Socialist League (ASL) developed a highly visible utopian counter-discourse to this new language of state and urban planning. Using a wide variety of media (including newspapers, pamphlets, graffiti and utopian novels), these radicals disseminated images of the violent restructuring of Australian cities that directly opposed the goals of federalism and imperialism alike. In his 1892 utopia, *The Melbourne Riots and How Harry Holdfast and His Friends Emancipated The Workers. A Realistic Novel*, bookseller and MAC founder David Andrade depicted rioting in the streets of Melbourne, describing the 'somber beauty of the charred and desolated ruins' of Sydney after the people's revolt against the oligarchs.[3] Andrade's narrative accuses the land monopolists of enslaving the workers and inciting riots; his imagined solution was the establishment of an anarcho-syndicalist agrarian commune near Healesville, Victoria, modelled after America's Fourierist Brook Farm community.

Two years later, Andrade's sometime associate Samuel Albert Rosa published his own utopia, in which he predicted a violent revolt among Australia's poor. *The Coming Terror, or, the Australian Revolution* (1894) describes the collapse of the cities under the weight of capitalism, the defeat of the British empire by Russia, and the emergence in Australia of a new federal republic under the leadership of one Oliver Spence. Initially, Spence reconstructs Australia according to collectivist principles, declaring the parliamentary government a farce and proclaiming all land free and all private property a crime. However, the benevolent leader grows despotic after the federal exploring party happens upon a lost race in the interior desert, a 'community of simple, honest, truthful, unsophisticated white people!' living in a federation of 'purely Democratic, self-governing communities'. In this anarchist microtopia nested within Rosa's nationalist utopia, '[t]here were no police, no military, no parliaments, no governments',[4] just a new Garden of Eden springing from artesian wells sunk into the Great Sandy Desert. Knowing a good thing when they see it, federation missionaries take over the lost society, and Spence's poorest subjects flock to the desert to find a better life. After a failed attempt to reclaim the splinter state, the dictator resigns himself to a policy of '[h]armonious co-operation' which, he assures his wife, is large enough to safely harbour and contain any anarchist element.[5] In his address 'To the Reader', Rosa is careful to point out that '[t]he writer is no Anarchist. He desires to see the inevitable change from capitalism to collectivism facilitated by the peaceful action of an enlightened populace voting at the polls', and not the 'violent and bloody upheaval sketched in this book'.[6] Despite this disclaimer, however, his future Australia figures ambivalently as both a new imperial centre and an autonomous anarchist federation.

This ambivalence perhaps represents Rosa's attempt to mediate the ideological differences that divided members of both the ASL and the MAC from 1888 on. Bob James has carefully delineated the factions that developed within these groups, painting the picture of a highly reactive collection of individuals whose political commitments evolved alongside frequent theoretical disagreements, interpersonal conflicts and regional political developments. Local concerns invariably inflected their understanding of imported anarchist theories, terminologies and practices, and club meetings were the occasion for frequent and heated arguments over the interpretation of various imported doctrines, such as the proper balance of individualism and collectivism. When Bruce Mansfield stated in 1956 that English radical thought 'carr[ied] so completely to the Socialist League in New South Wales' because, 'insofar as men read, they read similar books, and their dissatisfactions were similarly fashioned and moulded',[7] he underestimated the extent to which political theories developed outside Australia were adapted to suit conditions at home. Continental political texts frequently lost their foreign associations during transportation and local radicals, with a 'blindness to inconsistency', often ignored the distinctions found in sources as varied as Marx, Morris, Kropotkin and Mill.[8] Debates among members were exacerbated by concerns over their international reputations. When Benjamin Tucker, editor of Boston's anarchist paper *Liberty*, attacked W. H. McNamara of the ASL for being a 'State-Socialist and plagiarist', the latter responded that he and his League were in fact scientific socialists; Andrade, for his part, considered them to be evolutionary socialists, even though he was himself more properly a mutualist and Proudhonist after Tucker's example.[9] Overseas movements were often used as arenas for playing out their definitional tensions and power struggles, as when Rosa was accused of betraying the Haymarket martyrs during a visit to Chicago.

Although he never left Australia, MAC co-founder John Arthur Andrews did much to shape foreign impressions of local radicalism. A prison writer, slum journalist, epic poet and propagandist, Andrews is considered the most significant radical of the period by radical historian Bob James, whose biography documents Andrews's dismissal at an early age from the Victorian civil service, his affiliations first with the MAC and subsequently the ASL, and his widespread writerly activities. From the late 1880s until his death in 1903, Andrews penned articles on anarchist theory for the radical press in Australia, France, America and Portugal, which brought him into contact with figures like Jean Grave and Kropotkin. He also published three books of poetry, *Temple Mystic* (1888), *Poems of Freedom* (1894) and *Teufelswelt* (1896), and several short stories. His work documents the abuses of property and the suffering of the urban poor in various literary modes. Although his pseudonymous, incomplete or unpublished writings, and those effected in ephemeral media such as handbills and graffiti, make it difficult to gauge his complete oeuvre with precision, the generic and tonal diversity of Andrews's writings indicate that he wrote for a variety of purposes: his potboilers were probably penned simply to earn a bit of money and relief from his starvation diet,[10] while his foreign correspondence was aimed at maintaining links with comrades abroad, and his essays in Melbourne's *Tocsin* or Sydney's *Radical* engaged the divisive radical circles in the capital cities.

Andrews considered the city streets the proper site of revolutionary action and the source of a future anarchist utopia, as revealed in his unfinished utopian novel. 'The Triumph of Freedom: A Prospective History of the Social Revolution in Victoria', probably written in 1887, remains an important document for understanding Australia's transition from colony to nation, as well as the social alternatives eclipsed by that process. The remainder of this chapter will examine the extant fragments of 'The Triumph of Freedom' as they have come down to us. Rather than attempt to impose a coherence where none exists, I take the narrative's broken and uneven spatial form as iconic of both the cities in which Andrews actually lived and the utopian city he desired. Like the 'romantic anarchist' Walter Benjamin, Andrews marked capital's ongoing redevelopment of the city centre as presaging the final ruin of capitalism itself, seeing in the slums of Melbourne a dialectical link between communal societies of Australia's pre-capitalist past and a utopian, post-capitalist future. Whereas Benjamin knew that the anarchist utopia required the interruption of historical time and the temporal logic of modern progress, Andrews saw the additional need to disrupt the spatial organisation of colonial capitalism. As anticipatory exercises in spatial writing, his novel and various city texts not only described but also enacted the inevitable reconfiguration of the Australian metropolis in its future anarchist phase.

Two romantic anarchists, two worlds apart

While Rosa and Andrade saw the Australian city as an obstacle that must be destroyed to achieve a more balanced agrarian society, Andrews recognised the traces of a future utopia in the city streets. In his otherwise excellent study, historian Bruce Scates, one of the few to date to consider Andrews's utopian writings as such, erroneously groups Andrews with Andrade, Rosa and the widespread new arcadian movement that promoted intentional communes in rural areas in order to relieve the economic pressure on the cities during the depression of the 1890s.[11] To be sure, in his preparatory notes to 'The Triumph of Freedom', Andrews describes the 'organization of solidarity between farmers and industrial laborers': he writes that '[d]uring this period . . . a decentralising movement took place from the towns, and numerous highly developed village communities grew up'.[12] Scates imposes closure on the unfinished narrative by taking this intermediary stage as its final goal, even though Andrews quickly adds that '[t]his period was terminated by the imposition of the Single Tax'.[13] Given that Andrews elsewhere argued against Henry George's single tax solution,[14] it is unlikely that these village communities were meant to represent his final vision of utopia. In fact, in the novel's outline Andrews clearly indicates that syndicalism was to be merely an intermediary stage en route to the peaceful dissolution of the revolutionary government. After the syndicalist phase Andrews imagined a final 'revolutionary crisis', then 'collapse of the Government . . . restoration of order, and the inauguration of harmony . . . [T]he Government was neither overthrown by military force, nor terrorised into abdicating. It did not abdicate. It evaporated', leaving an indeterminate society in its place.[15]

Whereas Andrade and Rosa set their respective utopias in a pastoral retreat and a transformed desert interior, Andrews's own utopia was decidedly urban, a rare bias for a period in which the 'authentic' Australian character was still defined by the bush pioneer.[16] When poverty and the threat of prosecution for seditious libel forced him to flee Melbourne, he wrote to the British paper *Freedom* expressing his frustration at country life, 'where it is almost impossible to effect any propaganda . . . I can do no more than . . . write out posters for . . . two Melbourne comrades to stick up.'[17] Throughout his political and fictional writings, Andrews considers the city streets as the proper site of revolutionary action. In an essay on the Paris Communards, he anticipates the fearful yet heroic day when Australian workers 'may be butchered in the like cruel manner'.[18] He imagines this very scene in chapter three of his utopia, when the crowd of workers erects barricades, 'closing the street opening with wires supporting wire grilles, ironmongery and the like . . . At another part barricades were erected built of iron pipes and rails; at another again tramcars were taken out of the sheds, overturned, and filled with kerbstones and broken paving.'[19] This close detailing of the barricades shows a fascination with the material city and its potential for *détournement* toward revolutionary action.

It also reveals Andrews's close familiarity with the streets. No writer has mapped the nooks and byways of Melbourne in more detail, nor integrated the city more immanently into his writing and politics. He admired Zola, and assumed him to be an anarchist, 'since he goes into the nooks and streets [of Paris] to draw his descriptions from real life'.[20] The particular physiognomy of downtown Melbourne made it the perfect setting for

Andrews's own anarchist project. He positioned the antipodean metropolis at the centre of the battle against state capitalism, a struggle inscribed in its very streets though fought on a global field: 'Melbourne is in fact a Whitechapel, a Bermondsey and a Belgravia thrown together on the other side of the planet so as to form a centre of civilization. It contains some spacious thoroughfares and some narrow streets, mansions and hovels, alleys, courts and boulevards. It is a triumph of capitalism and a revolutionary centre.'[21] Here as elsewhere, he saw in the Australian capital's cosmopolitan marketplace its potential significance for international radicalism.

Graeme Davison and David Dunstan write that '[t]he city's sore spots seemed more heinous for being located at the very centre of the metropolis ... New commercial buildings often displaced old residential quarters ... Thus the contrast between the frontstage glamour of Collins and Bourke Streets [at that time, the primary shopping promenades] and the *backstage* squalor of the adjoining alleys and lanes became more and more pronounced.'[22] In a series of articles on the slums of Melbourne written for *Tocsin* in 1901, the year of federation, Andrews mapped the working-class hovels in the 'gridiron' of lanes between Bourke and Little Bourke Streets, byways that 'never appeared on any map of the city' but which contained '*secret passages*, occasioned by irregularities of building and fencing'.[23] He points out a theatre covering the spot where once stood 'the special quarter of the halt, the maimed and the blind', bourgeois entertainment halls squeezing out the suffering of the lumpen class. Andrews's vision of urban development is syncretic: he notes that '[t]he typical city slum features of that day have ... vanished ... but in some spots portions remained', providing 'a connecting link between the past and the present'.[24]

A half century later and half a world away, close to the centre of empire, Walter Benjamin would speculate on the 'dialectical images' arising from the connecting links between older urban architectures and contemporary commodity spectacles: the panoramas, the world exhibitions and, in particular, the shopping arcades. In the nineteenth-century arcades of Paris, icons of modernity that were already neglected by Benjamin's day, he famously sought 'to recognize the monuments of the bourgeoisie as ruins even before they have crumbled', the first step toward historical awakening.[25] These ruined monuments to consumerism evoked in their architecture the lost dream of Fourier's utopian phalanstery, and the key to understanding Benjamin's own particular blend of anarchism and utopianism. In the structure of the phalanstery, 'Fourier designs an alternative utopian world from the passages and *rue-galeries* that gets even with civilization. It is a dream city', made of the newest construction materials but having more in common with pre-historic, classless communities than modern capitalist society.[26] For Benjamin, the dilapidated shopping arcades recalled the phalanstery's 'porosity', an 'anarchical' spatial organisation characterised by 'a lack of clear boundaries between phenomena, a permeation of one thing by another, a merger of, for example, old and new, public and private, sacred and profane'.[27] This porosity enabled Benjamin's dialectical vision of the city, in which 'each private attitude or act is permeated by streams of communal life',[28] a long-lost utopia just visible beneath the transitory architectures and desires of the modern marketplace.

From the 1850s on, Melbourne built its own arcades in a fit of colonial mimicry.[29] Long before Benjamin recognised in the *passages couverts* traces of a Fourierist dream city and a monument to capitalism's impermanence and imminent demise, Andrews had mapped the thresholds of Melbourne's awakening from its capitalist dream not in the arcades proper, but in the so-called 'arcade system' formed by the adjacent laneways and back alleys. The laneway hovel was Andrews's transitional architecture, already disappearing in his day beneath the façade of redevelopment but still visible to the intrepid urban explorer. Andrews and Benjamin shared certain critical attitudes toward the modern metropolis, even though they were quite literally worlds apart. Both were refugees – one of the class war, the other of the Nazis; but Andrews was an engaged radical living in doss houses, in prison cells and on the streets, when not tramping through the Victorian countryside and going hungry for days on end; while Benjamin was a 'symbolic' anarchist, 'neither on the left nor on the right', who didn't grasp the hardships of being a beggar.[30] He documented new forms of commodity consumption and the bourgeois subjectivities they produced, while Andrews held largely to a Proudhonist critique of property and landed capitalism, breaking volubly with the individualist anarchists. For Benjamin, the international wares on display within the communicating walls of the arcades suggested a fantastic consumerist alternative to the reality of European national borders, 'which were anything but porous in Benjamin's life'.[31] By contrast, Melbourne's own porosity frequently seemed dystopian to Andrews: he exposed the pathos of Richmond dwellings 'divided by nothing more substantial than a wall of Hessian and paper',[32] and complained that 'every word said in the next house could be heard in ours'.[33] Like Fourier, Andrews saw the interconnectedness of the ruling class and the urban poor; but rather than imagine an alternative utopian society in every detail, he chose to uncover the poverty at the heart of commercial Melbourne, revealing the close communication of the marketplace with the slums in order to play on the repressed fears of his bourgeois readership. From the crumbling laneway hovels he inhabited, Andrews looked both backwards and forwards in history, marking capital's ongoing destruction of the city's old topography of slums while anticipating the final ruin of capitalism itself. He shared Benjamin's belief that, in the modern city, time as well as space was porous and susceptible to transition.

That the present consumerist dystopia and hope for a future communal utopia could coexist in the same social architecture made the arcades the perfect image for what Michael Löwy has called Benjamin's romantic

anarchism, 'a world-view characterised by a (more or less) radical critique
of industrial/bourgeois civilization in the name of pre-capitalist social,
cultural, ethical or religious values', that involved a 'nostalgic and desperate
attempt at re-enchantment of the world'.[34] Löwy situates Benjamin at
the centre of a network of anti-capitalist German-Jewish intellectuals
who, feeling no connection to an idealised medieval Germany, instead
looked to monastic communities of the past for a model of their future
anarchist utopia, which they located in a messianic era at the end of history.
Benjamin's outlook shared with Jewish messianism 'a revolutionary
catastrophist perspective of history, and a libertarian image of the Edenic
future'; instead of gradual reform, he sought an irruption of the historical
continuum as the precondition for a totally new society.[35]

Löwy's exposition of the network of philosophical correspondences that
led German Jews of the Munich circle to romantic anarchism is finally more
convincing than his assertion that these 'elective affinities' could have arisen
within this historical context alone. Given the growing internationalism of
anarchists after 1872 and the widespread millenarianism at the end of the
nineteenth century, it seems likely that a similar variety of romantic anarchism could well have arisen in other geographical or historical contexts.
I want to suggest that J. A. Andrews exhibits a fusion of anarchist ideals
with messianic utopianism similar to Benjamin's, albeit one rooted in theosophy rather than Jewish mysticism. Mark Hearn has demonstrated that,
throughout much of the 1890s, Andrews was strongly influenced by the
theosophical preaching of his friend John Dwyer, founder of Sydney's Active
Service Brigade and President of the Isis Lodge of the Theosophical Society
in Australasia. Dwyer's millenarian theosophical beliefs provided a vision
of a coming universal brotherhood of humanity that, when fused with
Andrews's anti-capitalism, resulted in a particular form of romantic anarchism calibrated to his colonial context.[36]

That the origin myths of theosophy should have appealed to Andrews is
understandable. As a colonial radical of British descent, Andrews was
excluded from the myth of an ideal community in his nation's past, not
unlike Benjamin. Whereas the latter would base his restorative vision of
a communal utopia on Johann Jakob Bachofen's descriptions of a prehis-
toric Golden Age, Andrews located his 'lost source of human liberation' in
pre-settler aboriginal society, a civilisation which, following vague theosophical precedents, he variously identified with either Ancient Egypt or
the mythical continents of Atlantis and Lemuria.[37] Benjamin saw the return
to a Golden Age as a break with history and modern temporality, but
he remained relatively uninterested in political geography or 'the international dimension of capitalism'; for Andrews, by contrast, the catastrophic
collapse of capitalism implied a post-imperial future with an entirely new
geospatial organisation:

[W]e are living on the crater of a volcano. Nothing in the remotest degree
approaching the same universality of the upheaval has been indicated since
the fall of the Roman Empire . . . We see a world about to crumble into ruins
at our feet . . . It is more than a cosmopolitan – it is a cosmical movement of
which we are not the motive power but the index.[38]

This connection between the cosmic and the cosmopolitan meant that
Australian rumblings could ripple out and grow into worldwide revolution.
Hearn argues that Andrews and Dwyer developed a dystopian image of the
capitalist state as the city of Babylon, an image of power that fascinated
them and reduced their own visions of utopia to a 'hazy fantasy',[39] but this
reading underestimates the detail with which Andrews repeatedly describes
the modern metropolis as a symbol of change. While 'The Triumph of
Freedom' critiques the centralisation of power in the State capitals, it also
proposes a peaceful and proactive reconstruction of the city along anarchist
principles:

New South Wales waited till her faulty and dangerous house fell about her
ears; and then, with brick-battered body, lay pondering new architecture
among the ruins. Victoria toilsomely built a new house, went to live in it, and
knocked the old hovel down without further inconvenience.[40]

Significantly, Andrews here reclaims urban renewal as a necessary part of
this evolutionary process, although he would later critique the redevelopment of London's slums as a mock remedy that merely displaced the suffering of slum tenants.[41] Nevertheless, this passage reveals that Andrews
did not seek to level all cities and restore a lost, pre-modern society but
rather, like Benjamin, tried 'to weave dialectical relationships between the
pre-capitalist past and the post-capitalist future, between archaic and
utopian harmony'.[42] The future utopia merely required a reorganisation of
city space to discharge the violence of state capitalism and reveal its hidden
communal destiny, a task that Andrews approached through his words
more than his deeds.

States of ruin: the city as (an)archive

The socio-historical forces that kept European cities in a condition of porosity had little to do with the unequal development of Melbourne; ruins
signified differently in Paris, France – the 'capital of the nineteenth century'
– than in the Paris of the South, an outpost of empire entirely unacquainted
with gothic cathedrals or crumbling abbeys. Still, as a text about ruins
that itself lies in a ruinous state, Benjamin's unfinished 'Arcades Project'
('*Passagen-werk*') provides both a formal and ideological model for understanding Andrews's utopia. As Graeme Gilloch notes, 'the ["Arcades

Project"] is best understood not as a description of the urban (text-about-city), but as itself fundamentally urban in character (text-as-city)'.[43] Andrews's utopia, 'The Triumph of Freedom', is similarly fragmented and incomplete: it exists in a single manuscript in the State Library of Victoria comprising a vague plot outline and a few completed chapters describing the revolution, followed, notably, by several false starts at depicting the reconstruction. Andrews could describe street violence and barricades in vivid detail, but he hesitated to predict the aftermath of revolution or trace the contours of a fully realised anarchist utopia; the revolutionary government, he notes, was not overthrown by force or 'terrorised into abdicating', but simply 'evaporated'.[44]

Hearn blames this lack of triumphal closure on the author's 'fatalism' and his 'siege mentality', noting that in general 'his imaginative response to the social and economic situation of the working class seemed to be more vividly stirred by the forces controlling workers, rather than by a vision of their liberation'.[45] I would instead argue that, unlike the vast number of contemporary utopias that articulate a clear social goal but are vague about the process of transition, 'The Triumph of Freedom' aims to foreground this process at the expense of any clearly articulated goals. The lacunae in 'The Triumph' represent the gap between Andrews's urge to provide an *abstract* utopia of compensatory fantasies in which present conditions are repaired, and his desire to write a *concrete* utopia of anticipated fulfilment in a 'radically other future', to use Ernst Bloch's distinction.[46] He could not complete his narrative of liberation because it sets out to describe a social revolution that is 'principally a series of evolutions, and, for the remainder, mostly a simple collapse of effete institutions . . . [T]he great change was effected without any of the sensational struggles and dramatic intrigues for personal or party power which characterised the revolutionary history of other Australian colonies.'[47] Following Kropotkin, Andrews frequently described the seamless transition to utopia as a natural, and therefore scientifically reasonable, process.

While he could not envision the liberation of property or the means of production generally, Andrews did imagine the workers' expropriation of the press as a first step toward utopia. In chapter two of 'The Triumph of Freedom' a member of the fictionalised anarchists' club recalls a thriving cooperative farm that 'had no elaborate machinery, yet they were able to construct a printing plant . . . and in short to give themselves a high civilisation' before the government taxed it away from them. Following the insurrection, the narrative gets only as far as envisioning the transformation of the 'Socialist press room' into a new 'State printing office' for the issuing of circulars, proclamations and manifestos essential to the creation of a new social order.[48] Although Andrews could not yet write his urban anarchist utopia, he could imagine the media apparatus necessary for its future creation. This emphasis on propaganda reflects his own radical practice:

Benjamin's *Arcades Project* may resemble a city in its disjointed architecture but Andrews's fragmentary texts were inscribed into the actual urban fabric of Sydney and Melbourne. He literally wrote in and on the city streets, disseminating propaganda through pamphlets, bill-posts and graffiti – what Benjamin would later call 'inconspicuous forms that better fit [literature's] influence in active communities than does the pretentious, universal gesture of the book'.[49] Through his bill-sticking campaigns which, Andrews boasted, were 'visible all over the city' and 'reported on in the daily papers', he rewrote the architecture of capitalism *in situ* – for instance, by pasting a bank with a poster bluntly reading, 'This is a house of robbery.'[50] True to form, in chapter one of 'The Triumph of Freedom' the anarchists counter their exclusion from the means of production by disseminating a 'Declaration vs. the Associated Capitalists':

> It is being circulated all over the place, and the people are sticking the copies on all the doors as fast as they get them. The whole city is being placarded. . . . It was printed on a sheet of gummed paper. . . .[51]

This desire to reconfigure the material city through print carries through into the spatial logic of his utopia. Early on in the narrative, the military surrounds discontented workers at the bank of the river by the new bridge at Studley Park, Melbourne, close to Queen's Wharf, the site of many a demonstration and stump speech in Andrews's day. Yet, for the climactic scene of revolution, he transposes the action to the theatre district, close by the arcade system but nowhere near the sites at which he and his fellow radicals actually assembled and agitated. Parks and public monuments were useful spaces for soapbox oratory, but for Andrews the downtown core was something more: it was *rewritable*. Andrews foresaw the coming revolution as primarily a form of information dissemination 'by speech and pen', and argued that publicising the inevitability of mass unemployment in the 1890s was, in fact, the only way to prevent any attendant rioting and bloodshed:[52] written descriptions of destruction, he felt, could forestall its actualisation. Indeed, the act of writing represented his ideal of mutual aid. In the appendix to his short story 'Arisen', Andrews exalts the experience of co-authorship, asserting that men who write together can stand only in the relation of 'thorough mutual confidence. In fact, the reason why so many prominent writers are Anarchists must be that they are familiar with the pleasure and advantage of Liberty, Equity and Fraternity amongst themselves.'[53]

Like Kropotkin, Andrews saw revolution as a means of achieving the free flow of opinion, and the city riot as prelude to a communications revolution. To him, the city straining under landlordism was like a spoiled typeset in need of reorganisation: using printers' terminology, he wrote that 'the Sydney streets resemble a form that has been "squabbled" and half "pied"' – that is to say, they resemble a scrambled-up typeset.[54] In a passage undoubtedly influenced by Edgar Allan Poe, he likens the social problem to a substitution cipher, bourgeois myths to typographical puzzles and the demystification of the proletariat to an act of cryptanalysis. These cabbalistic metaphors get at the root of his romantic anarchism. For Andrews, as for Benjamin, the contours of the future could be discovered only by deciphering the present, and not through descriptions of the ideal society. He stated in characteristically alphabetic imagery that the 'entire lesson of the present [has] been spelled out from word to letter' for the people to analyse, though they are 'liable to be led astray by constructive schemes'.[55] Although his arguments against property were replete with biological analogies and mathematical formulae for calculating the distribution of wealth, his concept of analysis at times appears closer to Poe's notion of literary ratiocination, in which texts are read for typographic clues or details that manifest themselves through ingenious acts of deduction, than to the scientism of Marx or Kropotkin. Andrews's insistence on analysing class relations by deciphering the hermetic text of the city can be seen as an instance of the 'restorative aspect' of romantic anarchism, in which '[t]hought focuses on the *restoration* of lost meanings, suppressed connections, and is often linked to a sense of redemption through language and through the reading of texts which reveal the hidden presence or traces of a Messianic epoch'.[56]

This translation of class struggle into exercises in typesetting and alphabetic substitution epitomised Andrews's revolutionary strategy: not to destroy the city but to disperse it textually. Thus, while the scrambling of his own utopian narrative could be explained away as a failure of imagination or archival entropy, I am rather inclined to read it as a cryptographic exercise, a strategic hesitation designed to clear a textual space between the remnants of the old colonial government and the blueprints for federation. He ultimately felt an anarchist society would arise only through permanent revolution, a collective project to reform all aspects of social life that no single-authored utopia could ever fully convey. Far from offering a satisfying conclusion, 'The Triumph of Freedom' must dissipate in order to be more easily integrated into the fabric of the newly liberated city, for Andrews struggled to see any future for anarchism beyond his own daily acts of revolution. Instead of the end of history, the MAC witnessed its own dissolution as its membership drifted into the ASL, which slid steadily towards parliamentary socialism as the new century approached.[57] Two years after federation, Andrews died of tuberculosis in Melbourne Hospital. The federalists would soon enough realise their blueprint for utopia in the rational geometries of Canberra; the anarchist vision, by contrast, survived only as 'disruptive traces', a collection of textual fragments destined for the archives.

And yet, as anticipatory fossils, the remaining fragments of Andrews's utopia prefigure the spectral state itself as an archive of ruin, disrupting the archive's function within national and colonial projects. Thomas Richards has described the archive in this period as a utopian repository of longings for national coherence. In the 1870s, he writes, the British imperial archive 'was not a building, nor even a collection of texts, but the collectively imagined junction of all that was known or knowable, a fantastic representation of an epistemological master pattern, a virtual focal point for the heterogeneous local knowledge of metropolis and empire'. This imperial master pattern was identified not with Egypt or Lemuria, but with Tibet, 'an imagined community that united archival institutions and persons in one hieratic archive-state'.[58] If the figure of the archive could contain the empire's utopian longings for coherence, then its destruction in a remote Australian outpost could prefigure an anarchist utopia that would dissolve both colony and empire. Andrews imagined the archive's destruction while writing at the public library under police surveillance: he wrote of 'the forcible throwing open of public museums and libraries' alongside 'the sudden demolition of buildings . . . and their re-erection in fitting localities as dwellings and workshops for those who now live in hovels'.[59] The question of the tenanted poor linked his anarchism and an-archival drive: indeed, his own collection of writings was not housed under a single *arkheîon*, but dispersed about the city, the continent and, through his contacts in the radical press, the world. Like Benjamin's arcades, Fourier's street-galleries or the working-class hovels of Melbourne's back alleys, Andrews's street writings inverted the logic of interior and exterior that is central to the archive, refusing to replicate the logic of home and property on which it depends.[60] Ironically, many of his writings finally found a permanent home in the state archives, safer lodgings than the author himself ever secured. The 1889 issue of *La Revolte* in which he first exposed Melbourne's 'obscure and foul passages [*passages obscures et puants*]' ended up in the Bibliotècque Nationale, where, decades later, Benjamin might well have seen it while gathering fragments of urban lore for his *Passagen-werk*.[61]

Here it becomes necessary to extend the definition of the romantic anarchist to include experimentation with revolutionary media. For the Benjamin of *One-Way Street*, those media were advertising and the cinema, both of which relied on a montage aesthetic borrowed from the anarchist's leaflets and placards. Andrews, too, believed that reason was the solution to the social problem, and that only through an 'individualistic medium' could reason 'transform itself into action'. He published *The Anarchist* (1891) on a printing press he fashioned from cigar-box wood and a tobacco tin, and claimed to have invented several new forms of inscription, including a process for inscribing patterns on walls using 'luminous photography', a 'poetical machine to consist of movable bars of rubber type' for producing rhymes with the turn of a handle, a system for carrying ink in matchboxes instead of a bottle, and a machine for efficiently 'casting and setting up type, one letter at a time'. He even imagined (one hopes with Swiftian irony) 'a machine for writing penny dreadfuls' that, given a single work as input, 'will produce from that one hundred and forty-four distinct and different

MSS., all superior to the original'.[62] By reinventing the tools of writing, he was also changing the future conditions of the archive.

After all, the archive is about the future as much as it is about the past: '[t]he technical structure of the *archiving* archive also determines the structure of the *archivable* content even in its very coming into existence and in its relation to the future'.[63] The future orientation of the historical archive suggests the problems Andrews faced in completing his utopian novel, and which confront the reader who encounters it today preserved in archive, isolated from the city streets. It is precisely because 'The Triumph of Freedom' remains forever stalled in the transitional phase between destruction and reconstruction that it perfectly captures the fleeting dream of an anarchist alternative to Australian colonial society at the precise moment that dream retreated before the advance of federation and national capitalism. Any attempt to reconstruct his narrative as a blueprint would risk transforming it into an abstract utopia more static and complete than that which Andrews, or any romantic anarchist, ever envisioned.

Notes

I gratefully acknowledge the assistance of the Social Sciences and Humanities Research Council of Canada, the University of Melbourne archives and the Merrifield Collection of the State Library of Victoria.

1   A. Maack, ' "It's All Contrary" – Utopian Projections in the Antipodes', *Antipodes* (December 2000), p. 125.
2   J. Docker, *The Nervous Nineties: Australian Cultural Life in the 1890s*.
3   D. Andrade, *The Melbourne Riots and How Harry Holdfast and His Friends Emancipated the Workers. A Realistic Novel*, p. 11.
4   S. A. Rosa, *The Coming Terror, or, The Australian Revolution: A Romance of the Twentieth Century*, pp. 29, 31.
5   *Ibid*. p. 34.
6   *Ibid*. n.p.
7   B. Mansfield, 'The Socialism of William Morris in England and in Australia', *Historical Studies*, 7 (November 1956), p. 289.
8   P. J. O'Farrell, 'The Australian Socialist League and the Labour Movement, 1887–1891', *Historical Studies*, 8:30 (May 1958), pp. 153–4.
9   B. James, *Anarchism and State Violence in Sydney and Melbourne, 1886–1896: An Argument about Australian Labour History*, pp. 68–9. I owe special thanks to Dr James for this thorough account of the lives and debates of the Melbourne Anarchists, his extensive editions of the writings of early Australian radicals, and his assistance in tracking down Andrews's sundry writings.
10 B. James, 'J. A. Andrews, 1865–1903: A Brief Biography', in J. A. Andrews, *What is Communism? and Other Anarchist Essays on 1889*, Melbourne, B. James (ed.), p. 12.
11 B. Scates, *A New Australia: Citizenship, Radicalism and the First Republic*, pp. 117–35.

12 J. A. Andrews, 'The Triumph of Freedom: A Prospective History of the Social Revolution in Victoria' (unpublished ms., 1887?), p. 5 (subsequent inferences: 'Triumph').

13 Scates, *A New Australia*, p. 121; 'Triumph', p. 5.

14 J. A. Andrews, 'The Single Tax', *Australian Radical* (April 1890), reprinted in B. James (ed.), *Reader of Australian Anarchism 1886–1896*.

15 J. A. Andrews, notes to 'Triumph'. The notes are in an itemised list of plot points in chapter 1: 'Evolution' on p. 5 of the manuscript, before the table of contents proper, after which pagination begins again at p. 1 with chapter 1: 'Trouble Brewing'. However, the table of contents, which Andrews seems to have written before the novel itself, still lists chapter 1 as 'Evolution'.

16 N. B. Albinski, 'Australian Utopian and Dystopian Fiction', *Australian Literary Studies*, 13:1 (May 1987), p. 16.

17 J. A. Andrews, 'A Cry from Australia', *Freedom*, 4:45 (August 1890).

18 J. A. Andrews, 'The Paris Commune', *Australian Radical* (16 March 1889), in *What is Communism?*, pp. 87–8.

19 'Triumph', p. 31.

20 J. A. Andrews, 'Melbourne Notes', *Australian Radical* (8 June 1889), in *What is Communism?*, p. 111.

21 J. A. Andrews, 'Revolutionary Melbourne', *Freedom* (June 1889), in *What is Communism?*, p. 22.

22 G. Davison and D. Dunstan, '"This Moral Pandemonium": Images of Low Life', in G. Davison, D. Dunstan and C. McConville (eds), *The Outcasts of Melbourne: Essays in Social History*, p. 43.

23 J. A. Andrews, 'Australia's Slums', *Tocsin* (5 September 1901), in *What is Communism?*, pp. 154–5.

24 Andrews, 'Australia's Slums', *Tocsin* (29 August 1901), in *What is Communism?*, p. 152.

25 W. Benjamin, 'Paris, Capital of the Nineteenth Century', in *Reflections: Essays, Aphorisms, Autobiographical Writings*, ed. P. Demetz, trans. E. Jephcott, p. 162.

26 B. Lindner, 'The Passagen-Werk, the Berliner Kindheit, and the Archaeology of the "Recent Past"', trans. C. B. Ludtke, *New German Critique*, 39, Second Special Issue on Walter Benjamin (Autumn 1986), p. 32.

27 G. Gilloch, *Myth and Metropolis: Walter Benjamin and the City*, p. 25. For a discussion of Fourier's connection to anarchism, see E. S. Mason, 'Fourier and Anarchism', *Quarterly Journal of Economics*, 42:2 (February 1928), pp. 228–62.

28 W. Benjamin, 'Naples', in *Reflections*, p. 171.

29 Andrew McCann has compellingly argued that the bohemian journalist Marcus Clarke anticipated Benjamin's *Arcades Project* 'as soon as he set foot inside the Royal Arcade' in 1869, foreseeing 'its gradual relegation to the tawdry, exhausted world of outmoded consumption'; in A. McCann, *Marcus Clarke's Bohemia: Literature and Modernity in Colonial Melbourne*, p. 85. There is perhaps some danger in universalising Benjamin's critique, which does not invest the Parisian arcades with timeless values, but rather treats them as allegories of an historically – and, I would add, geographically – specific process of commodification.

30 M. Löwy, *Redemption and Utopia: Jewish Libertarian Thought in Central Europe: A Study in Elective Affinity*, trans. F. H. Heaney, p. 100. On Benjamin's class status, see Gilloch, *Myth and Metropolis*, p. 33.
31 V. Burgin, *In/Different Spaces: Place and Memory in Visual Culture*, pp. 155–6.
32 Andrews, 'Australia's Slums', *Tocsin* (31 October 1901), in *What is Communism*, p. 187.
33 Andrews, 'Australia's Slums', *Tocsin* (7 November 1901), in *What is Communism?*, p. 189.
34 Löwy, *Redemption and Utopia*, p. 28.
35 *Ibid.* p. 101.
36 M. G. Hearn, 'Hard Cash: John Dwyer and his Contemporaries, 1890–1914' (PhD dissertation, University of Sydney, 2000).
37 *Ibid.* p. 247. For an account of Benjamin's debt to Bachofen, see Löwy, *Redemption and Utopia*, p. 117.
38 J. Kraniauskas, 'Beware Mexican Ruins! "One-Way Street" and the Colonial Unconscious', in A. Benjamin and P. Osborne (eds), *Walter Benjamin's Philosophy: Destruction and Experience*, p. 143. J. A. Andrews, 'Revolution and Physical Force (A Reply to W.R. Winspear)', *Australian Radical* (July–August 1889), in *What is Communism?*, p. 69.
39 Hearn, 'Hard Cash', p. 237.
40 'Triumph', pp. 3–4.
41 Andrews, 'Australia's Slums', in *Tocsin* (31 October 1901), pp. 185–6.
42 Löwy, *Redemption and Utopia*, p. 117.
43 Gilloch, *Myth and Metropolis*, p. 94.
44 'Triumph', p. 5.
45 Hearn, 'Hard Cash', pp. 241–2.
46 For a broader explanation of Bloch's terms in the context of spatial form, see P. Wegner, *Imaginary Communities: Utopia, the Nation, and the Spatial Histories of Modernity*, p. 21.
47 'Triumph', p. 2.
48 *Ibid.* pp. 19, 72.
49 W. Benjamin, *One-Way Street, and Other Writings*, trans. E. Jephcott and K. Shorter, p. 61.
50 Andrews, 'Melbourne Notes' *Australian Radical* (10 August 1889), in *What is Communism?*, p. 130; 'Some Small Matters', *Tocsin* (28 June 1900).
51 'Triumph', p. 8.
52 Andrews, 'Melbourne Notes', *Australian Radical* (9 March 1889), in *What is Communism?*, p. 86.
53 J. A. Andrews, 'Arisen', *Temple Mystic and Other Poems*, p. 177.
54 J. A. Andrews, 'Sydney and Thereabouts', *Tocsin* (26 September 1901), in *What is Communism?*, p. 166.
55 Andrews, 'Australia's Slums', *Tocsin* (26 September 1901), in *What is Communism?*, p. 166; 'Revolution and Physical Force', pp. 60–1.
56 A. Rabinbach, 'Between Enlightenment and Apocalypse: Benjamin, Bloch and Modern German Jewish Messianism', *New German Critique*, 34 (Winter 1985), pp. 84–5.
57 O'Farrell, 'The Australian Socialist League', pp. 164–5.

58 T. Richards, *The Imperial Archive: Knowledge and the Fantasy of Empire*, p. 11.
59 Andrews, 'Melbourne Notes' *Australian Radical* (28 September 1889), in *What is Communism?*, p. 145; 'Revolution and Physical Force', p. 71.
60 J. Derrida, *Archive Fever: A Freudian Impression*, p. 11 and *passim*.
61 J. A. Andrews, 'La Vie Sociale de Melbourne', *La Revolte*, 2:31 (14–20 April 1889), p. 1.
62 J. A. Andrews, 'Reason and the Social Question', Andrews Papers, Merrifield Collection, La Trobe Library, reprinted in *Reader of Australian Anarchism 1886–1896*; ' "Anarchist" Andrews as Inventor', *The Bulletin* (31 March 1900), 'The Red Page' (n.p.).
63 Derrida, *Archive Fever*, p. 17.

References

Albinski, N. B., 'Australian Utopian and Dystopian Fiction', *Australian Literary Studies*, 13:1 (May 1987), pp. 15–28.

Andrade, D., *The Melbourne Riots and How Harry Holdfast and His Friends Emancipated the Workers. A Realistic Novel* (Melbourne: The Author, 1892).

Andrews, J. A., 'The Triumph of Freedom: A Prospective History of the Social Revolution in Victoria', Andrews papers, Merrifield Collection, La Trobe Library (unpublished ms., 1887?).

——. 'Arisen', in John Arthur Andrews, *Temple Mystic and Other Poems* (Ballarat: F.W. Niven & Co., 1888), pp. 155–81.

——. 'Melbourne Notes', *Australian Radical* (22 December 1888 to 28 September 1889), in *What is Communism?*, pp. 76–148.

——. 'The Paris Commune', *Australian Radical* (16 March 1889), in *What is Communism?*, pp. 87–8.

——. 'La Vie Sociale de Melbourne', *La Revolte*, 2:31 (14–20 April 1889), pp. 1–2.

——. 'Revolutionary Melbourne', *Freedom* (June 1889), in *What is Communism?*, pp. 22–4.

——. 'Revolution and Physical Force (A Reply to W.R. Winspear)', *Australian Radical* (July–August 1889), in *What is Communism?*, pp. 59–71.

——. 'The Single Tax', *Australian Radical* (April 1890), in B. James (ed.), *A Reader of Australian Anarchism 1886–1896* (Canberra: B. James, 1979), www.takver.com/history/raa/raa14.htm, accessed 28 January 2007.

——.'A Cry from Australia', *Freedom*, 4:45 (August 1890), available at http://dwardmac.pitzer.edu/Anarchist_Archives/journals/freedom/freedom4_45.html, accessed 20 December 2007.

——. ' "Anarchist" Andrews as Inventor', *The Bulletin* (31 March 1900), 'The Red Page' (n.p.).

——. 'Some Small Matters', *Tocsin* (28 June 1900), available at www.takver.com/history/ aasv/aasv_app1.htm#june28, accessed 14 March 2007.

——. 'Australia's Slums', *Tocsin* (29 August 1901 to 7 November 1901), in *What is Communism?*, pp. 151–90.

——. 'Sydney and Thereabouts', *Tocsin* (26 September 1901), in *What is Communism?*, p. 166.

——. *What is Communism? and Other Anarchist Essays on 1889, Melbourne*, ed. Bob James (Prahran: Backyard Press, 1984).

——. 'Reason and the Social Question', Andrews Papers, Merrifield Collection, La Trobe Library, reprinted in *Reader of Australian Anarchism 1886–1896*, www.takver.com/history/raa/raa25.htm, accessed 12 February 2007.

Benjamin, W., *One-Way Street, and Other Writings*, trans. E. Jephcott and K. Shorter (London: NLB, 1979).

——. 'Naples', in *Reflections: Essays, Aphorisms, Autobiographical Writings*, ed. Peter Demetz, trans. E. Jephcott (New York: Schocken Books, 1986). pp. 163–73.

——. 'Paris, Capital of the Nineteenth Century', in *Reflections: Essays, Aphorisms, Autobiographical Writings*, ed. Peter Demetz, trans. E. Jephcott (New York: Schocken Books, 1986). pp. 146–62.

——. *Reflections: Essays, Aphorisms, Autobiographical Writings*, ed. Peter Demetz, trans. E. Jephcott (New York: Schocken Books, 1986).

——. *The Arcades Project*, ed. Rolf Tiedemann, trans. H. Eiland and K. McLaughlin (Cambridge, MA: Belknap Press of Harvard University Press, 1999).

Burgin, V., *In/Different Spaces: Place and Memory in Visual Culture* (Berkeley: University of California Press, 1996).

Davison, G. and D. Dunstan, ' "This Moral Pandemonium": Images of Low Life', in G. Davison, D. Dunstan and C. McConville (eds), *The Outcasts of Melbourne: Essays in Social History* (Sydney: Allen and Unwin, 1985), pp. 29–57.

Derrida, J., *Archive Fever: A Freudian Impression* (Chicago: University of Chicago Press, 1996).

Docker, J., *The Nervous Nineties: Australian Cultural Life in the 1890s* (Melbourne: Oxford University Press, 1991).

Gilloch, G., *Myth and Metropolis: Walter Benjamin and the City* (Cambridge, UK: Polity Press in association with Blackwell Publishers, 1996).

Hearn, M. G., 'Hard Cash: John Dwyer and his Contemporaries, 1890–1914' (PhD dissertation, University of Sydney, 2000).

James, B., *Anarchism and State Violence in Sydney and Melbourne, 1886–1896: An Argument about Australian Labour History* (Broadmeadow, New South Wales: Newey & Beath Printers Pty. Ltd, 1986).

Kraniauskas, J., 'Beware Mexican Ruins! "One-Way Street" and the Colonial Unconscious', in A. Benjamin and P. Osborne (eds), *Walter Benjamin's Philosophy: Destruction and Experience* (London: Routledge, 1994), pp. 139–54.

Lindner, B., 'The Passagen-Werk, the Berliner Kindheit, and the Archaeology of the "Recent Past" ', trans. C. B. Ludtke, *New German Critique*, 39, Second Special Issue on Walter Benjamin (Autumn 1986), pp. 25–46.

Löwy, M., *Redemption and Utopia: Jewish Libertarian Thought in Central Europe: A Study in Elective Affinity*, trans. F. H. Heaney (London: Athlone Press, 1992).

Maack, A., ' "It's All Contrary" – Utopian Projections in the Antipodes', *Antipodes* (December 2000), pp. 123–8.

Mansfield, B., 'The Socialism of William Morris in England and in Australia', *Historical Studies*, 7 (November 1956), pp. 271–90.

Mason, E. S. 'Fourier and Anarchism', *Quarterly Journal of Economics*, 42:2 (February 1928), pp. 228–62.

McCann, A., *Marcus Clarke's Bohemia: Literature and Modernity in Colonial Melbourne* (Carlton, Vic.: Melbourne University Press, 2004).

O'Farrell, P. J., 'The Australian Socialist League and the Labour Movement, 1887–1891', *Historical Studies*, 8:30 (May 1958), pp. 152–65.

Rabinbach, A., 'Between Enlightenment and Apocalypse: Benjamin, Bloch and Modern German Jewish Messianism', *New German Critique*, 34 (Winter 1985), pp. 78–128.

Richards, T., *The Imperial Archive: Knowledge and the Fantasy of Empire* (New York: Verso, 1993).

Rosa, S. A., *The Coming Terror, or, The Australian Revolution: A Romance of the Twentieth Century* (Sydney: S.A. Rosa, 1894).

Scates, B., *A New Australia: Citizenship, Radicalism and the First Republic* (Melbourne: Cambridge University Press, 1997).

Wegner, P., *Imaginary Communities: Utopia, the Nation, and the Spatial Histories of Modernity* (Berkeley: University of California Press, 2002).

PART IV

Free love: anarchist politics and utopian desire

Speaking desire: anarchism and free love as utopian performance in fin de siècle Britain

The most beautiful thing around or above
Is Love, true Love:
The beautiful thing can more beautiful be
If its life be free.

Bind the most beautiful thing there is,
And the serpents hiss;
Free from its fetters the beautiful thing,
And the angels sing.

(Louisa Bevington, 1895[1])

Free love, for many anarchists in late nineteenth-century Britain, was integral to any vision of a transformed society. A better world was on the agenda, and how to bring it about was the subject of intense anarchist debate. Then as now, anarchism was often characterised negatively as utopian, meaning unrealistic, unachievable. Anarchists often responded by trying to dissociate anarchism from utopianism, insisting that it was not 'an artificially concocted, fanciful theory of reconstructing the world' but based on 'truth and reality'.[2] Tolstoy and Kropotkin, whose ideas inspired several utopian communities in Britain, criticised such experimentation as a diversion from the wider struggle for change.[3]

Others, however, saw things differently:

> [P]ropaganda cannot be diversified enough if we want to touch all. We want it to pervade and penetrate all the utterances of life, social and political, domestic and artistic, educational and recreational. There should be propaganda by word and action, the platform and the press, the street corner, the workshop and the domestic circle, acts of revolt, and the example of our lives as freemen.[4]

This more inclusive approach to anarchist practice, with its emphasis on process, corresponds with the more dynamic and open-ended conceptions of anarchism – and utopianism – explored in this chapter. 'Utopia', says Ruth Levitas, 'is the expression of desire for a better way of being'. If, as she and others have argued, utopianism is the education of desire, then the propagandising of utopia, the processes of educating desire, may themselves be utopian, transformative, prefiguring a different world.[5] And desire, as queer theorist Elspeth Probyn says about sexual desire, is 'a method of doing things, of getting places'.[6] For utopian theorists and theorists of utopia, desire in its broad sense is both method and movement. Charlotte Wilson, writing in 1886 about anarchist revolution as a movement away from the darkness of the past and 'into the darkness of the future . . . toward the beckoning of a light of hope', evokes an image of anarchism as exploration, direction and destination: a form of utopian desire.[7]

Those anarchists in fin de siècle Britain who spoke out for free love believed that the transformation of intimate relationships was essential to social transformation, neither attainable without the other. They saw its practice as a form of demonstrative politics: a rehearsal or experimentation with new ways to live, an assertion that another world was possible. The main argument of this chapter is that just as the practice of free love can be a form of speech, a text of desire, so, conversely, to speak of free love can itself be the enactment or performance of utopian desire.

The trajectory of the chapter is from free love as a subject of private conviction in the 1880s to free love as an intrinsically public practice by the turn of the century. It begins by examining how a reluctant Charlotte Wilson eventually found a route to publicise her critique of marriage, and argues that she played an unacknowledged part in the process of opening up the discussion of free love. It goes on to show how subsequent anarchist debates on the subject interacted with debates in wider society, framed by the reporting of high profile events which helped shape public attitudes toward the new social movements of the period. Finally, a range of examples illustrates the richness and diversity that increasingly characterised the theory and practice of free love. Its advocates queered the pitch of normality, using rhetorical strategies that denaturalised traditional ideas and institutions of gender and sexuality. Some went further, and turned themselves from sexual spectacle into exemplars of a transformed sexual politics.

'Free love' is not a fixed concept but means different things in different contexts, and must be understood by what it is set against. Its advocates oppose it to its dystopian other, unfree love – itself a mutable and historically specific term. In the 1880s and 90s, its opponents represented free love as itself the dystopian other to an idyll of marriage and the family, an idyll teetering precariously on its pedestal as love, sex, marriage, reproduction and the relationship, if any, between them, became topics of increasing public concern.

Principle and reticence in the 1880s: Charlotte Wilson

> In the relations between men and women as in all others, I cry for freedom as the first step – and after freedom, knowledge, that each may decide for himself or herself how that freedom can best be used. (Charlotte Wilson, 1885)[8]

The old cliché that the Victorians never mentioned sex has been replaced by another: that Victorian society was saturated with discussions of it. The interesting questions, though, concern who spoke about it, what they could say, where and to whom – and, most neglected because hardest to answer, what effect did they have? The struggle to speak out on sexuality, especially for women, was about far more than free speech – it embodied a fundamental challenge to existing gender power relations.

Charlotte Wilson was a central figure in the emergence of English anarchism in the 1880s. At the time, open discussion of free love was rare, despite ongoing feminist campaigns around marriage law reform. Wilson (who refused to rely on her husband's money) argued for the importance of women's economic independence but was reluctant to speak out openly on sexual matters, citing the 'unclean', 'unhealthy' sensitivity which resulted from women's ignorance. Contemporary society, she thought, was too 'morbid' to deal with such issues.[9] Her reticence meant that her contribution to the free love debate has gone largely unrecognised.

In 1884, Karl Pearson, the socialist statistician, invited Wilson to speak at the new Men and Women's Club, founded for the private discussion of subjects to do with sex 'from the historical and scientific standpoint'.[10] She declined, and the first paper given was Pearson's 'The Woman's Question'. Although Wilson did not attend the meeting, she commented at length on this paper in her private correspondence with Pearson.

Motherhood, she argued, should be freely chosen. Many women, like her own mother (and, by implication, herself), were unsuited for it, and in a free society the majority of women might well choose not to have children. In any case, '[c]hildren apart – it is an intolerable impertinence that Church or State or society in any official form should venture to interfere with lovers. If we were not accustomed to such a thing it would appear unutterably disgusting.' Friendship between men and women is valuable in itself, and a woman who can select a lover from among her friends is more capable of choosing wisely. Only exceptionally, she adds, would free women want more than one lover.[11]

When Pearson asked her to present these arguments at the Club, she refused, pleading the mental strain of dealing with 'matters so trying to overstrung and unhealthy nerves'. But, she asked, is it even necessary to talk about such things? 'Have you not noticed that men and women of the New Society which is struggling into being within the old, naturally fall into healthy relations of cordial equality without very much theorising?' She concludes that she would rather work for political and economic freedom, from which true sexual freedom will follow.[12] Although that was the standard line on sex put forward by many socialists and anarchists, her comments are striking for their emphasis on everyday practice rather than theory as a way to change the relations between men and women; her letters to Pearson repeatedly insist on the interconnection of personal and political issues.

Pearson then gave another paper at the Club, entitled 'Socialism and Sex'. This seems to have incorporated verbatim passages from Wilson's letter, and when reproduced as a pamphlet it included the footnote: 'Some of the above remarks we owe to a woman friend; they express our own views in truer words than we should have found for ourselves.' A subsequent edition refers to the letter of 'a friend' – sex unspecified. Later versions fail to acknowledge Wilson's contribution at all.[13]

One of Pearson's purposes in setting up the Club had been to gain access to women's thoughts on sex questions: a kind of raw material for investigation.[14] From that perspective, citing a woman's letter in his pamphlet draws attention to this scarce source material. But then why obscure it in subsequent editions? Possibly as Pearson became better known he became unwilling to acknowledge women's contributions to his work. Perhaps this is an instance of the process of the male scientific investigator distancing himself from the female object of inquiry. Whatever the reason, there is no record of Wilson protesting Pearson's increasingly cavalier appropriation of her words.

Wilson believed at the time that anarchists should publish anonymously, signing herself in print as 'An English Anarchist'.[15] If she found it too stressful to speak publicly on sexual matters, such anonymity must have made it easier, and in 1885, soon after her exchange with Pearson, she helped to create a forum for debate in *The Anarchist*, a newspaper edited by Henry Seymour. Kropotkin joined them on the editorial committee, before leaving with Wilson to found the journal *Freedom*. Rumour has it that at this time Wilson and Kropotkin (who was also married) became lovers. Whether or not this was so, Kropotkin disapproved of public discussion of sexual matters, believing that men and women should work these out between themselves.[16] But under Wilson's editorship, *Freedom*, though concentrating on economic and political analysis, did make space for questions of sex and marriage as well.

The first time Wilson addresses these is – remarkably – in her review of 'Socialism and Sex' by 'K. P.' (i.e. Pearson). In a sort of multiple ventriloquism, Wilson's review quotes Pearson's unattributed quotations from her. This way she can discuss and develop her own ideas without explicitly acknowledging them as such. Her critique of marriage is more vehement than before: she refers to the torture, despair, pain and 'horrible degradation of human dignity' of 'the existing hypocritical and unnatural sexual relations'. It is not just state interference that is 'disgusting'; marriage itself is unnatural and unhealthy, contaminating all relationships between men and women. Expanding her earlier ideas, she urges the need to envision a different future. She rejects Pearson's proto-eugenicist views on state-regulated motherhood, arguing that social and reproductive freedom for women will transform gender relations: free love is part of a wider conception of a natural, healthy social world. Having, rather unconvincingly, claimed

Pearson as an anarchist, Wilson ends by justifying his right (and so, indirectly, her own) to speak about sex, as 'one who with clean hands and pure
heart, dares to scale heights of truth, and to approach every side of life with
the reverence of sincerity.'[17]

A year later an attack on marriage appeared in the *Westminster Review*'s
'Independent' section, reserved for controversial pieces. Its author, Mona
Caird (later a well-known novelist) was a feminist freethinker and radical
individualist associated with the Men and Women's Club. Her article
includes arguments and examples taken from Pearson; the final part extrap-
olates from his (i.e. Wilson's) views on how the relations between the sexes
might be transformed. 'First of all', Caird writes, 'we must set up an ideal,
undismayed by what will seem its Utopian impossibility.' Beginning with
an argument for 'free marriage' as a private, dissoluble contract, she draws
on evolutionary theory to suggest that, guided by science, limitless utopian
possibilities lie ahead. 'It will be found that men and women as they increase
in complexity can enter into a numberless variety of relationships . . . adding
to their powers indefinitely and thence to their emotions and experience.'[18]
Although this is sufficiently vague to be capable of different interpretations,
it could certainly be taken to imply that the 'numberless variety of relationships' includes sexual ones.

Caird's critique of marriage sparked off a major public debate when the
conservative *Daily Telegraph* relayed it under the headline: 'Is Marriage a
Failure?' 'The marriage controversy', as it became popularly known, was
widely taken up in the mainstream press. Thousands of readers responded,
filling correspondence columns for months with stories of unhappy and
desperate marriages.[19] All this gave Charlotte Wilson another opportunity
to return to 'Pearson's' ideas in a front-page *Freedom* editorial. Encouraged
by the widespread dissatisfaction with marriage, Wilson sought to extend
the critique: 'If the kernel [of society] may even be suspected of being
unsound, what of the whole nut?' Although women had benefited from
some recent legal and social changes, she argued, most still faced the unsat-
isfactory alternatives of chattel slavery in the home or wage slavery outside
it. Even if laws were changed, conventions defied, economic independence
gained, it would not be enough. She concluded:

> Women who are awake to a consciousness of their human dignity have every-
> thing to gain, because they have nothing to lose, by a Social Revolution. It is
> possible to conceive a tolerably intelligent man advocating palliative measures
> and gradual reform; but a woman who is not a Revolutionist is a fool.[20]

If marriage was the kernel of existing society, free love was arguably the
kernel of a new one. The marriage controversy focused primarily on the
wrongs of marriage, rather than the alternatives, but it helped open up
wider questions for public debate during the following decade, and Wilson's
ideas played a part in that process.

Sexual anarchy in the 1890s

> A teaching which would turn society into groups of harlots. (Lord Egerton, 1898)[21]

By the 1890s, anarchism, socialism and feminism were on the rise, prompting many anxious commentators to connect sexual and political dangerousness. Sexual anarchy was not just a metaphor: the fears and fascinations that the term evokes can be linked to public perceptions of increasingly visible anarchist activity.[22] Anarchists were responsible for a number of bombings and political assassinations in mainland Europe, and Britain, then something of a centre for international anarchism, was gripped by an 'anarchist panic': riots and strikes, bomb outrages and assassination attempts were all attributed to anarchist conspiracies. Scotland Yard set up its Special Branch to deal foremost with the dual menace of Fenianism and anarchism. Before long it seemed that no anarchist gathering was complete without a plain-clothes policeman taking notes and a reporter hoping for scandal; it was at this period that the stereotype of the anarchist with a black cloak and a bomb was propagated.[23]

Newspapers, novels, cartoons and learned articles represented anarchist men as mad bombers, deluded intellectuals or sensation-seeking aesthetes. Women tended to be characterised sexually: de-sexed fanatics like 'Red Virgin' Louise Michel; sexualised sirens with disordered morals and disorderly dress; or puzzlingly 'feminine' and normal-seeming. Anarchist advocacy of free love was seen as at best an excuse for promiscuity, and the women either seduced into this by unscrupulous men or themselves no better than prostitutes aiming to degrade all women.[24] Such images may perversely have contributed to the large audiences for anarchist women speakers, and to such episodes as the arrival of prurient sightseers demanding to view the women at Whiteway, an anarchist community in rural Gloucestershire.[25] The repeated association of anarchism with sexual licentiousness meant that anarchists were often forced, however reluctantly, to take a position on the subject. Anarchist women in particular had little choice but to address questions of sexuality: their very identification as *women* anarchists was already a form of sexual spectacle.

But they were not the only ones seen as a threat to sexual order. A more overt metropolitan subculture of male homosexuality caused alarm, as did the 'New Woman' phenomenon, then in its heyday. 'New Women' and 'effeminate men' were rhetorically linked with social and sexual 'anarchy' and actual anarchism. To its enemies, anarchism meant political and social chaos, and sexual freedom in turn would lead to anarchism – the destruction of all order. Anarchists, on the other hand, argued that chaos, disorder and immorality characterised the system that they aimed to undermine or overthrow, and that anarchism heralded a new order in sexual and social relations.

Sex and marriage were in any case becoming decidedly hot topics. The argument that marriage was often no more than licensed prostitution was commonplace among feminists and marriage reformers, as well as the anarchists who wanted to abolish it altogether. Most socialist and feminist groups, fearing the negative publicity that would damage their campaigning, endeavoured to dissociate their critiques of marriage from any suggestion of sexual irregularity. But many anarchists, women especially, saw free love as the basis of a wider struggle around issues of sexuality and gender, central to a critique of an unjust and authoritarian society. For them, it was not a subject for silence. The challenge was to change the terms of the debate.

Many located the discussion firmly within a feminist framework, and saw free love as part of an interconnected struggle around such issues as freedom of sexual expression, sex education, contraception, childcare, and women's economic and social independence. Although rejection of the state, its laws and institutions, should in theory include rejection of marriage, there was no consensus among anarchists about what this actually involved; the term 'free love' was used with a range of meanings, including monogamous but dissoluble partnerships, non-exclusive 'sexual varietism' and even – occasionally – passionate but non-sexual relationships.

However, although in theory the call for free love could create a space to speak of same-sex love, most discussion was strongly heteronormative; homosexuality, if mentioned at all, was usually seen as an unfortunate medical condition. The most notable exception to the general silence came from Edward Carpenter, who in 1895 published *Homogenic Love in a Free Society*, arguing that same-sex love was natural and socially progressive, and should not be persecuted.[26] But shortly afterward, amidst massive publicity, Oscar Wilde was tried and imprisoned for homosexuality; the spectacle intimidated and silenced many writers and publishers.

Freedom, though, ran an editorial attacking Wilde's persecutors as hypocritical and unjust, and published an article by Carpenter defending same-sex love. This suggested a more inclusive definition of free love, arguing that 'there can be no truly moral relations between people unless they *are* free'.[27] Although he did not spell it out in this article, for Carpenter free love included physical love. He lived openly with his male lover and argued against silence on sexual matters; in the aftermath of Wilde's downfall, few gay men in Britain showed such courage.

The Wilde case was only the first of several episodes giving a high profile to 'sexual anarchy'. Free love hit the headlines again in 1895, after Edith Lanchester, an activist in the Social Democratic Federation (SDF), announced to her respectable middle-class family that she was entering a free union with James Sullivan, an Irish factory worker. Outraged, her father and brothers had her forcibly incarcerated in a mental asylum. The doctor who committed her cited her socialism, her attachment to a 'lower class' man and her belief in free love – 'social suicide', he called it – as evidence of insanity, while her father claimed madness had been brought on by over-education. As the more uninhibited of her political comrades paraded outside the asylum, sounding trumpets and singing the Red Flag, influential friends worked behind the scenes, and amidst worldwide publicity – which can only have been boosted by the case's similarity to the plot of a gothic thriller – Lanchester was released. Many socialists, including some of her SDF colleagues, thought she had brought their cause into disrepute, and a number of former friends now ostracised her. The socialist press, while denouncing her incarceration, disapproved of her actions. *Freedom*, though, praised her assertion of sexual liberty: an 'anarchistic' act which would do more 'for the cause of human freedom . . . than a hundred years of political action'.[28]

A number of the noisy demonstrators were from the Legitimation League, which campaigned for the rights of illegitimate children. The Lanchester case boosted its activities, providing an opportunity to make free love a more explicit part of its agenda. Mona Caird was an active member, as were many anarchists, and Lillian Harman, an American anarchist feminist who had notoriously served a prison sentence for cohabiting with her lover, accepted an invitation to become Honorary President. When she came to Britain on a lecture tour, and was interviewed in the national press, the resulting publicity led to another surge in League membership.[29]

In its journal *The Adult*, Harman criticised novels such as Thomas Hardy's *Jude the Obscure* and Grant Allen's *The Woman Who Did* for their negative depictions of free love. Their unhappy endings, she said, were not true to reality: as her own life demonstrated, it was possible to live happily, without shame and regret, as a free woman and a free mother – the key was frankness.[30] In similar spirit the League encouraged members to make public announcements of free unions and any subsequent children, and a few did so, one pair of 'marriage resisters' even putting a notice in *The Times*.[31] Women, who made up around half the membership and regularly chaired League meetings, often contributed to *The Adult* praising free love and criticising male writers on the subject for their misogyny.

According to John Sweeney, an undercover policeman who infiltrated the organisation, the authorities feared that this 'open and unashamed' attack on marriage laws was the vanguard of an attack on all laws. After the national press published a letter signed by peers and clergymen urging the use of 'the strong hand of the law' against the free love movement, the police decided to make a move.[32]

They soon found their excuse. In 1898, the Watford University Press, publishers of *The Adult*, brought out *Sexual Inversion*, Havelock Ellis's book about homosexuality. George Bedborough, the paper's editor, agreed to distribute it. Detective Sweeney bought a copy, and the police pounced. They arrested Bedborough, seizing Ellis's book and another on free love by

Oswald Dawson, the League's founder, as well as copies of *The Adult*; all were condemned as obscene at the subsequent trial. The indictment included, as evidence of obscenity, poems and articles by women; the judge was outraged by women's active involvement with the paper and ordered female spectators from the courtroom. Henry Seymour organised a Free Press Defence Committee that included Edith Lanchester and Edward Carpenter, but much to its annoyance Bedborough did a deal, pleading guilty to avoid jail. Although Seymour, who had taken over editorship of The *Adult*, repudiated first free love and then anarchism, booksellers would no longer stock it. Soon both the paper and the League folded: to that extent, a success for the police who had, in Sweeney's words, aimed in one blow to crack down on the publication of material on homosexuality and to kill 'a growing evil in the shape of a vigorous campaign of free love and anarchism'.[33]

But although such cases had some deterrent effect, especially on the discussion of homosexuality, they also gave mainstream publicity to subversive ideas, and by the end of the 1890s marriage versus free love was a regular, if controversial, topic of debate in novels, plays and stories, newspaper articles and public meetings.

Speaking utopia

> A subject . . . in the vibrations of a first great awakening. (Voltairine de Cleyre, 1897)[34]

> I am not a mere theorist. I have lived that of which I write. (Lillian Harman, 1896)[35]

This period saw a general upsurge in utopian writing as well as experiments in living, and free love propaganda increasingly developed more explicitly utopian imagery to parallel its dystopian representation of conventional marriage. Louisa Bevington's poem 'The Most Beautiful Thing', with its echo of Blake, is characteristic of the romantic rhetoric used by many women, emphasising the 'love' in 'free love'.

Such romanticism did not preclude discussion of the obstacles to change. Most anarchists acknowledged the sexual oppression of women under existing social arrangements, and emphasised that change would benefit both sexes. But Charlotte Wilson was not alone in recognising that men and women often had different priorities, and many anarchist women complained, as did other new women, that new men were hard to find.[36] In 1896, the individualist *Free Review* ran an article by Aphra Wilson called: 'Wanted: A New Adam'. New woman, she argued, does not want the old Adam: 'She will not put a foot into Bondwoman's Lane . . . She shall take to herself a mate; with her shall lie the choice in childbearing . . . so shall she be the free mother of strong children.' She wants 'dual freedom' with a new Adam 'who has not used his sister, Woman; he has not abused her, so he is not her thrall; he is his own man', who will find freedom through restraint. Together they will travel in love on 'the Open Road . . . of perfect freedom – the heroic path of a divine Liberty'. Aphra Wilson identifies the enemies of this freedom as the priest, the licentious male and the man of science.[37]

In earlier years, it had been easier to see science as an essential part of the utopian project, a liberator bearing the light of truth into superstition's dark corners – and indeed this is how most radical men and many women continued to see it. For instance Henry Seymour, then a fervent free love propagandist, initially viewed science as something provisional and imperfect that might help free lovers to make a better choice of partner. By 1898, however, he depicted science as essential to any progress towards a new improved kind of human being, and advertised his services as a eugenic matchmaker: free choice was no use without professional guidance.[38]

Women tended to be more wary than men of pronouncements about gender and sexuality from scientists who, like Karl Pearson with his increasingly authoritarian eugenicist ideas about the control of women and motherhood, were entering contemporary debates about women's place with new ideas to justify the status quo. During the whole of the period under discussion the sexual double standard, despite constant attack, showed little sign of withering away – indeed it was ingeniously reconstituted in biological and evolutionary terms; Seymour and Pearson were among those arguing that nature, not society, dictated women's subordinated sexual role.

It was clear to Aphra Wilson and others that women would have to seek liberation on their own terms. Some adapted eugenicist arguments to claim that free love and free motherhood produce healthier and happier children, while others focused on the psychological benefits of sexual liberation, emphasising not just freedom from the legal and social bondage of marriage, but the positive virtues of choice, and the conditions in which love can flourish. Such women stressed that freedom was about control over their own bodies and desires, an argument which needed to be constantly remade in response to those opponents (and a few proponents) who thought that 'free women' meant women's sexual availability to men.

Charlotte Wilson, writing in the 1880s, had deployed the language of healthy versus morbid sexual and gender relations in a way that took up and reversed dominant medical and anthropological discourses, and this now became a regular tactic in free love debates. (Similarly, in his later writings Edward Carpenter would draw on evolutionary theory to argue that, far from being an index of biological degeneration, homosexuality could represent a higher social development, incorporating the best aspects of masculinity and femininity. This argument was taken up by others, who sometimes referred to Wilde himself as a representative of the higher humanity.[39])

Although Wilson's writings reveal her intellectual and emotional engagement with the subject of marriage and free love, it was only in private letters that she referred directly to her own experiences. But by the late 1890s, in the franker climate that she had helped to bring about, a new generation of anarchist women felt able to be more outspoken about living their politics, drawing on their own lives for propaganda.

At the forefront of this approach were Lillian Harman, Voltairine de Cleyre and Emma Goldman, anarchist feminists active in the USA who each attracted large audiences on their visits to Britain. All three used examples from their own lives to illustrate not just the need for but the possibilities of sex revolution. They confidently argued for a free and natural sexuality which might not be confined to one partner, and shifted the parameters of the debate by discussing the psychology of sexual relationships.

Goldman urged women to free themselves from internal as well as external tyrants, and brave public opinion to free their true natures as women and as mothers.[40] De Cleyre, herself a working-class mother, had a different take on tyranny, drawing on bitter experience to warn women that living with their lovers would mean becoming at best mere housekeepers, at worst slavish dependants: 'Men may not mean to be tyrants when they marry, but they frequently grow to be such. It is insufficient to dispense with the priest or the registrar. The spirit of marriage makes for slavery.' She praised the domestic arrangements of Mary Wollstonecraft and William Godwin, who lived apart during their marriage, as a model for preserving the spontaneity of love. On her speaking tour of Britain in the winter of 1897–8, de Cleyre spoke to large audiences, who applauded her most radical points on 'The Woman Question'. In Scotland, one of her most popular topics was 'The Life and Work of Mary Wollstonecraft'. De Cleyre called for an annual commemoration of Wollstonecraft: 'Let us have a little bit of she-ro worship to even things up a bit.'[41]

In the 1880s Charlotte Wilson and Karl Pearson had supported a project to republish Wollstonecraft's *Vindication of the Rights of Women*, and the Men and Women's Club was initially called the Mary Wollstonecraft Club; its name was changed because anxious members feared any implication that dangerous ideas might be not only discussed but acted on. Mainstream feminists continued to distance themselves from Wollstonecraft's life, even while reviving and extolling her writing. But many anarchist feminists of the 1890s extolled her life as a 'she-ro' of free love. Biography and autobiography were as important to them as theory in inspiring them to think or rethink their own lives. So Harman and Goldman represented themselves as positive role models for other women; while the sad example of Eleanor Marx, who killed herself after being betrayed by her lover, was taken as evidence of the need for changes that went deeper than legal reform.

Literature served as another prompt for social questioning. Goldman and Harman regularly discussed contemporary works, while in *Freedom* Charlotte Wilson (now signing herself C. M. W.) analysed Ibsen's plays in relation to marriage, women and social prejudice. The paper also carried items about free love in the life and work of Shelley, as well as highly selective extracts from *Jude the Obscure* and *The Woman Who Did*, setting out the case for free love – and omitting the unhappy endings.[42] This making and re-making of narratives was taken up with enthusiasm by a younger generation who wanted to live their politics, making their own stories part of the propaganda for a new life.

'Propaganda cannot be diversified enough if we want to touch all.'[43] There may have been general agreement about what was wrong with marriage, but there was no single alternative model of free love: instead, there were debates, aspirations, experiments, compromises; failures and successes, adaptation and change. The relationship between principle and practice was never straightforward.

Some anarchists continued to stand against any attempt to propagandise or practise free love – men most often on the grounds that it exploited women, while those few women who publicly opposed it argued that it diverted attention from more pressing issues. Some perhaps had more personally complicated reasons for silence or opposition. Nannie Dryhurst, for example, editor of *Freedom*'s propaganda column, spoke against free love in a public debate with Lillian Harman.[44] Dryhurst had a long and passionate affair with journalist Henry Nevinson; both were married with children, and despite much agonising, remained with their families. Personal difficulties did not necessarily inspire anarchists to publicly challenge the institution of marriage.[45] Nor did all free love advocates actually live in free unions – Henry Seymour, for instance, remained in a lifelong marriage despite his belief that it was practically a gentlemanly duty to provide sexual experience to unpartnered women whenever the opportunity arose.

Although women were more likely than men to favour monogamy – at least serial monogamy – over 'varietism' (multiple sexual partners), and love over sexual desire, this was certainly not always the case. While a section of mainstream feminists called for an end to the sexual double standard in the form of chastity for both men and women, most anarchist women still advocated free love as primarily a *sexual* choice. Hope Clare, for example, writing in the *Free Review*, used her own experience of unwanted celibacy to urge that women should be free to break the 'conspiracy of silence' and speak their desires to men.[46]

Some Christian anarchists, following Tolstoy's teachings, did see the physical expression of sexuality as an unfortunate diversion from spiritual development.[47] Others disagreed, hotly debating what they called 'the SQ' – the sex question. Tolstoyan Lilian Hunt Ferris wrote about her free union, contrasting the subjugation of women in legal marriage with a truly religious free marriage, which unites love, sex and spirituality. For her, free love meant a natural 'love without stint' and fidelity without compulsion.[48] In 1898, several women and men left a collective household set up by the Tolstoyan Brotherhood Church, disagreeing with, amongst other things, its anti-sex (and anti-woman) line. They founded Whiteway, an anarchist community which, with its spirit of tolerance and openness to change, was to see several generations of experiments with free love.[49]

It was the 'out and proud' approach to free love that made it, in contrast to other unorthodox sexual arrangements, a kind of deliberate propaganda; like marriage, it gave a public face to personal relationships. This often meant social repercussions, even if these were usually less dramatic than Lillian Harman's imprisonment or Edith Lanchester's incarceration: jobs and homes could be lost, families estranged, individuals ostracised. Lilian and Tom Ferris devised an unofficial 'marriage' ceremony for themselves, and were expelled from the Quakers as a result.[50] Oswald and Gladys Dawson, the individualist founders of the Legitimation League, were repeatedly threatened with eviction because of their highly publicised free union; Gladys was particularly vilified, especially by other women, and once had her face slapped in the street.[51] George and Louie Bedborough married for the sake of their families while agreeing between themselves to have an open relationship.[52] Having children was an added complication, and some women just took their partner's name and called themselves 'Mrs', for practical reasons. More often, though, women kept their own name even while committing themselves to lifelong partnerships.

Although social stigmatisation affected women in free unions more than their male partners, it may be that for some the loss of respectability (that relative and class-dependent term) was compensated for by the pleasures of transgression and the assertion of a liberated sexuality. However, the public avowal of free love ideals remained problematic for the politically isolated, or those who were involved in mainstream socialist or feminist campaigns where personal unconventionality was seen as a liability.[53] In practice, the most important factor in sustaining a commitment to free love was the creation of an alternative community, such as Whiteway, with shared views on morality and honour and the interdependence of the personal and the political.

If men and women even in such supportive environments did not always achieve the transformed relationships they had envisaged, free love nevertheless remained an ideal worth struggling for and transmitting to a younger generation, who in turn would adapt its meanings according to their own needs and circumstances. An example of this process of transmission can be seen in the relationship between Rose Witcop and Guy Aldred, both of them still children in the years of the New Woman and the utopian revival. In 1907, the young Aldred published a pamphlet arguing that as long as women are economically, legally and socially unfree, all sexual intercourse oppresses them; his solution was revolutionary celibacy. Then he met Witcop, who lived among other anarchists in London's East End. Both of her older sisters were in free unions, and she plied Aldred with Legitimation League pamphlets on free love and others, by Lillian Harman's father, Moses Harman, on birth control. She told him stories about Victoria

Woodhull, another notorious American feminist, who once stood for president of the USA on a free love ticket. Aldred was won over, abandoning celibacy; he and Witcop set up home and had a child together. Later, he continued the transmission of free love stories when he described their tempestuous, non-exclusive relationship in his autobiography.[54]

Clearly, for most of the individuals I have discussed, free love was crucial to social transformation. By representing marriage as immoral, unhealthy and unnatural, and free love as the moral, healthy and natural basis of a free society, their polemical interventions in the marriage debates reversed the terms of argument and drew attention to, made strange, what was taken for granted. These are classic utopian strategies, seeking to awaken simultaneously dissatisfaction with the existing world and desire for something better.

Such reversals of conventional thought can be immensely exhilarating, and the expression of the joys of free love and the horrors of its opposite gives a sense of what utopia *feels* like, rather than a plan or narrative of what it might be. To adapt a point from Richard Dyer's work on musicals, in these speeches and writings 'utopianism is contained in the feelings'.[55] In the gap between what is and what might be, the desire for change can take root and grow.

But persuasion with words was only part of a demonstrative politics that also relied on the powerful example of lived experience. As Lillian Harman said in an interview with the *Daily Mail*, 'My object . . . was to make it easier for others who might wish to follow in our path, and yet feared the difficulties in the way . . . What we want is liberty . . . so that people may arrive by experience at the most desirable form of relationship.'[56] The experiments in living that flourished at the end of the century rehearsed different possibilities for the future. And the telling and retelling of cautionary and inspirational stories of the relation between theory and practice became part of the education of desire. As sociologist Ken Plummer suggests in *Telling Sexual Stories*: in order to tell stories there must be a community to listen – and in order for there to be a community to listen there must be stories.[57] Such storytelling is part of the creation and recreation not just of specific utopian communities but of a wider community of utopians.

But telling about free love has significance beyond the stories themselves. Some queer theorists, following the work of Judith Butler, claim that sexual identity is created through performance – put simply, that it is what we do, not what we are. So for example, to say 'I am a lesbian' is not to express an inner truth, or to adopt a label, or to play a role: it is to create that self. This theory derives from J. L. Austin's concept of the performative utterance, in which to say something is to do it. Austin cites as a paradigm case the phrase 'I do' in the marriage ceremony: saying the words *is* the act of assenting to marriage.[58] Perhaps saying 'I don't' to marriage can similarly be a performative utterance – the creation of a dissident, utopian self.

For women and men in the late nineteenth century, to write or speak in public about their own sexual feelings, experiences and desires was still scandalous, as it was to speak publicly as anarchists. The automatic association of women anarchists with sexuality meant that to speak as an anarchist woman was to speak as a sexual woman. Their desire to speak of desire was a propulsion towards utopianism, and – in the desire for free love, free love as the expression of desire, the speaking of desire – such women were in effect performing desire, enacting anarchism, doing utopia.

Notes

Thanks to Lucy Bland, Laurence Davis, Ruth Kinna and Helen Lowe for detailed and helpful comments, and to everyone who encouraged the work while it was in progress and inspired me to think about it in new ways.

1   L. S. Bevington, *Liberty Lyrics*, p. 7.
2   British Library (hereafter BL), Additional MS 50511 fol.176, Charlotte Wilson to George Bernard Shaw, 5 May 1886.
3   See D. Hardy, *Alternative Communities in Nineteenth Century England*; N. Shaw, *Whiteway: A Colony in the Cotswolds*.
4   London Anarchist Communist Alliance, *An Anarchist Manifesto*, p. 11.
5   R. Levitas, *The Concept of Utopia*, p. 8.
6   E. Probyn, 'Queer Belongings: The Politics of Departure', in E. Grosz and E. Probyn (eds), *Sexy Bodies: The Strange Carnalities of Feminism*, p. 2.
7   BL Add. 50511 fo.176, Wilson.
8   University College London, Pearson Papers (hereafter UCL P) 900/6-10, Wilson to Karl Pearson, 8 August 1885.
9   UCL P, 900/6-10, 12-20, Wilson to Pearson, 8 August and 8 October 1885.
10 L. Bland, *Banishing the Beast: English Feminism and Sexual Morality 1885–1914*, p. 5. See also J. Walkowitz, *City of Dreadful Delight*, chapter 5.
11 UCL P, 900/6-10.
12 UCL P, 900/12-20.
13 K. Pearson, *Socialism and Sex*, p. 14; 'Socialism and Sex' in *The Ethic of Freethought: A Selection of Essays and Lectures*, p. 246.
14 L. Bland, 'Marriage Laid Bare: Middle Class Women and Marital Sex', in J. Lewis (ed.), *Labour and Love*; Bland, *Banishing the Beast*.
15 BL Add. 50510 fols 310–11, Wilson to Shaw, 10 December 1884.
16 See *Adult*, 2:2 (1898).
17 'Socialism and Sex', *Freedom*, 1:7 (1887).
18 M. Caird, 'Marriage', *Westminster Review*, 130 (August 1888), p. 200.
19 Bland, *Banishing the Beast*.
20 *Freedom*, 3:25 (1888).
21 J. Sweeney, *At Scotland Yard*, p. 181.
22 This connection is overlooked in E. Showalter's otherwise illuminating *Sexual Anarchy: Gender and Culture at the Fin de Siècle*.

23 H. Oliver, *The International Anarchist Movement in Late Victorian London*;
    J. Quail, *The Slow Burning Fuse: The Lost History of the British Anarchists*;
    H. Shpayer, 'British Anarchism 1881–1914: Reality and Appearance' (PhD,
    dissertation, University of London, 1981).
24 *Ibid.*
25 Shaw, *Whiteway.*
26 E. Carpenter, *Homogenic Love: And its Place in a Free Society* (actually pub-
    lished in January 1895 although the publication date is given as 1894).
27 *Freedom*, 11:94 (1895); *Freedom*, 9:95 (1895).
28 *Liberty*, 3:1 (1896); O. Dawson, *The Bar Sinister and Licit Love*; Elsa Lanches-
    ter, *Elsa Lanchester Herself*; *Freedom*, 9:99 (1895). See also K. Hunt, *Equivocal
    Feminists: The Social Democratic Federation and the Woman Question 1884–
    1911*; and Bland, *Banishing the Beast.*
29 Sweeney, *At Scotland Yard.*
30 L. Harman, 'Cast Off the Shell', *Adult*, 1:6 (1898); Harman, 'Eve and Her
    Eden', *Adult*, 2:2 (March 1898).
31 *Adult* 1:6 (1898); O. Dawson, *Personal Rights and Sexual Wrongs.*
32 Sweeney, *At Scotland Yard*, p. 181.
33 *Ibid.* p. 186; *Adult*, 2:7 (1898) and 2:9 (1898); *University Magazine and Free
    Review*, 10:6 (1898).
34 *Freedom*, 11:121 (1897).
35 Harman, 'Eve and Her Eden'.
36 For example, L. Harman, 'The New Martyrdom', *Adult*, 6:1 (1898).
37 *Free Review*, 5:4 (1896), 377, 386.
38 H. Seymour, *The Anarchy of Love or the Science of the Sexes*; H. Seymour,
    The Physiology of Love: A Study in Stirpiculture.
39 E. Carpenter, *The Intermediate Sex: A Study of Some Transitional Types of
    Men and Women*; E. Carpenter, *Love's Coming of Age*; E. Lees, *The New
    Horizon in Love and Life.*
40 E. Goldman, 'The Tragedy of Women's Emancipation' and 'Marriage and
    Love', in A. K. Shulman (ed.), *Red Emma Speaks: Selected Writings and
    Speeches by Emma Goldman.*
41 De Cleyre, cited in *Adult*, 1:6 (1898) pp. 143–5; *Freedom*, 11:21 (1897);
    Freedom, 11:20 (1897); P. Avrich, *An American Anarchist: The Life of Voltair-
    ine de Cleyre*, pp. 158–9.
42 *Freedom*, 4:39 (1890); *Freedom*, 3:33 (1889); *Freedom*, 6:70 (1892); *Freedom*,
    10:106 (1896); *Freedom*, 13:143 (1899); *Freedom*, 10:110 (1896).
43 London Anarchist Communist Alliance, *Manifesto*, p. 11.
44 International Institute of Social History, Amsterdam, Max Nettlau Papers 341,
    Agnes Davies, letter, 21 August 1898.
45 Bodleian Library, MS. Eng. misc. e.610/1-6, Henry Nevinson diaries.
46 H. Clare, 'Stagnant Virginity', *Free Review*, 7:3 (1896), p. 412.
47 Hardy, *Alternative Communities in Nineteenth Century England.*
48 L. H. Ferris, 'True Life and Free Love', in A. G. Higgins, *A History of the
    Brotherhood Church*, pp. 14–17.
49 Shaw, *Whiteway.*
50 *New Order*, 5:12, 5:14, 5:19 (1899).
51 *Freedom*, 11:120 (1897).

52 BL Add.7055 fols.69–74, George Bedborough to Havelock Ellis, 26 April 1922.
53 See, for example, Hunt, *Equivocal Feminists* and S. Pankhurst, *The Suffragette Movement*, pp. 30–1.
54 G. Aldred, *The Religion and Economics of Sex Oppression*; Aldred, *No Traitor's Gait!*
55 R. Dyer, 'Entertainment and Utopia', in R. Altman (ed.), *Genre: The Musical*, p. 177.
56 L. Harman, 'Apostle of Free Love', *Daily Mail* (16 April 1898), p. 3.
57 K. Plummer, *Telling Sexual Stories: Power, Change and Social Worlds*, p. 87 and *passim*.
58 J. Butler, *Bodies That Matter: On the Discursive Limits of 'Sex'*, p. 224; J. L. Austin, 'Performative Utterances' in *Philosophical Papers*.

References

Aldred, G., *The Religion and Economics of Sex Oppression* (London: Bakunin Press, 1907).
——. *No Traitor's Gait!* (Glasgow: Strickland Press, 1958).
Austin, J. L., 'Performative Utterances', in *Philosophical Papers* (Oxford: Clarendon Press, 1961).
Avrich, P., *An American Anarchist: The Life of Voltairine de Cleyre* (Princeton: Princeton University Press, 1978).
Bevington, L. S., *Liberty Lyrics* (London: Liberty Press, 1895).
Bland, L., 'Marriage Laid Bare: Middle Class Women and Marital Sex', in J. Lewis (ed.), *Labour and Love* (Oxford: Blackwell, 1986).
——. *Banishing the Beast: English Feminism and Sexual Morality 1885–1914* (Harmondsworth: Penguin, 1995).
Butler, J., *Bodies That Matter: On the Discursive Limits of 'Sex'* (London: Routledge, 1993).
Carpenter, E., *Homogenic Love: and its Place in a Free Society* (Manchester: Labour Press, 1894).
——. *Love's Coming of Age* (Manchester S. Clarke: 1906).
——. *The Intermediate Sex: A Study of Some Transitional Types of Men and Women* (London: Sonnenschein, 1908).
Dawson, O., *The Bar Sinister and Licit Love* (London: Legitimation League, 1895).
——. *Personal Rights and Sexual Wrongs* (London: Legitimation League, 1897).
Dyer, R., 'Entertainment and Utopia', in R. Altman (ed.), *Genre: The Musical* (London: RKP/BFI, 1981).
Ferris, L. H., 'True Life and Free Love', in A. G. Higgins, *A History of the Brotherhood Church* (Stapleton: Brotherhood Church, 1982).
Goldman, E., 'The Tragedy of Women's Emancipation' and 'Marriage and Love', in A. K. Shulman (ed.), *Red Emma Speaks: Selected Writings and Speeches by Emma Goldman* (New York: Vintage, 1972).
Hardy, D., *Alternative Communities in Nineteenth Century England* (London: Longman, 1979).

Hunt, K., *Equivocal Feminists: The Social Democratic Federation and the Woman Question 1884–1911* (Cambridge: Cambridge University Press, 1996).

Lanchester, E., *Elsa Lanchester Herself* (London: Michael Joseph, 1983).

Lees, E., *The New Horizon in Love and Life* (London: A. and C. Black, 1921).

Levitas, R., *The Concept of Utopia* (Hemel Hempstead: Philip Allan, 1990).

London Anarchist Communist Alliance, *An Anarchist Manifesto* (London: LACA, 1895).

Oliver, H., *The International Anarchist Movement in Late Victorian London* (Beckenham: Croom Helm, 1983).

Pankhurst, S., *The Suffragette Movement* (London: Virago, 1977).

Pearson, K., *Socialism and Sex* (London: W. Reeves, 1887).

——. 'Socialism and Sex', in *The Ethic of Freethought: A Selection of Essays and Lectures* (London: T. Fisher Unwin, 1888).

——. *The Ethic of Freethought* (London: Adam and Charles Black, 2nd edn, 1901).

Plummer, K., *Telling Sexual Stories: Power, Change and Social Worlds* (London: Routledge, 1995).

Probyn, E., 'Queer Belongings: The Politics of Departure', in E. Grosz and E. Probyn (eds), *Sexy Bodies: The Strange Carnalities of Feminism* (London: Routledge, 1995).

Quail, J., *The Slow Burning Fuse: The Lost History of the British Anarchists* (London: Paladin, 1978).

Seymour, H., *The Anarchy of Love or the Science of the Sexes* (London: H. Seymour, 1888).

——. *The Physiology of Love: A Study in Stirpiculture* (London: L. N. Fowler & Co., 1898).

Shaw, N., *Whiteway: A Colony in the Cotswolds* (London: C. W. Daniel, 1935).

Showalter, E., *Sexual Anarchy: Gender and Culture at the Fin de Siècle* (London: Bloomsbury, 1991).

Shpayer, H., 'British Anarchism, 1881–1914: Reality and Appearance' (PhD dissertation, University of London, 1981).

Sweeney, J., *At Scotland Yard* (London: Grant Richards, 1904).

Walkowitz, J., *City of Dreadful Delight: Narratives of Sexual Danger in Late-Victorian London* (London: Virago, 1992).

Visions of the future: reproduction, revolution, and regeneration in American anarchist utopian fiction

In 1898 an advertisement for a new novel appeared in the American anarchist and sex-reform journal *Lucifer, the Light-Bearer*. Describing the work as 'a story of surpassing interest, largely devoted to Sexologic and Sociologic problems', the editors called attention to its 'radically revolutionary ideals in regard to popular theories – sexologic, theologic, cosmologic, etc'. For $1.50, the 'substantially printed and artistically bound' novel could be purchased directly through the journal.[1]

A 'cosmologic' novel was not a work one would ordinarily associate with a radical newspaper. *Loma, a Citizen of Venus* is the story of a messianic extraterrestrial that comes to earth to share, in the words of its author William Windsor, 'the crude announcement of principles by which a true civilization can be reached'.[2] As Loma, the Venusian, reveals to an audience composed of a suicidal unwed mother, the narrator (a doctor, clearly meant to be Windsor himself), and the doctor's mother, the reorganisation of society is to be premised upon the exultation of motherhood and personal liberty. Once the earthlings have been tutored in Loma's ways, the alien returns to Colorado and ascends to Venus while his disciples watch. It is an unusual plot to be sure, and it contrasts sharply with the more formal socioeconomic tracts that were mainstays of anarchist publications. Within this idiosyncratic storyline, however, lay a substantive critique of late nineteenth-century society. Cloaked in a discussion of sexuality and social relationships was a detailed prescription for a utopia based upon a social, cultural, sexual, and political transformation of the United States.

Loma's Venus is a far cry from the popular understanding of anarchism. In the minds of most Americans, anarchism was (and remains) a philosophy associated with destruction and violence; indeed, the very term anarchy is frequently used as a synonym for chaos. The image of the anarchist is equally as identifiable: a foreign man with shaggy hair, a beard, a crazed look in his eyes, and, of course, a bomb in his hands.[3] There are a few points worth underscoring about this familiar image: it suggests destruction rather than construction; it frames anarchist radicalism as un-American; and in so doing, it portrays the movement as decidedly male.

Anarchists' writings suggest something else. This essay examines American anarchists' own visions of their ideal as reflected in the utopian fiction they produced at the end of the nineteenth century – works that until now have been virtually ignored by historians and literary critics.[4] Like their mainstream counterparts, anarchist utopian authors suggested an alternative future that simultaneously questioned the present and emphasised social planning and collectivism. More distinctive is the fact that gender played a central role in anarchists' visions of a new world order. This essay traces the contours of these anarchist utopian novels and explores their concern with the politics of gender in the form of maternalism, sexuality, and reproduction. The result is a very different picture of anarchism: one that is not only imaginative but constructive; one that articulates a regeneration of society in an American voice; and one that advocates a sexual revolution based upon feminine roles and relationships in the realisation of anarchy.

The utopian form was revitalised at the end of the nineteenth century, a time when industrial, agrarian, and feminist reform movements gained momentum alongside the escalation of political, economic, and social discontent. The resulting utopian literature bore testament to the tensions of its time while at the same time it imagined possible resolutions to them. As such this fiction became an important medium through which culture could be challenged and subverted.

Following the phenomenal success of Edward Bellamy's *Looking Backward* in 1888, anarchists produced their own fictionalised accounts of a model society. This is not surprising. While fiction was a popular propagandistic aid for many critics of turn-of-the-century American society – indeed, more utopian novels were written in the period from 1890–1910 than in the eighty years preceding and following it – the utopia held particular value for anarchists.[5] Since an anarchist society was never realised on a large scale, its proponents were frequently criticised for the ethereal quality of their rhetoric. Moreover, in the post-Haymarket era American anarchists faced the challenge of demonstrating to an unsympathetic populace that anarchism suggested construction, not destruction.[6] For anarchist authors, then, fiction was not only a form of artistic expression but an invaluable medium that even more than their polemical writings explicitly delineated their proposals for change in a popularly accessible form and language. Through the use of literature, anarchist writers hoped to introduce their visions to a larger audience. Author Rosa Graul asserted, '[M]y story was written not so much for those who are *already* possessed of the "New Ideal" as for those whom we wish to convert, to win, from the old to the new.'[7] Such efforts were often welcomed. Two women wrote to

Lucifer, the Light-Bearer, '[w]e find that many women – beginners – will read a story, while the other articles are "too dry" they say'.[8]

In the last decade of the nineteenth century, authors published four full-length anarchist utopian novels: Florence Huntley's *The Dream Child* (1892); Henry Olerich's *A Cityless and Countryless World: An Outline of Practical Co-operative Individualism* (1893); William Windsor's, *Loma, a Citizen of Venus* (1897); and Rosa Graul's *Hilda's Home: A Story of Woman's Emancipation* (1899). These works were serialised in or promoted by the English-language anarchist journals *Lucifer, the Light-Bearer* and *Free Society*, and some later in the most popular of all US anarchist journals, *Mother Earth*.[9]

The form of anarchist utopias varied from a pastoral Eden, a communal present, and, like contemporary science fiction, an extra-planetary future. Despite their vastly different settings and storylines, these novels shared a focus on the role of the individual in bringing about a broader social transformation. Each novel highlighted anarchism's basic tenet that personal liberty supersedes all other rights, and that the existing state (which anarchists perceived as an institution grounded in coercive authority) should be replaced by a new form of social organisation. Although American anarchists at the end of the nineteenth century were divided over the type of socioeconomic system needed to replace the capitalist state, their differences of opinion did not negate joint efforts to seek the means to those ends; accordingly, communist and individualist anarchists alike read the works examined here.

In fantastic stories about extraterrestrials and fallen women, anarchists posited both the means and the end of the revitalisation of society. These means were found not only in socioeconomic transformation but in sexual revolution. Accordingly, American anarchists underscored sexual politics – sex and gender issues concerning women's emancipation, marriage, free love, sexuality, and voluntary motherhood – in their ideal societies. Gender, anarchists realised, was integral to the issue of power; and in discussions of sexuality, the social organisation of intimate life, and the elimination of institutions that infringed upon individual liberties, anarchists found a construct that was both analogous to and symptomatic of the hierarchical relation between the individual and the state. In positing the reconstruction of society in gender-conscious terms, these anarchist authors envisioned a society in which maternalism would replace paternalism as the organising principle of society.

Maternalism, historians Sonya Michel and Robyn Rosen explain, is 'a political concept that accepts the principle of gender difference, specifically, women's identities as mothers, but maintains that women have a responsibility to apply their domestic and familial roles to society at large'.[10] It operates as a political ideology as well as a form of political economy. Other scholarship has shown how important these discourses can be in shaping social structures and organisations, including the characters of state institutions.[11] In the United States at the end of the nineteenth century, maternalism was the basis upon which women's private roles and duties generated their public activism – an activism, these scholars argue, that had a determining effect upon the evolution of the welfare state.

It is therefore fascinating to see the use of maternalist rhetoric for entirely different ends. At the same time as anarchists' contemporaries extolled the virtues of womanhood in their efforts to purify society, anarchists appealed to women's biological roles and domestic duties as a basis for the radical reorganisation of society. In their literature anarchists constructed a philosophy of maternalist politics, or the ways in which issues of gender and family – sexuality, reproduction, and parenting – were essential to their understanding of two key concerns: the relation of the individual to the state, and that between the social organisation of intimate life and the advent of socio-political revolution. American anarchists articulated a type of maternalist politics, then, to suggest a reconceptualisation of both intimate and public life. This maternalist vision is particularly evident in the utopian novel *Hilda's Home: A Story of Woman's Emancipation* by Rosa Graul.

Hilda's Home was originally serialised in *Lucifer, the Light-Bearer* in 1897 and was subsequently published in one volume by the journal's editor in response to repeated requests from his readership. It begins innocuously enough with a marriage proposal from one character to another; however, it quickly becomes clear that this is not a typical romance novel. Over the course of the book, the female characters discuss the ills of marriage and seek an alternative through their creation of a maternal commune with their male partners. By abolishing marriage and realising the sexual emancipation of women, Graul suggested, communal associations could be formed that would allow for the greater freedom of individuals. Even more specifically, she advised, it was through reproduction and the socialisation of the young into a new maternalist structure that a new society could both figuratively and literally be born. Thus, while Graul's utopia firmly grounded women in the domestic arena, it also proposed ways in which this sphere might be liberating rather than constraining were women to exert more control in determining the roles and relationships they would assume.[12]

This emphasis on domesticity was reflected in a more unusual way in Florence Huntley's *The Dream Child* (1892). Described in advertisements as 'a most charming and absorbing story dealing with the occult and to a certain extent metaphysical – Exceedingly interesting', this utopia is located within the dreams of Dian Varien, a wealthy woman who is institutionalised by her husband following years of living in a dream-like state.[13] Dian's fantasies begin following the accidental death of her daughter, Stella. In her dreams Dian is reunited with Stella in a motherland that exists on another planet, where Zanoni, her male spiritual guide, tells of a living arrangement based upon maternal and physical love. Gone are the competition of capitalism and the hierarchy of patriarchy; what replaces them are voluntary relationships between individuals. Eventually Dian abandons her earthly life in favour of her celestial dream world.

The use of an extraterrestrial prophet was a favoured technique of anarchist utopian authors. As in William Windsor's *Loma, a Citizen of Venus*, Henry Olerich's *A Cityless and Countryless World: An Outline of Practical Co-operative Individualism* embraced a maternalist vision of society in an otherworldly environment. Olerich, a farmer, teacher, and inventor, possessed both a vivid imagination and a love of meticulous organisation. These traits are evident in *A Cityless and Countryless World*, which relies upon an extraterrestrial 'Marsite', Mr Midith, to detail the faults of American society and posit an alternative socioeconomic system. The result is a utopia markedly free from the strife of late nineteenth-century America. It is based on the construction of voluntary but highly structured communities: in this Martian model, each community contains 120 extended families or 120,000 persons on a 144 square mile tract of land, living in dwellings accommodating 1000 people. In addition to reconfiguring the organisation of society, Olerich observed, social mentalities also had to be reconsidered. 'Paternalism stunts individuality', he wrote.[14] The answer was to replace paternalism with maternalism, in which sexual equality and affective relations would redefine public and private life.

In each of these novels, gender lay at the heart of socio-political transformation. 'In the new type of civilization', William Windsor wrote, 'the sweet influences of woman must have an equal value with those of man'. Accordingly, he maintained, 'the first step in the line of reform must be the emancipation of woman'.[15] The other authors agreed. In lengthy discussions of marriage, sexuality, and motherhood, these utopian writers insisted that social revolution could not be achieved until the 'sex question', as they termed sex and gender issues concerning women's emancipation, marriage, free love, sexuality, and voluntary motherhood, was resolved.

More than any other social construct, anarchists believed, marriage represented the invasion of the state into the lives of individuals. Because anarchists did not recognise the authority of religious or governmental institutions, its adherents perceived marriage as serving to state-sanction what was fundamentally a private affair between two individuals. The institution of marriage, then, was a political construct. Beyond their theoretical objections to marriage, some anarchist authors emphasised the fact that many people felt trapped in unhappy marriages. Rosa Graul repeatedly stressed in *Hilda's Home* and in later interviews that she drew from first-hand knowledge in her condemnation of marriage: 'There is *no true happiness in marriage*. My own experience has taught this. Marriage forbids its victims to grow, to broaden, to expand. Marriage prohibits admiration of lovable qualities in others besides the legal partner. Marriage possesses; marriage monopolises, and thereby cramps and finally destroys the pair.'[16]

Anarchists rarely blamed the individuals involved for the problems in a marriage. It was not because people were imperfect that marriages failed, but rather that the institution of marriage itself was inherently flawed. Because the state both regulated marriage and restricted divorce, marriage was interpreted by many anarchists as a form of bondage that in no way enhanced the ostensible reason for marriage, the love of two individuals. Loma tells an engaged couple that the 'degradation of marriage consists . . . in the fact that they [the married couple] violate nature by promising to do impossible things, by assuming ownership over each other, and by regarding the relationship as only terminable by the death or the criminal action of one or the other of the parties'.[17] Similarly, Huntley's extraterrestrial character Zanoni discerns, '[t]hough society, the church, and established civil law, recognize the true principle of marriage, they as yet misunderstand the application. The world recognizes the bonds but ignores the freedom; it perceives the duties but denies the rights. It talks of love and deals with lust. It seeks after marriage and forms legal partnerships.'[18] Anarchists found great irony in the popular conviction that marriage represented the civility of civilisation; instead, they argued, it masked the very source of the misery inflicted on the populace – the intrusion of the government into citizens' affairs – and in that way constituted a 'barrier' to progress.[19]

In *Hilda's Home* Imelda says to her suitor, 'I am afraid of a husband. Husbands are not lovers.'[20] Having condemned marriage in their utopias, American anarchists presented an alternative: free love. It was a term, radicals knew, that was subject to frequent misunderstanding, and in their novels authors hastened to explain the practice. Free love, the Venusian Loma states, 'does not mean promiscuous love, nor promiscuous sexual association, but it does mean the largest possible freedom in social intercourse'.[21] Because marriage was a civil and religious construction, anarchists argued, it could not dictate interpersonal relations. If people were to be entrusted with themselves, they must have the freedom to decide the nature of their involvement with another person. The unwritten double standard already allowed men a great deal of sexual freedom. What was novel about anarchists' argument for free love, then, was its demand that women have a definitive say in their sexual behaviour.

The asexual woman of the Victorian ethos had no place in anarchist utopian fiction; indeed, in these novels, the angel of the house was decidedly earthy.[22] Each of the anarchist utopias contained candid depictions of feminine passion and sexuality. *Hilda's Home* opens with a scene describing in great detail the passionate interlude of a young woman and her date in which in 'ecstasy' the woman 'gave herself up to the enjoyment of blissful consciousness'.[23] (Interestingly enough, it was at this moment that the young man chose to entreat the woman to marry him – an offer she refused.) 'Blissful consciousness' and unconsciousness were apparently endemic conditions for female characters in these novels. Myrtle, a young unwed mother, is overcome by Loma in one of many such scenes in *Loma, a Citizen of Venus*: 'Myrtle felt the wonderful thrill of her personal contact, and then as his lips met hers, she closed her eyes and sank upon his breast in blissful unconscious[ness]'. When Myrtle expresses guilt over her behaviour, Loma gently assures her, '[i]t is just as natural for a woman at your age to crave the loving caresses of pure and affectionate men as it is for her to breathe'.[24]

Even more radical for its time are the homoerotic overtones of this literature. Each of the male protagonists in these utopias is depicted as stunning in appearance. Mr Midith, the Martian of *A Cityless and Countryless World*, is described by the male narrator as being 'as nearly a model of human perfection as the world will probably ever be capable of producing'.[25] Similarly, Dr Bell notes that 'Loma . . . presented a picture of classic beauty'. Dr Bell does more than just admire Loma, however. The reader is informed that Dr Bell 'thrilled under the magnetism of Loma . . . [H]e felt that he himself was glowing with a corresponding emanation, which the association of Loma seemed to have suddenly called out. He was conscious of the most delicious sensations and he surrendered himself to them without reserve.' After one such scene, 'the doctor arose, and drawing Loma's arm through his own, conducted his distinguished guest to his own bedroom'.[26]

Nor were these descriptions confined to men. Mrs Bell and Myrtle are repeatedly depicted in amorous situations in *Loma, a Citizen of Venus*. Passion abounds when 'Mrs Bell rained kiss after kiss upon [Myrtle's] forehead and upon the golden hair'. Soon thereafter 'the loose robe which enveloped Myrtle's slender form slipped from her shoulders and fell to the floor'. Mrs Bell finds Myrtle's nudity 'enchanting', and 'in a moment she also was without adornment other than her own splendid person'.[27]

The homoeroticism in this fiction is significant in many ways. The very fact that these situations were included in utopian novels – ostensibly political works concerned with socio-economic transformation – indicates that their authors clearly deemed sexuality to have political implications. Not only did the writers' depictions of sexuality in these works attack the construct of asexual Victorian womanhood, but they went further to challenge the most basic of binary gender constructs, heterosexual pairing. In so doing, this fiction negated the importance of the nuclear family based on the monogamous, heterosexual couple. In fictional form, utopian anarchists publicly redefined the possibilities for the social organisation of intimate life. (It is important to note, however, that while anarchist utopias accepted homoeroticism as a legitimate expression of sexuality, they did not eliminate a heterosexual norm. In discussions of reproduction and childrearing, the heterosexual couple was the only unit specifically identified.)

Anarchists' celebration of sexuality and dismissal of marriage had obvious implications for motherhood, a concept that figured prominently in each work. In these novels anarchist authors broadened the notion of motherhood to refer not only to reproduction and the parenting relation itself, but also to serve as a metaphor for their idealised social organisation of the community. Specifically, the theme of voluntary motherhood was invoked repeatedly both as the literal control over one's body – or freedom from 'sex slavery', as anarchists termed it – and as a conceptual blueprint for the self-chosen, affective associations to be realised in an anarchist society.

In practical terms, anarchist authors discussed voluntary motherhood as a counter to patriarchy and the hierarchical structure of the family unit. Rosa Graul lamented in *Hilda's Home* that 'in enforced motherhood, unwelcome motherhood, is to be found the chief cause of the degradation that gives birth to human woe'.[28] Accordingly, anarchists insisted, women should be able to choose whether or not to bear a child as well as who the father of that child should be. In Henry Olerich's science fiction utopia *A Cityless and Countryless World*, the male Martian character Midith enthusiastically promotes the idea of female prerogative in sexual relationships: 'The Marsian idea and practice of sex relations is, that whenever, in due time the maternal instinct of procreation prompts a woman to become a mother, she has the full privilege of soliciting the love of any man whose propagative association she desires for that purpose.' He explains, '[t]his privilege, you see, throws the full control of motherhood in the hands of the woman. The *man* sexually co-operates *only* when his assistance is agreeably solicited or accepted. The Marsites can, therefore, have no unwelcome motherhood imposed upon the *woman* by the *man*.'[29] By reversing roles so that women would be the initiators of a sexual relationship, 'sex slavery' would be eliminated. Even more radical was Graul's assertion that 'if a woman desires to repeat the experience of motherhood, why should it be wrong when she selects another to be the father of her [second child], instead of the one who has once performed this office for her?'[30] Thus women were to have complete control over their sexuality and its products.

In this literature motherhood assumed great import as the founding basis for an anarchist society. At the peak of Graul's novel, the character Imelda rhapsodises about the significance of parenting relations in assuring societal transformation:

> When mothers are free to choose the fathers of their babes; when they can have just the conditions their hearts long for; when they can be free from care and anxiety; when every woman has learned the science of becoming a perfect mother; when every mother understands the fearful responsibility of being such; when every father is filled with a sense of the high honor that has been conferred upon him in being chosen to be such; when, in consequence, he recognizes the duties he owes to woman and her offspring, and when, in every act of his life he seeks to aid her in perfecting the coming being; then, and not till then, may we expect peace and joy and happiness.[31]

Voluntary motherhood was not a by-product of revolution but part of the means through which social transformation could be achieved. That this directly undermined the male prerogative inherent in patriarchy was not lost on these authors. In *The Dream Child* Mr Varien bitterly notes of the motherland to which his wife has fled, 'I had no part in it . . . From this enchanted land and from the reunited lives of Dian and her daughter, I, the husband, and father, was excluded and forgotten.'[32]

For a number of anarchists voluntary motherhood was also an issue of eugenics, a subject that received serious consideration in some anarchist circles. Put simply, many anarchists believed that children conceived in loving relationships by healthy parents would be superior to those who were not, and as a result were fond of invoking eugenic arguments in their proposals for social reform.[33] Such proponents argued that a child's character and strength were prenatally influenced by the physical and psychological condition of the mother in particular. Thus, Windsor's character Loma counselled, it was important that the mother desire the pregnancy so that she might 'impress the offspring with the germs of thought' and thereby bear 'offspring . . . of such superior quality'.[34]

Because a mother's happiness was deemed crucial in ensuring a child's 'quality', elaborate rituals were developed in Windsor's and Olerich's utopias to celebrate a woman's pregnancy. 'When the female has conceived', Loma describes, 'she is at once made the recipient of special attention and honor'.[35] Such honours bestowed upon the mother-to-be included private concerts, gifts of jewellery, and daily massages. Likewise the Martians of Midith's world rewarded a pregnant woman quite literally for her labour by paying her a wage for the length of her pregnancy: 'You see', Midith notes, 'we have become humane enough to recognize the bearing and nursing of offspring as *productive* labor'.[36] Although these utopias did not avoid biological determinism, they did attempt to suggest some ways in which reproduction need not result in sexual oppression.

This concern with maternity and maternalism reflects an extremely important shift in American anarchist political thought. For years anarchist tracts had relentlessly debated the possibilities for a new order in terms of political structure (or the lack thereof) and economic organisation. Despite this, radicals and conservatives alike frequently criticised anarchist political theory as romantic, idealistic, and essentially unrealistic.[37] How, critics asked, could political institutions and the superstructure of the state ever be eliminated without resulting in chaos and mayhem? Anarchist utopias emphasising motherhood addressed the concerns of these critics, albeit indirectly, by taking a familiar, trusted, indeed even deified role and placing it at the centre of their idealised society. Motherhood became the metaphor for an anarchist society, allowing love, creation, individual initiative, sexual egalitarianism, and, to a tempered degree, a form of social control based on affective relations. Rather than serving as a refuge from an external political arena, anarchists suggested, domesticity could encompass that arena.

In our own time, when domesticity and feminism are too often portrayed as locked in a binary relationship, some may find this aspect of anarchist utopianism troubling. How does it reconcile with the explicit feminism of the early twentieth-century anarchist movement, including its prescient championing of birth control and sexual liberation? The answer is complicated. Beyond the fact that movements, like individuals, are frequently inconsistent, it is important to bear in mind that for American anarchists a century ago, feminism and maternalism were not mutually exclusive philosophies; instead, they were intertwined expressions of individual freedom.

The answer also lies in the fact that anarchists' maternalism deviated significantly from that of other maternalist reformers. While many of their contemporaries embraced the idea that the expansion of feminine roles would engender social purification and progress, anarchists took this concept to a different end. What anarchists sought was not merely a feminisation of the public sphere but the abolition of public and private spheres altogether. While their mainstream counterparts used maternalism as a way to bolster the emerging welfare state, anarchists understood it as a means of transforming, not reinforcing, the patriarchal, nuclear family and the larger capitalist state. Far from suggesting a return to family values, anarchists took the familiar image of the family and inverted it; that is, while retaining the significance of socialisation and childrearing, they simultaneously rejected what many viewed as the bastion of organised society, the monogamous, heterosexual couple bound together through legal and religious institutions.

This radicalised maternalism represented quite a challenge to turn-of-the-century American society, as many Americans understood. In 1901 Senator Louis E. McComas of Maryland warned his colleagues of the threat anarchists posed to the family: 'Anarchists would abolish the family and marriage. More than any other land ours is the land of pure homes. In no other tongue or country are the words "father," "mother," "wife," "child," sweeter or more sacred.'[38] What McComas could not appreciate was that for some this was part of anarchism's appeal.

Modern readers might be inclined to underestimate the full political significance of these fantastic and surreal utopian novels. Turn-of-the-century anarchists, however, did take them very seriously. In a letter to one anarchist journal, T. O. Smith described the efforts of 'The Colorado Co-Operative Company' to create a communal society based on the vision presented in *Hilda's Home*. Smith urged 'social radicals' to join the venture so that 'while we are doing the pioneer work, blazing the trail, we can be cultivating the soil and sowing the seeds of liberty and freethought, until every home in our community shall be a "Hilda's Home" in principle'.[39] Such endeavours constituted an attempt to realise anarchism in the absence of a larger socioeconomic transformation. Both as a form of popular culture and as propaganda, the effects of anarchist utopian fiction were more widespread than their literary merits alone might suggest.

These novels brought together efforts at individual and social change and reflected and proselytised anarchists' dreams for the new century. In fictional form anarchists publicly redefined the possibilities for the social organisation of intimate life in a more detailed manner than their polemical tracts allowed. The special licence accorded by this medium was not lost on them. Upon hearing that yet another theoretical tract on free love and marriage had been held up by the zealous vice censor Anthony Comstock, *Free Society* editor Abe Isaak posed those who had ordered the condemned publication with an alternative: 'Shall we furnish instead "A Cityless and Countryless World", which contains the most advanced thought on the same subject and in language that we defy any idiot to call "lewd and obscene?" '[40] There is more than a little irony to the fact that the veil of the utopia allowed explicit discussion of the tabooed topics of the day.

With the fading popularity of the utopian genre in the first decade of the twentieth century, anarchist journals ceased to promote utopian novels and turned instead to allegorical and realist tales. This change, while in sync with the trends of the time, was not as accommodating of anarchists' efforts. Whereas the genre of the utopia suggested alternative re-conceptualisations of the state, realism retreated from a focus on the state to one on the individual. In so doing, the new genre served better to criticise than propose. Realism, such a powerful genre for others who challenged the status quo in American society, made manifest the fragmentation of anarchists' literary politics in the absence of the utopia. By 1914, fiction was virtually nonexistent in anarchist publications.[41] For a political philosophy like anarchism this was a crucial shift. Since an anarchist society existed only in the imagination, the silencing of American anarchists' literary voice limited their ability to convey the possibilities to be realised in anarchism.

Conclusion

For over a century anarchists have been dismissed as extra-legal and peripheral to the political mainstream, but through their fiction they revealed that they did not position themselves entirely outside of American culture. Indeed, this literature, despite its obvious radicalism, has analogues in other popular fiction of the period: like Edward Bellamy, many anarchist utopians posed their idealised present in the future; like Upton Sinclair and Theodore Dreiser, these authors used literature to critique contemporary society; and like Charlotte Perkins Gilman, they looked to mothers to create a new world order.

Yet study of anarchist fiction also exposes the challenge that anarchism posed to American culture and society. In utopian fiction anarchist authors used sexuality to suggest a reorganisation of intimate and public life and to posit a model for the reconstruction of both. The politics of maternalism were thus central to the propositions anarchists detailed in their fiction and highlight a distinctive aspect of the American anarchist movement: its emphasis on sex and gender, and particularly the use of motherhood as the basis for the transformation of society. It was this stress on gender in American anarchist publications that prompted the Russian anarchist prince Peter Kropotkin to complain to Emma Goldman of one anarchist journal: 'The paper is doing splendid work, but it would do more if it would not waste so much space discussing sex.' (Goldman's response is equally as memorable – after arguing with Kropotkin extensively about the importance of women's emancipation to the anarchist movement, she sighed, 'All right, dear comrade, when I have reached your age the sex question may no longer be of importance to me.')[42]

The true radicalism of American anarchists lay not only in their discussion of the destruction of the state but in the construction they hoped would replace it: a maternalist society in which free sexuality, voluntary motherhood, and affective relations would replace patriarchy and competition. As a result, what anarchists called into question was not just the structure of government but something far more immediate: the social organisation of intimate life. Perhaps, then, the anarchist as a woman bent on sexual revolution was a more subversive threat to the American status quo than the bomb-toting male nihilist would ever be.

Notes

I am indebted to Laurence Davis and Ruth Kinna, whose stimulating queries and generous comments have helped to strengthen this work. This essay is dedicated to Mark Julian and William Rhys Garman. Every day their enthusiasm and sense of wonder revitalise my faith in the possibilities for change.
  1 Advertisement for *Loma, a Citizen of Venus*, in *Lucifer, the Light-Bearer*, 19 January 1898, 439.
  2 W. Windsor, *Loma, a Citizen of Venus*, p. 2.
  3 For an excellent discussion of the caricature of the anarchist in the popular press, see F. Rosemont, 'A Bomb-Toting, Long-Haired, Wild-Eyed Fiend: The Image of the Anarchist in Popular Culture', in D. Roediger and F. Rosemont (eds), *Haymarket Scrapbook*, pp. 203–12.
  4 American anarchist fiction has received little notice. One of the foremost scholars of radical fiction, Walter B. Rideout, claims that anarchists – unlike many of their contemporaries in late nineteenth- and early twentieth-century North America – did not use fiction to creatively express their political philosophy. The reason for this omission was to be found in the anarchist character itself,

Rideout writes, because of 'the Anarchist "temperament," which expended itself more readily in personal reminiscence, critical analysis, short poems, and long arguments'. See W. B. Rideout, *The Radical Novel in the United States 1900–1954: Some Interrelations of Literature and Society*, pp. 90–1. One of the few studies to examine a work of anarchist fiction in this time period is Blaine McKinley's article on the 'anti-domestic' and semi-realist novel *Hagar Lyndon* by Lizzie M. Holmes: 'Free Love and Domesticity: Lizzie M. Holmes, *Hagar Lyndon* (1893), and the Anarchist–Feminist Imagination', *Journal of American Culture*, 13 (1990), 55–62. It is an excellent study of Holmes's rather contradictory (and ultimately quite pessimistic) views regarding the emancipation of women.

5 D. Bleich, *Utopia: The Psychology of a Cultural Fantasy*, p. 56.

6 The Haymarket affair established the association of anarchism with violence. In 1886 a bomb exploded during a labour demonstration at Chicago's Haymarket Square. Four anarchists were executed as a result of the offence, though the evidence against them was at best flimsy.

7 R. Graul, 'What "Hilda's Home" Means', *Lucifer, the Light-Bearer*, 15 December 1897, 395.

8 E. S. and J. W. D., 'Various Voices', *Lucifer, the Light-Bearer*, 15 April 1899, 111. Editor Moses Harman responded with a note: 'The question whether Lucifer should publish stories is one rather difficult . . . The paper is so small that many grudge the space taken by fiction, while on the other hand, others have become interested in Lucifer through the ideas presented in a story.' Harman, like many other anarchist editors, evidently decided to devote the space to fiction, for fiction appeared regularly in *Lucifer, the Light-Bearer* throughout the life of the publication.

9 The repeated advertisements for and discussions of these works attest to their dissemination within the American anarchist movement. We have no specific sales figures for this fiction, however, largely due to the fact that these novels were typically published by the authors and their friends and accordingly lacked an institutionalised means of recording circulation. What are more readily available are the circulations of the journals that serialised and promoted this fiction. *Lucifer, the Light-Bearer* had a distribution of 2000 in the late 1880s. The exact figures for *Free Society* are not known, but it is likely that they exceeded the 3000 of its predecessor, *The Firebrand*. At its height, *Mother Earth* claimed a readership of over 40,000 in 1911. See H. D. Sears, *The Sex Radicals: Free Love in High Victorian America*, p. 99; H. Addis, 'A True Story of American Officialism', *Free Society*, 21 November 1897, 1; and L. Veysey, *The Communal Experience: Anarchist and Mystical Communities in Twentieth-Century America*, p. 36.

10 S. Michel and R. Rosen, 'The Paradox of Maternalism: Elizabeth Lowell Putnam and the American Welfare State', *Gender and History*, 4 (1992), 364.

11 Maternalism is a concept of considerable debate in recent scholarship. The majority of works in this area look at the transformation of 'motherhood from women's primary *private* responsibility into *public* policy', in the words of Seth Koven and Sonya Michel, editors of *Mothers of a New World: Maternalist Politics and the Origins of Welfare States*, p. 2. Theda Skocpol's position significantly differs from Koven's and Michel's in important regards, but shares

their use of maternalism in understanding social welfare development in *Protecting Soldiers and Mothers: The Political Origins of Social Policy in the United States*. See also N. Fraser and L. Gordon, 'A Genealogy of *Dependency*: Tracing a Keyword of the U.S. Welfare State', *Signs*, 19 (1994), 309–36; L. Gordon, 'Gender, State, and Society: A Debate with Theda Skocpol', *Contention*, 2 (1993), 139–56; and T. Skocpol, 'Soldiers, Workers, and Mothers: Gendered Identities in Early U.S. Social Policy', *Contention*, 2 (1993), 157–83.

12 R. Graul, *Hilda's Home: A Story of Woman's Emancipation*.

13 F. Huntley, *The Dream Child*; the advertisement for the book is contained within it on p. 231.

14 H. Olerich, *A Cityless and Countryless World: An Outline of Practical Co-operative Individualism*, pp. 231, 114, 5–6.

15 Windsor, *Loma, a Citizen of Venus*, pp. 383, 145.

16 Graul, 'What "Hilda's Home" means', 395.

17 Windsor, *Loma, a Citizen of Venus*, p. 369.

18 Huntley, *The Dream Child*, p. 172.

19 Windsor, *Loma, a Citizen of Venus*, p. 144.

20 Graul, *Hilda's Home*, p. 3.

21 Windsor, *Loma, a Citizen of Venus*, p. 147.

22 The term 'angel of the house' derives from Coventry Patmore's popular poem by the same name. The poem, which was first published in 1854 and significantly revised thereafter, gained fame in the late nineteenth century as encapsulating the ideal of Victorian womanhood. It celebrated the role of the wife as a self-sacrificing and chaste help-mate to her husband – a concept underscored in American marital advice manuals, education, and sermons, historian Carroll Smith-Rosenberg notes in her influential study *Disorderly Conduct: Visions of Gender in Victorian America*, p. 25. In contrast, sexuality was given full expression both in and outside the marital bed in many anarchists' writings and discussions. For further discussion of this topic, see M. H. Blatt, *Free Love and Anarchism: The Biography of Ezra Heywood*; C. Falk, *Love, Anarchy, and Emma Goldman: A Biography*; and B. Haaland, *Emma Goldman: Sexuality and the Impurity of the State*.

23 Graul, *Hilda's Home*, p. 2.

24 Windsor, *Loma, a Citizen of Venus*, pp. 82, 133.

25 Olerich, *A Cityless and Countryless World*, pp. 18–19.

26 Windsor, *Loma, a Citizen of Venus*, pp. 16, 43, 114.

27 *Ibid.* p. 81.

28 Graul, *Hilda's Home*, p. 426.

29 Olerich, *A Cityless and Countryless World*, p. 264.

30 Graul, *Hilda's Home*, p. 425.

31 *Ibid.* pp. 287–8.

32 Huntley, *The Dream Child*, p. 26.

33 Moses Harman, editor of *Lucifer, the Light-Bearer*, was a leading advocate of eugenics; indeed, wearied after multiple censorship battles involving *Lucifer*, he reconfigured the journal as the *American Journal of Eugenics* in 1907.

34 Windsor, *Loma, a Citizen of Venus*, p. 60.

35 *Ibid.* p. 208.

36 Olerich, *A Cityless and Countryless World*, p. 264.

37 This was a point some anarchists themselves acknowledged. William Holmes tackled this question directly, and asked his fellow anarchists, 'Do we ignore the practical?'. He wrote, 'We have an ideal. A rare and beautiful picture of terrestrial beatitude is ever before us.' Nevertheless, he conceded, 'dream and hope and fancy as we may, the realization is still a long way off; our beautiful earthly paradise is still in the clouds, our picture still remains a picture. We are forced back continually to our practical workaday world; to a daily consideration of the great bread and butter prob'em; to the swamps and quagmires of human hideousness and treachery.' W. Holmes, 'Do We Ignore the Practical?', *The Firebrand*, 10 May 1896, 2.

38 L. E. McComas, *Progress of Anarchism – Federal Legislation Against Anarchists. Speech of Hon. Louis E. McComas, of Maryland, in the Senate of the United States, Thurs., December 5, 1901*, p. 17.

39 T. O. Smith, 'Where Hilda's Homes May Be Realized', *Lucifer, the Light-Bearer*, 21 May 1898, 55. There is ample evidence that many anarchists did attempt to realise these visions in their utopian colonies, of which Home, Washington, is the most famous example. For further discussion of Home, see B. Koenig, 'Law and Disorder at Home: Free Love, Free Speech, and the Search for an Anarchist Utopia', *Labor History*, 45 (2004), 199–223.

40 A. Isaak, 'Comstock's Ax Falls', *Free Society*, 26 December 1897, 5.

41 *Mother Earth*, the most prominent American anarchist journal in circulation and influence, published only one fictional piece after 1914: Ben Hecht's 'The Mob' (*Mother Earth*, May 1917, 92–6). Although the figure of the anarchist would frequently appear in fiction, it was in works about anarchists, not by anarchists. See, for example, Henry James, *The Princess Casamassima* (1886); Joseph Conrad, *The Secret Agent* (1907); Hutchins Hapgood, *An Anarchist Woman* (1909); Upton Sinclair, *Boston: A Documentary Novel of the Sacco-Vanzetti Case* (1928).

42 E. Goldman, *Living My Life*, p. 253. Kropotkin was referring to *Free Society*.

References

Addis, H., 'A True Story of American Officialism', *Free Society*, 21 November 1897, p. 1.

Advertisement for *Loma, a Citizen of Venus*, in *Lucifer, the Light-Bearer*, 19 January 1898, 439.

Blatt, M. H., *Free Love and Anarchism: The Biography of Ezra Heywood* (Urbana: University of Illinois Press, 1989).

Bleich, D., *Utopia: The Psychology of a Cultural Fantasy* (Ann Arbor: UMI Research Press, 1984 [1970]).

Falk, C., *Love, Anarchy, and Emma Goldman: A Biography* (New Brunswick: Rutgers University Press, rev edn, 1990).

Fraser, N. and L. Gordon, 'A Geneology of *Dependency*: Tracing a Keyword of the U.S. Welfare State', *Signs*, 19 (1994), 309–36.

Goldman, E., *Living My Life* (New York: Dover Publications, 1970 [1931]).

Gordon, L., 'Gender, State, and Society: A Debate with Theda Skocpol', *Contention*, 2 (1993), 139–56.

Graul, R., 'What "Hilda's Home" Means', *Lucifer, the Light-Bearer*, 15 December 1897, p. 395.

——. *Hilda's Home: A Story of Woman's Emancipation* (Chicago: M. Harman and Co., 1899).

Haaland, B., *Emma Goldman: Sexuality and the Impurity of the State* (Montreal: Black Rose Books, 1993).

Hecht, B., 'The Mob', *Mother Earth* (May 1917), 92–6.

Holmes, W., 'Do We Ignore the Practical?', *The Firebrand*, 10 May 1896, 2.

Huntley, F., *The Dream Child* (Boston: Arena Publishing Co., 1892).

Isaak, A., 'Comstock's Ax Falls', *Free Society*, 26 December 1897, 5.

Koenig, B., 'Law and Disorder at Home: Free Love, Free Speech, and the Search for an Anarchist Utopia', *Labor History*, 45 (2004), 199–223.

McComas, L. E., *Progress of Anarchism – Federal Legislation Against Anarchists. Speech of Hon. Louis E. McComas, of Maryland, in the Senate of the United States, Thurs., December 5, 1901* (Washington, DC: n.p., 1901).

McKinley, B., 'Free Love and Domesticity: Lizzie M. Holmes, *Hagar Lyndon* (1893), and the Anarchist–Feminist Imagination', *Journal of American Culture*, 13 (1990), 55–62.

Michel, S. and S. Koven (eds), 'The Paradox of Maternalism: Elizabeth Lowell Putnam and the American Welfare State', *Gender and History*, 4 (1992), 364–86.

——. *Mothers of a New World: Maternalist Politics and the Origins of Welfare States* (New York: Routledge, 1993).

Olerich, H., *A Cityless and Countryless World: An Outline of Practical Co-operative Individualism* (Holstein: Gilmore and Olerich, 1893).

Rideout, W. B., *The Radical Novel in the United States 1900–1954: Some Interrelations of Literature and Society* (Cambridge, MA: Harvard University Press, new edn, 1992).

Rosemont, F., 'A Bomb-Toting, Long-Haired, Wild-Eyed Fiend: The Image of the Anarchist in Popular Culture', in D. Roediger and F. Rosemont (eds), *Haymarket Scrapbook* (Chicago: Charles H. Kerr Publishing Co., 1986).

S., E. and J. W. D., 'Various Voices', *Lucifer, the Light-Bearer*, 15 April 1899, 111.

Sears, H. D., *The Sex Radicals: Free Love in High Victorian America* (Lawrence: Regents Press of Kansas, 1977).

Skocpol, T., *Protecting Soldiers and Mothers: The Political Origins of Social Policy in the United States* (Cambridge, MA: Harvard University Press, 1992).

——. 'Soldiers, Workers, and Mothers: Gendered Identities in Early U.S. Social Policy', *Contention*, 2 (1993), 157–83.

Smith, T. O., 'Where Hilda's Homes May Be Realized', *Lucifer, the Light-Bearer*, 21 May 1898, 55.

Smith-Rosenberg, C., *Disorderly Conduct: Visions of Gender in Victorian America* (New York: Oxford University Press, 1985).

Veysey, L., *The Communal Experience: Anarchist and Mystical Communities in Twentieth-Century America* (Chicago: University of Chicago Press, new edn, 1977).

Windsor, W., *Loma, a Citizen of Venus* (St Paul: The Windsor and Lewis Publishing Co., 1897).

Intimate fellows: utopia and chaos in the early post-Stonewall gay liberation manifestos

Guilt, by reminding us what we musn't do, shows us what we want and what we want to want. (Adam Phillips, 1996)[1]

So I cannot take the Gross National Product very seriously, nor status and credentials, nor grandiose technological solutions, nor ideological politics, including ideological liberation movements. For a starving person, the world has got to come across in kind. It doesn't. I have learned to have very modest goals for society and myself: things like clean air, green grass, children with bright eyes, not being pushed around, useful work that suits one's abilities, plain tasty food, and occasional satisfying nookie. (Paul Goodman, 1979)[2]

This essay examines utopian and anarchist impulses in a set of texts written by gay men in the early years following the Stonewall Rebellion. ('Stonewall', a riot in Greenwich Village at the end of June 1969, is often hailed as the birth of the modern US lesbian and gay liberation movement, at least as a major media event.[3]) The texts looked at here all appeared in the collection *Out of the Closets: Voices of Gay Liberation*, edited by Karla Jay and Allen Young, first published in 1972. These texts make an important contribution to our understanding of how recently liberated (at least ostensibly liberated) gay men attempted to articulate and embody new conceptualisations of intimacy, community, masculinity and gender roles, and sexual politics, without the help of any satisfactory existent models of how to establish meaningful and conscientious relationships with each other. They often found themselves embroiled in conflicts between their desires as emotional and sexual beings and their political commitments. Such commitments were formed in the broader context of widespread calls for the radical transformation of society that emerged in the 1960s and early 1970s. Of course, the project of inventing and reinventing meaningful relationships is an ongoing one; this essay seeks to illuminate the struggles these writers faced – not only for their inherent historical value but also for the relevance of their stories to contemporary concerns that we all have about how best to go about cultivating intimate relationships.

These early gay activist writers were faced with the complicated task of negotiating the relation of sex and pleasure with notions of happiness during this period in America. They faced, for instance, not only the difficulty of defining 'manhood' in America at that time, but also an inherited legacy of deep-rooted cultural anxieties about gender, intimacy, and sexuality in general, including attitudes toward monogamy and promiscuity that might be described as conflicted and hypocritical at best.[4] The distinction between what we want and what we want to want, when they differ, as they so often do, is crucial in analysing the relation of political ideals to desire as gay men struggled to be sexual, liberated, and good all at the same time. Not only can you not always *get* what you want, but you sometimes cannot even *be* what you want to be, a frustration that will be discussed in detail below. Gay men in this period were therefore dealing not only with the challenge of figuring out what it means to be gay and to be a man, but also with moral considerations about how one 'ought to' structure one's affectional and social life according to the ideological principles of 'liberated sexuality' at the time, including, for instance, the injunction against treating each other as sexual objects. In short, they wanted to be conscientious and to get laid at the same time, a prospect that was not always as easy as it may have seemed to the authors of these autobiographical texts.

One major figure whose thinking influenced not only this generation of gay activism but also the wider New Left and the counter-culture is Paul Goodman. Goodman's critique of what he calls the 'organized society' (most famously in *Growing Up Absurd* in 1960), and the impoverished, sterile and unnatural alternatives for living it offers, contains insights from both the utopian and anarchist traditions: a utopian call for a notion of local community that fosters the free – libertarian – expression of natural human impulses. These insights are very useful for analysing what was at stake as the authors of these gay liberation texts tried to figure out how to create freer and more dignified lives after years of stifling oppression, fear, and shame.

The main argument of this essay is that the project of mapping out specific strategies and often rigid guidelines for how to structure and inhabit new identities as gay men with a sense of radical freedom as their main common rallying point proved difficult. For one thing, the attempt to articulate principles for what a truly liberated gay identity should resemble failed to accommodate the vast differences between men who often had in common only their homosexuality (race, class, and age are but a few obvious examples of such differences). Visions of utopias put forward in these post-Stonewall texts were flawed: the aim was to determine a preconceived and highly prescriptive end rather than to see utopia as a process (as articulated by Angelika Bammer, below). But many also contain an anarchist impulse that focuses on radical sexual freedom (without harming others) as the sole preconceived requirement, and thus offer a welcome corrective to the ideological confines of the more prescriptive demands.[5] Here, Paul Goodman's open-ended libertarianism offered an approach to gay liberation that was especially promising.

This essay is divided into four sections. The first examines a set of complicated questions facing gay men following Stonewall and Paul Goodman's utopian and anarchist insights that shed light on attempts to answer these questions, though some of the authors fail to find sufficiently persuasive answers. The second section raises the problem of individual and community identity formation; some men found it extremely difficult to figure out how to understand themselves and their desires now that they were ostensibly liberated, and some were very ambivalent about aspects of the emerging gay community. Section three evaluates a critique of one element of pre-Stonewall gay life as being reactionary and damaging to the liberation project. Section four accompanies a group of men who attempt to form a living collective; they begin with a set of very specific political ideals and struggle to make their everyday life experiences fit the ideals.

Introduction: 'we can work it out'

In the early post-Stonewall manifestos, the most significant debates were over sexism, the legacy of gender roles, and other sources and consequences of internalised homophobia. The need to confront sexism especially, including their own sexist attitudes, was seen as central to developing gay men's understandings of their own oppression. There were also tensions between generations. On the one hand were typically older, closeted men who lived double lives, along with the assimilationist homophile activists who sought to convince straight society that homosexuals are 'just like you' and deserve to be free from discrimination under the law. On the other hand were a new generation of activists who called for an all-out social revolution in solidarity with blacks, feminists, the New Left, and the anti-war movement. They believed that the oppression of homosexuals could not end under the conditions of white, middle-class, capitalist, sexist, heteronormative society; hence, liberation would mean a transformation of the entire society; and this transformation would begin, in part, with a reconceptualisation of the possibilities of relationships between self-identified gay men.

The universal demand was for sexual freedom without shame. But what exactly would this mean in practice, and how would it affect gay male relations not defined simply or exclusively in sexual terms? What is liberated sexuality; what is liberated friendship? And what of love? Romance? Is there any place in post-Stonewall gay consciousness and sexual–political life for monogamy? Promiscuity? Anonymous and/or public sex? These questions were raised and scrutinised in many early manifestos, and would continue to be so through the onset of HIV/AIDS, and, of course, very much so through the present. Especially in the earliest texts, however, it seemed quite a bit easier to articulate pointed critiques of the past – a legacy of 'lifestyles' and identities that were no longer desirable. The articulation of positive alternatives, and any common core of values upon which these might be built, was rarer, more contentious, and less concrete.

One area of serious contention for these writers is the appropriate relationship between sex and sentiment. Might sex and sentiment be or become (indeed, should they be or become) unified in the persons of their affection? Should one's lovers and tricks and friends be the same people? Or are sexual desire and emotional attachment, or should they be, quite mutually exclusive, or at least separable at will? This question is closely linked to one's attitude toward monogamy and promiscuity. The relation between sex and sentiment, and monogamy and promiscuity, and their relation to various conceptions of gender, are themes present throughout these texts. Regardless of one's position on these questions, the project of putting forth theoretical or political claims about correct behaviour assumes the ability of people to control their desires and emotions, and to shape their sexual activities for the sake of abstract principles (e.g. deciding whom one should find attractive as a potential partner, or friend, or not – all of which assumes the possibility of living lives that correspond with these imposed desires). Related to this demand is the implied requirement that men somehow reinvent personas – public faces – to go along with their new, sometimes still only semi-internalised identities as liberated gays. Here, the activities of self-monitoring and consciousness-raising are more often assumed and asserted as inherently worthy rather than being explored or debated. If one oughtn't to be a nelly queen or a hyper-masculine butch, then what ought one to be? A central tension here is the requirement that not only must behaviour and interactions be reprogrammed, but so must how you feel about yourself – a sort of imposed internal identity. While several writers at least acknowledge the difficulties involved with such self-transformation, many write assuming it to be a very manageable task (e.g. 'so just stop chasing after sixteen-year-olds'; 'so just stop waving your arms and talking that way'). Few are able to articulate what the new ideal might be like.

Again, Paul Goodman is an important figure who began writing about freedom, sexuality, and liberation some decades before Stonewall. One widely quoted passage from 'The May Pamphlet' published in 1946 in *Art and Social Nature* sums up his basic political position: 'Free action is to live in present society as though it were a natural society.'[6] In other words, we must proceed *as though* present society were not corrupted by the oppressive and unnatural 'system' with its exploitation, discrimination, stifling of creativity, and hypocritical sexual prohibitions. Goodman calls his libertarian position millenarian rather than utopian because it does not propose a programme for some better future state of affairs but re-imagines the present – to make it better now. Goodman puts it this way: 'Merely by continuing to exist and act in nature and freedom, the libertarian wins the victory, establishes the society.'[7]

As noted above, Goodman's thought can be characterised as combining elements from both the anarchist and utopian traditions. In *Demanding the Impossible*, Peter Marshall provides the following formulation of the basic tenets that unify various strains of anarchist philosophy:

> All anarchists reject the legitimacy of external government and of the State, and condemn imposed political authority, hierarchy and domination. They seek to establish the condition of anarchy, that is to say, a decentralized and self-regulating society consisting of a federation of voluntary associations of free and equal individuals. The ultimate goal of anarchism is to create a free society which allows all human beings to realize their full potential.[8]

Goodman's writing certainly champions such a free (and, he would add, *natural*) society. As for his utopianism, he was not always comfortable with the term 'utopian thinking' because of its often perverted use by those who seek to naturalise the existing state of affairs as being the only state of affairs possible.[9] Goodman would, however, embrace Angelika Bammer's notion of utopia as a process, especially as it involves actively working toward some indefinite, but better and freer, state of affairs. In *Partial Visions: Feminism and Utopianism in the 1970s*, Bammer describes the new utopianism as 'an idea of the future *as possibility* rather than as preset goal'. Thus, there is no specific programme or set of principles that would dictate rigidly defined modes of behaviour ahead of time. Rather, she describes it in these terms: 'Experimental rather than prescriptive, speculative rather than predictive, this new utopianism propose[s] a politics of change cast in the subjunctive instead of the imperative mode. It [is] a politics that dare[s] to leave questions open, a politics of the "what if . . .".'[10]

This experimental, speculative perspective is precisely the sort of utopianism that Goodman would welcome in thinking about the project(s) of gay liberation, though he wrote little specifically about post-Stonewall gay activist politics (he died in 1972, the same year the collection of texts considered here was published). He was, however, suspicious of ideological demands about how people ought to behave. In his sexual politics, Goodman was ahead of his time, and a precursor to the Beats, in that he refused to hide his bisexuality, to the point of being fired from teaching positions for seducing students. He lived the sexual revolution he wrote about; and his concerns with individual freedom and the creation of natural communities resonate throughout the struggles and imaginings of the authors of the autobiographical texts to be discussed in the rest of this essay.

'One is the loneliest number': the formation of individual identities and the gay community

One major point of contention in these texts is the relationship between the consciousness of the individual, as having and acting on homosexual desires and/or being a self-proclaimed liberated gay man, on the one hand, and the idea of 'the gay community' on the other. Questions arise: Is the mere fact of sharing sexual and affectional attractions an adequate basis for a political movement? Is there some pre-existent or newly forming community that one wants or needs or should want to belong to and participate in? Since gay men and lesbians constitute such a diverse group of people, why should they expect to share more than same-sex attraction? (For example, apart from their sexuality, Log Cabin Republicans in the US appear to have little else in common with progressive politicos and poor and minority homosexuals[11]).

Paul Goodman's writings seem to offer ambivalent perspectives about what might be the proper attitude toward gay community-building. While Goodman's anarchism rejects large-scale social projects with centralised authority and a conformist ethic, including governmental regulation of private lives and individual behaviour (except to protect others from undue harm), he does believe that human beings are naturally social creatures and that most people are probably happiest in local, small-scale communities in which decisions are made by consensus – what he calls 'unanimity'.[12] But he was also sceptical of rigid ideological programmes (even ideological liberation movements, as noted in the epigraph) that would promote conformity and put restrictions on that free action best suited to an individual or a small community with common interests and shared desires. Likewise, the writers of these gay liberation texts seem generally to desire some form of community, or at least a connection with other gay men, but some find it hard to achieve. Moreover, some are willing at least to attempt to subscribe to various forms of ideological demand (for example, to broaden their range of attraction to include more potential mates or otherwise reprogramme their sex lives).

One moving tale of struggling with such questions is Konstantin Berlandt's saga of the vanishing of his soul.[13] At first, Berlandt begins to illuminate the sheer pleasure and excitement of anonymous sexuality, though in a narrative filled with ambivalence about what to feel and how to behave. Beyond its refreshing honesty and lack of any obvious polemical agenda, the power of Berlandt's story, and its keen ability to portray the complexity and ambiguity of various sorts of intimate encounters, comes in large part through its form. It is a highly personal autobiography with a freedom of form that allows the text to imitate the flux of moving from encounter to encounter and back into the straight world; and from guilt to exaltation; from normality to radicality; from hot sex – some form or other of intimacy – in the moment, to the wish for love in bed the morning after – and, ultimately, to gay liberation. What such liberation might mean for Berlandt is clearly a quandary. He seems to enjoy 'cruising' for public, anonymous sex, but wonders whether it is enough in the end. This is a question that has puzzled many who engage in such behaviour. Goodman, for instance, speaks fondly of cruising for sex as a chance for encounters with other men that enrich rather than desensitise gay men's lives, though he laments on occasion the tremendous amount of time he spent over the years, daily hunting on the streets – time that might have been spent on more productive pursuits.[14]

Berlandt-as-narrator begins as a college student interviewing homosexuals for a project, and discovers himself surprised – 'I'm going back next week to interview another one' – using the ugly yet somehow quaint pronoun, 'another *one*'; but soon he becomes all 'too involved'.

> I left the bar high, excited, jumping, running. I greeted my friends with a huge grin. I've just discovered a whole new world: Homosexuals are people, beautiful people who really exist, party, rap, hold each other tight when riding motorcycles. I'm going back next week to interview another one.
>
> But the following Saturday afternoon I am an intrepid boy on an AC Transit bus from Berkeley.
>
> I'm too involved. My cock starts to rise. Just an interview for a sociology project and a newspaper article, but my cock starts to rise. The fear climbs up around me. I have always loved going to San Francisco. Now it is frightening, crawling with homosexuals, old men who want to make me. I don't want anybody to see me, and yet I've worn a bright shirt and tight Levis. The city is dark, the shadows hanging over the patches of sun.[15]

Berlandt provides such a poignant and utterly realistic portrait of the transformation involved in coming out – to himself first (gradually, almost unconsciously), and then to other gay men. *Now*, San Francisco is frightening, and crawling with lusty homosexuals (as opposed to the last time he visited) – this may be the beginning of a libratory epistemological victory. This is the confusion of being at once attracted and repelled – the whole scene, at least as he imagines it, is at once so dirty and so inescapably magnetic. Berlandt wonders how he is supposed to feel when his cock starts to rise in new environments, with new, and maybe longtime, objects of desire suddenly thrust into full relief. He finds himself in the anarchist–utopian position of freedom in which the only judgement on how he should feel or proceed is his own, except that he has not yet fully freed himself from the old shame associated with homosexual desire that follows him as he gradually comes out of the closet.

This must have been the experience of so many in the post-Stonewall period – different from earlier experiences of coming into one's own homosexual desires because there had then been virtually no publicised debate with one side saying that one should be proud to be gay, that gay might perhaps be good. No, this personal moment is not unique in the intensity and ambivalence of its emotions and desires, but unique in that it now includes the 'sociological' knowledge that a whole community of people is being public and political about it.

I'd be ashamed for people to know I jacked off in the john, I blew a man through a glory hole, I blew a man at all.

I like making it in a restroom. There's romance in the fear of being caught, the excitement of making it with a complete stranger, someone you don't know, and you can be so close, so sexually intimate and unafraid to put your cock in his mouth and taking his in yours and feeling strong because you can fuck. If I can't ever show my cock in public now, I can show it to a public stranger who loves it.[16]

The dichotomies are telling; they are not placed in opposition, but act in concert in the service of a restroom sexual experience at once shameful and pleasurable: romance in fear and romance in being unafraid; romance in anonymous cocks and romance in intimacy; and strength, whether reinforcing his own version of masculinity or challenging it.

The passage below shows the tension between participation in a subculture that often seems to value genital contact and orgasm above all else, on the one hand, and wanting to make longer-lasting contact, on the other. The object of attraction changes from 'it' to 'him', and from the narrator's penis to the other's. And is the cup of coffee Berlandt imagines them having in the midst of their erotic scene for getting to know one another, or just to make sure they're not cops? Does the narrator even distinguish between these possibilities, or choose in his mind, as he contemplates what to ask first himself and then the other?

Exercise: Stand at the urinal and look at the cock of the man standing next to you. Is it ugly? Is it beautiful? Do you want to make it feel good? You'll never see him again. You might be in love with him. Let him look at your cock. Is it ugly? Is it beautiful? Do you want to make it feel good? Is it getting hard? Yes, it is. Let's go get a cup of coffee and reassure each other we're not cops.[17]

The saddest part of Berlandt's story is the following tale of lost love. It's such a common experience in gay male relations, and was perhaps even more so in the rush of the early days of liberation. What keeps them from getting together? They both seem to want to. But it's as though something deep and common prohibits closeness and emotional vulnerability – as if they don't know how to negotiate or express their emotions, oftentimes a quandary for men of all sexual orientations. This is the moment in the piece where it sounds as though he might want monogamy on some level, might be capable of what society tends to call love:

My last night in New York I met a man who had just gotten out of the army. He had a wife and three children. It was 3 a.m. and we talked by the sunrise on the Hudson River until 9 a.m. when my father had gone to work and we went to my house and made love. Six hours of anticipation as he became more and more beautiful and then he fucked me and it felt so good.

I wrote him three letters from California. He finally answered one pledging that while 'most gay relationships don't last, our love would last forever.' I don't remember answering his letter.[18]

This is the sort of failure to establish a satisfactory connection for which an open-ended utopia as process has little specific remedy to offer. And, of course, even the most liberated gay relationships are not free from many of the troubles involved in the drama of human relating in general.

While apparently focused more than Berlandt on a single issue of contention within the emerging gay liberation movement, the following piece by Ralph Schaffer, 'Will You Still Need Me When I'm 64?', ultimately portrays a man in a similar state of disillusion, except that he opts out of participation in 'the movement' because, in his eyes, it refuses to meet his needs as an 'older' gay man.[19] His sense of isolation and loneliness, though, very much echoes Paul Goodman's experience. Goodman writes: 'Frankly, my experience of radical community is that it does not tolerate my freedom. Nevertheless, I am all for community because it is a human thing, only I seem doomed to be left out.'[20] While Schaffer applauds progress made by gay men in confronting many elements of their own oppression, and that of women, he remains unhappy with what he calls the 'youthism' of many gay men of all ages in the movement:

> Gay liberation has covered wide terrain – geographically and intellectually. We gay people have recognized our oppression and, in different ways, are dealing with it. We are also confronting our male chauvinism toward women and each other, and our racism. We are coping with gender identities and gender chauvinism . . .
>
> Now I'm beginning to get a little pissed. I think it is about time that gay liberation come to grips with youthism. It is the most vicious and entrenched of our fuck-ups left over from our oppression. It is tragic because it leaves half our gay people lonely, alienated, and unwanted.[21]

Schaffer's claim that 'youthism' is the most vicious of all oppressive fuck-ups is incredibly important. While there can be no fruitful quantitative or qualitative comparison to adjudicate between all the various 'fucked-up-nesses' of gay oppression, nor a hierarchy of blame put on gay liberation activists for not considering the needs of everybody, his point is well taken in that youthism does affect so many people (as do racism, classism, fashionism, culturism – for example, fairy princesses v. hipsters). But the oppression against the elder brothers was especially divisive and short-sighted, not only because it made so many feel left out, but because it neglected the wisdom of experience and potentially viable and sorely needed role models. He makes the point that most gay men will some day be in their late thirties (and even older); this is incredibly important in 1971, when the hipster sentiment, as represented by the popular media, was 'never trust anyone over thirty' – and, Schaffer might add, don't sleep with them; besides, they're unattractive by that age. Schaffer goes on to ask about the older person:

> Who is the older person? Well, I remember two sweet young guys complaining to me at a gay liberation dance that this dirty old man was bothering them.

The 'dirty old man' was 24 years old! And why is it when an older man cruises he is dirty? . . .

And so what if a guy does have a pot belly? A pot belly has its own kind of beauty, if you would look for it. So does baldness, grayness, wrinkledness, etc . . .

I have quit the gay liberation movement after being extremely active for a full year. In gay liberation, I've known more gay people than in all my life. I have never been so lonely. What a tragic comment on gay liberation.

Gay liberation is masturbation.[22]

Schaffer's complaint about what he sees as rampant discrimination against the old in the movement – at least as potential sex partners – is extremely important. Especially if one were to decide *on principle* that anybody over a certain age was unattractive, then such a position would be obviously wrong and hurtful. But Paul Goodman, for instance, took it in stride that he was less attractive to many as he aged.[23] He didn't see it as a moral oversight on the part of other gay men, but as a natural part of their particular preferences in any unique encounter. (Ralph Schaffer was murdered on 27 August 1972, while working on the Gay Will Funky Store project of the Gay Community Services Center in Los Angeles. He was 44 years old. There is no evidence one way or the other whether Schaffer's murder was a hate crime[24]).

'Is that all there is?': rejection of the tired old trip

Even harsher than Schaffer's criticism of the gay liberation movement for its youthism is the scathing critique by Craig Alfred Hanson, 'The Fairy Princess Exposed'.[25] Hanson describes a purported type of gay mentality – very delusional and destructive, according to him – in strongly accusatory terms:

It used to be that when most male homosexuals came out of their closets they headed straight for that gay fairyland somewhere way over Judy Garland's rainbow and set up housekeeping as fairy princesses. The gay liberation movement has been an escape from the old fairyland, and Judy Garland, and from the traditional gay subculture . . .

Fairyland is still alive and well in Hollywood and for most of those half-de-closeted gays over 30, and I don't think most of our older gay brothers will ever escape from it.[26]

At first glance, this rant could be seen as merely the displeasure of one man directed at a particular stereotype of homosexual men (regardless how widespread in reality). In this scenario, we have a writer rejecting the Judy Garland cult and its associations with femme-identification and fantasy. Maybe the man is personally not attracted to or repelled by these 'princess' types. Perhaps he thinks they give homosexual men a bad name; possibly his is an implied call for masculinity and normality.

On a closer reading, however, the passage contains a lot of problematic cultural assumptions about gender and identity conflation, not to mention outrage at what he claims is a looming threat – of a huge trap to be avoided at all cost. To regard a group of one's fellows as culturally conservative and even egocentric, and to identify a certain pattern of tastes and behaviour as 'a tired old trip' seem fair enough. But Hanson attacks a huge population here, and calls their fate *inescapable*, while appearing to blame the victims for their deep malaise. Hanson continues his rant about the failure of these elders to recognise and live according to 'what being gay is all about'. He goes on to make a rather unspecified claim about reality and rationality:

> We must make our gay brothers realize that the princess trip is a rotten one, a self-deluding flight into a past that never was, an artificiality, and an escape from reality. It is a selfish, self-serving, irrational and materialistic journey which shuns real human relations for past images and things material, and human relations are what being gay is all about.[27]

What is Hanson so bitter about and threatened by? And what might be his own version of possible positive relationships? And what would it take, by way of a cultural shift, to satisfy Hanson's demands? If all older gay men suddenly stopped listening to Judy Garland and began to identify with the hip movement, listening instead to Jimi Hendrix as many of them did, would this be enough? Perhaps it would be, and was. Perhaps embracing the counter-culture and its egalitarian and revolutionary ideology helped the project of gay liberation, at least for a short moment. But perhaps it was just another fantasy world – the anti-establishment hipster instead of the fairy princess – yet another spurious inner world, yet another escape from reality. This is exactly the sort of prescriptiveness that Goodman objected to in the often rigid demands made by some gay activists. Yet if Hanson is right that the hipster is an improvement on the fairy queen, then at least the hipster could say that 'gay is good' and perhaps engage to some degree in dialogue, out of the closet, not only with other gays but with the dominant heteronormative society.

'Those were the days, my friend': one experiment in collective living

While Schaffer writes from the perspective of a lonely 'older' man, and Hanson generalises about the dangerous, fantastical inner-lives of many older gay men, John Knoebel tells of the loneliness he experienced as a member of a group of younger men in 'Somewhere in the Right Direction'.[28] Age doesn't seem to be an obstacle in the way of this group's becoming intimate, though there is a slight gap between the youngest and eldest. Rather, major obstacles include their diverse life experiences and, more crucially, the difficulty of moulding their desires and behaviour to fit the ideological imperatives they have set for themselves. The experiment of this collective is an attempt to create a small, local community that would both respect the needs and desires of the individuals involved (the sort of free, natural community that Goodman may have envisioned) and also grapple with the challenges of the main ideological principles of many of the liberation movements of the day. But the collective was also challenged by the lack of models to look to for guidance, and the need to give some collective content to their sense of radical freedom and their vision of how to go about creating a new form of togetherness:

> I found out quickly enough that the others' ideas about collective living were just about as vague as mine. This was not difficult to understand: we were the first gay male living collective in the country. We were creating something that had never been tried before, and this meant we largely had to create it as we went along. Of course we thought of collective living as sharing everything equally: expenses, housework, ideas and feelings . . .
>
> We brought every aspect of our lives to group discussion. If I was reading a good book, it was my responsibility to share it with the group, as well as my mother's letters. If I had to make a decision about something that affected me alone, like an argument with a friend, I still brought it to the group. As it turned out, almost nothing that happened to me did not in some way affect the group. Yet as this loss of individuality became part of our experience, we recognized that the need to spend time alone once in a while was legitimate and tried to provide for it.[29]

Knoebel was by no means alone in his scepticism about the loss of individuality and privacy. Several voices in texts from this period raise concerns about feeling stifled by socialistic, consciousness-raising ideology – for example, that utter candour and forced sharing of all thoughts and feelings was a trap, and that confessions were sometimes used later as weapons. And Gary, a member of Knoebel's 95th Street Collective, 'often talked about wondering what it would be like to live alone', just the sort of doubt about the feasibility of their project that would ultimately lead to its demise.[30] But they made a sincere and extended effort to make it work for all of them, as Knoebel goes on to demonstrate:

> We were a tight group. We spent as much time as we could together and were constantly telling each other what had happened to us while we were apart. In the evenings we often took walks in Riverside Park, all of us holding hands. It was romantic, in a very different way than any of us had experienced before.
>
> Whenever there was a disagreement between any of us, everyone would gather together. We never allowed any two members to argue by themselves. This sometimes meant getting dragged out of bed or off the phone, but it was something we all agreed to do. In the presence of the group, arguments soon turned into reasonable discussions. Everyone's opinion was solicited.[31]

Such idealistic aspirations for conflict resolution and the group process ultimately led to the dissolution of this collective (as it finally became impossible for them to sustain their 'all for one, for the good of the group' philosophy in practice), as well as the swift disintegration of the Gay Liberation Front, the organisation at whose meetings the members of Knoebel's group first met. They also struggled with how to handle sex, both within and without the group. First, they fret about sex with outsiders:

> None of the relationships inside the group were sexualized . . . Having no internal sexual outlet, we were forced to go outside the collective for sex and the exception to the rule [which allowed for unannounced guests to be brought home only in the case of sexual partners] protected our ability to do so. But since we were almost always together as a group and felt our emotional involvement to be with the collective, this did not say much for the nature of the sexual encounters we had outside. For myself, I often thought it strange that living in a gay male collective in the midst of a busy gay movement, I had so little sex. I complained that I began to feel like a professional homosexual: being gay was my work, not my life.[32]

This passage includes several important examples of questions that raised the possibility, in very practical terms, that perhaps the group had expectations that were impossible to satisfy. The mandate that all visitors be scheduled ahead of time *except* for sexual partners imposes incredibly harsh restrictions on how such liaisons might be known to be sexual before the fact of the visit, as though the member and his sex partner would have had to negotiate the nature of their encounter *beforehand* (that it would be understood that they would be fuck-buddies of some sort, nothing more and definitely nothing less, or the rule would be violated). It's a bizarre manner of separating sex and sentiment ahead of time, and deciding theoretically that they *are* in fact separate and separable. Moreover, though the members of the collective recognised the need for privacy and time alone, they didn't manage to have much of either, and such time couldn't be spent with a nonmember unless it was sexual time. Presumably they would be required to tell the group about their sex lives and confess to any emotional attachments that might develop with a nonmember; and what if the nonmember fell in love with the member sex-partner? Was it stated, or merely assumed by the author, that their emotional involvement was with the collective? How can rules be made about such things, and how could they be enforced, either for oneself or for another? Finally, why might he have had so little sex, if he really wanted to have sex more often? Is this something one can decide ahead of time, and keep consistent, or change so voluntarily or easily in any direction?

The group was well aware of some of these difficulties, and tried various strategies to work them out, but in the end was unable to solve enough of the serious problems to remain together:

Of course, we often discussed the need to be sexual together. This was some-thing we did not expect to accomplish right away, as it meant coming to understand the nature of our sexuality and attempting to change our sexual programming. We tried to be physical together: holding one another, kissing each other in greeting. We learned to be naked together, around the apartment and sitting at meetings. This in itself was difficult, for it meant we had to overcome being shy and ashamed of our bodies. Several times we moved mattresses into the living room and slept together. But we were very afraid and hesitant to do much more. We knew we should be in theory, but theory was not supported by our feelings. [33]

Thus, sex and sentiment must be both separate and united simultane-ously. And the collective's members must be both promiscuous enough with outsiders *and* devoted and loyal enough to each other. As for their inability to be sexual with each other, the mind is dazzled by possible strategies they might or might not, should or should not, have employed (or did employ) *while* they were all lying on a mattress together naked, or milling around the apartment together. Were they incapable of actually touching each other's penises, asses, nipples, earlobes, or whatever zone imaginable and sexualisable, or unable to achieve or sustain erections? What is the defini-tion of the sexual that Knoebel laments they were unable to achieve? The point here is not to expect Knoebel to be more explicit or descriptive, but to explore the realm of the possible which the collective may have under-estimated or failed to experiment with sufficiently. Why wasn't it enough simply to sleep together and be physically intimate and affectionate? In some ways, their nonsexual togetherness seems to fulfil many libratory ideological requirements (working against obvious roles, inequalities, and oppressive modes of exclusivist coupling).

Through the process of consciousness-raising and continued experimen-tation with living arrangements and the management of daily tasks, members of the collective attempt to develop strategies for dealing with issues that are central concerns in many of these early post-Stonewall texts, whether practical, theoretical, political, emotional, or material – and part of the challenge they face is that these categories are not always cleanly distinct. They quickly decide they need another member to help with the workload, as basic household upkeep and their extensive community service work become overwhelming. John Knoebel falls in unrequited love with a man named Lane, who they all agree should be the new member. Lane moves in and begins an affair with Robert, which violates collective principles. John is jealous. Robert and Lane have problems with their need for privacy and their inability to remain loyal to the group decision-making process as they negotiate their private relationship together. They all agree that it no longer feels like a collective but like a pair of lovers with three hangers-on. The decision is made that Robert should leave. His sudden departure breaks the utopian spirit in which the collective began. John Knoebel asks himself what principles are good for if they force people apart and make everybody feel awful. The remaining members begin to criticise each other in new ways. Quickly the collective falls apart and they decide to disband in a heartbreaking goodbye scene. In the end, they were overcome by conflicts between personal and political pressures, including the need for privacy, for personal lives.

The struggles of this group of men to achieve intimacy within the confines of politically appropriate non-gendered, or at least re-imagined, gendered identities and attitudes toward sexuality echo throughout these texts. They had no role models to begin with; and they were very conscious of their experiment: of making it up as they went along. But even in such a thoughtful and dedicated community, sustaining intimate relationships proved an impossible task on account of members' intractable desires and their ultimate need to express or maintain their individuality, even at the expense of what may have been best for the collective.

The demise of this experiment in collective living may be seen as emblematic of the fate of early post-Stonewall gay liberation aspirations in general. As the 1970s wore on, the gay circuit culture became commodified and the revolutionary impulse of earlier notions of gay liberations waned. Political concerns of many gay activists shifted from calls for broad social transformation to a narrower focus on specific 'gay rights' issues. Then came the horror of the HIV/AIDS health crisis, whereupon humanitarian political energies and resources became often, and necessarily, focused on more immediate, local, and personal needs.[34] The writers of the texts treated in this essay could not, of course, have foreseen such developments.

Yet for all their disappointments and frustrated ideals back then, representations in these manifesto texts contributed to the discourse of what might be possible and desirable. They helped establish the terms of the debate for the post-Stonewall community about the relationship between gender and sexuality, and the importance of these categories to intimate relationships between self-identified gay men. This complicated debate would be a central concern of voices from this community through the 1970s and, indeed, it continues today – for instance in discussions among so-called radical queers, many of whom intend to create their utopias in anarchist–libertarian communities, and others who want to marry, settle down, and to assimilate into mainstream, 'normal' culture.

Notes

Many thanks to Laurence Davis and Ruth Kinna for their thoughtful comments and encouragement. Special thanks to Dagmar Herzog and Katherine McCracken for their inspiration and guidance along the way.

 1 Adam Phillips, *Monogamy*, p. 45.
 2 Paul Goodman, *Nature Heals: The Psychological Essays of Paul Goodman*, ed. T. Stoehr, p. 222.

3   Anecdotal reports about the uprising at the Stonewall Inn abound in the gay and mainstream media. One compelling and probably reliable account is E. Marcus, S. Thomas and L. Witt (eds), *Out in All Directions: The Almanac of Gay and Lesbian America*, pp. 208–17, which relies largely on first-hand interviews and puts Stonewall in the context of other protests.

4   For a discussion of the historicity of 'manhood', see E. A. Rotundo, 'Epilogue: Manhood in the Twentieth Century' in *American Manhood: Transformations in Masculinity from the Revolution to the Modern Era*, pp. 284–93. For insights into the legacy of cultural anxieties about sex, see L. Berlant (ed.), *Intimacy*, especially the essay by Berlant and M. Warner, 'Sex in Public', pp. 311–30.

5   See John D'Emilio's discussion of this prescriptiveness in K. Jay and A. Young (eds), *Out of the Closets: Voices of Gay Liberation*, p. xxviii.

6   P. Goodman, *Art and Social Nature*, p. 1.

7   *Ibid.* p. 7.

8   P. Marshall, *Demanding the Impossible: A History of Anarchism*, p. 3.

9   For his concerns about the term 'utopian' see P. Goodman, *Utopian Essays and Practical Proposals*, pp. 3–12.

10 A. Bammer, *Partial Visions: Feminism and Utopianism in the 1970s*, pp. 48–51.

11 Log Cabin Republicans are a group of gay Republicans.

12 P. Goodman, *Drawing the Line: The Political Essays of Paul Goodman*, ed. T. Stoehr, pp. 36–45.

13 K. Berlandt, 'My Soul Vanished from Sight: A California Saga of Gay Liberation', in Jay and Young, *Out of the Closets*, pp. 38–55.

14 P. Goodman, *Nature Heals*, ed. T. Stoehr, pp. 223–4.

15 Berlandt, 'My Soul Vanished from Sight', pp. 40–1.

16 *Ibid.* p. 44.

17 *Ibid.* p. 46.

18 *Ibid.* p. 47.

19 R. Schaffer, 'Will You Still Need Me When I'm 64?', in Jay and Young, *Out of the Closets*, pp. 278–9.

20 Goodman, *Nature Heals*, p. 217.

21 Schaffer, 'Will You Still Need Me When I'm 64?', p. 278.

22 *Ibid.* pp. 278–9.

23 Goodman, *Nature Heals*, pp. 18, 22.

24 W. Leyland (ed.), *Gay Roots: Twenty Years of Gay Sunshine: An Anthology of Gay History, Sex, Politics, and Culture*, p. 236.

25 C. A. Hanson, 'The Fairy Princess Exposed', in Jay and Young, *Out of the Closets*, pp. 266–9.

26 *Ibid.* p. 266.

27 *Ibid.* p. 269.

28 J. Knoebel, 'Somewhere in the Right Direction: Testimony of My Experience in a Gay Male Living Collective', in Jay and Young, *Out of the Closets*, pp. 301–15.

29 *Ibid.* pp. 303–4.

30 *Ibid.* p. 303.

31 *Ibid.* p. 305.

32 *Ibid.* p. 306.

33   *Ibid.* It should be noted here that Knoebel and a member, Robert, had a brief
     sexual affair at the very start, but that the attraction, at least in Knoebel's
     telling, disappeared for them both.
34   Among the many discussions of these shifts in lesbian and gay politics, see
     D'Emilio in Jay and Young, *Out of the Closets*, pp. xi–xxiv and U. Vaid, *Virtual
     Equality: The Mainstreaming of Gay and Lesbian Liberation.*

References

Bammer, A., *Partial Visions: Feminism and Utopianism in the 1970s* (New York:
    Routledge, 1991).
Berlant, L. (ed.), *Intimacy* (Chicago: University of Chicago Press, 2000).
Goodman, P., *Art and Social Nature* (New York: Vinco, 1946).
——*Utopian Essays and Practical Proposals* (New York: Random House, 1952).
——*Growing Up Absurd: Problems of Youth in the Organized Society* (New York:
    Vintage Books, 1960).
——*Drawing the Line: The Political Essays of Paul Goodman*, ed. T. Stoehr
    (New York: Dutton, 1979).
——*Nature Heals: The Psychological Essays of Paul Goodman*, ed. T. Stoehr
    (New York: Dutton, 1979).
Jay, K. and A. Young, (eds), *Out of the Closets: Voices of Gay Liberation*
    (New York: New York University Press, 1992 [1972]).
Leyland, W. (ed.), *Gay Roots: Twenty Years of Gay Sunshine: An Anthology of Gay
    History, Sex, Politics, and Culture* (San Francisco: Gay Sunshine Press, 1991).
Marcus, E., S. Thomas and L. Witt (eds), *Out in All Directions: The Almanac of
    Gay and Lesbian America* (New York: Warner Books, 1997).
Marshall, P., *Demanding the Impossible: A History of Anarchism* (London: Fontana
    Press, 1993).
Phillips, A., *Monogamy* (London: Faber and Faber, 1996).
Rotundo, E. A., *American Manhood: Transformations in Masculinity from the
    Revolution to the Modern Era* (New York: Basic Books, 1993).
Vaid, U., *Virtual Equality: The Mainstreaming of Gay and Lesbian Liberation*
    (New York: Anchor Books, 1995).

PART V

Rethinking revolutionary practice

Anarchism, utopianism and the politics of emancipation

In this chapter I will explore the paradoxical relationship between anarchism and utopianism, and examine the significance of utopian thinking for radical politics more generally. I will suggest that there has always been a utopian dimension in anarchist thought, not only in the more consciously utopian imagination of Le Guin, Morris and Landauer, but even in the 'scientific' anarchism of Kropotkin and Bakunin. However, in the case of the latter, I would argue that two opposed understandings of utopianism are at work here: first, the utopianism that is to be found in the positivist and rationalist paradigms present in classical anarchism – the idea of a rational social objectivity and an essentialist human subject whose unfolding coincides with a social revolution aimed at liberation of all humanity and the establishment of an anarchist society (this is what I have termed 'scientific' utopianism); and second, the utopianism that is to be found in the idea of revolutionary spontaneity, Bakunin's contempt for scientists and in the critique of certain paradigms central to Marxism – such as the bourgeois and authoritarian ideas of class and party, and Marxism's unquestioning embrace of industrial technology and factory discipline (this I have called the 'utopianism of revolt').

I see both these utopianisms as present in the discourse of classical anarchism; and yet, if we explore their implications for radical politics, we can also see a significant tension between them. The first sees revolutionary action as largely determined by historical and social forces that are understood rationally and in a scientific sense; moreover, it suggests an immanent movement towards an anarchist form of social organisation. The second understanding of utopianism sees revolutionary action as spontaneous and indeterminate – as something that is always present in every upsurge, every rebellion – perhaps as a spontaneous will to revolution: here we have, for instance, Bakunin's 'negative dialectics' – 'the urge to destroy is also a creative urge'; as well as the idea that a revolution must be libertarian in form as well as aim. In other words, there is an understanding of utopia as *here and now*, and as affirming a radical break with the present – rather than

the more deterministic idea of revolution as emerging from social and economic contradictions and always deferred into the future.

I would argue that it is this second understanding of utopianism –
utopianism as a disruption of the present that is also in the present – which
is much more relevant to radical politics today, especially at a time when
the positivist, dialectical and economistic 'grand narratives' of revolutionary
thought can no longer be sustained and have been subject to rigorous theoretical criticism. Moreover, we live in a time when the very idea of utopia
seems to have been discredited. However, it is precisely for this reason, I
would argue, that we need to retain some sort of utopian dimension to
radical politics – some idea of an alternative space – because this introduces
a kind of radical heterogeneity and disruptive opening into the economic,
social, political and ideological constellation that goes by the name of global
capitalism. Thus, my position here can best be summed up by Frederic
Jameson's phrase: anti-anti-utopianism.[1]

The ideology of anti-utopianism

Global capitalism presents us today with a closed, sterile, claustrophobic
space rather than an open horizon. In its colonisation of every region on
earth and every social and economic relation, it increasingly appears as a
system without an exterior, without an outside. Cultural and national differences, it would seem, no longer present any real obstacle or contradiction
to this economic logic – all these are commodified: indeed, as Deleuze and
Guattari pointed out, capitalism *thrives* even on its own contradictions.[2]
Moreover, the dominant ideology today is that which proclaims the inevitability of capitalism and free markets – the idea that, as Margaret Thatcher
infamously put it, 'there is no alternative'. We hear this constantly from
global politico-economic elites and the media: the refrain that capitalism is
here to stay, that free markets and neo-liberal deregulation are not only
inevitable but actually beneficial, that everyone will prosper (eventually),
and so on. We find this neo-liberal consensus on both the political left and
right today – these two sides of politics have become virtually indistinguish-
able in their endorsement of, or at least their resignation to, the exigencies
and structural requirements of global capitalism. Governments today set
about restructuring their national economies in accordance with these
'requirements': in order to attract investment, they deregulate their economies and labour markets, cut corporate taxes, reduce social welfare spend-
ing, and so on. Indeed, Marx's claim that governments are the simple
business agents of capital seems never more true than today.[3]

So this is a time that is conditioned by the eclipse of the radical and
utopian projects of the past – a time of quiet resignation to the 'realities'
of the global economy. A Fourier or Saint-Simon would be largely unthink-

able today. It is here that the word utopia has a precise ideological function: it operates as a way of stigmatising alternative political and economic visions as, at best, unrealistic and naive, and, at worst, dangerous.[4] It is enough simply to invoke the idea of the gulag, planned economies and other economic and political catastrophes of the socialist project to instantly dismiss any idea of even significantly reforming global capitalism. The spectre of communism continues to haunt us – no longer as a threatening future but rather as a ghostly past; moreover, rather than trying to exorcise this spectre, the politico-economic elites of today use it to ward off any future that is different from theirs.

So we live in a time characterised, at the formal ideological level at least, by the death of utopia. The collapse of the communist systems nearly two decades ago represented the snuffing out of the last frontier, the last space outside the global capitalist system – and with this, the embodiment of an alternative political imaginary. I am not saying here, of course, that the 'actually existing' state socialist systems did not in every sense amount to a betrayal of socialism; but nevertheless they symbolised a kind of petrified forest of utopian desire – a conviction that another form of society was once thinkable.

At the same time, however, we could say that this anti-utopian global ideology has its own ecstatic utopian dimension: is there not a hopeless utopianism and idealism in the dream of frictionless capitalism, in the idea that free markets can break down barriers between people and bring prosperity to everyone? Indeed, it is with quite astonishing conviction that the high priests of global capitalist ideology cling to their dreams in the face of overwhelming evidence to the contrary: the promise of global free trade seems to find its answer in economic colonialism, the exploitation of poor countries by rich countries and the consigning of vast sectors of humanity to crushing poverty; the promise of a universal liberal peace ends up in a situation of total and permanent war; the promise of a world without borders leads to the strengthening of old borders and the emergence of new ones, both between and within national territories, and so on. On the terrain of capitalist globalisation we find re-territorialising forces everywhere – the supposedly free circulation of goods, labour and capital seems to lead only to new barriers, divisions and communitarian identifications; the nationalism and anti-immigrant racism present in so many societies today has to be seen as much a symptom of globalisation as free trade agreements and 'cultural exchanges'. The economic interconnectedness of the world seems to be resulting in growing disconnectedness and outright hatred, and yet the utopian dream of the big finance capitalists is all-pervasive and almost religious in its fervour.

So rather than the utopian liberal capitalist dream being accepted by everyone, as Fukuyama predicted, it has only led to new antagonisms: the emergence of religious fundamentalism, terrorism and virulent nationalism can only be seen as reactions against this utopianism, as can the overwhelming 'no' to the EU free market ideal – to, as Baudrillard puts it, the imperialism and arrogance of 'divine' Europe.[5] However, even these forces contain their own utopian dimension: do they not cling on to some imaginary lost life-world of religious beliefs and 'traditional' values that has been eroded by modernity? The religious ecstasies of the suicide bomber and the Christian fundamentalist, and the neoconservative reassertion of God and the family into political and social debates, suggest another kind of utopian thinking is at work here at the limits of our modern secular liberal world.

Imprisoned in the present

It is perhaps with a view to countering these reactionary 'utopianisms' that radical politics today should assert its own utopian dimension. However, rather than cling on to utopian dreams of the past, I would suggest here that the very notion of political utopianism needs to be rethought. It is here that I would like to situate the discussion of radical politics today, and particularly the significance of anarchism: many have suggested that anarchism – which for a long time had been overshadowed by Marxism – is increasingly presenting itself as the radical politics of the future. This is particularly so because many of its ideas about decentred and non-hierarchical forms of politics seem to be reflected in contemporary global anti-capitalist struggles. Indeed, the strength of anarchism lies partly in its strong utopian dimension: in its belief that another kind of society – based on egalitarian and non-authoritarian relationships – is possible; that it is possible to live without the state and without capitalism. So we need to take a closer look at this utopian moment in anarchism and how it functions as part of its political imaginary.

First, however, we must ask whether utopianism is still possible in radical politics – and whether utopianism is something that might actually constrain radical political thinking today. One might argue that under the theoretical conditions of postmodernity, in which the grand narratives of universal human emancipation are questioned and in which Enlightenment ideas of rationality, social objectivity and human essence are thrown into doubt, utopian thinking is no longer credible: that it is no longer credible, for instance, to imagine a future society in which power relations would be completely absent, in which the subject would be completely liberated, and in which social forces would become harmonised and reconciled with themselves. There are a number of problems with the postmodern position, however – not least of which is the extent to which it contains its own hidden utopian dimension: for instance, the postmodern idea of the fully liberated 'hybrid' subject, in which the individual can inhabit an endless plurality of different subject positions – an experience which certain postmodern thinkers equate with the supposedly boundless universe of cyberspace – can be seen as another kind of utopia, equally idealistic. There is a sense in which postmodernism, in its celebration of the decline of the grand narrative, posits its own grand narrative, its own utopian imaginary.[6]

However, there are certain aspects of postmodernism's, or at least poststructuralism's, critique of political utopianism that we should take on board. In an interview in 1977, when Foucault was asked about what sort of alternative there could be to the current system – the eternal question of 'what replaces the system?' – he replied: 'I think that to imagine another system is to extend our participation in the present system.'[7] In other words, one of the problems with utopian thinking is that to imagine some sort of future society which would replace the current one is only to project our current political and conceptual conditions into the future and thus to remain caught within the paradigms of the present. Rather than utopian thinking being a release from the current order, it simply reaffirms, inexorably, our place within it – it does not allow any sort of escape from the present. Here Foucault gives the example of the Soviet Union, and the way that the Bolshevik Revolution, so far from ushering in a completely new revolutionary society, only reinvented many of the old institutions and practices that characterised the tsarist regime: particularly in the organisation of the Red Army, the return to realism in art, family morality, and the Taylorist system of factory discipline. 'The Soviet Union returned to the standards of bourgeois society in the nineteenth century, and perhaps, more as a result of utopian tendencies than a concern for realities.'[8] In other words, according to Foucault, it was the utopian desire of the Bolsheviks to revolutionise society – to invent something new – that led them, paradoxically, to relying on the old power structures and practices. It was utopian desire itself that led to the undermining of the revolution – to the lost opportunity for a real transformation of social conditions. As an alternative to utopian blueprints and plans for a future society, Foucault suggests that the possibility for real change might emerge from actual experiences with alternative realities:

> I would rather oppose actual experiences than the possibility of a utopia. It is possible that the rough outline of a future society is supplied by the recent experiences with drugs, sex, communes, other forms of consciousness, and other forms of individuality. If scientific socialism emerged from the Utopias of the nineteenth century, it is possible that a real socialization will emerge, in the twentieth century, from experiences.[9]

I will return to this idea of alternative experiences later. But what Foucault seems to be suggesting here is another way of thinking about utopia – not so much as the projection of a society of the future, but rather as a sort of *enacted* utopia that emerges in the present, from present conditions, and that, at the same time, affirms a radical break *with* the present and the invention of something completely new.

Anarchism

This bears directly on the discussion of anarchism and its relation to utopian thought. Similarly to Foucault, anarchists have been critical of Marxism and Marxist-Leninism: they have argued that it was the authoritarian and centralist thinking that characterised this revolutionary imaginary that led to the installation of an authoritarian political system in the Soviet Union. Indeed, Bakunin, during his debates with Marx in the First International in the nineteenth century, famously warned that a Marxist revolution would end up perpetuating a form of state authority that would turn out to be even more oppressive than the one it replaced.[10] Anarchists like Bakunin and Kropotkin argued that it was simply utopian to believe that the state would 'wither away' after the revolution, or even that the state could be used as an instrument of emancipation if it was controlled by the 'dictatorship of the proletariat'. In the words of Bakunin: 'They [the Marxists] do not know that despotism resides not so much in the form of the State but in the very principle of the State and political power.'[11]

However, at the same time, anarchism itself does not escape the pitfalls of utopian thinking – particularly those that Foucault drew attention to. Yet here I think it is possible to tease out two utopian moments in anarchism – two utopian tendencies which are, at the same time, at odds with one another. Indeed, it is by exploring the tension between them that we can arrive at a new understanding of radical political utopianism.

The first of these utopian dimensions I would call 'scientific utopianism'. Despite the conflict that existed between the anarchism and Marxism, classical anarchists shared with Marx an indebtedness to an Enlightenment paradigm of thinking – one that brought with it its own utopianism, particularly in its scientism and positivism. Both classical anarchism and Marxism are characterised by a strong positivist faith in science and rationality: both revolutionary projects were seen by their exponents as scientific (as opposed to utopian). Indeed, anarchists such as Bakunin were critical of what they saw as 'utopian socialism' – claiming, like Marx, to have founded their socialism on 'scientific' and 'materialist' principles:

> Having shown how idealism, starting with the absurd ideas of God, immortality and the soul, the *original* freedom of individuals, and their morality independent of society, inevitably arrives at the consecration of slavery, I now have to show how real science, materialism and socialism – the second term being but the true and complete development of the first, precisely because they take as their starting point the material nature and the natural and primitive slavery of men, and because they bind themselves to seek the emancipation of men not outside but within society, not against it but by means of it – are bound to end in the establishment of the greatest freedom of individuals and the highest form of human morality.[12]

Central here is the notion that socialism, and the liberation of humanity, has a materialist and scientific basis: there was a rational logic at work in society and history, a logic that was only intelligible through science. For Bakunin, this logic consisted of what he saw as 'immutable' natural laws which formed the basis of humans and social development. For Kropotkin, this rational social logic could be found in a natural sociability that he observed in humans and animals – a 'permanent instinct' towards cooperation which be believed could provide the foundation for a new ethics of mutual aid and a new conception of justice and morality.[13] Related to this also is the idea of human essence: central to anarchism is the idea of a natural development of the individual from a state of animality to a state of full humanity, in which the full development of rational and moral faculties would coincide with a social revolution against all external forms of oppression.

Classical anarchism can therefore be understood as an Enlightenment-based radical political philosophy, at the heart of which is a developmental relationship between freedom and authority. The possibilities of human freedom in anarchist theory have their basis in an essential rational harmony which has been disrupted by the operation of 'artificial' political authority. However, this harmony constitutes the objective truth of social relations – a truth that lies dormant, waiting to be rediscovered. That is why the secret of the subject's freedom, in anarchist theory, lies in revealing the meaning of this social essence, of rediscovering its laws and restoring harmony and transparency to social relations. Therefore, the subject's struggle for freedom is determined by the unfolding of this rational truth and the overcoming of the external limitations of political power and authority. Once centralised political authority is destroyed, social relations will become transparent. Thus, the anarchist revolution would involve a destruction of authority, but in this destruction there would be, at the same time, the *restoration* of a rational social order. In other words, the anarchist transgression of authority is inseparable from a 'return' to a lost social fullness.

So in this discourse we can see a strong utopian dimension: particularly with this notion of a rational harmony that has always existed in society, yet which has been repressed by political authority, and therefore which can serve as the basis of social organisation after political authority has disappeared. So here we see nineteenth-century anarchists developing all sorts of plans for the future 'rational' organisation of society: Bakunin conceived of future anarchist societies which would be based on free and autonomous collectives where the family and the institution of marriage would be abolished, where children would become the collective responsibility of society, where property would be owned in common and where everyone would work. Proudhon conceived of a form of social and administrative organisation based on federalist lines. Kropotkin also imagined industry and farming in a future anarchist society as being based on decentralisation, deriving his arguments from an extensive study of current industrial and agricultural techniques, scientific principles and political economy.[14] He said: 'No destruction of the existing order is possible, if at the time of the overthrow, or of the struggle leading to the overthrow, the idea of what is to take the place of what is destroyed is not always present in the mind.'[15] Moreover, what is central to the anarchist utopian vision is the general absence of power relations and any form of coercion. However, the possibility of a society without power relations has been cast doubt on by Foucault, for instance, who sees power as coextensive with any form of social organisation – even though, in an anarchist society, power relations would presumably be more reciprocal and egalitarian than in other societies.

However, there is also a second utopian tendency in anarchist thinking which is somewhat at odds with the first. For instance, there is also a strongly anti-scientific and spontaneist element in Bakunin's thinking, despite him claiming that his anarchism was 'scientific': he warned of the dangers of allowing revolutionary politics to be determined by scientists and technocrats, arguing that the Marxist revolutionary programme risks ending up with a dictatorship of scientists.[16] He saw life as being too complex and spontaneous to be mutilated on the Procrustean bed of scientific knowledge. Instead of scientific determinism, Bakunin emphasised what he saw as man's natural urge to revolt, his natural rebelliousness, which could not be contained by revolutionary dogmas and programmes. Furthermore, we could point here to Bakunin's 'negative' dialectics: unlike Hegel, who posited the dialectic reconciliation between thesis and antithesis, between positive and negative, Bakunin's dialectics emphasised the victory of the negative and the triumph of man's destructive urge: his most famous aphorism is 'the urge to destroy is also a creative urge'. So in opposition to Marx's Hegelian schema in which each epoch contained the conditions for its own transcendence – so that the elements of the old society could be used to facilitate the transition to the next – Bakunin argued for an absolute break with existing conditions: the revolution could only come about through a destruction of the old society and the building of something completely new. This referred directly to the question of the state: for Marx, the state – if it was in the hands of the proletariat – could be used to revolutionise society and to build socialism; whereas for Bakunin, and anarchists generally, the state – which was always oppressive no matter which class controlled it – was the main obstacle to revolution.

Anarchism's utopianism lies in the idea that liberation is immediately present in the revolution itself; it is not something that has to emerge in planned stages after a long process. There is no slow withering away of the state in anarchism; rather the state was to be destroyed as the first revolutionary act. Here we also see the insistence that the revolution must be libertarian in its form as well as its aims. In other words, if authoritarian institutions like the state are used to liberate society, this will only perpetuate authoritarianism. This is also why anarchism rejected the authoritarian structures of the revolutionary party, which, with its centralised bureaucracy and decision-making apparatus, anarchists saw as a microcosm of the state – a future state in waiting.

Anarchists also rejected the idea of Taylorism and factory discipline which Marx and Lenin saw as being necessary to harness the powers of industrial production. Instead, anarchists saw this as a remnant of bourgeois society that should be abolished if workers were to liberate themselves. Even the concept of class itself – and the primacy of the industrial proletariat as the only truly revolutionary class – was questioned here: anarchists saw this as exclusivist and bourgeois, and instead emphasised the heterogeneity of revolutionary subjectivity. Bakunin preferred the concept of a mass to a class – and spoke of a revolutionary mass that would include not only workers, but also peasants, intellectuals déclassé and even the lumpenproletariat that Marx had referred to in *The Communist Manifesto* as the 'social scum, that passively rotting mass thrown off by the layers of the old society'.[17]

So here we can see another utopian tendency in anarchism – that which emphasises spontaneity, personal liberation and heterogeneity. Here revolution is seen in terms of its immediacy and its radical break with the present, rather than as something which emerges dialectically or developmentally and is deferred until conditions are ripe. This is somewhat different from the first understanding of utopia: rather than a future society which develops according to the unfolding of a rational social logic, this is a utopia of the *here and now*, a utopia which is present in every rebellion or insurrection. It is utopia as a radical disruption of the present rather than a deferred projection into the future.

This second understanding of utopia comes close to Baudrillard's vision of a radical politics that would break with economist or 'scientific' Marxism:

> The cursed poet, non-official art, and utopian writings in general, by giving a current and immediate content to man's liberation, should be the very speech of communism, its direct prophecy. They are only its bad conscience precisely because in them something of man is immediately realised, because they object without pity to the 'political' dimension of the revolution.[18]

According to Baudrillard, there is a utopian and aesthetic dimension in radical politics that Marxism has always repressed and derided. These utopian energies should be released – they are the very language of revolution and communism. This is because they reject the whole means–ends logic of Marxist political strategy. Instead, they suggest an immediate liberation, a liberation that is present in every struggle whether or not the time is officially 'ripe' for revolution.

It is this second dimension of utopian thinking which I would emphasise here – especially as many of the theoretical categories of Marxism are now redundant – particularly its scientism, economic determinism and class essentialism. Radical politics today seems to be more heterogeneous and less deterministic than this Marxist model. Paradigmatic, perhaps, of this new radical politics would be the 'anti-globalisation' or anti-capitalist movement that has exploded across our horizon in recent years. This is one of the most significant political innovations for a long time. It goes beyond the particularistic logic of identity politics: it is no longer about the assertion of a particular and differential identity – based on sexuality, gender or ethnicity – and the demand for recognition. It once again invokes a universal horizon of emancipation – from capitalism and the state – affirming notions of global economic democracy and social justice. At the same time, it cannot be seen as simply a reinvention of Marxism: the proletariat as a class is no longer seen as central to the struggle; nor is there a party at the helm playing the vanguard role. Moreover, the new forms of direct action and 'network activism' which the movement embodies suggest completely different modes of political organisation, mobilisation and identity.[19]

It is possible to see the anti-capitalist movement as a deliberately utopian politics: its slogan is, after all, 'another world is possible'. However, I would suggest its utopianism is more like the second understanding I have described: it is a form of politics that affirms a kind of radical disruption of the current order through the invoking of the idea of an alternative, without at the same time setting out what this alternative actually is (this is perhaps its weakness as well as its strength). The slogan 'another world is possible' functions in this sense as an 'empty signifier', as Ernesto Laclau would put it.[20] In other words, it suggests a kind of alternative empty horizon that can take different shapes and be interpreted by different people in different ways: for environmentalists, it might mean a world without massive environmental degradation or in which there is a more sustainable balance between industry and nature; for workers it might mean a world in which pay and conditions are significantly improved, where there is greater job security and full employment, or where workers have a greater influence over the productive process; for indigenous groups, it might mean a world where their rights and autonomy are respected, and where their attachment to native lands is recognised, and so on. These different demands and visions are brought together around a shared imaginary which is at the same time empty and without definite content. So at this stage, the anti-capitalist movement remains a kind of open political horizon – and its importance and force lie in precisely this: in showing that there is an alternative to global neo-liberal capitalism (whatever it might be), that there is an outside to this system – that this is not a closed system at all, but one which is fundamentally contested and resisted.

Moreover, the anti-capitalist movement represents a kind of 'enacted utopia' which might be seen in its massive demonstrations, and different and innovative forms of protest and direct action – tactics which involve not only confrontations, but also theatre, alternative spectacles, parody, *detournement* or cultural subversion, street parties and festivals.[21] Of particular interest here is the reclamation of physical spaces by groups such as Reclaim the Streets, and their transformation, even if only temporarily, into autonomous zones. The central idea with these symbolic occupations is that an autonomous space can be created that is beyond the immediate control of the state and in which new forms of social interaction can emerge spontaneously. We might think here of the more permanent autonomous zones established by the Zapatistas in Mexico or the landless movement in Brazil, as well as alternative spaces such as food cooperatives, communes, squats and independent media centres. Behind such experiments is the idea that rather than confronting global capitalism and the state head on, the best way to overcome them is to work around them, to gradually take over spaces and build a new society from the ground up. So here we can see a kind of enacted utopia – an attempt to realise utopia in the current moment, rather than waiting for a revolution.

Perhaps in examining the political significance of such spaces, we could consider briefly Foucault's idea of heterotopias. Heterotopias are different from utopias because rather than being imagined places in the future – projecting an image of a perfected society – heterotopias are real places within society as it currently is, but which are radically different or heterogeneous to it. They are actually realised utopias within the existing social order:

> There are also, and probably in every culture, in every civilization, real places, actual places, places that are designed into the very institution of society, which are sorts of actually realized utopias in which the real emplacements, all other real emplacements that can be found within a culture are, at the same time, represented, contested and reversed.[22]

Foucault gives several examples of heterotopias: 'crisis heterotopias' of primitive societies which were sacred or forbidden places reserved for people in some form of crisis – adolescents, menstruating women, women in labour, old people; heterotopias of the nineteenth century, such as schools and military academies for boys and 'honeymoon' hotels for girls; modern 'heterotopias of deviation' such as rest homes and psychiatric hospitals; brothels, colonies and even ships. One of the key dimensions of such spaces is their discontinuity with the existing world, not only aesthetically but also temporally: they represent an absolute break with the existing course of things, with the existing stages in one's life.

Perhaps this notion of heterotopias can be used to characterise the utopian dimension of contemporary radical politics that I have been discussing here. Can we not see the enacted utopias that can be found in mass demonstrations, as well as direct action networks, 'reclaimed spaces' and 'autonomous zones', precisely as political heterotopias – spaces in which a radical discontinuity is introduced into the current order, and in which new forms of politics, new ways of being together are possible?

Conclusion

In this chapter I have tried to address the problem of utopia in radical politics, and specifically in anarchism. While a utopian dimension to radical and emancipative politics must be retained, I have suggested that it must also be rethought. Radical political utopianism can no longer consist in the drawing up of blueprints for future societies, nor can it be about establishing the scientific and historical laws of revolutions. Rather, radical political utopianism must be that which breaks with all determinism, positivism and historical materialism – and which affirms what is heterogeneous to the current order. In other words, it can be seen as a disruption of the current order which, at the same time, emerges from *within* the current order, and which introduces a moment of radical indeterminacy and unpredictability in which anything is possible. Rather than a society of the future, utopia is an *event* which takes place in the present.

Notes

1 F. Jameson, *Archaeologies of the Future: The Desire Called Utopia and other Science Fictions.*

2 Deleuze, G. and F. Guattari, *Anti–Oedipus: Capitalism and Schizophreria*, trans. R. Hurley, p. 37.

3 See J. Rancière, *Dis-agreement*, p. 113.

4 A similar point is made by Alain Badiou, who talks about the way that today, emancipatory politics is subordinated to the ethical ideology of human rights. Here, the very idea of emancipatory politics, every attempt to construct, in Badiou's terms, a collective will around a good, is immediately condemned as a potential evil: 'Such is the accusation so often repeated over the last fifteen years: every revolutionary project stigmatized as "utopian" turns, we are told, into a totalitarian nightmare.' See *Ethics: An Essay on the Understanding of Evil*, p. 13.

5 See J. Baudrillard, 'Divine Europe', *International Journal of Baudrillard Studies*, 3:1 (2006).

6 Here it is important to consider Badiou's powerful critique of the concept of postmodernity, which he refers to as the 'age of the poets'. He suggests that the postmodern discourse of the collapse of the metanarrative is itself another metanarrative, another totalising discourse: 'The announcement of the "End of

Grand Narratives" is as immodest as the Grand Narrative itself, the certainty of "the end of metaphysics" proceeds within the metaphysical element of certainty.' See A. Badiou, *Manifesto for Philosophy*, pp. 30–1.

7 See interview with M. Foucault, 'Revolutionary Action: "Until Now"', in *Language, Counter-Memory, Practice*, pp. 218–33.

8 *Ibid.* p. 230.

9 *Ibid.* p. 231.

10 See M. Bakunin, *Marxism, Freedom and the State*, p. 32.

11 M. Bakunin, *Political Philosophy: Scientific Anarchism*, p. 221.

12 *Ibid.* p. 146.

13 P. Kropotkin, *Ethics: Origin and Development*, p. 45. See also *Mutual Aid: A Factor of Evolution*.

14 See P. Kropotkin, *Fields, Factories and Workshops*.

15 P. Kropotkin, *Revolutionary Pamphlets*, pp. 156–7.

16 See M. Bakunin, *Selected Writings*, p. 266.

17 K. Marx and F. Engels, 'Manifesto of the Communist Party', The Marx–Engels Reader, p. 482. It is interesting to see Bakunin's idea of a heterogeneous mass that is no longer subsumed under the category of class being reinvented today in various ways as 'the people' or 'the multitude' by contemporary post-Marxist thinkers. See, for instance, M. Hardt and A. Negri, *Multitude: War and Democracy in the Age of Empire*.

18 J. Baudrillard, *The Mirror of Production*, p. 164.

19 Indeed, as David Graeber has argued, the forms of non-hierarchical organisation and direct democratic and consensus forms of decision-making that characterise anti-capitalist politics exhibit clear anarchist tendencies. See 'The New Anarchists', *New Left Review*, 13 (Jan./Feb. 2002), 61–73.

20 See E. Laclau, 'Why do Empty Signifiers Matter to Politics?', in *The Lesser Evil and the Greater Good: The Theory and Politics of Social Diversity*, pp. 167–78.

21 For an extensive discussion of this, see R. J. F. Day, *Gramsci is Dead: Anarchist Currents in the Newest Social Movements*.

22 See M. Foucault, 'Different Spaces', *Foucault: Essential Works Vol. 2: Aesthetics*, J. Faubion (ed.), p. 178.

References

Badiou, A., *Manifesto for Philosophy*, trans. N. Madarasz (ed.) (Albany NY: State University of New York Press, 1999), pp. 30–1.

——*Ethics: An Essay on the Understanding of Evil*, trans. P. Hallward (London: Verso, 2001), p. 13.

Bakunin, M., *Marxism, Freedom and the State*, trans. K. J. Kenafick (London: Freedom Press, 1950).

——*Selected Writings*, A. Lehning (ed.), (London: Cape, 1973).

——*Political Philosophy: Scientific Anarchism*, G. P. Maximoff (ed.), (London: Free Press of Glencoe, 1984).

Baudrillard, J., *The Mirror of Production*, trans. M. Poster (St Louis: Telos Press, 1975).

—— 'Divine Europe', trans. L. Nyssola (originally appeared as 'L'Europe Divine' in *Liberation* on 17 May 2005), *International Journal of Baudrillard Studies*, 3:1 (2006), www.ubishops.ca/baudrillardstudies/vol3_1/baudrillard.htm.

Day, R. J. F., *Gramsci is Dead: Anarchist Currents in the Newest Social Movements*, (London: Pluto Press, 2005).

Deleuze, G. and F. Guattari, *Anti–Oedipus: Capitalism and Schizophreria*, trans. R. Hurley (London: Continuum, 2004).

Foucault, M., 'Revolutionary Action: "Until Now"', in *Language, Counter-Memory, Practice*, D. Bouchard (ed.), (Oxford: Basil Blackwell, 1977), pp. 218–33.

—— 'Different Spaces', *Foucault: Essential Works Vol. 2: Aesthetics*, J. Faubion (ed.), (New York: The New Press, 1998), pp. 175–85.

Graeber, D., 'The New Anarchists', *New Left Review*, 13 (Jan./Feb. 2002), 61–73.

Hardt, M. and A. Negri, *Multitude: War and Democracy in the Age of Empire* (New York: Penguin, 2004).

Jameson, F., *Archaeologies of the Future: The Desire Called Utopia and other Science Fictions* (London: Verso, 2005).

Kropotkin, P., *Fields, Factories and Workshops* (New York: Benjamin Blom, 1913).

—— *Ethics: Origin and Development*, trans. L. S. Friedland (New York: Tudor Publishing, 1947).

—— *Mutual Aid: A Factor of Evolution* (Boston, MA: Extending Horizons Books, 1955).

—— *Revolutionary Pamphlets*, R. N. Baldwin (ed.), (New York: Benjamin Blom, 1968).

Laclau, E., 'Why do Empty Signifiers Matter to Politics?', in *The Lesser Evil and the Greater Good: The Theory and Politics of Social Diversity*, J. Weeks (ed.), (Concord, MA: Rivers Oram Press, 1994), pp. 167–78.

Marx, K. and F. Engels, 'Manifesto of the Communist Party', *The Marx–Engels Reader*, 2nd edn, R. C. Tucker (ed.), (New York: W. W. Norton, 1978), p. 482.

Rancière, J., *Dis-agreement*, trans. J. Rose (Minneapolis: University of Minnesota Press, 1999), p. 113.

Anarchism and the politics of utopia

There is a curious paradox at the heart of contemporary debates about the relationship between utopian and anarchist studies. While anarchistic ideas have gained some purchase in utopian studies, there is a strong anti-utopian trend in modern anarchism. What is puzzling about this paradox is that both positions seem to be shaped by a common set of concerns. The anarchistic aspect of modern utopianism is marked by an engagement with an imaginative and open-ended exploration of alternative ways of being. Valérie Fournier's embrace of 'grass roots utopianism' flows from a rejection of utopias that prioritise 'destinations' over 'journeys' and 'better states' over 'movement and process'.[1] The anti-utopian bent of modern anarchism is shaped by a worry that utopianism threatens precisely these kinds of practice. Jason McQuinn's anarchist treatment of utopianism is informed by a suspicion of ends. All preconceived ideals, he argues, necessarily constrain free thought. Anarchists must, therefore, take particular care when discussing the nature of anarchy for any such discussion runs the risk of embedding in the analysis an 'idealized, hypostatized vision'.[2]

It is possible to explain this paradox by looking at the different anarchist traditions to which these parties appeal. The former find inspiration in what might be called a romantic–anarchist tradition, exemplified – within political anarchism – by Gustav Landauer. Anarchist anti-utopians, by contrast, base their critiques of utopianism on a rationalist, scientific strain of anarchist thought, usually associated with Peter Kropotkin. Both sets of scholars might agree with Fournier that it is possible and necessary to distinguish 'utopianism' as a way of thinking about qualitatively better states, opening up 'new conceptual spaces', from 'utopia' if this is understood as a perfectionist, highly prescriptive or monistic attempt to delineate ' "a" vision of "a" better society'.[3] But anarchistic utopians and anarchist anti-utopians part company in their understanding of the earlier generation's ability to hold these ideas apart.

If this explanation of the paradox is correct, it begs questions about the manner in which the two anarchist traditions have been represented. To what extent is it possible to distinguish a romantic from a rationalist tradition in anarchist thought? In this chapter I discuss these early anarchist conceptions of utopianism and argue that the differences have been exaggerated. Certainly, Landauer and Kropotkin followed different paths, but they formulated their responses to utopianism in the same context, specifically through a political engagement with Marxism and an ideologically charged debate about scientific socialism. Landauer met this claim by rejecting science as a paradigm for anarchist debate and trumpeting utopianism. Kropotkin instead tried to expose the fraudulence of scientific socialism by contrasting its metaphysical underpinnings to the positivist foundations of his own anarcho-communism. These two responses could be harnessed easily within a single framework. Indeed, Landauer's concern that anarchists give content to the future in an effort to counter Marxism's projected development and Kropotkin's attempt to show that genuine science was neither teleological nor prescriptive came together in Warlam Tcherkesov's work. Nineteenth-century anarchists were utopians in the sociological sense that their thought had a transcendent, transformative character, but neither Landauer nor Kropotkin fits easily into the categorisations suggested by contemporary utopian or anarchist anti-utopian thought. My contention is that their approach to anarchist utopianism has something to offer both.

Utopianism and anarchist anti-utopianism

The contrasting impressions that modern theorists of utopianism and anarchist anti-utopians have of historical anarchism stem from the critical frameworks each have adopted for their treatments of utopianism rather than any strong divisions in early anarchist thought. At the turn of the twentieth century, there was a strong consensus about the problems and possibilities of utopia in anarchist circles. This consensus is well documented but it has been mediated by a modern engagement with Marxism. On one side of the debate, modern theorists of utopianism have turned to anarchist (or anarchistic) ideas in order to re-inject Marxism with a creative dimension that Marx and Engels are said to have wrongly overlooked. On the other, anarchist anti-utopians argue that nineteenth-century anarchists, albeit unwittingly, introduced into anarchism a theory of history as deterministic as Marx's.

To start with the consensus: the common thread that runs through nineteenth-century anarchism is the rejection of blueprint utopia. Proudhon's pithy 'reform forever, utopias never' encapsulates the general view, but within this, it is possible to distinguish two main concerns.[4] Some anarchists associated blueprints with notions of moral perfection or what Frank Manuel has called the 'eternal Sabbath' of utopia.[5] Others were more disturbed by *phalansterisme*: the overly prescriptive design of the social order.

At the heart of the first complaint was a suspicion of abstract ideals. Proudhon's reflection on 'association' is indicative of this view. Like all abstract ideas, he argued, 'association' was wrongly understood as 'something finished, complete, absolute, unchangeable' – in other words, a utopia. Those 'who have taken up this Utopia have ended, without exception, in a SYSTEM'. The view chimed in with the critique of 'critical–utopian socialism' in the *Communist Manifesto* though Proudhon cast his net more widely than Marx, capturing Cabet, Leroux, Blanc, Babeuf, Morelly, More, Campanella and Plato under the banner of utopianism as well as the familiar triumvirate: Owen, Fourier and St Simon.[6] Rudolf Rocker's objection to utopia followed in much the same vein. Anarchism, he argued, offers 'no patent solution for all human problems, no Utopia of a perfect social order . . . since on principle it rejects all absolute schemes and concepts'.[7]

The second complaint – of *phalansterisme* – was that utopians mistakenly believed that it was possible to design an ideal social order and somehow to escape existing social arrangements by the construction of these ideals. This critique also dovetailed with Marx's and it found expression in arguments about the wisdom of community-building and about the designation of anarchists by their commitment to particular (usually economic) goals: so-called anarchists-without-adjective worried that disputes between anarcho-communists, individualists and collectivists suggested the pre-determination of anarchy whereas, Voltairine de Cleyre argued, '[l]iberty and experiment alone can determine the best forms of society'.[8]

Neither critique of blueprint utopia prevented anarchists from thinking about the future anarchist society. Indeed, even those who professed themselves anti-utopians believed that anarchist anti-utopianism was consistent with the exploration of anarchy or utopia. Colin Ward offers a modern defence of this position. By probing private dreams, he argues, we reflect on the particularity of our desires and thus make room for other people.[9] Nineteenth-century anarchists followed a slightly different tack, couching the argument in terms of the educative possibilities of utopia rather than its discursive function. For David Andrade education meant practical experimentation and it was a necessary part of securing revolutionary change. 'When a few persons in any community are sufficiently educated in social principles, there need be no delay in carrying into practice the plan of campaign.'[10] Andrade's own cooperative scheme was offered as just one model they might follow. In other circles, education was inspirational and it attached itself to elevated, idealistic aims.

> By education, by free organisation, by individual and associated resistance to political and economic tyranny, the Anarchist hopes to achieve his aim . . . Even our bitterest opponents admit the beauty of our 'dream', and reluctantly confess that it would be well for humanity if it were 'possible.' Anarchist Communist propaganda is the intelligent, organised, determined effort to realise the 'dream', and to ensure that freedom and well-being for all *shall* be possible.[11]

These late nineteenth-century anarchist responses to utopianism were ably captured in Marie Louise Berneri's *Journey Through Utopia*. Utopias, she argued, can be sorted into one of two categories: 'authoritarian' and 'anti-authoritarian'. The first seek 'the happiness of mankind through material well-being' but sink 'man's individuality into the group, and the greatness of the State'. The second demand 'a certain degree of material comfort' and consider that 'happiness is the result of the free expression of man's personality and must not be sacrificed to an arbitrary moral code or to the interests of the State'.[12] Utopia and anarchy are not irreconcilable ideas, but are consistent only when 'utopia points to an ideal life without becoming a plan, that is, a lifeless machine applied to living matter'. As a non-planned ideal, utopia 'truly becomes the realisation of progress'.[13] In their classic study *Utopian Thought in the Western World* the Manuels similarly describe the anarchist position as a rejection of blueprint utopia that falls short of anti-utopianism. There is, they note, no 'significant utopian novel or full-bodied description of a future utopian society whose author would identify himself as an anarchist'. And the reason is that anarchists viewed 'the world of anarchy' as 'a spontaneous creation of the free, untrammelled spirit of the men . . . not fettered to any previously formulated plans or dogmas'. A blueprint of anarchy, they continue, 'would be self-contradictory, internally inconsistent, and anathema to anarchists'.[14] Yet just as Berneri identifies an anti-authoritarian trend in utopian thought, the Manuels also describe anarchism as a 'utopian condition'. Nineteenth-century anarchists were 'seduced . . . into utterances about what an ideal world should look like after the great outburst of destruction that would bring the new man into being'.[15]

The distinction between blueprint utopia and utopianism resonates in modern utopian theory, though the links between it and nineteenth-century political anarchism are indirect. The attraction of modern utopian theory to anarchism can be explained as a response to Marx's anti-utopianism, famously captured in his refusal to consider recipes for the cookshops of the future on the grounds that socialism would be shaped by the inevitable crisis of capitalism and proletarian class struggle. For Steven Lukes, this position was contradictory. Marx and Engels could hardly claim ignorance about the form(s) socialism was likely to take while also claiming insight into the development of history. Their mistake was to downplay the utopian implications of their thought; and the costs were 'disastrously' high. Believing that 'the ends would somehow call forth the appropriate means', Marxism 'almost totally failed to bring social and political imagination to bear upon real-life problems'.[16] The leaders of so-called 'actually existing socialism' instead forcibly adjusted socio-economic conditions to suit the theoretical assumptions of the historical model.

Since the 1970s, William Morris's *News From Nowhere* has been seen as one of the earliest attempts to make up for the lacuna in Marx's – and perhaps more pointedly, Engels' – imagination. Nevertheless, the most concerted effort to shift the balance within Marxism from science to utopia came (at around the same time) with a resurgence of interest in the Central European Jewish libertarian thought of the inter-war period. Michael Löwy's pioneering work argued that there was an elective affinity between Jewish messianic thought and libertarian utopianism which challenged the vulgar Marxist idea that history could be reduced to a 'mechanical, repetitive and quantitative accumulation' and suggested that social transformations were open to active interventions and 'utopian novelty'.[17] Löwy pointed out that the inherently libertarian quality of Jewish messianic thought was not anarchist in any strict sense. Indeed, Ernst Bloch and Walter Benjamin – Marxist socialists – were two of the movement's central thinkers. Nonetheless, there was an important link to political anarchism through the work of Gustav Landauer, a significant figure both in his own right and, after his murder in 1919 at the hands of Bavarian counter-revolutionaries, through the profound influence he exercised on other members of the group, notably Martin Buber, as well as Bloch and Benjamin.[18]

The attractiveness of Landauer's work to modern theorists of utopianism stems from the poetic and mystical dimensions of his thought. As Löwy notes, Landauer's political thought was underpinned by a pantheistic religiosity, itself shaped by an interest in medieval Christianity and eighteenth-century Jewish mysticism. With these influences he fused a profound sense of nostalgia for community, inherited from German romanticism, a Nietzschean revolt against the philistinism of modern bourgeois society and a Rousseauean embrace of moral freedom. The result was a form of socialism that was at once conservative, libertarian and revolutionary and, more to the point, one that emphasised creativity, imagination, passion, intuition and free expression. These ingredients provided a perfect vehicle for utopianism. As Buber argued, Landauer understood that socialism 'can never be anything absolute. It is the continual becoming of human community in mankind, adapted and proportioned to whatever can be willed and done in the conditions given.'[19]

The largely negative response of modern anarchists to nineteenth-century anarchism reflects a theoretical worry about the status that nineteenth-century anarchists attached to the idea of historical development. The problem here is not, as Lukes argues in respect of Marx, that the anarchists overplayed the concept of history and consequently disregarded utopia, but that they transformed what were intended to be educative models of anarchy into rigid utopias owing to a misplaced faith in natural scientific method and a conviction that history could be read like a rune. The charge, which is part methodological and part political, bears some of the hallmarks of liberal anti-totalitarianism associated with Popper, Hayek and others.[20] But whereas liberal critics recommended empirical methods to safeguard against utopianism, anarchist anti-utopians add an epistemological complaint derived from post-structuralism and postmodernist thought to argue that rationalism and empiricism are the fast tracks to utopia.

The story told by the Manuels is that nineteenth-century anarchist anti-utopianism was rooted in an 'ardent' belief 'in reason and the scientific method'.[21] As Frank Manuel points out, the resulting utopias were typically 'open-ended' and 'virtually all . . . have continued metamorphoses built into their very frame'.[22] Critics disagree. Fastening on Kropotkin's work, they dismiss nineteenth-century anarchism as naturalistic scientism. According to this critique, anarchist theoreticians combined the language of science with a faulty understanding of scientific method to develop an evolutionary social science that was, in Popper's terms, historicist. Anarchists – Kropotkin's Darwinian theory of mutual aid is a prime target – came to believe that it was possible to describe laws of history and use these laws to make predictions about the future. The result was not so much a blueprint as a straitjacket. With knowledge of the course of evolution, anarchists had no more need of recipes for the future than Marx. They believed that there was no alternative future to the one history – anarchist theory – prescribed. Moreover, in their optimism and certainty that they had placed anarchism on a scientific foundation, these anarchists wrongly believed that evolution pointed towards the eradication of all social conflict. Robert Nozick, Jon Elster and Isaiah Berlin have all argued that utopia requires an unreasonable degree of consensus of its citizens, that it ignores trade-offs between competing moral values and leaves no room for genuine pluralism. This is the essence of the charge against Kropotkin's anarchist science: it breeds a utopianism that is both rigid and impossible.

> Although Kropotkin's anarcho-communism . . . lacks any invisible, hidden or directing hand, it promises to be the evolutionary culmination of the better side to human nature. The causal teleology is . . . finalistic and illegitimate; its locus is in a self-directed evolutionary process whose goal is Kropotkin's utopia. We are all urged to give the process a helping hand, which in the absence of any power to direct it would have to be a receptive frame of mind so general as to constitute a universal consensus.[23]

Twenty-first-century anarchist anti-utopian critics have resurrected these arguments, largely because of a political concern that nineteenth-century anarchists failed to distance themselves sufficiently from Marxism. Saul Newman has recently made the case, rejecting the nineteenth century's scientific and rationalist frameworks and, in particular, Kropotkin's theory of mutual aid. His broad claim is that the anarchists fell 'into the same reductionist trap as Marxism'.[24]

Newman identifies three errors in traditional anarchist thought: a commitment to the 'idea of a rational social "object" that determines the revolutionary process', a Manichean conception of liberation as the removal or abolition of state power, and an ideal of a rational and moralised post-revolutionary subject. In sum:

classical anarchism . . . is sustained . . . by the utopian idea of society of the 'other side' of power – a society . . . without the distortions and dislocations wrought by power and authority. That is to say, there is a utopian fantasy of an Edenic state of fullness and reconciliation that would prevail in society once power relations have been eliminated. Furthermore, there is, in anarchism, an idealization of the subject – the subject is seen as embodying an inherent morality and rationality . . . which has been distorted by political authority. In other words, there is a political fantasy that sustains the revolutionary desire at the heart of anarchism – this fantasy consists of a Manichean division between the subject and authority, and the promise of a return to a lost rational and moral social objectivity once this authority has been eliminated.[25]

Like the earlier generation of liberal and libertarian critics, Newman associates this vision of anarchy with stultifying uniformity. Classical anarchism is based on 'the fantasy of society without dislocation and antagonism'.[26] Franco Ferrarotti advances a similar case. Classical anarchists, he argues, were not utopians in the modern sense of the word because they could not see social change as a 'piece-meal transformation which is constantly under the control of community judgment, in order to strike the best connection between what is ideally desirable and what is today already possible'. Their utopianism was based on a 'grandiose, but highly unrealistic, dream of a totally liberated world through a cathartic revolution and a consequent palingenesis'.[27] Anarchists in the mould of Kropotkin thus rejected blueprints but remained as utopian, or in Berneri's terms, 'authoritarian', as any other schemers. This utopianism was the very opposite of the diverse, unbound utopianism that Löwy and others associate with Landauer. It was neither open-ended, nor offered a corrective to scientific socialism. Kropotkin failed to escape the scientific paradigms of the period and constrained anarchist hopes and dreams about the future in a utopian fantasy.

Anarchism, Marxism and utopianism

As modern theorists suggest, Landauer's and Kropotkin's relationship to utopianism was mediated by an understanding of scientific socialism, a term they associated with Marxist social democracy. And it is through the examination of their critical responses to Marxism that their relationship to utopianism can best be understood.

Landauer and Kropotkin elaborated their responses in the 1890s, when the ideological boundaries within European socialism were becoming less permeable. The issue that galvanised the socialist movement and helped sort socialists into more clearly delineated camps was political action. This described a policy of constitutional engagement in bourgeois politics and a commitment to parliamentarism as a means of securing revolutionary change. Social democrats, following the model favoured by Engels and the German Social Democratic Party (SPD), spearheaded the policy, arguing that electoral struggle offered socialists a route to power and therefore a means to bring about socialist transformation. Opponents, many of whom did not think of themselves as anarchists, contested this view, typically arguing that participation in bourgeois politics was likely to breed reformism. To this argument the anarchists added another: the problem with parliamentarism was that it pointed to an inadequate conception of the state. Reiterating Bakunin's complaint that Marx's socialism required only shift of power within the state rather than the state's abolition, anarchists argued that statelessness had an organisational as well as a class dimension that socialist party politicking completely overlooked.[28] Landauer captured this view perfectly, attacking the model of social democracy pioneered in Germany as 'intolerant and despotic'. The party enjoyed phenomenal popular support but the strategy had 'hitherto led to miserable failure and shall always fail' because the structures of the state were replicated in the party's own organisation. Germany, Landauer argued, was the 'home of monarchism and militarism' and far from challenging these pillars of the state, the SPD exploited them.

> [T]he German Social Democratic party in the most shameful way used this reactionary tendency of an oppressed people, this dependence of the masses, as the basis upon which an extremely strict party rule could be constructed, strong enough to crush on every occasion the rising germs of freedom and revolt.[29]

Social democrats, led by Engels, forged the link between anarchist anti-parliamentarism and utopianism by arguing that the policy of political action was informed by Marx's discovery of historical materialism. Marx had conclusively shown that all systems of production were subject to internal contradictions and that these could be resolved only through class struggle. When socialists entered into electoral competition they were not, therefore, entering into bourgeois politics but waging class war in a political system that was about to explode in revolution. The Russian social democrat, George Pleckhanov, referred to the *Manifesto* to make the point:

> The true revolutionists of our days . . . 'everywhere support every revolutionary movement against the existing social and political order of things;' which does not prevent them (but quite the contrary) from forming the proletariat into a party separate from all the exploiter parties, opposed to the whole 'reactionary mass.'[30]

Those, like Bakunin, who failed to see the oppositional and revolutionary force of political action simply showed that they were unable to digest the materialist conception of history. Their critique of political action was based on an assessment of 'the bourgeois parliamentary environment', not the 'environment of the *electors*, the environment of a working-class party, conscious of its aim and well organised'.[31] The anarchist view was unscientific and, therefore, utopian. Following Engels' re-conceptualisation of utopianism in *Socialism Utopian and Scientific*, Pleckhanov concluded:

> The Anarchists are Utopians. Their point of view has nothing in common with that of modern scientific Socialism. But there are Utopias and Utopias. The great Utopians of the first half of our century were men of genius; they helped forward social science, which in their time was still entirely Utopian. The Utopians of to-day, the Anarchists . . . have nothing to do with social science, which, in its onward march, has distanced them by at least half a century. Their 'profound thinkers', their 'lofty theorists', . . . are the decadent Utopians, stricken with incurable intellectual anaemia. The great Utopians did much of the development of the working class movement. The Utopians of our days do nothing but retard its progress.[32]

The anarchists were not slow to respond. Tcherkesov led the charge:

> For a long while we have been told that men of genius, of German extraction, have created a truly scientific idealism founded upon the metaphysics of Hegel . . . But I long ago felt somewhat doubtful about it, because I knew that neither the metaphysics of Hegel nor the dialectical method so praised by Mr. Engels have had much influence among learned and thoughtful men [. . .]
>
> I was very doubtful if anything really scientific could come of a philosophy rejected by science, condemned by historians . . . by . . . Marx himself . . . But under the influence of the fabricators of a pretentious legend it is attempted to impose upon the workers . . . this reactionary and aristocratic rubbish as a 'scientific' basis for modern socialism. It is true that enlightened men of independent minds have pronounced against the evil attempt of Liebknecht, Engels, Plekhanoff, [Plekhanov] and others; but the tide of reaction rises rapidly. It is urgent to oppose it, to show the workers that their good faith is being abused, and that instead of humanitarian ideas, authority, bureaucracy, and officalism are being pressed upon them.[33]

Landauer's and Kropotkin's efforts to reveal the flaws of social democracy were based on different logics. Landauer rejected the new pejorative spin the social democrats put on utopianism and openly attacked the notion that science provided a useful or appropriate foundation for socialism. In contrast, Kropotkin attempted to exploit the evaluative force of science but detach it from social democracy.

Landauer based his critique of Marx's thought on an idea of spirit. Spirit was the 'inner compulsion' which animated individuals, drawing them into collective actions and voluntary association; it was better thought of as a feeling than a concept. For example, spirit was expressed in the words: '*I know, I can, I may, I will, it must, and I should*'.[34] It was the 'grasping of the whole in a living universal', the 'unity of separate things, concepts and men'. In periods of change, spirit was 'ardent enthusiasm, courage in the struggle . . . constructive activity'.[35] In all its myriad forms, spirit contrasted with the 'unspirit' – the 'external force, regimentation', the 'centralism of command' and discipline – of the state.[36] And in none of them could it be confused with the idealism or 'travesty of real spirit, namely Hegelian philosophy' which provided the foundation for Marx's 'eccentric and ludicrous scientific superstition'.[37] Landauer located the difference between these two conceptions in the idea of immanence. Instead of describing the indwelling, inherent, permanently pervading and sustaining spirit of the Christian scholars, 'immanence' in the Marxist tradition meant that 'nothing requires special efforts or mental insights, everything follows smoothly from the social process'. Specifically, it meant the 'so-called socialist forms of organization are already immanent in capitalism'.[38] In this guise, spirit was closely related to its opposite and it signalled the replacement of 'cultural will' with 'politics and party'.[39]

Whereas spirit gave full scope to desire and will as the motors of revolutionary change, Landauer linked Marxist un-spirit to an idea of revolution that tied action to phases of development outside human control. This idea raised problems of agency and it also pointed to a lack of revolutionary ambition. Properly understood, he argued, socialism was 'the tendency of will of unified men to create something new for the sake of an ideal'.[40] It was supposed to make real things that were 'otherwise hidden in our soul, in the structures and rhythms of art, in the faith-structures of religion, in dream and love, in dancing limbs and gleaming glances'.[41] Marxists failed to appreciate this dimension of socialism and were mere 'executive organs of the law of development'.[42] To illustrate the poverty of Marxism Landauer contrasted the attitude of the socialist to the dry, mechanistic method of the politician. Socialists were poets, Marxists, plotters. Socialism was prophetic, Marxism predictive. The socialist knows the 'whole of society and of the past; feels and knows whence we come and then determines where we are headed'. Marxists knew only economics. Socialism was 'a cultural movement, a struggle for beauty, greatness, abundance of the peoples'.[43] 'Philistine' and 'pigmy-socialism' described 'the uncultured plodder who knows nothing more important, nothing more splendid, nothing more sacred than technology and its progress'.[44] The father of Marxism was not will or longing, but steam.[45]

Not only did Landauer conclude from this analysis that the achievement of classlessness in social democracy would leave the fabric of the capitalist state intact (the 'broad, centralized state', he argued, 'already resembles his state of the future quite closely'),[46] he also suggested that Marx and the social democrats warmly embraced this kind of socialism, using science to cloak the normative implications of their theory. In particular, Landauer feared that the practical result of social democracy would be the imposition of a technologically advanced, highly industrialised system of production and the eradication of all traditional, rural and communal practices. In

1896, as the Second International voted to make the commitment to political action a condition of entry, he put this resolution to the alternative Anarchist conference:

> The Anarchists no longer believe in the fatalistic and jesuitical doctrine of Marx, which declares the spread of Capitalism on a large scale and the elimination of all smaller producers to be necessary conditions for the realisation of Socialism.
>
> As to the land question:
> 1. We reject State aid . . .
> 2. We want to spread the principles of Free Socialism among labourers and peasants as well
> 3. We desire that the peasants hinder proletarisation [sic] by associating themselves with their labourers in agricultural co-operative associations . . . and creating organisations which might be the nuclei of socialistic Society.
> 4. Considering that the desire just expressed can in many cases not be realised, we advise in the meantime labourers, as well as farmers and peasants, to unite for an energetic economic struggle against their exploiters.[47]

Though Marx represented himself as a scientist, Landauer's analysis suggested that he was a utopian of sorts – a utopian in Popper's sense. 'Utopianists', Popper notes, 'believe that their aims or ends are not a matter of choice, or of moral decision, but that they may be scientifically discovered by them within their fields of inquiry.'[48] Landauer's premises were, of course, at odds with Popper's, but his conclusion was not dissimilar: Marx did not need to elaborate a clear vision of the future because his theory of history pointed to an image that was so familiar it hardly needed fleshing out. Marxists denied that 'their doctrine is merely a product of technical centralisation of enterprises'. However, it was clear to Landauer that 'all these forms of desolate, ugly, uniform, restrictive, and repressive centralism were . . . exemplary for Marxism'.[49] Marx's utopia was a 'mirror image of the Utopia of the sated bourgeois' and the 'product of undisturbed laboratory development of capitalism'.[50] It was no accident that Marxist science designated capitalism as a necessary stage of historical development and a foundation for socialism, because Marx's socialism was only a form of the bureaucratic, centralised and militarised capitalist state. Marx was a dreamer but 'never was a dream emptier and drier'. Indeed, of all 'unimaginative fantasists', Landauer argued, 'the Marxists are the worst'.[51]

Keen to disassociate himself from this kind of utopianism, Landauer tied his own brand of socialism to the tradition Marx claimed to have superseded:

> Yes . . . we want to do what you call experiments. We want to make attempts. We want to create from the heart, and then we want, if it must be, to suffer shipwreck and bear defeat, until we have the victory and land is

sighted . . . Ashen-faced, drowsy men . . . are leading our people . . . Where
are the . . . victorious Reds who will laugh at these gray faces? The Marxists
don't like to hear such words, such attacks, which they call relapses, such
enthusiastic unscientific challenges. I know, and that is exactly why I feel so
good at having told them this.[52]

The tone of Kropotkin's critique of Marx was very different and it had
a methodological as well as philosophical dimension, fastening on two
issues: first Marx's indebtedness to Hegelian metaphysics and, second, his
rejection of natural scientific methods. These related ideas pointed to two
different problems. Whereas the Hegelian legacy wrongly suggested that
history followed a predictable path, Marx's preference for metaphysics over
natural science led him to a faulty understanding of the future.

Drawing on Comte's sociology, Kropotkin painted Hegelian philosophy
as an outmoded form of thinking that rested on the mistaken assumption
– attributable, in modern times, to Kant – that it is possible to distinguish
phenomena from noumena; 'the domain of physics' from what Kropotkin
confusingly called 'mental phenomena'.[53] Accepting this distinction, meta-
physicians like Hegel at once attempted to overcome it. Kropotkin admitted
that his ideas were 'sometimes poetical' and, moreover, they had succeeded
in generating some useful generalisations about 'the unity of physical
and "spiritual" nature'.[54] But the shortcomings were considerable: 'the
dialectic method' was 'despairingly vague' and 'mostly based on naïve asser-
tions'. Hegel's 'total absence of proofs' was 'concealed by the vagueness of
the arguments . . . nebulous reasonings . . . and grotesquely heavy style'.[55]
Kropotkin found one example of nebulousness in the concept of innate-
ness.[56] Echoing Landauer's critique of 'immanence', Kropotkin argued that
this concept enabled Hegelians to claim that there was a logic to history
while disagreeing about its content. Hegel's generalisations were so 'abstract
and cloudy' that 'one could deduce from them . . . the revolutionary spirit
of Bakunin . . . the revolutionary Jacobinism of Marx, and the "Recognition
of what exists," which led so many "right wing" Hegelians to make "Peace
with reality"'. Yet, these same generalisations were also 'easily exaggerated,
and . . . represented as indisputable *laws*'.[57]

Kropotkin found Marx's materialist theory of history even less satisfactory than Hegel's idealist version. On the one hand, advances in knowledge
showed the bankruptcy of the science Marx claimed to have discovered.
On the other, the path of development traced by Marx's theory highlighted
just how out of step with popular aspirations his brand of socialism really
was. Kropotkin fleshed out the first complaint by contrasting dialectical
reasoning with natural science. The latter was predicated on two principles:
that all phenomena could be understood by the same method of inquiry
and that knowledge was based on the application of 'inductive–deductive'
method. In *Modern Science and Anarchism* he explained:

We have heard of late very much about the dialectic method, recommended to us by Social Democrats in order to elaborate the Socialist ideal. But we no more admit this method than would natural science. The dialectic method reminds the modern naturalist of something very antiquated that has had its day and is forgotten . . . No discovery of the nineteenth century, in mechanics, astronomy, physics, chemistry, biology, psychology, or anthropology, has been made by the dialectic method. All the immense acquisitions of the century are due to the use of the inductive–deductive method – the only scientific method. And as man is a part of Nature, as his personal and social life is a natural phenomenon . . . there is no reason why we should . . . abandon the method which till then has been so useful, and look for another method in the realms of metaphysics.[58]

Pursuing his second complaint, Kropotkin argued that Marx's failure to understand modern science led him to append to his theory of history an illiberal and unworkable ideal. Like Landauer, he represented this ideal as 'the worship of the centralised State'.[59] More precisely, in social democracy Kropotkin argued that this basic tenet supported a policy of gradual change '*to mitigate* . . . exploitation' by means of 'legal limitations' and a commitment to the state nationalisation of major services. The result, Kropotkin argued, was '*State Capitalism*'.[60] Had Marx been a genuine scientist and based his political theory on deductions supported by careful empirical observation he would have realised, as Kropotkin did, that the tendency of history was towards anarchy – the abolition of the state and capitalism – not its capture and control. He would have understood that the desire for liberation, evidenced in countless popular revolutionary movements, was not a locomotive of history but merely the expression of a strong human drive which, through the advances of modern science, nineteenth-century activists now knew could be satisfied. And finally, he would have understood that the purpose of science was not to uncover a law of development, but to find 'an answer to a plain question well put'.

The question put by Anarchism might be expressed in the following way: 'Which social forms best guarantee in such and such societies, and in humanity at large, the greatest sum of happiness, and therefore the greatest sum of vitality?'[61]

Wrapping anarchism in the mantel of science, Kropotkin did not exploit the pejorative understanding of utopia in order to denigrate Marxism. Instead, returning to the history of socialism, he challenged the basis of the dichotomy Engels had promoted. Socialists, he argued, were never properly divided into scientists and utopians but primarily into authoritarian and anti-authoritarian camps. For example, of the so-called utopians, St Simon fell in the first division and Fourier and Owen in the second.[62] Marx, too, was an authoritarian, though Kropotkin traced his lineage from Babeuf, Blanqui and the 'secret political organisation of the "Materialist

Communists"' which burgeoned in the 1830s and 40s, rather than St Simon.[63] Tracing his intellectual inheritance to Proudhon, with whom Owen had 'joined hands', he put himself squarely in the anti-authoritarian camp. Thus, just as Landauer tied anarchism to a pre-Marxist experimental form of socialism, Kropotkin used his analysis of science to demonstrate his links with early anti-authoritarian pre-Marxist socialists and to highlight the superiority *of his vision* to the social democratic alternative.

Kropotkin's attempt to place anarchism on a scientific foundation was not historicist in the sense in which Landauer accused Marx. Using admittedly contestable arguments about the process of scientific inquiry and the unity of scientific methods, Kropotkin claimed that natural science provided a foundation for the kind of creative exercises at the heart of Landauer's work. To return to the analogy with Popper, he combined piece-meal social engineering – a desire to 'design . . . remodel and service . . . social institutions' without regard for the 'ends . . . of human activity' – with revolutionary ambition.[64] The important difference between his work and Landauer's was that Kropotkin believed that the centralisation of production and the exploitation of the existing technology anticipated by the social democratic state reflected Marx's *political preferences*, not a scientifically informed view. In contrast, Landauer believed that Marx's science had some validity; left unhindered western societies were sure to develop along the alienating, industrially advanced lines that Marx described. Nevertheless, both Landauer and Kropotkin defended utopianism as a tool to consider the possibilities of socialism and elaborate the principles of anarchist organisation.

The themes explored by Landauer and Kropotkin were brought together in the work of Warlaam Tcherkesov. In *Pages of Socialist History* Tcherkesov argued that the claims social democrats made about the distinctiveness and originality of Marx's science were baseless. If Marx contributed anything original to socialism it was, as the economist Vladimir Simkhovitch argued, 'his systematic coordination of ideas'.[65] The 'cornerstone' of Marx's socialism, the theory of capitalist concentration, Tcherkesov argued, was the unhappy result of blending so-called French utopian socialism with German philosophy. Bluntly, Marx and Engels had plagiarised the writings of the Fourierists Eugène Buret and Victor Considerant and mixed their ideas with Hegel's 'reactionary metaphysics'.[66] In his study of Considerant, Jonathan Beecher argues that Tcherkesov's claim should be dismissed since Marxism has at its heart 'an argument concerning the laws of historical change and the necessity of revolution which is not to be found in Considerant'.[67] Tcherkesov's argument was not, however, that Marx – still less Engels – remained faithful to the spirit of French socialism, but that his Hegelianism seriously distorted its arguments. Whereas Considerant 'so clearly indicated and formulated capitalist concentration of capital as a great social evil', Marx 'turned it into a beneficent social law which would mechanically and peacefully liberate human society without any effort on its own side'.[68] Simkhovitch's objection was that this interpretation badly underestimated the importance Marx attached to revolutionary class struggle – 'a conception that permeates the whole Marxian system'.[69] On this point, Tcherkesov argued that though it was Engels, not Marx, who denied the need for force in the revolutionary process,[70] the discovery of the 'law of capitalistic concentration' had established an 'economic fatalism' which encouraged Engels' view.[71] In contrast to the revolutionaries of the 1840s – 'Blanqui, Dejacques, Flocon and others' – and, indeed, 'peaceful French socialists' like Considerant, Marx rejected calls for 'immediate revolutionary action and social revolution' and 'immediate social reform', substituting in their stead a bloodless idea of spontaneous evolutionary change.[72]

Turning to the substance of Marx's work, Tcherkesov questioned the arguments for concentration. In general, he argued that genuine – that is, natural, inductive – scientific methods suggested that the processes of social transformation were a good deal more complicated than Marx's theory suggested.[73] Marx claimed to be a materialist, but his 'evolutionary generalisations' were based on 'economism' – not the same thing at all.[74] In particular, he argued that economic indicators lent no support to Marx's theory. Looking at data from 1840 to 1900, Tcherkesov concluded that the 'numbers neither of potentates of capital nor of smaller capitalists are diminished'.[75] As Max Nettlau pointed out, Tcherkesov's analysis ran parallel to Eduard Bernstein's revisionism.[76] However, whereas Bernstein questioned the idea of capitalist concentration in order to encourage a wholehearted embrace of parliamentarism, Tcherkesov advocated its abandonment and a return to revolutionary struggle. The theory of concentration, he argued:

> lies at the root of the parliamentary tactics of State Socialists. From this point of view, the solution to the social question . . . becomes delightfully simple and easy. No need for an economic struggle . . . no need to begin here and now to practice brotherly relations between man and man; . . . It is enough that the workers should vote for members of parliament who call themselves Socialists, that the number of these M.P.s should increase to the extent of a majority in the House, that they should decree State Collectivism or Communism, and all exploiters will peaceably submit to the decision of parliament. The capitalists will have no choice . . . for . . . their numbers will be reduced to an infinitesimal proportion of the nation.[77]

Once socialists realised the fallaciousness of Marx's theory, Tcherkesov's hope was that they would use genuine – that is, natural – scientific methods to help them make their own history and return, as Landauer suggested, to utopian notions of desire. Pleckanov's definition of a utopian, he noted, was 'one who, starting from an abstract principle, seeks for a perfect social organisation'. Tcherkesov's lengthy response is worth quoting in full:

Read that sentence carefully, and you will discover that utopians are men of principle, and that they wish to reorganize present society, based on exploitation, ignorance, and oppression, in order to make out of it a solidary [sic] and communistic society, where the individual will have liberty, education and happiness among his fellow men, likewise, free enlightened, and happy. I confess to being a utopian. I am even afraid of not being so enough; for I might be suspected of being a man without principles, like Engels and his disciples, and like them, of being capable of distorting scientific terminology, the conception of Socialism, and lastly, instead of preaching emancipation and solidarity, of being capable of dishonouring myself so far as to preach the organization of the army of labour, especially of agriculture, discipline, subordination; in a word, Social Democracy.[78]

Anarchism, utopianism and anti-utopian anarchism

What does the analysis of these anarchist critiques of scientific socialism show about the nature of Landauer's and Kropotkin's utopianism? In different ways, Landauer, Kropotkin and Tcherkesov identified two flaws in Marxism: it was fatalistic and it pointed to a picture of socialism that was deeply unattractive. Politically, they argued, Marx's so-called science supported a misguided and futile strategy. Landauer also accused Marx of adopting a theoretical framework that was alienating and uncreative, recommending that socialists jettison science in favour of imagination. In contrast, Kropotkin and Tcherkesov argued that Marx's reasoning was unscientific and that natural science indicated that it was possible to resist social democracy. As Kropotkin explained, there was no certainty that it could be resisted: 'we do not consider as "laws" certain "correlations" indicated by them'.[79] Indeed, it was 'possible that we are wrong, and they [the Marxists] are right',[80] notwithstanding the economic trends Tcherkesov detected. The answer, then, was to think about how to exploit knowable trends to meet desirable goals. Here, Kropotkin, Tcherkesov and Landauer were agreed. As Landauer put it: the socialist 'feels and knows whence we come and then determines where we are headed'.[81] Each had a clear idea of what they wanted anarchy to look like. None of them wanted to prescribe how all should live. Landauer, then, had an image of anarchy and was not quite the open-ended utopian of modern utopian theory. Kropotkin was confident that science demonstrated that anarchy was a viable alternative to social democracy, but contrary to anarchist anti-utopian critics, relied on the struggles of real people in the real world to give it content and ensure its delivery. For both, utopianism was an essential part of the revolutionary struggle.

In the 1960s Bruce McSheehy argued that 'in a world in which utopianism has become universally stigmatised, [utopianism] is still necessary'. 'Toward what goal', he asked, 'is socialism reaching?' 'No society', he suggested, 'can exist without a goal, without a fulfilment.'[82] Landauer and Kropotkin would have agreed. Perhaps, though, Tcherkesov should have the last word: 'And you also, friend and reader, I wish with all my heart that you should always remain a man of principle. Every honest man must have principles and if this quality belongs to utopians, be a utopian.'[83]

Notes

I am grateful to the participants of the 2006 Tarragona Utopian Studies Society conference for their feedback and encouragement and to Laurence Davis for his comments and careful reading of the final draft.

1   V. Fournier, 'Utopianism and the Cultivation of Possibilities: Grassroots Movements of Hope', in M. Parker (ed.), *Utopia and Organisation*, p. 192.
2   J. McQuinn, 'Primitivism as ideology'.
3   Fournier, 'Utopianism', p. 192. Fournier adopts a harder stance on 'utopia'; nevertheless, the distinction between 'utopia' and 'utopianism' usefully captures the central issues of this debate. I am grateful to Laurence Davis for drawing my attention to the nuances of 'utopia' and 'utopianism'.
4   P. J. Proudhon, *Theorie de l'Impot*, pp. i, 5. I am grateful to Alex Prichard for drawing my attention to this comment.
5   F. E. Manuel, 'Toward a Psychological History of Utopias', *Daedalus*, 94:2 (1965), 304.
6   P. J. Proudhon, *The General Idea of the Revolution*, p. 79.
7   R. Rocker, *Anarcho-syndicalism*, p. 20.
8   V. de Cleyre, 'The Making of an Anarchist', in *Quiet Rumours: An Anarcha-Feminist Anthology*, p. 51.
9   C. Ward, *Utopia*, p. 8.
10   D. Andrade, *An Anarchist Plan of Campaign*, p. 2.
11   'Anarchist Communism: Its Aims and Principles', *Freedom* (August–September 1902), p. 40.
12   M. L. Berneri, *Journey Through Utopia*, p. 2.
13   *Ibid.* p. 8.
14   F. E. Manuel and F. P. Manuel, *Utopian Thought in the Western World*, p. 737.
15   *Ibid.* p. 737.
16   S. Lukes, 'Marxism and Utopianism', in P. Alexander and R. Gill (eds), *Utopias*, p. 166.
17   M. Löwy, *Redemption and Utopia: Jewish Libertarian Thought in Central Europe*, p. 208.
18   *Ibid.* p. 138.
19   M. Buber, *Paths in Utopia*, p. 56.
20   For a discussion see B. Goodwin, 'Utopia Defended against the Liberals', *Political Studies*, 28:3 (1980), 384–400.
21   Manuel and Manuel, *Utopian Thought*, p. 737.
22   Manuel, 'Toward a Psychological History of Utopias', p. 304.
23   C. J. Erasmus, *In Search of the Common Good: Utopian Experiments Past and Future*, p. 289.

24 S. Newman, 'The Place of Power in Political Discourse', *International Political Science Review*, 25:2 (2004), 142.
25 S. Newman, 'Interrogating the Master: Lacan and Radical Politics', *Psychoanalysis, Culture and Society*, 9:3 (2004), 304.
26 *Ibid.* p. 308.
27 F. Ferrarotti, 'Foreshadowings of Postmodernism: Counter-cultures of the Apocalypse', *International Journal of Politics, Culture and Society*, 9:2 (1995), 260.
28 See S. F. Bloom, 'The "Withering Away" of the State', *Journal of the History of Ideas*, 7:1 (1946), 113–21; R. Adamiak, 'The Withering Away of the State: A Reconsideration', *Journal of Politics*, 32:1 (1970), 3–18.
29 G. Landauer, *Social Democracy in Germany*, p. 2.
30 G. Plekhanov [Plechanoff], *Anarchism and Socialism*, trans. E. Marx Aveling, p. 97.
31 *Ibid.* pp. 98–9.
32 *Ibid.* p. 127.
33 W. Tcherkesov, 'Socialism or Democracy', *Supplement to Freedom* (June 1895), pp. 18–19.
34 G. Landauer, *For Socialism*, trans. D. J. Parent, p. 51.
35 *Ibid.* p. 45.
36 *Ibid.* p. 43.
37 *Ibid.* p. 46.
38 *Ibid.* p. 68.
39 *Ibid.* p. 46.
40 *Ibid.* p. 44.
41 *Ibid.* p. 21.
42 *Ibid.* p. 48.
43 *Ibid.* p. 45.
44 *Ibid.* p. 64.
45 *Ibid.* p. 65.
46 *Ibid.* p. 61.
47 'Report of Anarchist Conference', *Supplement to Freedom* (August–September 1896), p. 2.
48 K. Popper, *The Poverty of Historicism*, p. 68.
49 Landauer, *For Socialism*, p. 66.
50 *Ibid.* p. 72.
51 *Ibid.* p. 67.
52 *Ibid.* p. 63.
53 P. A. Kropotkin, *Modern Science and Anarchism*, p. 24.
54 *Ibid.* p. 27.
55 *Ibid.* p. 27.
56 *Ibid.* p. 26.
57 *Ibid.* p. 28.
58 *Ibid.* p. 40.
59 *Ibid.* p. 61.
60 *Ibid.* p. 67.
61 *Ibid.* p. 41.
62 *Ibid.* pp. 52–5.

63 *Ibid.* p. 51.
64 Popper, *The Poverty of Historicism*, p. 59.
65 V. G. Simkhovitch, *Marxism Versus Socialism*, p. 151.
66 W. Tcherkesov [Tcherkesoff], *Pages of Socialist History: Teachings and Acts of Social Democracy*, p. 82.
67 J. Beecher, *Victor Considerant and the Rise and Fall of French Romantic Socialism*, p.164.
68 Tcherkesov, *Pages of Socialist History*, p. 24.
69 Simkhovitch, *Marxism Versus Socialism*, p. 148.
70 Tcherkesov, *Pages of Socialist History*, p. 76.
71 *Ibid.* p. 13.
72 *Ibid.* p. 24.
73 *Ibid.* p. 15.
74 *Ibid.* p. 68.
75 *Ibid.* p. 32.
76 M. Nettlau, *German Social Democracy and E. Bernstein*, p. 14.
77 Tcherkesov, *Pages of Socialist History*, p. 23.
78 *Ibid.* p. 86.
79 Kropotkin, *Modern Science and Anarchism*, p. 78.
80 *Ibid.* p. 79.
81 Landauer, *For Socialism*, p. 45.
82 B. McSheehy, 'Anarchism and Socialism', *Monthly Review*, 21:4 (1969), 59.
83 Tcherkesov, *Pages of Socialist History*, p. 86.

References

Adamiak, R., 'The Withering Away of the State: A Reconsideration', *Journal of Politics*, 32:1 (1970), 3–18.

Andrade, D., *An Anarchist Plan of Campaign* (Melborne: Co-operative Publishing Company, n. d.).

Anon., 'Anarchist Communism: Its Aims and Principles', *Freedom* (August–September 1902), p. 40.

Beecher, J., *Victor Considerant and the Rise and Fall of French Romantic Socialism* (Berkeley, Los Angeles and London: University of California Press, 2001).

Berneri, M. L., *Journey Through Utopia* (London: Freedom Press, 1982).

Bloom, S. F., 'The "Withering Away" of the State', *Journal of the History of Ideas*, 7:1 (1946), 113–21.

Buber, M., *Paths in Utopia*, trans. R. F. C. Hull (Boston: Beacon Press, 1958).

de Cleyre, V., 'The Making of an Anarchist', in *Quiet Rumours: An Anarcha-Feminist Anthology* (London: Dark Star, n. d.), pp. 48–55.

Erasmus, C. J., *In Search of the Common Good: Utopian Experiments Past and Future* (New York: Free Press, 1977).

Ferrarotti, F., 'Foreshadowings of Postmodernism: Counter-cultures of the Apocalypse', *International Journal of Politics, Culture and Society*, 9:2 (1995), 237–61.

Fournier, V., 'Utopianism and the Cultivation of Possibilities: Grassroots Movements of Hope', in M. Parker (ed.), *Utopia and Organisation* (Oxford: Blackwell Publishing/The Sociological Review, 2002), pp.189–216.

Goodwin, B., 'Utopia Defended against the Liberals', *Political Studies*, 28:3 (1980), 384–400.

Kropotkin, P. A., *Modern Science and Anarchism* (London: Freedom Press, 1912).

——*Social Democracy in Germany* (London: n. p., 1896).

Landauer, G., 'Report of Anarchist Conference', *Supplement to Freedom* (August–September 1896), pp. 1–3.

——*For Socialism*, trans. D. J. Parent (St Louis: Telos Press, 1978).

Löwy, M., *Redemption and Utopia: Jewish Libertarian Thought in Central Europe*, trans. H. Heaney (London: The Athlone Press, 1992).

Lukes, S., 'Marxism and Utopianism', in P. Alexander and R. Gill (eds), *Utopias* (London: Duckworth, 1984), pp. 154–67.

Manuel, F. E., 'Toward a Psychological History of Utopias', *Daedalus*, 94:2 (1965), 293–366.

Manuel, F. E. and F. P. Manuel, *Utopian Thought in the Western World* (Oxford: Basil Blackwell, 1979).

McQuinn, J., 'Primitivism as Ideology', http://primitivism.com/ideology/htm, 15 March 2004.

McSheehy, B., 'Anarchism and Socialism', *Monthly Review*, 21:4 (1969), 58–60.

Nettlau, M., *German Social Democracy and E. Bernstein* (London: Freedom Press, 1900).

Newman, S., 'Interrogating the Master: Lacan and Radical Politics', *Psychoanalysis, Culture and Society*, 9:3 (2004), 298–314.

——'The Place of Power in Political Discourse', *International Political Science Review*, 25:2 (2004), 139–57.

Plekhanov [Plechanoff], G., *Anarchism and Socialism* trans. E. Marx Aveling (Chicago: Charles H. Kerr and Company, n. d.).

Popper, K., *The Poverty of Historicism* (London: Routledge, 2002).

Proudhon, P. J., *Theorie de l'Impot* (Paris: E. Dentu, 1861).

——*The General Idea of the Revolution*, trans. J. B. Robinson (London: Pluto, 1989).

Rocker, R., *Anarcho-syndicalism* (London: Phoenix Press, n. d.).

Simkhovitch, V. G., *Marxism Versus Socialism* (New York: Columbia University Press, 1913).

Tcherkesov [Tcherkesoff], W., 'Socialism or Democracy', *Supplement to Freedom* (June 1895), pp. 18–19.

——*Pages of Socialist History: Teachings and Acts of Social Democracy* (New York: C. B. Cooper, 1902).

Ward, C., *Utopia* (Harmondsworth: Penguin, 1974).

13 Judith Suissa

'The space now possible': anarchist education as utopian hope

Introduction

The failure by many commentators to pay adequate attention to the central role of education in anarchist thought has contributed to a great deal of confusion and misunderstanding surrounding anarchist theory, especially regarding the commonly made claim that anarchists hold a naive view about the possibility of maintaining a just, decentralised society without institutional control. This claim, often associated with the dismissal of anarchism as 'utopian', overlooks the central and ongoing role of education in fostering and maintaining the moral foundations that the social anarchists deemed necessary to support such a society.

I have argued elsewhere[1] that the social anarchists' acknowledgement of the need for a substantive educational process, designed along clear moral principles, goes hand in hand with their contextualist account of human nature, thus turning what might otherwise be regarded as a sort of naive optimism into a complex and inspiring social hope. Here, I argue that articulating a social anarchist perspective on education can add an important dimension to discussions of utopianism. In developing this argument, I draw a distinction between 'utopia' and 'utopianism'. Specifically, I believe that posing the question 'what does anarchism's utopianism consist of?' can help to rebut some critiques of anarchism and challenge certain notions central to liberal thought and the liberal theory of education.

Anarchist education

Contrary to common assumptions, most anarchist thinkers, especially the nineteenth- and early twentieth-century social anarchists who were involved in the long tradition of radical educational experiments, were not libertarians when it came to children's education. The sheer volume of anarchist literature devoted to educational issues, and the efforts invested by anarchist activists in educational projects,[2] are evidence of the fact that for anarchists, schools and education in general are a valuable part of the project for social change, rather than just one more aspect of state bureaucracy to be abolished as soon as possible.

In what follows, much of my discussion will be focused on schools, but I assume a broad conception of education that is not restricted to institutional settings. Indeed, part of my argument is that articulating an anarchist perspective on education highlights the significance not just of formal aspects of schooling such as control and content of the curriculum, classroom management and pedagogy, but of what I will describe as the 'educational space' created by the relationship at the heart of any educational encounter. Although the relationship between teachers and students in schools is typical of this type of encounter, I believe an anarchist perspective allows us to include other types of educational relationships within the scope of this discussion.

The anarchist schools founded in the late nineteenth and early twentieth century by anarchists and sympathisers in Europe and the United States were very different places from mainstream schools in their emphasis on non-coercive pedagogy, co-education and non-hierarchical organisation. Nevertheless, they offered a substantive curriculum. Although generally sympathetic to the agenda of libertarian thinkers, most anarchists did not reject all planned and direct intervention in the moral and intellectual development of children. At Paul Robin and Sebastien Faure's schools in France, Francisco Ferrer's *Escuela Moderna* in Barcelona and the Modern Schools set up in New York and Stelton after Ferrer's execution, children were actively encouraged to value brotherhood and cooperation and to develop a keen sense of social justice, and the curriculum carried explicitly anti-capitalist, anti-statist and anti-militarist messages. *La Ruche*, Sebastien Faure's school, set up in 1904, was run as an independent agricultural cooperative, teaching children through first-hand experience the value of syndicalist principles, and at Ferrer's school in Barcelona the children were regularly taken on visits to factories to learn about the evils of the capitalist wage system.[3] At the same time, the notion of integral education, first used by Charles Fourier and later developed by Kropotkin, was a key feature of anarchist schools in Europe and the USA, where it was explicitly intended as a way to break down the distinction between 'brain work and manual work' that anarchist thinkers regarded as the basis for the class-related occupational divisions of capitalist society.[4] Many anarchist schools also taught Esperanto to promote international solidarity.

Behind these radical educational experiments lay a faith in the anarchist vision – some would say, the utopia – of a society without injustice, without oppressive hierarchical social structures, where individual freedom and mutual aid would flourish. Anarchist educational theorists and practitioners saw the anarchist school both as an embryo of this future society and as proof that, even within the authoritarian structures of the capitalist state, an alternative was possible; thus that the anarchist society, while utopian in the sense of transcending current social and political reality, was not unattainable.

Yet in conceiving education this way, the social anarchists were not regarding it simply as a means to an end. The relationship between education and utopia in anarchist thought is very different from that in Plato's *Republic* where, as John Dewey noted, utopia serves as a final answer to all questions about the good life, the state and education being constructed so as to translate it immediately into reality.[5]

Unlike Plato's utopia, the anarchist utopia is not an end-state model, but has the commitment to constant experimentation and flux built into it. For this reason, anarchist thinkers have typically rejected blueprints and have been suspicious of programmes which, like Marxism, claim to offer a scientific theory of social change. In defending the alternative, organic image of social change, Bakunin famously attacked Marx as follows:

> Revolution is a natural fact, and not the act of a few persons; it does not take place according to a preconceived plan but is produced by uncontrollable circumstances which no individual can command. We do not, therefore, intend to draw up a blueprint for the future revolutionary campaign; we leave this childish task to those who believe in the possibility and the efficacy of achieving the emancipation of humanity through personal dictatorship.[6]

Indeed, it is this point which lies behind the dismissal of social anarchism by Marxist socialists as unscientific and lacking a theory of revolution, a dismissal captured in the pejorative use of the word 'utopian'.

It is certainly true that the very idea that there may be something constructive and valuable in positing an ideal of a radically different society whose form is determined not by predictable historical progress but by human experimentation, itself constitutes a rejection of the basic Marxist materialist assumption that consciousness is determined by the material conditions of life – specifically, by the relations of production. The anarchist position implies that, *contra* Marx, life may, to some extent at least, be determined by consciousness.

On the Marxist view, until the relations of production themselves are radically changed, 'the possibility of an alternative reality is not only impossible, but literally unthinkable',[7] for our thought structures are determined by the reality of the base/superstructure relationship. However, in anarchism, an alternative reality is not only 'thinkable' but, in an important sense, already here. Social anarchists believe that the human capacity for mutual aid, benevolence and solidarity is reflected in forms of social relations which exist even within the capitalist state and which, reinforced by a substantive but non-coercive process of education, have the potential to create radical social change.

The anarchist project, then, is not one of rejecting the past in favour of an imagined future, but of transforming the present as part of an organic process in which already existing tendencies are built on, nurtured and actively engaged with. The anarchist view of human nature, which David Morland[8] has described as 'contextualist', forms the basis of the insistence, and the faith that the future society is to be constructed not by radically transforming human relations and attitudes, but from the seeds of existing social tendencies. This is in contrast to the Marxist vision, where, as Zygmunt Bauman points out, 'the attempt to build a socialist society is an effort to emancipate human nature, mutilated and humiliated by class society'.[9]

Many contemporary critics of anarchism, from both the liberal and the socialist end of the political spectrum, continue to dismiss it as utopian for similar reasons to those originally put forth by early Marxists. Likewise, many political theorists criticise anarchism for its apparent reliance on an unrealistically optimistic view of human nature as a basis for a society without coercion. Thus Jonathan Wolff states that 'to rely on the natural goodness of human beings to such an extent seems utopian in the extreme'.[10] While such accounts often overlook or simply misrepresent the anarchist account of human nature as developed by Bakunin, Kropotkin and Proudhon,[11] they also, crucially, fail to take account of the central and ongoing role of education in fostering and maintaining an anarchist society. Erin McKenna, for example, offers a rich account of the utopian imagination and defends what she calls 'process models' of utopia, with which anarchist visions have some affinity as, on her account, 'they do see multiple possibilities for the future rather than a final, static, homogeneous end-state'.[12] However, McKenna argues that such visions 'do not provide a method through which to prepare people to participate in the ongoing experiment'.[13] As suggested here, there is a sense in which anarchist educational practice can be seen as constituting just such a method. Yet it is important to understand exactly how this is so.

The educational approach implemented in the anarchist schools of the late nineteenth and early twentieth centuries was not libertarian in the sense promoted by educators like A. S. Neill, who famously argued that children must be allowed to 'determine their own values, in culture as in morality'.[14] Anarchist schools explicitly promoted, through school ethos and curriculum, a substantive set of values and social virtues – equality, solidarity and mutual aid – that they regarded as the foundations of the social anarchist society. However, these values served not to delineate the exact contours of a pre-conceived model of social organisation without the state, but to lay the ground for an organic development and continued reinvention of such a model, by fostering the attitudes that underpin it. This may seem like a subtle distinction, but it is an important one and one which, I suggest, lies at the very heart of anarchism's 'utopianism'. Thus the utopian aspect of anarchist thought cannot be adequately grasped without an appreciation of anarchist educational ideas and practice.

Apart from the general sense in which anarchism can be regarded as utopian in its very rejection of the assumed inevitability of the nation state, there are two important aspects of its utopianism that require further exploration in light of the above discussion. One has to do with the refusal to subscribe to a systematic programme of social change, and to allow the aspirations for an alternative political reality, the means by which to bring about this reality, and the moral and political values underpinning it to interact dynamically as part of the educational process itself. The other has to do with the perspective, common to most utopian thinkers, that regards social reality as essentially malleable. In order to fully grasp the significance of the first point, I turn to a discussion of the analytic distinction between means and ends.

Means and ends

As mentioned above, many theorists sympathetic to some aspects of anarchism have offered important rebuttals to charges of the 'naivete' or 'utopian impracticality' of anarchism by developing rich accounts of the anarchist theory of human nature,[15] and by pointing out the significant differences between the anarchist utopian stance and 'end-state' utopias associated with Plato, Huxley and Bellamy.[16] Yet such theorists often ultimately dismiss anarchism as incoherent, arguing either that there is a conceptual tension between the different values promoted by anarchist thinkers,[17] or that 'neither history nor human nature can afford a bond that will deliver an anarchist society'.[18] I have already noted how such critiques often completely overlook the role of education in anarchist theory and practice. I want now to focus on the way anarchist educational thought and practice in fact embody a particular conception of the relationship between means and ends, thus allowing us to appreciate how social change is understood in anarchism. It is, I suggest, because they implicitly assume a simplistic conception of the relationship between means and ends that critics such as Erin McKenna argue – mistakenly – that 'the anarchist vision lacks a developed method of change'.[19]

The ends/means distinction has received considerable attention in the tradition of liberal analytic philosophy of education, where it is often associated with the justification of a liberal – as opposed to a narrow, vocational – conception of education. Richard Peters famously argued, in 'Must an Educator Have an Aim?',[20] that the inherently normative aspect of the concept 'education' should not mislead us into thinking of education in terms of a model 'like building a bridge or going on a journey', where all experiences and processes leading up to the stated end are regarded as means to achieving it. Peters and other liberal philosophers are anxious to avoid a notion of aims that implies a simple means–ends model and thus an apparent willingness to employ any means necessary in order to achieve a given end. He gives as an example of what he calls a 'very general aim', the political aim of equality, arguing that the type of people who regard this as important, lured by the picture of a society without inequalities, often advocate all sorts of drastic structural measures in order to achieve it. When employed as a 'principle of procedure', equality would yield far more moderate results – for example, the insistence that 'whatever schemes were put forward must not be introduced in a way which would infringe his procedural principle'.[21] The second type of reformer, as Peters notes, would not have any 'concrete picture to lure him on his journey'.[22] At the same time, liberal educators from Peters on have stressed the centrality of intrinsically worthwhile activities in any process deserving of the name 'education', thus contrasting the idea of liberal education with forms of training or vocational education in which educational achievements are pursued for some aim (economic success, social prestige, job qualifications) extrinsic to the educational process itself.

It is important to note that the fact that there is always a risk of aims being interpreted rigidly is not an argument against having 'concrete aims' as such, but against trying to impose them without any critical evaluation or sensitivity to existing conditions. As John Dewey notes, it is when aims are 'regarded as literally ends to action rather than as directive stimuli to present choice' that they become 'frozen and isolated'.[23]

Yet on the liberal view, one is often left with the impression that the central analytic distinction – a distinction which has, in fact, become something of an orthodoxy in liberal educational thought – is that between education as a means to an end, and education as an end in itself. The work of John Dewey, while not entirely avoiding this distinction, goes some way towards demonstrating just how problematic it is.

Crucially, for Dewey, the means to an end cannot be determined in advance but are in constant interplay with it, and the aim, far from being a fixed point in the distance, is constantly a part of present activity; not 'an end or terminus of action' but something which directs one's thoughts and deliberations, and stimulates action. 'Ends are foreseen consequences which arise in the course of activity and which are employed to give activity added meaning and to direct its further course.'[24] Furthermore, the original aim is constantly being revised and new aims are 'forever coming into existence as new activities occasion new consequences'.[25]

This Deweyan idea goes some way towards capturing what I believe is the anarchist perspective on the relationship between education and social change. Crucial to this perspective is the insight that while aims and goals play an important role in the educational process, they do so not in the simple sense of ends, to which educational activities are conceived as a means.

The point here is not simply that the social anarchist utopian stance rejects the type of social engineering so abhorred by theorists such as Popper – who in fact saw it as characteristic of 'utopian thought' – in favour of a more piecemeal approach. It would indeed be a mistake to characterise anarchist thinkers as favouring a piecemeal, tactical approach to social change over a strategic one. Yet it would be equally mistaken to argue, with Todd May, that such thinkers, faced with the need to adopt either a strategic or a tactical position, have to opt for the former due to their reductionist view of power and their humanist ethics.[26] Rather, what I am suggesting is that the anarchist approach transcends the ends–means dichotomy and thus allows us to conceive of the relationship between utopian hope and social change in a different light.

What the anarchist perspective suggests is that one can be, and in fact has to be, both tactical and strategic. In other words, anarchism, in transcending the ends–means dichotomy, transcends Popper's contrast between 'utopian social engineering' and 'piecemeal social engineering'. It is utopian in that it offers a radically different vision of society – albeit one without a fixed blueprint. Yet at the same time, it is 'piecemeal' in the sense that it advocates a form of gradual restructuring, being concerned with 'searching for, and fighting against, the greatest and most urgent evils of society, rather than searching for, and fighting for, its greatest ultimate good'.[27] For, as Paul Goodman remarks, '[a] free society cannot be the substitution of a "new order" for the old order; it is the extension of spheres of free action until they make up most of social life.'[28]

Thus the model whereby education and other social processes are regarded merely as means to achieving social or political ends is an inadequate tool for understanding the anarchist position. Change is inherent in the anarchist stance, for the social anarchist utopian vision is based on a radical challenge to current social arrangements. But the fact that utopia is not, for the anarchist, a clearly articulated end-state, means, among other things, that the locus of change is situated not primarily in organised (class) action or revolutionary programmes, but in moments of change at the level of human interaction, of which educational encounters are an important example. It is this perspective that is captured in Colin Ward's remark that in anarchism 'there is no final struggle, only a series of partisan struggles on a variety of fronts'.[29]

The educational space can be one such 'front'. For committed anarchists, it is a space where the transformative power of the anarchist utopian vision is manifested, as participants in the educational process play out both their (shared and differing) understandings of the contours of this vision, the ways in which it seeks to transform existing reality, and the steps necessary to achieve this.

On this view, it is not true to say that 'on the anarchist view we cannot even begin to explore what the "good life" is until everyone is free and equal'.[30] Exploration of what the good life consists of, articulation and affirmation of moral values, and experimentation with the ways in which these values can and should lead to social and political change are part and parcel of the same dynamic, interactive process that is anarchist education.

In short, what Todd May refers to as the anarchists' 'ambivalence' between a purely strategic and a purely tactical stance is in fact the essence of their position. I am suggesting that this position is exemplified by anarchist educational practice, wherein education is seen neither as the means to achieving social change, nor as an end in itself, but as a space for utopian experimentation with ends and means. Chomsky indicates this idea in commenting:

> In today's world, I think, the goals of a committed anarchist should be to defend some state institutions from the attack against them, while trying at the same time to pry them open to more meaningful public participation – and ultimately, to dismantle them in a much more free society, if the appropriate circumstances can be achieved. Right or wrong – and that's a matter of uncertain judgement – this stand is not undermined by the apparent conflict between goals and visions. Such conflict is a normal feature of everyday life, which we somehow try to live with but cannot escape.[31]

The educational dimension of anarchist utopianism

I have argued that an appreciation of the role and nature of education in anarchist thought can serve to rebut some critiques of anarchism and can contribute to our understanding of just what anarchist utopianism means. I now wish to take this discussion one step futher and to suggest that while a consideration of education can enrich our understanding of anarchism, it is also true that a consideration of anarchist utopianism can enrich our understanding of education.

Education, in many ways, is all about the interplay between the possible and the desirable. All those who see themselves as educators (and I include here teachers and parents, formal and informal educators), have, in Chomsky's words, goals and visions of what they want for the children they are educating. These may be radical in their departure from current reality, or more conservative; they will, inevitably, embody some of their own personal aspirations and hopes, and, crucially, they cannot be entirely separated from more general social and political aspirations. The question of what kind of education we think children should receive cannot be coherently cut off from the question of what kind of society we want to live in. Thus the educational encounter is a complex and frustrating balancing act between goals, visions and possibilities.

A linear understanding of social change, and a dichotomous view of ends and means, not only misrepresent the anarchist position but also fail to

reflect the complexity of actual educational experience. We often find ourselves exploring what our aspirations and values mean within educational
encounters, playing with the boundaries between the possible and the desirable. Thus many parents, for example, feel that they cannot fully articulate
what they want for their children until they come to know not only their
children's dispositions and inclinations, but also their own traits, desires
and hopes, with which they interact in a changing daily context; likewise,
their sense of what they want is constantly challenged by their understanding of what is possible and their conception of their own place within the
possible.

In daring to see education in this way, rather than acquiescing with
a view that regards it simply as a means to a predefined political goal, a
form of training, preparation for the workplace or the transmission of a
set of values, we exercise what Rorty has described as a 'willingness to
substitute imagination for certainty'.[32] This conception emphasises the need
for active engagement on the part of social agents, articulating a desire 'to
create new ways of being human . . . over the desire for stability, security
and order'.[33]

My account of this conception of education is not intended just as a
normative argument about what education should be like – although it is,
too, a plea for a different kind of teaching. I believe that this idea both
illustrates the stance adopted by anarchist educators, thus allowing us to
grasp the essential significance of anarchist utopianism, and also, importantly, captures the real experience of educators in a variety of different
contexts.

Political education and the utopian imagination

Several writers on utopia have emphasised the transformative element of
utopian thinking, arguing that the study of utopias can be valuable as it
releases creative thought, prodding us to examine our preconceptions and
encouraging speculation on alternative ways of conceptualising and doing
things which we often take for granted. 'Utopia', Goodwin and Taylor
argue, 'is in a privileged position, perhaps uniquely so, for generating constructive and dynamic critical thought, with its projection of an alternative
or future which is supposedly immediately attainable.'[34] Likewise, the critical function of utopia is often noted; indeed there is an obvious sense in
which 'every utopia, by its very existence, constitutes an *ad hoc* criticism
of existing society'.[35] Such analyses suggest that the utopian form has a
powerful educational role. However, the focus of work by writers on utopia
is often on the form and content of particular utopias, or on utopia as a
literary genre. As far as anarchism goes, while most theorists refer to
the utopianism of the anarchist position, it is far more difficult to talk of

'the anarchist utopia' than it is, for example, to discuss classic works of utopian fiction.

The main reason for this is the anarchist aversion to blueprints and the open-ended nature of the anarchist utopia. As a result of this stance, writers such as Kropotkin, Bakunin and Proudhon, while sharing a radical rejection of the basic structures of the state and positing an alternative, stateless reality founded on principles of justice, freedom, equality and mutual aid, never spelled out the contours of this alternative reality in anything like the detail with which utopian writers such as More and Fourier developed their visions.

This is not to say that the anarchist utopian ideal cannot be explored as a theoretical construct, taking into account its substantive features and underlying values. Indeed, the work of political theorists such as David Miller, Alan Ritter and Michael Taylor does just this, addressing the theoretical tensions between, for example, the anarchist concept of individual freedom and the necessity of some form of communal censorship.[36] While such attention by political theorists to the principles and values inherent in anarchism constitutes a welcome and valuable commentary on the work of anarchist thinkers, it often focuses on a critique of 'the anarchist utopia', or even 'the anarchist model of utopia',[37] as if this were in some way analogous to More's model of utopia.

In focusing on the theoretical tensions inherent in the form and content of the 'utopia' at the heart of anarchism, many critics have taken inadequate account of the central role and nature of education, thus overlooking one of the main ways in which anarchism's utopianism manifests itself. Furthermore, looking at what I have called the educational space as a locus for utopian practice and experimentation can add an important dimension to debates on utopia by focusing on the question of what *utopianism* means for people operating in such a space, rather than on the content and implications of *utopia*.

The above discussion of nineteenth- and early twentieth-century anarchist education illustrated the important role of education in bringing about and maintaining an anarchist society. It also led to a discussion of the complex conception of the relationship between education and social change in anarchism, transcending the traditional means–ends distinction. However, the substantive, some may even say dogmatic, curricula of typical anarchist schools such as Ferrer's, with their explicit rejection of anything associated with religion or the capitalist state, may seem to some a betrayal of the anarchist commitment to open-ended experimentation. While Ferrer was adamant that he would teach children 'not what to think but how to think',[38] liberal theorists, sensitive to issues of pluralism, may be sceptical as to how non-coercive and genuinely pluralistic such an educational environment could really be. Anarchist educators were under no illusions that education could be politically or morally neutral, and rejected extreme libertarian views; yet the question of how successfully they managed to achieve a balance between promoting substantive ethical commitments and offering a genuinely open, non-coercive educational process is one which still demands further exploration. In the present context, I want to suggest that, even within a school where a particular ethical and political stance is promoted through both formal and informal aspects of the educational process, there is still an important role for the kind of utopian imagination so essential to the second key feature of anarchist utopianism mentioned above: that of regarding social and political reality as essentially malleable.

Direct examples of this type of utopian imagination are hard to come by in historical accounts of anarchist schools, yet it is, I suggest, not merely a valuable feature of utopia, but an aspect of anarchist utopianism that can be exemplified particularly clearly in educational practice. My focus in the remaining section of this chapter shall be on some specific, practical ways in which this utopian stance so typical of anarchism can be played out in an actual educational situation.

What distinguishes anarchism from other utopian movements, and consequently what makes anarchism a clear counter-example to the restrictive definition of utopia offered by theorists such as Popper, is the inherent malleability and commitment to constant experimentation of its social vision. Indeed, one could argue that it is this very stance which constitutes the essence of anarchism's utopia. As Paul Goodman once remarked, in a climate where 'experts plan in terms of an unchangeable structure, a pragmatic expediency that still wants to take the social structure as plastic and changeable comes to be thought of as "utopian"'.[39]

Many writers on utopia have reflected this position, discussing how the very form of utopian writing prompts the reader to regard social reality as malleable. As Zygmunt Bauman puts it, '[u]topias relativise the present. One cannot be critical about something that is believed to be an absolute.'[40] I would like, though, to look at an example of an educational approach which takes as its starting point not an existing literary utopia, but the exercise of trying to imagine, articulate and defend a possible utopian vision.

My example comes from a small pamphlet entitled *Design Your Own Utopia*.[41] I believe the educational approach suggested here captures the stance that I regard as constitutive of anarchist utopianism.

Although there is no systematic treatment of a programme for political education in the historical accounts of anarchist schools, nor in the theoretical works on education by leading anarchist theorists, political education, in some form or another, clearly permeates anarchist educational experiments. Whether in the course of visiting factories at Ferrer's school, or of planting and managing their own vegetable crops at Stelton, pupils were encouraged to develop a critical awareness of the problems and complexities of the existing political system and to speculate on alternative models of socio-economic organisation. However, for political education to have a uniquely anarchist significance, it must reflect the utopian element of anarchist thought.

Thus while a liberal perspective on political education may, for example, focus on notions like autonomy or democracy, aspiring to greater democratisation of the workplace, the school and other social institutions, the anarchist perspective, in contrast, implies a radical 'leap of faith'. This involves not just the faith that a stateless society is possible, but also the utopian hope that the very imaginative exercise of encouraging people to conceptualise the exact form of this society, and to constantly engage with and experiment with its features, is itself a central part of the revolutionary process.

Design Your Own Utopia outlines a question-posing programme for political education whereby each question answered (by the group or individually) leads, by way of a consideration of various options and implications, to further questions. Along the way, students are invited to engage in a thought experiment, articulating and defending their values and commitments and exploring their possible practical implications.

The starting point of the discussion is not the existing structures and institutions of the state, but the general question of 'What would the good life, or a good society, look like?'

The programme begins with the question of scope. Students are asked to consider whether their utopia would be a global utopia, a nation state, a village, a city, a bio-region or some other type of community.[42] Further on, they are asked: 'What would be the fundamental values of your utopia?' and, interestingly, 'Would individuals choose their own goals and values or would their goals and values be those of your utopian ideology?' By way of this discussion, students are presented with questions about the specific content of their utopia and encouraged to think through their implications. For example: 'What would the rights and duties of members of the utopia be?'; 'Would the number of children per parent be limited?'; 'What would your decision-making process be?'; 'How would production and distribution be organised?' and 'Would the roles of men and women vary?'

Such questions invite discussion of ideas of community and individual freedom and other connected notions and, by their very nature, suggest an exploration of far broader issues than those usually covered in political education or citizenship courses. The recent Qualifications and Curriculum Authority (QCA) recommendations on teaching citizenship in schools, for example (the nearest thing in the British National Curriculum to political education), are built around the idea of fostering the knowledge, understanding and skills needed for 'the development of pupils into active citizens'.[43] Although it is hard to find fault with this idea as an educational aim, the perspective from which it is formulated is clearly one of understanding and reinforcing the current political system, rather than radically questioning it.

In the utopian exercise described here, students are asked to speculate on the feasibility of political structures other than the state and their relationship to each other not as an informative exercise, but as an imaginative one. One can find passages in QCA documents, as well as in the work of some writers on citizenship education,[44] that emphasise the need for an active, participatory role on the part of future citizens, and attach considerable importance to 'student empowerment'.[45] However, utopian thought experiments add a valuable dimension to the idea of empowering students through 'experiments in active democracy', in that they are constructed so as to 'help us to understand that the present social, political and economic systems are human inventions, and that we, collectively, have the power to change them'.[46]

While a political education programme along these lines would clearly have to be thought out in further detail and with a great deal of caution, and may be more suited to older children who have already got some grasp of basic social and political concepts, it could be incorporated into a political education programme involving familiarisation with political concepts. As such, it could constitute an attractive alternative – or at least a supplement – to conventional teaching of political issues to children. It could also be incorporated into political philosophy and theory courses intended for older students.

For example, I am currently teaching a course in political philosophy to a group of MA students, most of whom have no background in philosophy. A central topic on the course is John Rawls' *Theory of Justice*.[47] In order for the students to engage in a critical debate about Rawls, it is essential that they grasp the key elements of his theory and the conceptual distinctions on which he relies. Nevertheless, even in the midst of explaining Rawls' conceptual points and the framework of his thought, I find myself engaged in a normative and speculative discussion with my students which could serve as a springboard for the kind of exercise in utopian imagination discussed above.

The question which concerns Rawls is what principles will allow people to live together in a just and stable society, even though they disagree on many fundamental issues and have different socio-economic positions. His *Theory of Justice* revives the idea of the contract theory as a hypothetical device for establishing the kinds of principles to which rational people would agree. At the heart of this work is the device known as 'the original position', a thought experiment whereby free and rational individuals under a 'veil of ignorance' are asked what rules they would choose to govern themselves under fair conditions. The point of the 'veil of ignorance' is that it supposedly neutralises factors which may, in any given social reality, influence people's choices of governing principles – for example, their socio-economic status, their natural talents, and so on. This move reflects the intuition that if an individual does not know how she will end up in a future society, she most probably will not privilege any one class of people but rather will develop a scheme of justice that treats everyone fairly. And indeed, the principles of justice defended in Rawls' account reflect the intuition that it is unfair to reward people according to natural assets, and that political society is to be regarded not as a competition in which the talented and those lucky to have been born into favourable circumstances are rewarded, but as a fair system of social cooperation.

However, although the 'original position' is supposed to create a situation of ignorance, it in fact has an awful lot built into it. For example, it is an unexamined assumption of Rawls' whole approach that a certain amount of socio-economic inequality is not only inevitable but necessary to ensure the efficient functioning of society. Likewise, the 'circumstances of justice' which constitute the context for Rawls' defence of political liberalism are underpinned by the assumption, common to all classic economic theories, of a basic scarcity of resources. Anarchist theorists such as Kropotkin, in contrast, developed ideas about global economy based on the assumed availability of sufficient resources to satisfy all basic needs.

Such problematic features of Rawls' 'veil of ignorance' generally prompt a lot of difficult questions from my students: Why are these people defined in the way they are? Are Rawls' assumptions about the incentives necessary for social–economic stability built on a conception of human nature, or are they a result of capitalist ideology? And is stability even something to be valued? And so on. I could avoid engaging substantially with these questions, focusing rather on an explanation of Rawls' account. This would be a lot less risky, but it would also be a lot less challenging, and would not really encourage students to think creatively and constructively about their own political reality, their beliefs, their aspirations for changing this reality, and the extent to which these may or may not be feasible.

Interestingly, Goodwin and Taylor, in their taxonomy of political theories, refer to Rawls' theory as an example of the type of theory which leads to 'justification of the present by reference to a hypothetical present' – in contrast to utopian theories which, it is argued, involve 'constructive criticism of the present via an ideal alternative (future or present)'.[48]

Yet what I want to suggest here is that it is not the theory itself which offers utopian possibilities in terms of encouraging imaginative, creative thinking about the good life, but how one engages with the theory. The educational setting is a key arena for the kind of utopian imagining which treats existing social structures as essentially malleable and open to question.

'Utopia', Goodwin and Taylor write, 'offers a precise account of an imaginary future susceptible of immediate realisation in the present'.[49] But in an educational context, what brings this alive is the fact that one can, at one and the same time, imagine the future and begin to conceptualise present change. The future is revolutionary and utopian in the sense that it represents a complete departure from present arrangements. Yet the contours of this future are, in the process of articulation, questioned, revised, and their relationship to present principles and structures made the subject of imagination. This, surely, is what good political education should be, and the complex intertwining of ends and means which it implies is also, inevitably, a part of any truly educational relationship. It is this idea which Buber wanted to capture:

> The anarchist desires a means commensurate with his ends; he refuses to believe that in our reliance on the future 'leap' we have to do now the direct opposite of what we are striving for; he believes rather that we must create here and now the space now possible for the thing for which we are striving, so that it may come to fulfilment then; he does not believe in the post-revolutionary leap, but he does believe in revolutionary continuity.[50]

For educators to engage in a project which involves, in Rorty's words, a 'willingness to substitute imagination for certainty' is a risky business. For committed anarchists, this risk is the essence of their utopian hope. Yet even for educators not necessarily convinced of the feasibility or the desirability of a stateless society, I would suggest that orienting one's educational endeavours around the aspiration for a better – although never perfect – society may perhaps provide a more motivating starting point than that of educational projects characterised by the concern to formulate comprehensive goals and procedural principles. For the interplay between our hopes, our aspirations and our immediate objectives is not a conflict to be decided in advance, but an interesting tension that can itself be seen as part of educational practice. Education, on this view, is not a means to an end, nor an end in itself, but simply one of many arenas of human relationships in which we constantly experiment with our ends, our goals, the means we choose to pursue them and the relationship between them.

Goodwin and Taylor[51] address the problems faced by those seeking to reinstate utopianism as an important intellectual current, one approach being that of conceptualising utopia as a 'unique brand of speculative theory'. In this approach, the idea is to reinforce the potential of utopian thought to create 'lateral possibilities'.[52] Such a methodological approach involves 'games of contingency'.[53] Yet on Goodwin and Taylor's account, these games seem to take place in the minds of those intellectually engaging with the theory. What I am suggesting is that focusing on education as one of the loci where such 'games of contingency' take place captures an essential aspect of anarchist utopianism and, in doing so, assigns these ideas more than a methodological or theoretical status. Yet education does not receive even a passing mention in Goodwin and Taylor's discussion.

Although they talk of 'mental exploration' as part of the value and the contribution of utopias, educational processes go beyond this idea because they are, crucially, conducted in a context of a dialogical, pedagogical relationship, involving both the dynamic thinking and the acting-out of the utopia. Anarchist educational experiments such as those discussed above often tried to embody this idea in both creating experimental utopian communities and educating children in a spirit of critical, imaginative political engagement. Admittedly, the pedagogical practices of some of these communities left some doubt as to whether the education was truly non-coercive and accommodating of multiple possibilities. But ideally, such exploration would take place in a community which is simultaneously trying out different forms of social engagement that challenge the existing system.

The pedagogical practice suggested by the anarchist position is, in an important sense, in keeping with the ideas and practice developed by writers within the tradition of radical pedagogy. Thus, drawing on the work of Paulo Freire, Peter McLaren talks of Freire's pedagogy as embodying a form of utopian imagination which, he argues, 'drives forward the multiple levels of human desire while at the same time it is the result of an unconscious ontological pulling from the "not-yet" of the still inarticulate future. The utopian imagination has, consequently, a subversive and emancipatory function.'[54]

As my above examples illustrate, one can be subversive in teaching political ideas in the sense that one reaches, with one's students, an understanding that our current political arrangements are possibly not the best or the only way to achieve certain desirable political aspirations. A type of political education such as that suggested here can at the same time be emancipatory in implying that there is a way to alleviate human suffering and injustice by social change.

Conclusion

I have argued that understanding the position embodied in anarchist educational experiments and ideas is key to grasping the essence of the anarchist position on social change. The anarchist perspective, indeed its very utopianism, cannot be appreciated independently of this educational context. At the same time, I have suggested that a reflection on anarchist utopianism can enrich our understanding of educational relationships and their social and political significance.

In discussing the theoretical value and meaning of utopia, Goodwin and Taylor suggest that 'utopias reflect the tension between being and becoming'.[55] Surely education, if it means anything at all, means negotiating exactly this tension.

Notes

I am grateful to Laurence Davis and Ruth Kinna for their very helpful comments on an earlier version of this chapter.

1　J. Suissa, *Anarchism and Education: A Philosophical Perspective.*
2　P. Avrich, *The Modern School Movement: Anarchism and Education in the United States.*
3　M. Smith, *The Libertarians and Education*, pp. 44–50; Avrich, *The Modern School Movement*, pp. 18–24.
4　Smith, *The Libertarians and Education*, pp. 54–7.
5　J. Dewey, *Democracy and Education: An Introduction to the Philosophy of Education*, pp. 105–6.
6　S. Dolgoff (ed.), *Bakunin on Anarchy*, p. 357.
7　A. Block, 'Marxism and Education', in R. Martusewicz and W. Reynolds (eds), *Inside/Out: Contemporary Critical Perspectives in Education*, p. 65.
8　D. Morland, *Demanding the Impossible? Human Nature and Politics in Nineteenth Century Social Anarchism.*
9　Z. Bauman, *Socialism: The Active Utopia*, p. 101.
10　J. Wolff, *An Introduction to Political Philosophy*, p. 34.
11　See Suissa, *Anarchism and Education*; Morland, *Demanding the Impossible?*
12　E. McKenna, *The Task of Utopia; A Pragmatist and Feminist Perspective*, p. 163.
13　*Ibid.*
14　R. Hemmings, *Fifty Years of Freedom: A Study of the Development of the Ideas of A.S. Neill*, p. 35.
15　See for example Morland, *Demanding the Impossible?*; D. Miller, *Anarchism.*
16　See McKenna, *The Task of Utopia.*
17　See A. Ritter, *Anarchism: A Theoretical Analysis*; M. Taylor, *Community, Anarchy and Liberty.*
18　Morland, *Demanding the Impossible?*, p. 199.
19　McKenna, *The Task of Utopia*, p. 65.
20　R. Peters, *Authority, Responsibility and Education*, p. 123.
21　*Ibid.*, p. 127.
22　*Ibid.*
23　J. Dewey, 'The Nature of Aims', in R. D. Archambault (ed.), *John Dewey on Education*, p. 73.
24　*Ibid.*, p. 72.
25　*Ibid.*, p. 76.
26　T. May, *The Political Philosophy of Poststructuralist Anarchism*, pp. 63–6.
27　K. R. Popper, *The Open Society and Its Enemies*, p. 158.
28　Quoted in C. Ward, *Anarchy in Action*, p. 18.
29　*Ibid.*, p. 26.
30　McKenna, *The Task of Utopia*, p. 65.
31　N. Chomsky, *Powers and Prospects; Reflections on Human Nature and the Social Order*, p. 75.
32　R. Rorty, *Philosophy and Social Hope*, p. 88.
33　*Ibid.*

34   B. Goodwin and K. Taylor, *The Politics of Utopia: A Study in Theory and Practice*, p. 27.
35   *Ibid.*, p. 29.
36   See Taylor, *Community, Anarchy and Liberty*.
37   See McKenna, *The Task of Utopia*, p. 49.
38   Avrich, *The Modern School Movement*, p. 20.
39   P. Goodman, *Utopian Essays and Proposals*, pp. 18–19.
40   Bauman, *Socialism: The Active Utopia*, p. 13.
41   C. Bufe and D. Neutopia, *Design Your Own Utopia*.
42   *Ibid.*, p. 3.
43   QCA, *Education for Citizenship and the Teaching of Democracy in Schools*, Final Report of the Advisory Group on Citizenship, p. 2.
44   See for example K. Fogelman (ed.), *Citizenship in Schools*.
45   V. Lynch and K. Smalley, 'Citizenship Education', in Fogelman (ed.), *Citizenship in Schools*, p. 171.
46   Bufe and Neutopia, *Design Your Own Utopia*, p. 1.
47   J. Rawls, *A Theory of Justice*.
48   Goodwin and Taylor, *The Politics of Utopia*, p. 24.
49   *Ibid.*, p. 26.
50   M. Buber, *Paths in Utopia*, p. 13.
51   Goodwin and Taylor, *The Politics of Utopia*, p. 84.
52   *Ibid.*
53   *Ibid.*
54   P. McLaren, 'Postmodernism and the Death of Politics; A Brazilian Reprieve', in P. McLaren and C. Lankshear (eds), *Politics of Liberation; Paths from Freire*, p. 208.
55   Goodwin and Taylor, *The Politics of Utopia*, p. 85.

References

Avrich, P., *The Modern School Movement: Anarchism and Education in the United States* (New Jersey: Princeton University Press, 1980).
Bauman, Z., *Socialism: The Active Utopia* (New York: Holmes and Meier, 1976).
——*In Search of Politics* (Oxford: Polity Press, 1999).
Block, A., 'Marxism and Education', in R. Martusewicz and W. Reynolds (eds), *Inside/Out: Contemporary Critical Perspectives in Education* (New York: St. Martin's Press, 1994).
Buber, M., *Paths in Utopia* (Boston: Beacon Press, 1958).
Bufe, C. and D. Neutopia, *Design Your Own Utopia* (Tuscon: See Sharp Press, 2002).
Chomsky, N., *Powers and Prospects; Reflections on Human Nature and the Social Order* (Boston: South End Press, 1996).
Dewey, J., *Democracy and Education: An Introduction to the Philosophy of Education* (New York: Macmillan, 1939).
——'The Nature of Aims', in R. D. Archambault (ed.), *John Dewey on Education* (Chicago: Random House, 1965).
——'The Need for a Recovery of Philosophy', in J. A. Boydston (ed.), *The Middle Works*, Vol. 10 (Carbondale: Southern Illinois University Press, 1980).

Dolgoff, S. (ed.), *Bakunin on Anarchy* (New York: Knopf, 1973).

Fogelman, K. (ed.), *Citizenship in Schools* (London: Fulton, 1991).

Goodman, P., *Utopian Essays and Proposals* (New York: Random House, 1952).

Goodwin, B. and Taylor, K., *The Politics of Utopia: A Study in Theory and Practice* (London: Hutchinson, 1982).

Hemmings, R., *Fifty Years of Freedom: A Study of the Development of the Ideas of A.S. Neill* (London: George Allen and Unwin, 1972).

Kelly, H., 'The Meaning of Libertarian Education', *The Modern School*, 1:5, (1913).

——Editorial, *The Modern School*, 1:3, (1914).

——'What is the Modern School?' *The Modern School*, 33:3, (1916).

Kropotkin, P., *Anarchism: Its Philosophy and Ideal* (London: J. Turner, 1897).

——*Fields, Factories and Workshops Tomorrow* (London: George Allen and Unwin, 1974).

——*Mutual Aid: A Factor of Evolution* (London: Freedom Press, 1987).

Lynch, V. and K. Smalley, 'Citizenship Education', in K. Fogelman (ed.), *Citizenship in Schools* (London: Fulton, 1991).

May, T., *The Political Philosophy of Poststructuralist Anarchism* (University Park: Pennsylvania State University Press, 1994).

McKenna, E., *The Task of Utopia; A Pragmatist and Feminist Perspective* (Lanham, MD: Rowman and Littlefield Inc., 2001).

McLaren, P., 'Postmodernism and the Death of Politics; A Brazilian Reprieve', in P. McLaren and C. Lankshear (eds), *Politics of Liberation; Paths from Freire* (London: Routledge, 1994).

Miller, D., *Anarchism* (London: Dent, 1984).

Morland, D., *Demanding the Impossible? Human Nature and Politics in Nineteenth Century Social Anarchism* (London: Cassell, 1997).

Peters, R., *Authority, Responsibility and Education* (Plymouth: George Allen and Unwin, 1959).

——*Ethics and Education* (London: Allen and Unwin, 1966).

Popper, K. R., *The Open Society and Its Enemies* (London: Routledge and Kegan Paul, 1945).

QCA, *Education for Citizenship and the Teaching of Democracy in Schools*, Final Report of the Advisory Group on Citizenship (London: QCA, 1998).

Rawls, J., *A Theory of Justice* (Oxford: Oxford University Press, 1973).

Ritter, A., *Anarchism: A Theoretical Analysis* (Cambridge: Cambridge University Press, 1980).

Rorty, R., *Philosophy and Social Hope* (London: Penguin, 1999).

Smith, M., *The Libertarians and Education* (London: George Allen and Unwin, 1983).

Suissa, J., *Anarchism and Education: A Philosophical Perspective* (London: Routledge, 2006).

Taylor, M., *Community, Anarchy and Liberty* (Cambridge: Cambridge University Press, 1982).

Ward, C., *Influences; Voices of Creative Dissent* (Bideford: Green Books, 1991).

——*Anarchy in Action* (London: Freedom Press, 1996).

Wolff, J., *An Introduction to Political Philosophy* (Oxford: Oxford University Press, 1996).

Utopia in contemporary anarchism

'Utopia is on the horizon', says Fernando Birri. 'I take two steps towards it, and it retreats two steps. I walk ten steps and the horizon moves ten steps further back. However much I walk, I will never reach it. What then is utopia for? It is for this: for walking'. (Eduardo Galeano, 1997)[1]

For anarchists, utopia has always meant something more than a hypothetical exercise in designing a perfect society. As an artefact in the collective mythology of a movement for social change, the anarchist utopia is umbilically connected to the idea of social revolution – anarchist utopias are perforce places created by the actions of individuals and communities taking history into their own hands. But if the anarchist utopia is the product of social revolution, what remains of either when they are placed on the intraversable horizon? While ultimately intended to suggest a permanent and productive tension between what is and what could be, Fernando Birri's allegory also reflects some of the most troubling anxieties facing anarchists and their allies today. It raises serious questions about the very meaning of the revolutionary project, where 'walking' designates a lifetime of dedication to resisting injustice and realising radically different human relations. How does the idea of an interminable and inherently imperfect revolutionary–utopian endeavour sit with central anarchist concerns? Can anarchism contain such disturbing notions of perpetual struggle and striving-but-never-arriving? And do the concepts of utopia and revolution even retain any meaning for anarchism today? Coming to grips with these questions requires us to radically re-imagine the nature of the utopian terrain and of the 'moment' of qualitative social transformation which marks the passage into it.

The purpose of this chapter, then, is to offer some theoretical markers for re-examining the role and significance of the utopian idea in contemporary anarchism. It argues that the revival of anarchist politics in recent decades has seen a thorough destabilisation of the status of utopia in the movement's political imaginary. The context for this destabilisation is the rise of a strongly open-ended tendency in anarchist thinking, which lacks any expectation of an eventual closure of the revolutionary project – the promise of an unproblematic resolution of social relations 'after the revolution'. In what follows I discuss the sources of this approach, examine its conceptual and political underpinnings, and look at its ramifications for anarchist attitudes and strategies towards social change.

I begin by tracing the destabilisation of the utopian idea to two prominent trends in the re-emergence of anarchist politics in recent decades, which create two distinct challenges to ideas of revolutionary closure and utopian perfectibility. The first section examines the generalisation of the anarchist target of resistance from the state and capitalism to all forms of domination. This generalisation creates an unanswerable conceptual challenge to the idea of revolutionary closure, since it must necessarily allow for the possibility of forms of domination that are hidden from us today and that will only become apparent in the future. The second section examines the rise of diversity to the status of a core anarchist value, and the resultant endorsement of pluralistic and heterogeneous paths to human liberation. This creates a practical challenge to the idea of closure since it raises the possibility of stagnation and renewed hierarchies even in a society where present structures of inequality have been abolished. The third and final section examines the ramifications of utopian destabilisation in relation to contemporary anarchism's emphasis on constructive direct action and prefigurative politics and the revival of anarchist individualism. Here it is argued that these features point to a discursive absorption of the revolutionary/utopian horizon into the present tense, whereby the proper site of utopian realisation is seen not in a perfectionist, post-revolutionary future scenario, but in the imperfect and present-day context of the practices and achievements of the revolutionary movement itself.

Domination: the conceptual argument

The discussion of utopia in contemporary anarchism offered here is based on an appreciation of the social processes through which the movement itself has been revived in recent decades. The anarchist movement as we see it today in advanced capitalist countries is not a direct genealogical descendant of the nineteenth- and early twentieth-century thread of libertarian–socialist militancy, which was effectively wiped out by the end of the second world war. Rather, the mainspring of today's anarchism can be found at the intersection of other social movements whose beginnings were never consciously anarchist – including radical ecology and feminism, black and queer liberation, and the anti-neoliberal internationalism launched by movements in the global south, most celebrated of which are the Mexican Zapatistas. The process of network- and ideological convergence among these movements involved a rediscovery, reframing and re-articulation of anarchist values and concepts, leading up to the fusion of a global anarchist movement network around the turn of the millennium. While often drawing directly on the anarchist tradition for inspiration and ideas, the re-emergent anarchist movement is also the site of manifold re-configurations that distinguish it from previous cycles of left-libertarian political expression. Networked forms of organisation replace formal federations and unions, a stronger emphasis is given to prefigurative direct action and cultural experimentation, and the commitment to modernity and technological progress is no longer widely shared. These qualitative changes add up to something of a paradigm shift in anarchism, which is now a heterodox and praxis-grounded formulation based on new logics of social movement protagonism.

Perhaps the most prominent feature of this new formulation is the generalisation of the target of anarchist resistance from the state and capitalism to all forms of domination in society – a generalisation which has significant implications for the anarchist utopian idea. Since the late 1960s, the movements at whose intersection contemporary anarchism has been reconstituted were creating linkages in theory and practice between various campaigning issues, pointing beyond specific grievances towards a more basic critique of stratified and hierarchical social structures. With the rise of multi-issue movements working on diverse agendas – economic justice, peace, feminism and ecology to name a few – activists progressively came to see these agendas' interdependence, manifest along various axes such as ecological critiques of capitalism, feminist anti-militarism, and the interrelation of racial and economic segregation. Accompanying the convergence of campaigning issues in the radical community was the growing emphasis on the intersections of numerous forms of oppression. Autonomous black feminist movements played a particularly important role in highlighting the concept of 'simultaneous oppression' – a personal and political awareness of how race, class and gender compound each other as arenas of exclusion, in a complex and mutually reinforcing relationship. The diversification of the gay rights movement in the 1980s, for its part, saw lesbian and bisexual activists tying feminist and gay liberation agendas, while queer women and men of colour founded their own organisations and were structuring their struggles explicitly around the intersections of racism, hetero-sexism, patriarchy and class.

The rootedness of contemporary anarchism in the convergence of these diverse radical orientations has led it to be attached to a generalised discourse of resistance, gravitating around the concept of *domination*. The word domination today occupies a central place in anarchist political language, designating the paradigm which governs both micro- and macro-political relations. The term 'domination' in its anarchist sense serves as a generic concept for the various systematic features of society whereby groups and persons are controlled, coerced, exploited, humiliated, discriminated against, and so on – all of which dynamics anarchists seek to uncover, challenge and erode. The function of the concept of domination, as anarchists construct it, is to express the encounter with a family resemblance among the entire ensemble of such social dynamics, or, more precisely, among the articulations of these dynamics by those who struggle against them.[2] Understood in this way, the term domination draws attention to the multiplicity of partial overlaps between different axes of inequality, constructing a general category that maintains a correspondence between them even as they remain grounded in their own particular realities. The systematic nature of domination is often expressed in reference to a number of overarching 'forms', 'systems' or 'regimes' of domination – impersonal sets of rules regulating relationships between people – rules which are not autonomously constituted by those individuals placed within the relationship (including the dominating side) – prominent examples of which are patriarchy, white supremacy and the wage system.[3]

On such a reading, institutions such as the state and the capitalist organisation of ownership and labour – as well as the nuclear family, the school system and many forms of organised religion – are where the authoritarian, indoctrinatory and disciplinary mechanisms which perpetuate regimes of domination are concretely exercised and normalised through the 'reproduction of everyday life'.[4] Thus any given act of resistance is, in the barest sense, 'anarchist' when it is perceived by the actor as a particular actualisation of a more systemic opposition to domination. For example, resistance to police repression or to the caging of refugees and illegal immigrants becomes anarchist when it is more broadly directed towards the state as such, the latter being the ultimate source of policing or of immigration policies.

The generalisation of anarchist resistance to all forms of domination in society moves its notions of social transformation beyond their previous formulation as the abolition of institutions to the redefinition of social patterns in all spheres of life, institutional or otherwise. This is important in the present context, since such a generalisation also means a shift in the understanding of the horizons of the anarchist project. While it is possible to at least imagine the abolition of concrete institutions, the way in which anarchists have come to conceptualise domination presents us with a concept to which the idea of abolition is not so easily attached. This is for a simple reason: in order to speak of the abolition of domination as such, we need to possess the complete list of all its forms and systems, the entire range of possible patterns of social inequality and exclusion. However, we can never be sure that we have such a complete picture: how can we know that there are no forms of domination that remain hidden from us today, just as some that we do recognise were hidden from our predecessors?

To clarify this, think about the cognitive dissonance we experience when realising that many of the authors of the US Declaration of Independence, who proclaimed that 'all men are created equal', were at the same time slaveholders and benefactors of the genocidal dispossession of North America's indigenous peoples. While the apparent contradiction displayed here may be easily attributed to hypocrisy or voluntary blindness, we can still honestly wonder whether the American 'founding fathers' truly realised the grave injustice of social relations that they considered natural and normal. Anarchists too have not always been very good at appreciating the full implications of their own conceptions of liberation, and instances of outright racism, sexism and homophobia are far more abundant in anarchist history and literature than many anarchists would care to recall. Pierre Joseph Proudhon was, on any modern assessment, a blatant misogynist and anti-Semite, writing that 'man's primary condition is to dominate his wife and to be the master [while] women know enough if they know how to mend our socks and fix our steaks'[5] and that 'the Jew is the enemy of humankind. It is necessary to send this race back to Asia, or exterminate it.'[6] Bakunin's writings are also famously rife with anti-Semitic and anti-German attitudes.[7] Did such statements stem from mere hypocrisy, or do they rather reflect short-sightedness on the part of these anarchist 'founding fathers' who remained unaware of the contradiction in their own positions? Another example: in 1935, the prominent Spanish anarchist periodical *Revista Blanca* carried the following, typically homophobic editorial response to the question '[W]hat is there to be said about those comrades who themselves are anarchists and who associate with inverts [*sic*]?':

> They cannot be viewed as men if that 'associate' means anything apart from speaking to or saluting sexual degenerates. If you are an anarchist, that means that you are more morally upright and physically strong than the average man. And he who likes inverts is no real man, and is therefore no real anarchist.[8]

Again, were the editors of *Revista Blanca* being hypocritical and conveniently ignoring the bigotry of their own statements? Or were they in fact simply unaware of this bigotry and of the regime of heterosexist domination which it expressed? These are only illustrative examples – whatever our judgement on them, the conceptual argument remains valid: anarchists today have every reason to endorse a healthy scepticism about the comprehensiveness of their own accounts of domination. Admittedly, we might have a better idea about forms of domination today simply because there are more voices expressing resistance to them. Movements endorsing indigenous, queer and youth liberation have taken their place much more vividly in the public sphere over recent years, and thus contributed to the articulation of resistance to domination in forms that have not been explored before. But this is not enough to ensure us that all possible axes along which domination operates have been exposed. As a result, the idea of an end to 'all' forms of domination becomes nonsensical. We simply cannot think such a state of affairs since we do not possess the full list of features that should be absent from it.

The consequence of this conceptual argument is that an anarchist critique and praxis targeting domination as such, rather than concrete institutions, has no place for notions of revolutionary closure. As Noam Chomsky remarks, this makes anarchism 'an unending struggle, since progress in achieving a more just society will lead to new insight and understanding of forms of oppression that may be concealed in traditional practice and consciousness'.[9] Thus if utopia is identified with a culmination of anarchist militancy then it is an empty concept, since such militancy will potentially always be necessary to confront previously unregistered forms of domination. This is not to say that no other account of anarchist utopianism is possible – only that utopia can no longer be identified with the 'happy ending' of the story of resistance.

Diversity: the vigilance argument

A second, more practical challenge to the notion of utopia as revolutionary closure stems from contemporary anarchism's unprecedented commitment to diversity and individual self-realisation. This commitment is traceable to the same process of anarchist reconvergence discussed above. As a result of the immense diversity of movements, campaigns and approaches which gave rise to contemporary anarchism, the movement itself came to be based on diverse, ad-hoc coalitions – giving rise to a pluralist orientation which disemphasises unity of analysis and vision in favour of multiplicity and experimentation. While several movements simultaneously purported to provide overarching, totalising perspectives as a vantage point for their analysis and action (as in the case of deep ecology or certain strands of feminism), their agendas' feeding into anarchism induced many activists to turn away from the requirement for theoretical unity towards a theoretical pluralism that was prepared to accord equal legitimacy to diverse perspectives and narratives of struggle. This ushered in a bottom-up approach to social theorising and a parallel interest in manifold creative articulations of social alternatives.

Another important contributing factor to this orientation was the rootedness of the emergent anarchist movement in western subcultures. Throughout the twentieth century, anarchist ideas had attracted subcultural and artistic movements such as Dada, Surrealism and the Beats. From the 1960s, this affiliation escalated with the advent of large-scale counter-cultures. The punk movement has been the most significant breeding ground for anarchists throughout the last two decades, due to its oppositional attitude to mainstream society and close affiliation with anarchist symbolism. Radical environmental groups such as *Earth First!*, for their part, borrow from many spiritual traditions including paganism, Buddhism, and various New Age and Native American spiritualities. Besides initiating multiple spaces of alternative cultural and social reproduction – from communes and squats to festivals and 'zines – subcultures also provided an impetus for the recognition of a great degree of diversity in the type of socio-cultural orientations that could be envisioned for a non-capitalist, stateless society.

The result of these developments is that diversity in itself has ascended to the status of a core value in contemporary anarchism, reflected not only in the diversity of the movement itself but in the diversity of visions for alternative social relations that it has place for. As Hakim Bey expresses this, prescribed and fixed models for a free society only attest to their originators' 'various brands of tunnel-vision, ranging from the peasant commune to the L-5 Space City. We say, let a thousand flowers bloom – with no gardener to lop off weeds & sports according to some moralizing or eugenical scheme!'[10]

While this orientation has come to high prominence and poignant expression in contemporary anarchism, the idea itself is not new, as can be seen from the following quote from Rudolf Rocker:

> Anarchism is no patent solution for all human problems, no Utopia of a perfect social order, as it has so often been called, since on principle it rejects all absolute schemes and concepts. It does not believe in any absolute truth, or in definite final goals for human development, but in an unlimited perfectibility of social arrangements and human living conditions, which are always straining after higher forms of expression, and to which for this reason one can assign no definite terminus nor set any fixed goal.[11]

Rocker bases his stance on the refusal of absolutes and the assertion that social arrangements display an inherent proclivity for change. For him, however, the change in question is regarded in optimistic terms – it tends towards improvement, and for this reason cannot be limited in scope. However, there is also a pessimistic side to this coin: in anticipating a constant flux of relationships between diverse and decentralised communities in a radically different social world, anarchists must also remain open to the possibility that even such societies might see the renewal of patterns of exploitation and domination, however encouraging the prevailing conditions may be for sociability and cooperation.

This type of argument has long been evaded by many anarchists, who have endorsed the expectation, inspired by Kropotkin, that a revolution in social, economic and political conditions would encourage an essentially different patterning of human behaviour – either because it would now be able to flower freely under nurturing conditions, or because revolution would remove all hindrances to the development of human beings' cooperative/egalitarian/benevolent side. However, there is room for doubt whether even the most favourable conditions would mean the eradication of the will to power and the creation of an eternally unproblematic arrangement of social life. The acknowledgement that patterns of hierarchy and exploitation may always re-emerge, even in societies oriented against them, means that there is a potential need for anarchist agency under any conditions. If this is the case, then a severe practical challenge is created to the notion of a closure of the revolutionary project. At most, an 'anarchist society' would be one in which everyone is an anarchist, that is, a society in which every person wields agency against rule and domination. To be sure, the frequency of the need to do so may hopefully diminish to a great extent, in comparison to what an anarchist approach would deem necessary in present societies. Still, one has no reason to think that it can ever be permanently removed.

The self-distancing from an anticipated closure of the 'successful' revolutionary project is very strongly apparent in modern anarchist-inspired works of a utopian nature. Ursula Le Guin's novel *The Dispossessed*, perhaps the most honest attempt at portraying a functioning anarchist society, is one prominent example. Referring to the work as an 'anarchist utopia', however, is misleading precisely for this reason, since the society it deals with is far from perfect or unproblematic. The protagonist, Shevek, is driven to leave his anarchist society on the moon of Anarres, not because he rejects its core anarchist ideals but because he sees that some of them are no longer adequately reflected in practice, while others need to be revised in order to give more place to individuality. In the hundred and seventy years since its establishment, following the secession of a mass of revolutionary anarchists from the home planet of Urras, Anarresti society has witnessed the growth of xenophobia, informal hierarchies in the administrative syndicates, and an apparatus of social control through custom and peer pressure. All of these create a widespread atmosphere of conformity that hinders Shevek's self-realisation in his pursuit of his life project, the development of a ground-breaking approach in theoretical physics. Shevek embodies the continuing importance of dissent even after the abolition of capitalism and government. Through his departure and founding of the Syndicate of Initiative, he becomes a revolutionary within the revolution and initiates change within the anarchist society. As he says towards the end of the story, '[I]t was our purpose all along – our Syndicate, this journey of mine – to shake up things, to stir up, to break some habits, to make people ask questions. To behave like anarchists!'[12]

Shevek's project renews the spirit of dissent and non-conformism that animated the original creation of the anarchist society on Anarres in the first place. As Raymond Williams observes, this makes *The Dispossessed* 'an open utopia: forced open, after the congealing of ideals, the degeneration of mutuality into conservatism; shifted, deliberately, from its achieved harmonious condition, the stasis in which the classical utopian mode culminates, to restless, open, risk-taking experiment'.[13]

The idea that diversity itself, when taken to its logical conclusion, nullifies the possibility of revolutionary closure is exemplified by the anarchist-inspired vision of an alternative society offered by the Zurich-based writer P. M. in his book, *bolo'bolo*. Again the application of the term 'utopia' to this book is to be handled with care, since it not only acknowledges but treasures the instability and diversity of social relations created by the removal of all external controls on the behaviour of individuals and groups. P. M. argues that most modern utopias are in fact totalitarian, mono-cultural models organised around work and education. In contrast, the world anti-system called *bolo'bolo* is a mosaic in which every community (*bolo*) of around five hundred residents is as nutritionally self-sufficient as possible and has complete autonomy to define its ethos or 'flavour' (*nima*) – be it monasticism, Marxism or sado-masochism. Some measure of stability is afforded by a minimal but universal social contract (*sila*), enforced by reputation and interdependence. This contract guarantees, for example, that every individual (*ibu*) can at any time leave their native *bolo*, and is entitled to one day's rations (*yalu*) and housing (*gano*) as well as medical treatment (*bete*) at any *bolo*. It even suggests a duel code (*yaka*) to solve disputes between individuals and groups.[14] However,

> There are no humanist, liberal or democratic laws or rules about the content of *nimas* and there is no State to enforce them. Nobody can prevent a *bolo* from committing mass suicide, dying of drug experiments, driving itself into madness or being unhappy under a violent regime. *Bolos* with a bandit-nima could terrorize whole regions or continents, as the Huns or Vikings did. Freedom and adventure, generalized terrorism, the law of the club, raids, tribal wars, vendettas, plundering – everything goes.[15]

While many anarchists might not want to go this far, the point here is that any anarchist theory which looks forward to the absence of law and authority, and to the maximum autonomy (literally 'self-legislation') of individuals and communities, must also respond to the possibility that patterns of domination may re-emerge within and/or among them. So from this perspective 'eternal vigilance is the price of liberty',[16] and anarchist utopianism cannot be equated with chiliasm and closure – the diverse and inherently un-enforceable nature of the anarchist project leaves it necessarily open to change and challenge from within.

Utopia and prefigurative politics

The conceptual and practical challenges reviewed so far render unsustainable the idea of utopia as the closure of the anarchist revolutionary project. If anarchists are against domination as such then they can never know that it has been abolished in all its forms, and in a diverse society lacking enforcement there is always a potential for the re-emergence of familiar hierarchies that may have been removed in the past. Nonetheless, here in this final section I want to suggest that there is a sense in which the utopian idea remains highly significant in contemporary anarchism. This has to do with the ethos of prefigurative politics, or constructive direct action, through which anarchist utopian aspirations are transposed from the future to the present tense.

Direct action has been an ever-present hallmark of anarchist politics, and is often defined as action without intermediaries, whereby an individual or a group uses their own power and resources to change reality in a desired direction, intervening directly in a situation rather than appealing to an external agent (typically the state) for its rectification. Most commonly, direct action is viewed under its preventative or destructive guise. If people object, for instance, to the clear cutting of a forest, then taking direct action means that rather than (only) petitioning or engaging in a legal process against it, they would physically intervene to prevent the clear cutting – by chaining themselves to the trees, or pouring sugar into the fuel-tanks of the bulldozers, or other acts of disruption and sabotage – their goal being directly to hinder or halt the project.

However, direct action can also be invoked in a constructive way, whereby anarchists directly pursue not only the prevention of injustices, but also the creation of alternative social relations free of hierarchy and domi-nation. This constructive form of direct action is also known as prefigura-tive politics – a term combining both dual power strategies for creating a new society 'within the shell of the old', and the ethical commitment on the part of activists to 'be the change' they want to see in society, recursively building their goals into their daily activities, collective structures and methods of organisation. Emphasising the latter aspect, prefigurative poli-tics has thus been defined as the idea that 'a transformative social movement must necessarily anticipate the ways and means of the hoped-for new society',[17] or as the 'commitment to overturning capitalism by only employ-ing a strategy that is an embryonic representation of an anarchist social future'.[18] On such a reading, alongside the ongoing resistance to injustices and the general confrontation with capitalism, patriarchy, militarism and so on, there is a need to nurture the communities, networks and collectives that emerge in the course of social struggle and to realise non-hierarchical relations within their fold. This perspective echoes Gustav Landauer's famous statement of 1910:

> One can throw away a chair and destroy a pane of glass; but . . . [only] idle talkers . . . regard the state as such a thing or as a fetish that one can smash in order to destroy it. The state is a condition, a certain relationship among human beings, a mode of behavior between men [sic]; we destroy it by con-tracting other relationships, by behaving differently toward one another . . . We are the state, and we shall continue to be the state until we have created the institutions that form a real community and society.[19]

The emphasis on prefigurative politics and constructive direct action has significant implications for the contemporary anarchist view of revolution and utopia. While Bakunin looked forward to 'a universal, worldwide revolution . . . the simultaneous revolutionary alliance and action of all the people of the civilized world',[20] anarchists today would tend to look at revolution not as a future event to be worked towards, but as a present-day process and a potential dimension of everyday life. As a result, anarchists often explain their actions and modes of organisation as intended not for the sake of a distant hope of generalised social transformation, the traditional movement through revolution to utopia, but primarily as a present-tense activity of individual and collective self-liberation. As New Zealander activist Torrance Hodgson expresses this,

> The revolution is now, and we must let the desires we have about the future manifest themselves in the here and now as best as we can. When we start doing that, we stop fighting for some abstract condition for the future and instead start fighting to see those desires realized in the present . . . Whether the project is a squat, a sharing of free food, an act of sabotage, a pirate radio station, a periodical, a demonstration, or an attack against one of the institutions of domination, it will not be entered into as a political obligation, but as a part of the life one is striving to create, as a flowering of one's self-determined existence.[21]

Such an approach promotes anarchy as culture, as a lived reality that pops up everywhere in new guises, adapts to different cultural climates, and should be extended and developed experimentally for its own sake, whether or not we believe it can become, in some sense, the prevailing mode of society. This, then, is the remaining significant sense of utopia in contemporary anarchism: an imperfect and present-tense experiment in alternative social relations, a sustained collective effort that looks forward to proliferation as a larger-scale practice, but which can also manifest itself in fleeting moments of non-conformism and carefree egalitarianism, in temporary autonomous zones which can take manifold forms: 'a quilting bee, a dinner party, a black market . . . a neighborhood protection society, an enthusiasts' club, a nude beach'.[22] Thus utopian modes of social interaction – non-hierarchical, voluntary, cooperative, solidaric and playful – are seen as realisable qualities of social interaction here and now.

This present-tense orientation also marks a revitalisation of the individualist element in anarchism, elevating projects of self-realisation and the liberation of desire to a pivotal place in the process of social transformation. In the words of US anarchist publishing collective CrimethInc.,

> Our revolution must be an immediate revolution in our daily lives . . . it is crucial that we seek change not in the name of some doctrine or grand cause, but on behalf of ourselves, so that we will be able to live more meaningful lives. Similarly we must seek first and foremost to alter the contents of our

own lives in a revolutionary manner, rather than direct our struggle towards world-historical changes which we will not live to witness. In this way we will avoid the feelings of worthlessness and alienation that result from believing that it is necessary to 'sacrifice oneself for the cause', and instead live to experience the fruits of our labors . . . in our labors themselves.[23]

On such a reading, a central motivation for anarchist action – not least so in its prefigurative idiom – lies in the desire to *inhabit*, to the greatest extent possible, social relations that approximate anarchists' ideals for society as a whole. Such a re-contextualisation of anarchist individualism in the present tense and its concretion in empirical subjects reflect back on anarchism's (anti-)political content. An anarchist individualism which demands realisation within society as it exists today, rather than as it could be, defines its realisation as-against this existing society and serves as an immediate impetus for action. Hence personal liberation and the confrontation with a homogenising and oppressive social order can each be seen to supply the other's motivation: the individual's own experience of restriction supplies a direct impulse for social action, whereas the experience of struggle itself becomes a site of present-tense liberation.

As the anarchist revolutionary–utopian horizon recedes into the present tense, revolutionary commitments, in turn, come to reflect and respond to the aspirations of living, experiencing individuals. Attitudes that militate against the individual's unfreedom and celebrate her or his self-realisation are no longer content to do so in the abstract. They must insist on the centrality of immediate liberation, to the extent to which it can be achieved, in order to have any relevance for an anarchist 'revolution in everyday life' and the imperfect, open utopian spaces it creates.

Conclusion

This chapter has looked at the destabilisation of the utopian idea in contemporary anarchism, discussing trends in the movement's political culture and discourse which have eroded the notion of utopia as a post-revolutionary resting point. As a result of these developments, efforts to delegitimise the existing system and to build alternatives from the grassroots are valorised today, not only in light of their role in a grand scheme of social revolution, but also (and more importantly) in their immediate contribution to the empowerment and self-realisation of the participants – absorbing the revolutionary–utopian nexus into the present tense. To return to the language of Fernando Birri's allegory, we can say that on a contemporary anarchist reading it is not enough to be drawn to the horizon; rather, the process of walking itself must be saturated with utopian becoming.

In closing, let me confront what seems to be the central objection to this perspective, namely that the demand for self-liberation and intrinsic value in any political endeavour is a self-absorbed and narcissistic preoccupation which does nothing more than create escapist pockets of alternative sub-culture and poses little challenge to the system.[24] Isn't the type of present-tense utopianism explored here a dangerous attitude which necessarily leads to abandoning the thankless but necessary work of building a mass revolutionary movement and propagating radical ideas in wider society?

There are two responses to this concern, one optimistic and one pessimistic. The optimistic response is that the nurturing spaces created by activists, which facilitate individuals' self-realisation and provide them with an environment for overcoming alienation and entrenched oppressive behaviours, are in fact a very strong form of anarchist propaganda by deed (I use this term in a general sense to refer to the potentially exemplary nature of any anarchist activity). The most effective anarchist propaganda will always be the actual implementation and display of anarchist social relations – the practice of prefigurative politics. It is much easier for people to engage with the idea that life without bosses or leaders is possible when such a life is displayed, if on a limited scale, in actual practice rather than merely argued for verbally or on paper. No less importantly, people would be much more attracted to becoming part of a movement that enriches their own lives in an immediate way, than they would be by joining a mass movement in which their desires and needs are suspended in anti-cipation of future rewards that they may never live to reap. Thus the emphasis on present-tense utopian politics can equally be seen as an invalu-able contribution to the growth and strengthening of a widespread anarchist movement.

The pessimistic response, on the other hand, departs altogether from the vision of a revolutionary process discussed above, in favour of what could be termed a strategy of survival and rebuilding. It is based on the premise, which today may seem more realistic than ever, that between peak oil and climate change we have simply run out of time to create the thoroughgoing social transformation needed to avert ecological and social collapse. Over the past few years there has been a surge of studies indicating that the point of historic maximum global oil production is imminent, and evidence is very strong that we are already beginning to experience the alteration of climatic systems due to anthropogenic global warming. Thus the pessimist response argues that the long-term global trajectory which anarchists should take as their working assumption is the protracted, crisis-ridden and irre-versible decay of industrial civilisation.[25]

This does not invalidate the anarchist project as a whole, but casts it into a new framework. Activist projects and initiatives involving mutual-aid structures and practical ecology are still as relevant as ever – only that now they are seen not as the seeds of a new society within the shell of the old, but as the seeds of a new society that can be built amid its collapse and among its ruins. Under this set of assumptions, anarchists are taking advantage of their foresight in order to build sustainable, utopian spaces that can enhance their own chances of survival as well as helping to develop and proliferate the skills, infrastructures and forms of social organisation that will allow communities to attain food and energy self-sufficiency and to flourish despite the surrounding collapse. Given such a scenario, the anarchist project comes to be seen as a drive to build proverbial lifeboats and to prepare libertarian and egalitarian social reconstruction, rather than allowing social–ecological collapse to usher in a 'Mad Max' scenario of all-against-all. Here the lack of belief in revolutionary closure becomes a strength rather than a liability; having let go of long-term utopian aspirations, activists are already partially equipped with the mental and emotional resources they need to carry on with their work despite the bleak prospects they might anticipate for global society in the coming decades. Time will tell how successfully we stand up to this challenge.

Notes

1   Eduardo Galeano, *Walking Words*, p. 326.
2   On the concept of family resemblance see L. Wittgenstein, *Philosophical Investigations*, §§65-7.
3   The terms 'patriarchy' and 'white supremacy' are preferred here to 'sexism' and 'racism' because the reference is to structural patterns in social relations rather than to individual persons' attitudes of prejudice and bigotry.
4   F. Perlman, *The Reproduction of Everyday Life*.
5   P. J. Proudhon, 'Pornocracy, or Women of Modern Times', cited in E. Hyams, *Proudhon: His Revolutionary Life, Mind and Works*, p. 274.
6   P. J. Proudhon, 'Les Carnets', cited in S. Edwards (ed.), *Selected Writings of Pierre Joseph Proudhon*, p. 228n.
7   M. Bakunin, *Statism and Anarchy*, pp. 104ff. and 175ff.
8   Cited in R. Cleminson, 'Male Inverts and Homosexuals: Sex Discourse in the Anarchist Revista Blanca', in G. Hekma, H. Oosterhuis and J. Steakley (eds), *Gay Men and the Sexual History of the Political Left*, p. 272.
9   N. Chomsky, 'The Soviet Union versus Socialism', *Our Generation*, 17:2 (1986), pp. 47–52.
10 Hakim Bey, 'Psychic Paleolithism and High Technology: A Position Paper', in *The Temporary Autonomous Zone*.
11 R. Rocker, 'Anarchism: Its Aims and Purposes', in *Anarcho-Syndicalism*, p. 30.
12 U. Le Guin, *The Dispossessed*, p. 316.
13 R. Williams, 'Utopia and Science Fiction', *Science Fiction Studies*, 16 (5:3) (1978).
14 P. M., *bolo'bolo*, pp. 68–70.
15 *Ibid.* pp. 77–8.
16 A saying attributed, in various phrasings, to Edmund Burke, Andrew Jackson and the abolitionist Wendell Phillips.
17 B. Tokar, 'Review of Joel Kovel, *The Enemy of Nature*', *Tikkun*, 18:1 (2003).

18 J. Carter and D. Morland, 'Anti-capitalism: Are We All Anarchists Now?', in J. Carter and D. Morland (eds), *Anti-capitalist Britain*, p. 79.
19 G. Landauer, 'Schwache Stattsmänner, Schwacheres Volk', cited in E. Lunn, *Prophet of Community: The Romantic Socialism of Gustav Landauer*, p. 226.
20 M. Bakunin, 'The Revolutionary Catechism', in S. Dolgoff (ed.), *Bakunin on Anarchy*.
21 T. Hodgson, 'Towards Anarchy'.
22 Hakim Bey, 'The Willimantic/Rensselaer Questions', in M. Gunderloy and M. Ziesing (eds), *Anarchy and the End of History*, pp. 87–92.
23 CrimethInc., 'Alive in the Land of the Dead'.
24 For the loudest expression of this position see M. Bookchin, *Social Anarchism or Lifestyle Anarchism: An Unbridgeable Chasm?*
25 Readers might find this scenario less far-fetched after a glance at recent books like R. Heinberg, *Powerdown: Options and Actions for a Post-carbon World*; J. Kunstler, *The Long Emergency: Surviving the End of Oil, Climate Change, and Other Converging Catastrophes of the Twenty-first Century*; A. McBay, *Peak Oil Survival: Preparation for Life after Gridcrash*. See also www. sinkingfeeling.net.

References

Bakunin, M., 'The Revolutionary Catechism', in Sam Dolgoff (ed.), *Bakunin on Anarchy* (New York: Knopf, 1971 [1866]).
——*Statism and Anarchy* (Cambridge: Cambridge University Press, 1990 [1873]), http://dwardmac.pitzer.edu/Anarchist_archives/bakunin/catechism.html.
Bookchin, M., *Social Anarchism or Lifestyle Anarchism: An Unbridgeable Chasm?* (Edinburgh: AK Press, 1995), http://dwardmac.pitzer.edu/anarchist_archives/ bookchin/soclife.html, accessed 3 December 2007.
Carter, J. and D. Morland, 'Anti-capitalism: Are We All Anarchists Now?', in J. Carter and D. Morland (eds), *Anti-capitalist Britain* (Gretton: New Clarion Press, 2004).
Chomsky, N., 'The Soviet Union versus Socialism', *Our Generation*, 17:2 (1986), 47–52, http://zmag.org/chomsky/articles/86-soviet-socialism.html, accessed 3 December 2007.
Cleminson, R., 'Male Inverts and Homosexuals: Sex Discourse in the Anarchist *Revista Blanca*', in G. Hekma, H. Oosterhuis and J. Steakley (eds), *Gay Men and the Sexual History of the Political Left* (Binghamton, NY: Haworth Press, 1995).
CrimethInc. 'Alive in the Land of the Dead', in *Days of War, Nights of Love: CrimethInc. for Beginners* (Olympia, WA: CrimethInc., 2001), www.crimethinc. com/library/english/alive.html, accessed 3 December 2007.
Galeano, Eduardo, *Walking Words* (New York: WOW. Norton, 1997).
Hakim Bey, 'The Willimantic/Rensselaer Questions', in M. Gunderloy and M. Ziesing (eds), *Anarchy and the End of History* (San Francisco: Factsheet Five, 1991).

——'Psychic Paleolithism and High Technology: A Position Paper', in *The Temporary Autonomous Zone* (New York: Autonomedia, 2003), www.hermetic.com/bey/taz2a.html, accessed 3 December 2007.

Heinberg, R., *Powerdown: Options and Actions for a Post-carbon World* (Gabriola Island: New Society Publishers, 2004).

Hodgson, T., 'Towards Anarchy' (web forum posting), http://groups.msn.com/AnarchistAlliance/towardsanarchy.msnw, accessed 3 December 2007.

Kunstler, J., *The Long Emergency: Surviving the End of Oil, Climate Change, and Other Converging Catastrophes of the Twenty-first Century* (Berkeley, CA: Grove/Atlantic, 2006).

Landauer, G., 'Schwache Stattsmänner, Schwacheres Volk', cited in E. Lunn, *Prophet of Community: The Romantic Socialism of Gustav Landauer* (Berkeley, CA: University of California Press, 1973 [1910]).

Le Guin, U., *The Dispossessed* (London: Gollancz, 2002 [1974]).

McBay, A., *Peak Oil Survival: Preparation for Life after Gridcrash* (Guilford, CT: Lyons, 2006).

P. M. *bolo'bolo* (New York: Autonomedia, 1985).

Perlman, F., *The Reproduction of Everyday Life* (Detroit: Black and Red, 1969), www.spunk.org/library/writers/perlman/sp001702/repro.html, accessed 3 December 2007.

Proudhon, P. J., 'Les Carnets', cited in S. Edwards (ed.), *Selected Writings of Pierre Joseph Proudhon* (London: Macmillan, 1969 [1843–64]).

——'Pornocracy, or Women of Modern Times', cited in E. Hyams, *Proudhon: His Revolutionary Life, Mind and Works* (London: John Murray, 1979 [1875]).

Rocker, R., 'Anarchism: Its Aims and Purposes', in *Anarcho-Syndicalism* (London: Pluto, 1989 [1938]).

Tokar, B., 'Review of J. Kovel, *The Enemy of Nature*', *Tikkun*, 18:1 (2003), www.social-ecology.org/article.php?story=20031202102552690, accessed 3 December 2007.

Williams, R., 'Utopia and Science Fiction', *Science Fiction Studies*, 5:3 (1978), www.depauw.edu/sfs/backissues/16/williams16art.htm, accessed 3 December 2007.

Wittgenstein, L., *Philosophical Investigations* (Oxford: Blackwell, 2003).

Index